L............., LIGHTSHIPS, and the GULF of MEXICO

David L. Cipra

Cypress Communications
Alexandria, Virginia
1997

Printed in the United States by Thomson-Shore, Inc., Dexter, Michigan

10 9 8 7 6 5 4 3 2 1

Library of Congress Catalog Card Number 96-072414
ISBN 0-9636412-1-2

Front cover: *Illustration entitled, "First Order Lt. Houses for Trinity Shoal & Timbalier, Gulf of Mexico." Signed by George H. Elliot, Major of Engineers, Engineer Secretary, Office of the Light House Board, August 1871. Note that the Trinity Shoal Lighthouse was never completed to this plan; a lightship was used instead. (Courtesy of National Archives)*

Cypress logo is from a woodcut by Dean Bornstein. Lighthouse location maps were created by Susan Browning.

Designed, produced, and published by Cypress Communications, 35 E. Rosemont Ave., Alexandria, VA 22301. Single copies of this book are available from the publisher for $24.95. *Women Who Kept the Lights: An Illustrated History of Female Lighthouse Keepers* by Mary Louise Clifford and J. Candace Clifford, is also available for $19.95. Shipping is free for prepaid orders.

Table of Contents

Chapter 8: America's Marine Highway: Delta to Natchez (Louisiana)

Foreword

In the late 1970s the Coast Guard published a small booklet written by David Cipra, titled *Lighthouses and Lightships of the Northern Gulf of Mexico*. I met the author around 1980 when he was first transferred to the 12th Coast Guard District offices in San Francisco as an enlisted man in the public affairs field. At the time I was Assistant Chief, Aids to Navigation Branch. I was becoming interested in the history of lighthouses, primarily because hundreds of queries on that subject came to the Public Affairs office. Dave pointed me in the right direction in answering them and always provided knowledge and assistance in a manner which was casual and humorous. He was an even-handed character without a mean bone in his body.

During his years in San Francisco with the 12th Coast Guard District, Dave spend thousands of hours at the Bancroft Library researching the lighthouses and lightships of our Gulf Coast. Once I asked him why the focused attention and dedication to that particular coast line? He replied, "Because it's virgin territory; nobody has covered the lighthouses of that area." And he was right. Northeast lighthouses, particularly New England, have been covered to a fair-thee-well. Numerous books have also been written about the Great Lakes and West Coast lighthouses. Until Dave Cipra wrote that Coast Guard booklet, however, nothing had been written about the Gulf. In recent years the overwhelming wave of popularity surrounding lighthouses has produced a few regional books on Gulf lighthouses: one on Texas and a few covering Florida lighthouses, but not a comprehensive book on the entire coast.

Unfortunately, Dave Cirpa died too young, before he could finish his life's work. Fortunately, he left ample notes, which allowed a few close friends to fill in the blanks and complete a seamless text.

This book covers that 'virgin territory' in a thorough manner and in a style that is a pleasure to read. I was delighted to learn that Dave's dream is, at last, being realized. His wife and children will reap the rewards of his tireless effort: his thousands of nights at libraries with a pocket full of quarters for the copier, his thousands of hours at the computer have all come together, and well. The sad note is that he will never hold this wonderful book in his hands, as you are doing at this moment.

Nice job, Dave.

Wayne C. Wheeler, President
U.S. Lighthouse Society, San Francisco, California

Preface

Dave Cipra joined the United States Coast Guard in 1966 and retired as the Master Chief of Public Affairs in 1986. After retirement, he immediately began work as a civilian for the Coast Guard's Office of Health and Safety. At his death, he had enjoyed a 28-year association with the Coast Guard. Dave had become well-known by most of the members of the lighthouse community as the foremost expert on Gulf Coast lighthouses. He authored the short but important work entitled *Lighthouses and Lightships of the Northern Gulf of Mexico.*

Before his death, Dave devoted 20 years to combing archives and secondary sources to compile the text of this book. Tragically, he never lived to see his life's work complete. Chapter one, parts of chapter two, and the notes of his last four chapters remained unfinished. We have completed the manuscript using the notes and the unfinished portions of the manuscript. Dave's notes sometimes lacked the detail that would quickly lead the researcher to the exact source. Rather than delay or abandon the publication of the book, we have given the most complete citations possible based on his notes. This is not the book it might have been had Dave been able to complete it and edit it himself; however, it is the best that two of his friends, lacking Dave's wealth of knowledge, were able to piece together.

This book, however, is unlike any other book on lighthouses. It not only brings to life the lighthouses and the people who tended the lights in the Gulf, but it also examines the reasons, both political and financial, for the establishment of these important aids to navigation. This is by far the most complete and well-documented study of Gulf Coast lighthouses and lightships to be published.

Everyone who knew Dave soon learned that one of his greatest attributes was his willingness to assist friends and other interested persons. As he wrote the book, his helpfulness spawned many reciprocal friendships of the type that all authors find necessary to complete their works. There are dozens of people whom Dave would have mentioned for their help with this manuscript. However, we do not have a complete list and fear leaving out many who made significant contributions. We choose to say a collective, heartfelt thank you to all who helped Dave. Those who shared their knowledge, or gave guidance and advice, will recognize their contributions as they read through the text.

Robert M. Browning, Jr., Chief Historian, U.S. Coast Guard

Robert L. Scheina, Professor of History, National Defense University

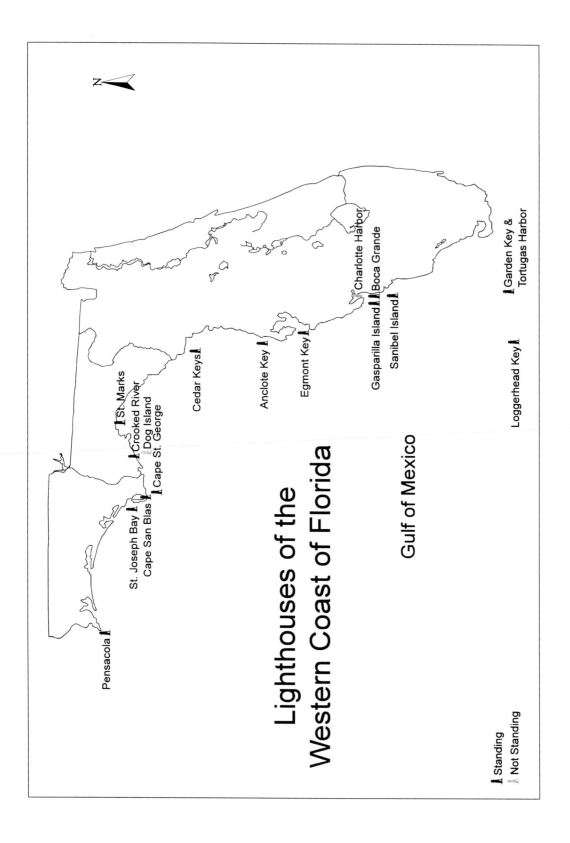

Lighthouses of the
Western Coast of Florida

Gulf of Mexico

Pensacola

St. Marks
Crooked River
Dog Island
St. Joseph Bay
Cape San Blas
Cape St. George

Cedar Keys

Anclote Key

Egmont Key

Charlotte Harbor
Boca Grande
Gasparilla Island
Sanibel Island

Garden Key &
Tortugas Harbor

Loggerhead Key

Standing
Not Standing

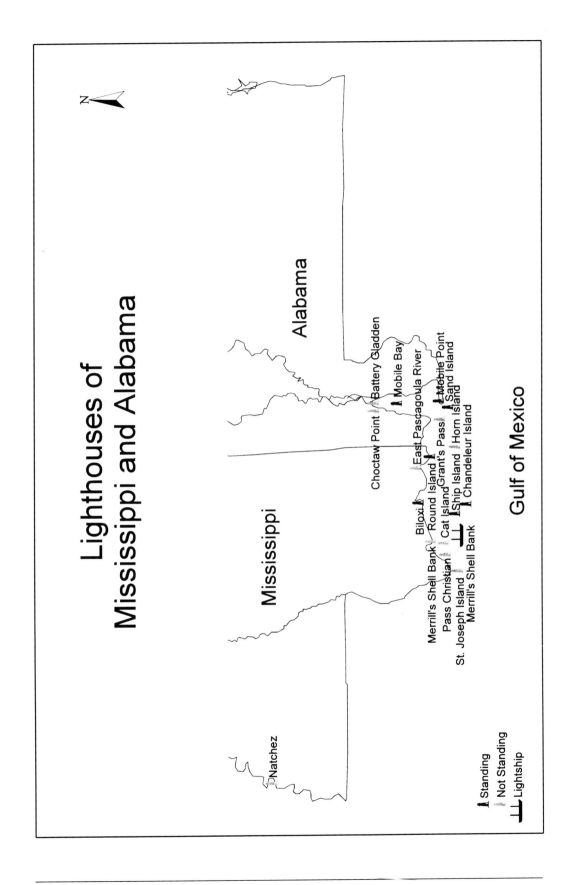

Lighthouses of Mississippi and Alabama

Mississippi

Alabama

Natchez

Choctaw Point
Battery Gladden
Mobile Bay
East Pascagoula River
Mobile Point
Sand Island
Biloxi
Round Island
Grant's Pass
Cat Island
Ship Island
Horn Island
Chandeleur Island
Merrill's Shell Bank
Pass Christian
St. Joseph Island
Merrill's Shell Bank

Gulf of Mexico

Standing
Not Standing
Lightship

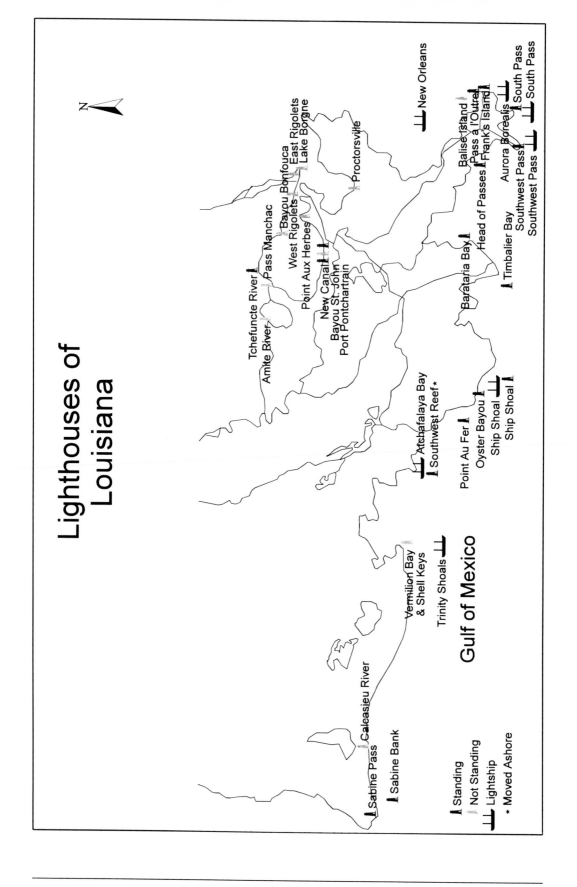

Lighthouses of Louisiana

N

New Orleans

East Rigolets
Bayou Bonfouca
Lake Borgne
West Rigolets
Point Aux Herbes

Proctorsville

Tchefuncte River
Pass Manchac

Amite River

New Canal
Bayou St. John
Port Pontchartrain

Balise Island
Pass a l'Outre
Head of Passes
Frank's Island
Aurora Borealis
South Pass
South Pass
Southwest Pass
Southwest Pass

Barataria Bay

Timbalier Bay

Atchafalaya Bay
Southwest Reef *

Point Au Fer
Oyster Bayou
Ship Shoal
Ship Shoal

Vermilion Bay
& Shell Keys

Trinity Shoals

Gulf of Mexico

Sabine Pass Calcasieu River

Sabine Bank

Standing
Not Standing
Lightship
* Moved Ashore

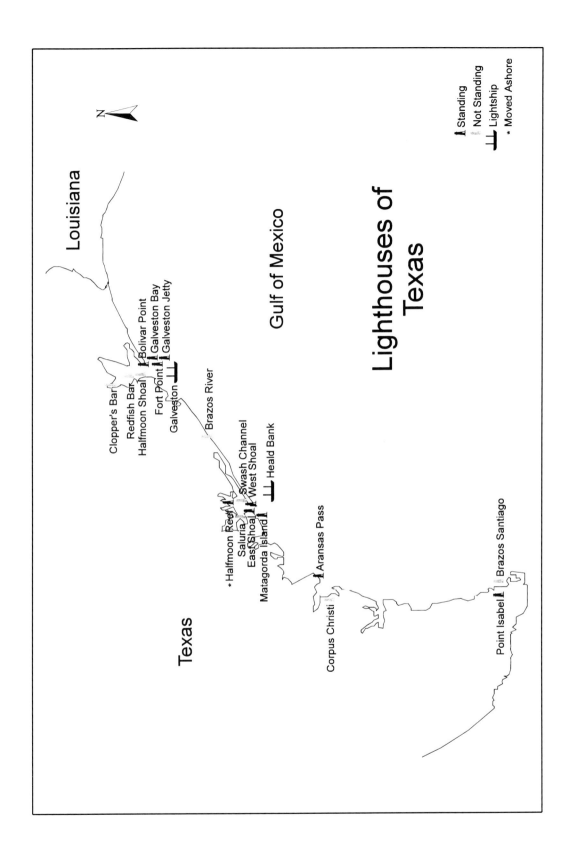

Lighthouses of Texas

Louisiana

Gulf of Mexico

Texas

Clopper's Bar
Redfish Bar
Halfmoon Shoal
Fort Point
Galveston
Bolivar Point
Galveston Bay
Galveston Jetty

Brazos River

Swash Channel
West Shoal
Heald Bank

* Halfmoon Reef
Saluria
East Shoal
Matagorda Island

Aransas Pass

Corpus Christi

Point Isabel
Brazos Santiago

N

Standing
Not Standing
Lightship
* Moved Ashore

The development of steam-powered boats significantly accelerated commerce on the Gulf and the need for lighthouses. Ship Island Lighthouse, shown at left, was established on the Mississippi Sound in 1853.

Chapter 1

The Gulf Coast of the United States before the Civil War

The history of the Gulf Coast has received too little attention within the context of U.S. maritime development. Yet the commerce which flowed through Gulf ports in the 19th century virtually bankrolled the bold young republic of the United States. By 1860 raw materials gleaned from half a continent flowed down the Midwestern rivers and through the shallow sounds and bays into the Gulf. And until the maturing of railroad networks in the second half of the century, the river system was the preferred route for both people and trade into the interior of America. The building of lighthouses and other aids to navigation was a vital step in the burgeoning of this commerce.

The colonial era

Although the first documented lighthouse built in North America was constructed by the Massachusetts Colony in Boston Harbor in 1716, the Spanish and French may have already built lighthouses at St. Marks, Florida, and at the Mississippi River entrance in Louisiana before this date.[1] Two hundred years elapsed between the time those doughty Europeans first explored the Gulf Coast and the time their settlements took root. All early pioneers on that coast must have bemoaned the dearth of landmarks, however. How were they to find their way through endless expanses of shifting shoals and bars, unstable islands, and winding bayous?

Spain sought and found fabulous wealth in the New World, but when Juan Ponce de Leon landed at Charlotte Harbor on the Florida coast in 1513, he found only hostile Indians. As a consequence, no lasting Spanish settlement took root on Florida's west coast for centuries. In 1519 Alonso Alvarez de Piñeda discovered a great river, thought to be either Mobile Bay or possibly the Mississippi. He also mapped the Texas coast. Finally, Spanish settlements took root at St. Marks, Pensacola, and Mobile. Nonetheless, Spain never got a true economic foothold in Florida, although a handful of defensive outposts did spread Christianity. Spanish colonial authorities planned the region's first lighthouse for the Mississippi River in about 1721; the light was not constructed for many years, however, as higher priorities drained the royal treasury.[2]

The French attempted to link their northern colony in Canada with the Gulf Coast, discovering the mouth of the Mississippi River in 1682 and erecting the first documented navigational marker. It was apparently

---

made of stone (in spite of the fact that no stone was located within hundreds of miles of the probable site) and bore the French coat of arms. In 1699 the French built Fort Boulaye (later called La Balize, the old French word for beacon or seamark) five miles from the mouth of the Mississippi; surviving documents do not indicate if a light was displayed. In 1721 Adrien de Pauger erected a 62-foot wood pyramid to guide ships to the mouth of the Mississippi, but nothing indicates whether it held a light. The French also planned a monumental hexagonal lighthouse inside a crescent-shaped fort, but the project was never carried through.[3]

Early aids to navigation might consist of a small ship's lantern or large banner flown from a watchtower or blockhouse.

The French did build America's first crude jetty to channel water through Balize Bayou. This project apparently was unsuccessful because of the limitations of 18th-century technology. Documentation suggests there may have been French colonial lighthouses on Lake Pontchartrain and at the bayou known as the Rigolets. These would have serviced the French trading network, which reached far inland, as well as a few plantations near rivers, which grew sugar, indigo, and eventually cotton— all export crops.[4]

The English moved into the Gulf primarily to challenge the claims of France and Spain, beginning their advance into the region in about 1760 as a consequence of the French and Indian War (1754-63). Great Britain attempted to establish homestead colonies resembling those it had created along the North Atlantic seaboard. A crude wooden lighthouse was built at about this time, but it was apparently not continued by the Spanish when the British moved out. There is no evidence of a colonial lighthouse at England's oldest holding, Pensacola. A royal mapmaker did recommend a lighthouse at the southern tip of the Florida Reef, probably at Dry Tortugas, with a fort to guard the entrance of the Gulf of Mexico. A lighthouse built with 18th-century technology at such an exposed location would not have withstood the hurricane-force winds, however, even had Great Britain carried out the suggestion.

The new republic of the United States

The United States acquired the Louisiana Territory in 1803 for many reasons. It was a great buy; the nation was already beginning to think of "Manifest Destiny" (although the term would not be coined for a few more decades); and the United States wanted to prevent the British from acquiring control over the Mississippi River. The boundaries of the Louisiana Purchase were ill-defined, allowing the United States to make the best of the opportunity. The United States claimed Mobile Bay and opened a port of entry within the bay for foreign commerce.[5] Three months after the purchase, Congress funded the most expensive American lighthouse authorized up to that time at the mouth of the Mississippi River on Frank's Island. Because it took 20 years to complete, it was not lit until after the Bayou St. John Light. At the same time, Congress funded a survey of the Louisiana Territory for other lighthouse sites. In 1805 Benjamin Latrobe designed a magnificent but outlandish stone lighthouse for the Mississippi River. No contractor was willing to attempt its construction on the spongy muck of the Delta. On May 1, 1810, Congress authorized $2,000 for a lighthouse at Bayou St. John at the site of an old Spanish fort. Some historians have speculated that the United States simply modified an existing tower, but no documentation supports this contention.[6]

In 1811 an event occurred which would significantly accelerate the economic development of the Gulf and, as a consequence, the building of lighthouses. In that year a steam-powered boat first operated on the Mississippi. Over the next five decades a growing fleet of riverboats brought the goods of river and coastal ports to the Gulf for transshipment abroad, with a fleet of tugs to push the seagoing sailing ships upriver or into the shallow restricted waters of the Gulf. The steamboat would eventually open the heartland of America to the Gulf and to the world.

The War of 1812 interrupted commerce as well as lighthouse construction throughout the nation. The effects were felt even on the far-away Gulf Coast. In May 1813 the British blockade of America's coast was extended to the mouth of the Mississippi. The war, however, had positive influences: it unified the United States, diversified its industry, and called attention to the Gulf region. Although regionalism was strong, the new nation nonetheless withstood the test of war against a very powerful enemy and as a consequence developed a strong national pride. The war cut off trade between Europe and the United States, forcing the North, which possessed adequate manpower and waterpower (fast-flowing streams), to begin to industrialize. And the Battle of New Orleans focused the nation's attention on the Mississippi River and its tributaries spanning half a continent. No longer was New Orleans considered a foreign port under the U.S. flag. It was now the portal of the American water highway into the interior of the continent and would become America's commercial window to the high seas.[7]

With the end of the war, abundant English capital again flowed into the United States, the seas were freed from impressment, and England's appetite for U.S. cotton became insatiable. Also, the ending of the Napoleonic Wars (1797-1815) unleashed a wave of migration. Many of these European newcomers settled in the wilderness recently wrested from the Native Americans. The produce of their new farms moved to the world market down the Mississippi and was carried out of Gulf ports, primarily in American merchant ships.

Shippers and ship captains demanded aids to navigate the treacherous coast. Lighthouse construction was renewed with greater vigor. In 1816 Henry Latrobe redesigned his father's Mississippi River edifice, but its bulk would be so heavy that no one dared undertake its construction upon soft Delta land. Finally, Winslow Lewis tried to build it, but his creation sank into the mud and cracked before it was completed.[8]

In 1817 the steamboat *Washington* sailed from New Orleans to Louisville, pioneering the flow of commerce in both directions on the river. Typically the steamboat could travel at 25 miles per hour downriver and a remarkable 16 miles per hour upstream. As travel increased and steam engines became more efficient, the cost to passengers and freight dropped sharply.

The next major land acquisition filled the maritime gap between the Louisiana Purchase and the young United States. Florida, acquired under the Transcontinental Treaty (1819), was another source of raw materials, spurring the construction of lighthouses in the Gulf.

With increasing shipping, the mouth of the Mississippi understandably received continuing attention. But lighting the Delta was no easy task because of its width and soft, mushy terrain. In 1820 the first coastal lighthouse on the Gulf (and the second in Gulf coastal states) was built at the mouth of the Mississippi River. Probably lit in 1823 (possibly earlier), it replaced a temporary beacon installed in about 1817 on a blockhouse watchtower at the nearby La Balize. Also in 1820, a lightship was placed at the entrance to the river. Another lightship was placed at Craney Island, Virginia, in the same year; it is unclear which was the nation's first. It soon became apparent that lightships were fragile and susceptible to damage, as well as much more expensive to maintain than lighthouses.[9]

Administering the lights

Between 1790 (when lighthouses were taken over by the federal government) and 1820, they were in the charge of local commissioners of revenue or under the direct supervision of the Secretary of the Treasury. The Department of the Treasury was responsible both for collecting revenues and for improving the nation's infrastructure, which would increase foreign trade. By 1820 the lighthouse system, which had been continually expanded, required more attention than the Secretary of the Treasury could devote to it. He passed responsibility for the administration of lighthouses to the Fifth Auditor of the Treasury, who continued this supervision for 32 years. He oversaw the construction of more than 250 lighthouses, most of them in New England and in the Great Lakes, but a fair number in the Gulf as well.[10]

In 1820 the first lighthouse was funded for Alabama at Mobile; it was completed two years later. The upper Mississippi received its first lighthouse at Natchez, Tennessee, in 1827. The light was considered useless by river pilots, however, and when it was blown down by a tornado, it was not replaced. An 1829 survey between Lake Pontchartrain and Mobile Bay recommended lighthouses at West Rigolets, Sand Island, Southwest Pass (twin towers), and South Pass. It also recommended a lightship for St. Joseph's Island and a buoy for Round Island.

During these early years of the republic, the federal government used contractors to supply, inspect, and build lighthouses. These contractors in turn often sublet the work to others who had no direct responsibility to the federal government.[11] Some two dozen contracts

Mississippi Sound's first coastal lighthouses were built to mark the anchorages and channels used by trade vessels headed for New Orleans. Cat Island Light marked the approach to New Orleans.

won by Winslow Lewis for lighthouses in the Gulf were technologically the most challenging construction projects of their day.[12]

The importance attached to lighthouse structures by the Congress is indicated by an 1825 law which stipulated the death penalty for those caught burning a building on lighthouse property. This law was probably aimed at "wreckers"—predators who intentionally misled ships with false lights, luring them to wreck and then looting their cargoes. The keepers and their families were far less protected. The penalty for murder, rape, or robbery was a mere five years in jail and a $1,000 fine.[13]

Technology and cotton

The opening up of the Midwest spurred a boom in commercial activity. Land sales in the Mississippi basin reached $25 million in 1835, the only year they exceeded U.S. customs receipts from import duties. Two years later Chicago was organized as a city. More immigrants came, pushing Native Americans farther west. Ports handling outbound cotton and inbound consumer goods grew rapidly. By the 1830s the small ports along the Gulf were shipping as much cotton as the entire state of South Carolina; within 30 years, cotton accounted for 57 percent of all U.S. exports—virtually all of it shipped out of the Gulf.

The cotton trade spurred the lighthouse building boom in the 1830s. Native Americans had been pushed out of western Georgia, Alabama, and Mississippi, allowing land-hungry farmers to move, clear the land, and buy cotton seed. Steam-powered riverboats were becoming increasingly common. The rivers became the "interstate highways" of the first half of the 19th century. As the century progressed, the United States spent less and less on the construction of canals and toll roads (turnpikes) and more and more on the improvement of aids to navigation, especially lighthouses. The introduction and perfection of steam dredging permitted the Corps of Topographical Engineers to deepen the Gulf's shallow harbors. The federal government scrambled to light up the waterways and the new ports that were drawing in so much foreign income—St. Marks, Apalachicola, St. Joseph, Pensacola, Mobile, Mississippi Sound, Lake Pontchartrain, the Mississippi River, and Atchafalaya Bay.[14]

Architect Robert Mills published his classic *The American Pharos* in 1832 with sailing directions for each of the lighthouses in the United States. The most common advice given for the Gulf Coast was to avoid navigation at night. The extremely poor performance of the lighting system in use throughout the United States made night navigation very hazardous. Typically the American system of lamps and reflectors projected a beam of light only a few miles. Yet in Europe the French-manufactured Fresnel lens focused a light visible some 20 miles.

Screwpile technology permitted construction of lighthouses in shallow water on a mud, sand, or coral bottom. Fort Point Lighthouse in Galveston Harbor, Texas, was first lit in 1882. (National Archives photo #26-LG-36-5)

The rapid development of technology in the decades just before the Civil War influenced trade patterns in the Gulf and consequently the need for and location of new lighthouses. Elias Howe invented the sewing machine in 1846 and within a few years it was significantly improved upon by Isaac Singer. This further increased the demand for cotton.[15]

The first passenger train west of the Allegheny mountains began operation in 1832 between New Orleans and Port Pontchartrain, a distance of about five miles. As a consequence, Milneville was established and a lighthouse built at Port Pontchartrain; within a few years four other lights were added on Lake Pontchartrain. The surge of railroads throughout the heartland increased trade flowing into and out of the Gulf. In general, small shallow ports (many in Texas) became less important and, as a consequence, less was spent for their aids to navigation. Conversely, large ports burgeoned as railroads brought goods for shipment to the East Coast or abroad. Their need for improved aids to navigation increased apace.[16]

By the 1850s technology had a direct impact on lighthouse construction. The new "screwpile" foundation was introduced into the Gulf. This permitted, for the first time, the erection of lightweight structures (compared to stone and brick) in shallow, slow-moving water, on a mud, sand, or coral bottom. Three screwpile lighthouses were built in Galveston Bay in 1854. Also, where ground firmness would permit, brick lighthouses were built taller because the myth that ground haze would obscure the light was dispelled.[17]

In 1851, a provisional lighthouse board surveyed the Gulf and recommended that 14 new lights be added. The goal was to place a light every 50 miles along the coast. Lighthouses were built at 10 of the sites and the others were marked by unmanned, minor lighted aids.[18]

In 1852 the responsibility for administering lighthouses was transferred from a single executive (the Fifth Auditor of the Treasury) to a permanent board. The magnitude and complexity of the job had outgrown a single bureaucrat's time and talent. Initially the new board was composed of two naval officers, one officer each from the Corps of Engineers and the Corps of Topographical Engineers of the Army, and two civilians possessing advanced scientific credentials. The nation was divided into 12 lighthouse districts, three of which (the Seventh, Eighth, and Ninth) were in the Gulf. Each district was assigned a naval officer as an inspector for operations and an Army officer as the superintendent of construction and repair. The new U.S. Light-House Board also oversaw installation of the more efficient Fresnel lens to replace the system of Lewis lamps and reflectors in American lighthouses. The Fresnel lenses generally required larger lanterns to accomodate them and varied in size, the largest being a first order, the smallest, a sixth order.

At the turn of the decade before the Civil War, with commerce still booming, the potential for additional lighthouse construction in the Gulf looked bright. New Orleans was the fifth largest city in the United States; bumper crops of cotton were carried out of Gulf ports in both 1859 and 1860. Cotton was king. The saga of lighthouses in the Gulf radically changed on July 8, 1861, when Confederates seized Ship Island, renamed it Fort Twiggs, and extinguished the light in the lighthouse. With the beginning of the Civil War, other lighthouses were extinguished one by one and a darkness fell on the Gulf Coast that would last for over five years.

Chapter 2

The Civil War and beyond

As the clouds of civil unrest gathered on the horizon, the South, perhaps more than the North, was dependent on navigable and safe ports which lighthouses helped provide. The North linked its population centers with a web of railroads, while the South enjoyed a system of natural marine highways, the Gulf Coast portion of which drained two-thirds of the United States and its territories. The few Southern roads and rails mostly connected its ports and rivers to the interior. In contrast to Northern deepwater ports, Gulf Coast harbors were generally choked by bars at the mouths of rivers and bays. Lighthouses were critical to the navigation of the winding channels in the shallow bays and sounds.

The great wealth of the South of course grew on the cotton plant. Few Americans, however, realize that the U.S. economy was for a long time based on Southern exports. Cotton was the great American commodity, accounting for far more than half the value of all U.S. exports in 1860 and about 75 percent of the revenue of the nation's treasury. The leading cotton states bordered the Gulf of Mexico. Just before the Civil War, they moved almost a million tons of the white fluff by sea annually. Aids to navigation along the Southern coast were critical to this commerce. Mississippi Congressman Jefferson Davis had worked diligently in the 1840s to ensure that Southern coasts were well marked by a system of efficient lighthouses.

The United States needed its southland, the South needed lighthouses, and the towers were built. By 1859, the U.S. Light-House Board had nearly completed its modernization of the country's lighthouse system. Every chandelier of ancient reflectors had been removed and modern Fresnel lenses installed. Inefficient lightships had been replaced everywhere on the Gulf Coast by offshore screwpile lighthouses or by more powerful lights ashore. Tall, first-order lighthouses such as the 200-foot tower at Mobile's Sand Island had just started to settle into the tidewater sands. At the outbreak of war, only two Gulf lighthouse sites approved by Congress remained to be marked, both delayed by clouded real estate titles. The American lighthouse system was approaching its zenith when political hostility halted its progress.

The attack on Sabine Pass, September 8, 1863, illustrated in Harper's Weekly, *October 10, 1863.*

Lighthouses under the sovereign states

A corollary to secession from the Union was sovereignty over former federal facilities, which Southerners knew had been financed by revenues from Southern ports. Seceding states moved quickly to seize forts, arsenals, customhouses, and lighthouses. Lighthouses must continue "business as usual" to keep vital trade flowing without interruption. In Alabama, one of the first states to follow South Carolina in seceding, the governor issued immediate orders inviting former U.S. government employees to continue their duties under state control. U.S. Navy Lieutenant Edward L. Handy, lighthouse inspector at Mobile, declined the offer. The state collector delivered a polite ultimatum on January 21, 1861: "To obviate difficulties and to prevent embarrassments that may arise from conflicting authorities in the Light House Establishment within the limits of the State of Alabama, I do hereby notify you that in the name of the Sovereign State of Alabama, I take possession of the several Light Houses within the State...." Alabama appointed its own inspector, Lieutenant Robert T. Chapman, and, lacking local directives, instructed state keepers: "In the discharge of your duties, you will be governed by the [c. 1857] laws, rules & regulations of the United States ... so far as they are applicable."[1]

State by state, lighthouses passed peacefully from Union to local control, with the exception of towers in the Florida Keys, which were held by Union forces throughout the war. Neither keepers nor mariners saw any difference in operations. Inspectors inspected, engineers repaired, and keepers were paid—with state funds.

The Confederate States Light House Bureau

By February 1861, the secession movement was well under way, tying the states together into a loose organization similar to the "firm league of friendship" created by the 1777 U.S. Articles of Confederation. On February 8, delegates adopted essentially the U.S. Constitution, appropriately edited to preserve the values of the South, and all U.S. laws which did not contradict the new law of the land. One of these laws was the 1789 act authorizing federal support of lighthouses to encourage prosperity and maritime commerce. Central control was not immediately established, however. Local customs collectors continued to manage lighthouses under their jurisdiction, often remaining under state control until the Confederate States Treasury Department was able to take over.

Information about their status filtered down slowly to often-confused keepers. On March 31, keeper Manuel Moreno at the isolated Southwest Pass of the Mississippi River had heard of the secession of the states. Hearing rumors of coming action from pilots on steam tugs, he wrote imploring the New Orleans collector Frank Hatch to enlighten him as to what he might expect. If his nation was arming, he felt he and his assistants should have muskets, pistols, and ammunition so that they might resist any attack that might come.[2]

The U.S. government attempted to negate the Southern activities and, at least on paper, administered a parallel lighthouse establishment throughout the war. Lighthouse inspectors for the U.S. Eighth and Ninth Districts sat out the conflict at the lighthouse depot on Staten Island, New York. When U.S. Navy Lieutenant Joseph E. Fry, inspector at New Orleans, resigned his commission on January 26, the date of Louisiana's secession, the secretary of the U.S. Light-House Board asked the Treasury Department if a replacement should be requested. The question was almost rhetorical and may have indeed been intended to test the Union government's attitudes toward Southern officers who resigned their commissions.[3]

The secretary of the U.S. Light-House Board, Commander Raphael Semmes, U.S.N., was an Alabamian and sailor of reputation who had felt for years that he had been wasted in a dismal desk job. A Confederate congressional committee invited Semmes to resign his Federal commission and accept one in the South. On February 15, 1861, he reported to Montgomery for duty in the Confederate States Navy, two days after the Electoral College affirmed Abraham Lincoln as U.S. President. Semmes' first assignment was to buy gunboats in the North. The Confederate Congress passed an act on March 6 establishing the Confederate States Light House Bureau, its chief officer to be a captain or commander of the Confederate Navy.[4]

Confederate Treasury Secretary Christopher G. Memminger recommended Semmes as bureau chief to President Jefferson Davis on April 10, 1861, although it appears that Semmes had already reported for duty as early as April 4. Semmes recommended a Southern lighthouse organization similar in makeup to the U.S. Light-House Board. For the sake of efficiency and out of disdain for soldiers, it would be smaller and under the complete control of the Navy. For Semmes, being a bureau chief meant a new desk but the same old sedentary job, at a time when his new nation needed men of salt and action. "I had barely time to appoint the necessary clerks, and open a set of books," he recorded in his memoirs, "before Fort Sumter was fired upon, and the tocsin of war was sounded." Officially, Semmes served four days as head of the Confederate States Light House Bureau.[5]

His only action in the bureau, recommending division of the Confederacy into four lighthouse districts, was of minor significance. District boundaries and headquarters are unclear in surviving documents, since the districts endured only a few months. The First (New Orleans) and Third (Mobile) Districts were in the Gulf of Mexico, constituting about half the nation's coast and all the largest, most strategic cotton ports. The Second and Fourth Districts were apparently on the Atlantic Coast. Since his plan was presented and accepted by April 15, these districts may not have included the "border states" of Virginia (which seceded April 17) and North Carolina (May 20).[6]

Had the Confederate Light House Bureau not begun disintegrating almost immediately, it might have later incorporated scientists and Army specialists as did the U.S. Light-House Board. Semmes quickly submitted the names of four top Navy lieutenants to fill the posts of district inspector. He had no use at all for engineers, and did not recommend any Army officers. Semmes did hire a civilian chief clerk, Edward F. Pedgard, just before departing for his first command afloat. Semmes left Montgomery on April 18 to outfit and command the commerce raider CSS *Sumter* at New Orleans.[7]

Secretary Memminger reported to President Jefferson Davis that Semmes was "withdrawn from the Light House Bureau for active service" and that several of the lieutenants he recommended were also wanted by the Navy Secretary. He recommended Commander Ebenezer Farrand of Perdido, Florida, to replace Semmes as bureau chief, and Lieutenants William G. Dozier for the First District inspector, James D. Johnson for the Third District, and John R. Eggleston for the Fourth District. The Second District inspector job remained vacant for the remainder of the war; one can guess that it was located at Key West, a Union stronghold. Inspectors were returned to the Confederate Navy on July 11, 1861, because of the threat of the Union warships, with the caveat, "Whenever the lights are restored, their services will again become necessary."[8]

As national events moved at a rapid pace, they disrupted the Light House Bureau. The Treasury Secretary appointed Thomas E. Martin as chief clerk, replacing Pedgard on May 1. Four days later, Farrand reported to take charge. Most of the next three weeks were apparently spent in preparing for the move of the capital from Montgomery, Alabama, to Richmond, Virginia. Squabbles there over precious office space took some precedence over whether the infant Confederacy would be able to maintain its system of lighthouses.[9]

No sooner had the bureau settled into its offices than its impossible task became apparent. The tiny U.S. Navy, 42 ships strong, had begun what would become a strangulating port blockade that would eventually help defeat the South economically. By the end of May 1861, blockaders had been assigned to the largest ports to cut off the cotton exports and prevent the importation of crucial war supplies. For the next few years, the blockade exposed the South's greatest vulnerability and constituted the Union's "greatest strategic success."

The Union fleet was rather slow in paying visits to Gulf Coast light stations. Into the third week of blockading, much to their comfort several coastal lights were still in full operation. Soon, however, Confederate customs collectors began extinguishing lighthouses, in one case dismantling a tower, in hopes the enemy ships would founder on unlit shoals. Bureau chief Farrand issued instructions for collectors to safeguard lighthouse property, especially the fine Fresnel lenses. At the Egmont Key Lighthouse guarding Tampa Bay, keeper George Rickard was instructed by the Confederate States collector to deceive the Union Navy and "keep up such relations with the fleet as would induce them to allow him to remain in charge until such time as the [lens and lamps]

The USS Mississippi *firing a Confederate steamer off Ship Island Lighthouse near the mouth of the Mississippi.*

could be safely removed." Union blockaders soon went off in chase of sails, and Rickard immediately stripped the lighthouse station, burying the lens near Tampa. By the end of July 1861, Southern mechanics had carefully removed Confederate States lamps and lenses to prevent Yankee "predations." Union gunboats responded by seizing all United States lighthouse property expropriated by the brazen rebels. The coast fell dark.[10]

Both Union and Confederate forces raided towers at the three Mississippi River passes, sometimes only hours apart. Semmes, now commanding CSS *Sumter*, sent boats on June 23, 1861, "to the different light-houses to stave in the oil casks and bring away the lighting apparatus to prevent the enemy's shipping from using the lights. I found that the lights at Pass a l'Outre and South Pass had been strangely overlooked and that they were still being nightly exhibited." When his men revisited one station on July 11 to remove the lens, they found that a whaleboat from the steam sloop USS *Brooklyn* had removed everything of value a few hours before.[11]

Most collectors had already seen to it that lenses and supplies were properly crated, inventoried, and removed to warehouses. A few simply left darkened stations in the charge of unarmed keepers. In perhaps a case of overreaction, the Galveston collector paid a contractor $250 to dismantle an 80-foot tower. The iron Bolivar Point Lighthouse was taken down bolt by bolt and plate by plate, with the one-inch iron skin probably used to satisfy the South's need for iron.[12]

The Confederate Light House Bureau started to implode only six months after its inception. With only four lighthouses still in operation, Farrand left the bureau and returned to Confederate Navy duty by September 20, 1861. Thomas Martin was quickly appointed as Chief of the Light House Bureau, *ad interim*, and served optimistically and loyally in that capacity until the government surrounding the bureau simply dissolved.[13]

Martin acted quickly to preserve Confederate property for the anticipated relighting, once the Union forces recognized the futility of the blockade. In his first week on the job, he proposed a letter from the Treasury Secretary requiring collectors to remove and safeguard all property and provide inventories of all government property. He also required more formal transfers of lighthouse vessels to the Confederate Navy and Army, often with the provision that they "be returned in good order to the Light House Bureau whenever required for that service." On April 30, 1862, Secretary Memminger approved Martin's plans to have all lighthouse materials shipped 150 miles inland, or to a point each collector felt was safe from Yankees. Six days earlier, U.S. Flag Officer David G. Farragut had run past the forts below New Orleans, proving that no place along the coast could be considered secure from invasion.[14]

Coastal lighthouses became favored sites for Confederate heavy gun emplacements or picket posts. The tall towers were usually the only vantage point on the low Gulf coastline and were well situated for defensive forces to spy on blockader movements or advancing enemy troops. The Dog Island station became a Union coaling station, bathing resort, and smoking lounge for blockade-weary Union sailors, visited by "ladies of Apalachicola." The Chandeleur Island keeper was arrested by naval authorities when he was caught sending flag signals to Confederate blockade runners.

As military assets, the lighthouses were also military prey. In most cases, lighthouses were damaged through individual acts: vandalism, accidental fires, or desperate attempts at destroying fortifications during a landing or retreat. The Mobile Point Lighthouse was simply in the way during exchanges of fire and was damaged by shot.

One of the greatest dangers to lighthouse stations was neglect. Shoreline erosion refused to pause for the war effort. There was only one documented instance on the Gulf Coast where mass destruction of lighthouses was deliberate and coordinated. General John Bankhead Magruder, commanding Confederate forces in Texas, issued explicit orders for field commanders to destroy every standing lighthouse on the state's oceanfront. Soldiers burned or mined with explosives the towers at Point Isabel, Padre Island, Port Aransas, Pass Cavallo, Saluria, and Matagorda Island.[15]

The Confederate States Light House Bureau's activity dwindled until November 1862, when the last known Confederate States lighthouse was extinguished on Choctaw Point at Mobile. On releasing the last keeper, Eliza Michold, the Bureau was reduced to only one employee, its interim chief, Thomas Martin. He continued to track, when he could, where strategic lighthouse apparatus were stored.[16]

Martin's last annual report, submitted January 25, 1864, sadly advised Secretary Memminger:

> The operations of the Light House Establishment during the past year have been very limited in extent, being confined almost exclusively to the care and preservation of the Light House property which has been taken down and removed to places of safety. Instructions were given to the various Superintendents of Lights to cause the illuminating apparatus and other fixtures to be carefully removed, boxed and conveyed to different points of the interior, removed from the depredations of the enemy. I am happy to report that with two or three exceptions the efforts made in this regard were entirely successful, so that when any order may be issued by you for the resumption of the active operations of the Light House Establishment (which time I trust is not far distant) no great difficulties will arise in replacing the machinery and carrying out the designs for which the Bureau were created.[17]

Thomas Martin was assigned two days later to the drudgery of paying war bond interest with worthless Confederate paper in the Office of the Treasurer, and then to the staff of the First Auditor of the Treasury. He had already been displaced from his comparatively plush offices by the head of the Bureau of Surgery and Medicine.[18]

Light House Bureau duties now were minimal. Martin's greatest challenge from this time onward was keeping valuable sperm oil out of the hands of his own countrymen. Until the Light House Bureau folded, the Confederate Navy requisitioned the precious oil for gunboats, presumably for engine room lubrication, and for lighting interior waterways not yet under Union control. The Bureau doubted that such expensive oil was being used efficiently, however. In one case the Confederate ram CSS *Baltic* had consumed 100 gallons, never even weighing anchor in Mobile Bay. "This quantity of oil cannot be procured at any price," Martin complained. The South's economy was in such a state that salt nearly equaled silver in value. Suspecting that many a poker hand had been lit by a whale-oil lamp, he flatly refused more requests for precious lighthouse oil "to avoid the embarrassment that would result from a total absence of oil when orders may be given to relight." To the end, Martin was hopeful the Confederacy could survive and that his lighthouses would help restore the prosperity and dignity the South had once known.[19]

Union troops removed lenses from many lighthouses, including the tower at Southwest Pass.

Confederate States Light House Bureau records dwindled as territories came under the Stars and Stripes. The National Archives file ends abruptly with an insignificant document recording the storage of minor lighthouse property at Mobile, dated December 31, 1864. Martin had by that time joined a battalion of clerks and bureaucrats, drilling each Wednesday after luncheon for a desperate attempt to defend the capital.[20]

Exactly when and how the C.S. Light House Bureau ended is unrecorded. On April 2, 1865, with all the Confederate coastline but Mobile in Union hands, President Davis and several government officers abandoned Richmond for a more secure capital in North Carolina. It is doubtful that a Light House Bureau chief was required there to help the cause. The last breath of the Confederacy was spent a month later during a skirmish in Texas, a few miles from the ruins of the Point Isabel Lighthouse.

Activities of the U.S. Light-House Board during the Civil War

The earliest efforts to relight the Southern coast were made by Union blockaders. Although many ships carried pilots experienced in sailing the shoal waters of the Gulf, much of the Union fleet was in constant fear of grounding and capture as they probed unfamiliar waterways. The few charts they carried dated to surveys begun, but never finished, one or two decades before on a coast reshaped almost yearly by hurricanes.

The first Gulf Coast lighthouse the U.S. Navy captured intact and relit was the strategic tower at the north end of the Chandeleur Islands. Captain Melancton Smith, commanding USS *Massachusetts*, removed the lens on July 9, 1861, and returned two months later to fortify the island and place the light back in operation. The anchorage behind the island was briefly the only port available to the blockading fleet. A few months before the Chandeleur Light was secured, sailors from the USS *Brooklyn* and USS *Powhatan* had visited the Southwest Pass and Pass a Loutre lighthouses in the Mississippi Delta, removing their lenses but not placing the stations in operation. For the remainder of the first year of the war, Union landing parties visited isolated lighthouses, only to find the lenses, oil, and other materials removed. They often reported these stations damaged, attributing much of the destruction to rebel vandals, when in reality much of the work had been done by previous Union visitors. At least one lighthouse served as a target for Union gunnery practice.[21]

By the end of the first year of the conflict, the Union had taken no significant Gulf Coast ports. Indeed, President Abraham Lincoln pressed his forces for any land or sea victories. Northern morale swelled when Flag Officer Farragut steamed past the forts below New Orleans in late April 1862 and forced the city to surrender. On July 5, the acting U.S. customs collector at New Orleans sent an urgent dispatch to the Light-House Board in Washington requesting immediate assistance in repairing recently captured lighthouses. The Board immediately dispatched an engineer, Captain William A. Goodwin. When he arrived on August 5, he found that U.S. Treasury special agent Maximillian F. Bonzano had already begun collecting and repairing lenses found at the New Orleans Mint. Goodwin recommended that Bonzano serve as acting engineer and inspector for the Eighth and Ninth Lighthouse Districts, consisting of the Gulf Coast from St. Marks, Florida, to the Mexican border. Bonzano filled all four positions until well after the war and became solely responsible for rebuilding towers on virtually the entire Gulf Coast during the most traumatic era in United States lighthouse history.[22]

Working out of a repair shop at the U.S. Mint, Bonzano fitted up 11 lighthouses in the four months following his arrival, most of them marking the approaches to New Orleans. Technically, he acted under congressional mandates to establish and operate lights at designated sites on Gulf waterways. In reality, he set his priorities by Army or Navy pleas for navigation aids in support of the war effort. Because of his isolation from Washington and the pressing needs of local commanders, he was delegated uncommon authority. Early on, Bonzano paid keepers, workers, and suppliers with $15,000 from his own pocket before funds arrived from the Light-House Board. He eventually drew from an ample pot of Union funds, and appointed and fired keepers or workers without the usual close scrutiny of Washington. The tasks ahead were challenging, to say the least.[23]

As far as Bonzano was concerned, Gulf Coast lighthouses were divided into three theaters of operation. Much of the territory surrounding New Orleans was firmly in Union hands by May 1862, the only Federal land west of Pensacola's Fort Pickens. His lighthouses marked the approaches to New Orleans by the end of 1862, with only Cat Island and Lake Pontchartrain's north shore remaining dark.

To the east, only Pensacola had been secured. Mobile was the scene of an intense Union blockade and would not be completely in Union hands until after General Robert E. Lee surrendered at Appomattox. Sovereignty over most other waterways between New Orleans and the Dry Tortugas was contested until the last days of the war.

On the western front was the grand invasion of Texas by the Union army. Here Army transports needed the aid of lighthouses to disembark troops at the jumping-off point in Barataria Bay and along the shallow Louisiana coast. With the exception of a tiny lighthouse built at the Brazos Santiago, Union sailors did not benefit from aids to navigation in Texas.

Even though Bonzano carried out his rebuilding operations only in secure locations, his crews were not immune from danger. In 1862, after Union troops landed at New Orleans, keeper Vincenzo Scorza was taken prisoner and his wood lighthouse at Bayou Bonfouca burned. At the time, Scorza was technically employed by the Confederate States Light House Bureau. He escaped from Camp Moore, and reported to the U.S. customhouse in New Orleans in July 1862. At the West Rigolets Lighthouse, keeper Thomas Harrison "was shot from off the L.H. wharf

The fate of the keeper at the Sand Island lighthouse is not recorded, if a keeper was even assigned. The light was exhibited with a temporary lens in December 1862, and was blasted to pieces by Confederate soldiers two months later.

on the 2d night after his arrival." Bonzano was not sure if he "was shot by rebels, contraband Negroes or some of our own soldiers." The lighthouse lay only a few hundred yards from the Union-occupied Fort Pike. The Union lighthouse tender *Martha*, running through Chandeleur Sound on July 16, 1864, was captured as she headed to Pensacola via stations on the Rigolets. Her crew was taken as prisoners to Mobile, where the master and his son escaped.[24]

Four dozen lighthouses were in operation on the Gulf of Mexico at the time of secession. Of these, the two at the Dry Tortugas operated throughout the war under Union control. The United States restored 11 others on their original towers by the end of 1862, and another seven by war's end. It would not be until 1875 that the Gulf's lighthouses would stand again in their pre-war state. After a gap in progress of 14 years, the first new Gulf Coast light station was added in 1874, the year the Civil War ended for lighthouses on the Gulf of Mexico.[25]

The recovery of trade

Without economic recovery in the South following the Civil War, new lighthouses would not have been built in the Gulf. And recovery was not easy. Many in the North, which controlled the federal purse strings, held ill will towards the recently defeated South. Also, the rapidly expanding railroads were challenging the cost-effectiveness of waterborne transportation. Although the number of steamboats using the river system which drained into the Gulf dramatically declined during the second half of the 19th century, the volume of goods carried by water increased as powerful towboats pushed and pulled barges, each one doing the work of several side-wheel steamers. By the 1880s, barges carried one-third of all cargo on the lower Mississippi, and the percentage continued to increase. Waterborne trade on the upper Mississippi and its tributaries declined as new railroad lines increasingly made Chicago the hub of the Midwest. Also, cotton gave way to coal as the most important cargo, and that in turn gave way to petroleum produced during the second half of the 20th century. Although these new trade patterns had a negative impact on the shipbuilding industry in the Gulf, the need for lighthouses and other navigational aids to guide the barge traffic increased. Also, Louisiana had once again become the state through which the most waterborne traffic passed.[26]

New lighthouse technology

The administrative change from the Fifth Auditor to the newly created Light-House Board in 1852 sparked the most productive and creative era in lighthouse construction. Along with the rest of the nation, the Gulf Coast was a beneficiary of this change. Although screwpile lighthouses had been introduced into the Gulf before the Civil War, this technology did not spread throughout the Gulf until after the war. Gasparilla Island Lighthouse and Charlotte Harbor Lighthouse are examples of post-Civil War screwpile lighthouses in the Gulf.

In 1870 two new districts were created in the heartland to cover the Mississippi, Missouri, and Ohio Rivers.

The next lighthouse construction technology to be introduced in the Gulf was that of cast-iron towers. Like the screwpile, a few had been built before the Civil War, but none in the South. Cast-iron tower construction offered numerous advantages over the classic stone and brick towers. First, it was lighter and could be made watertight. Second, it could be produced and prefabricated in the convenience of a workshop and then transported to the building site. Third, a cast-iron tower was strong and allowed for the standardization of designs. Fourth, it could be dismantled and moved if threatened by erosion. The first tall, skeleton tower lighthouse to be built in the Gulf was completed at Southwest Pass, Louisiana, in 1873. This design possessed the same advantages as the conical cast-iron tower but was lighter.

In 1910 Congress abolished the Light-House Board and created the Bureau of Lighthouses. The top four positions were appointed by the President and this new administrative system provided more direct control from Washington. On July 1, 1939, the Bureau was transferred to and consolidated within the U.S. Coast Guard, which to this day is responsible for administering the nation's lighthouses.[27]

The Tortugas Harbor Light was erected atop a staircase at Fort Jefferson in 1876. It is now part of the National Park Service's Fort Jefferson National Monument. (NPS photo by George A. Grant, 1937)

Chapter 3

Florida's West Coast: Dry Tortugas to Cedar Keys

The Turtle Islands

The Dry Tortugas are the most westward group of islets in the Florida Keys, guarding the mouth of the Gulf of Mexico. Here oceangoing ships make their turn into or from the Gulf. Until a channel was charted through the reef in 1847, shallow-draft vessels were at considerable risk when taking the northwest passage shortcut between Key West and the Tortugas.

The Florida Keys are the world's second-largest ocean reef; only Australia's Great Barrier Reef is more extensive. The keys are made even more dangerous by the swift Gulf Stream passing close by shore and by the notorious hurricanes and violent squalls which have battered ships since the days of Spanish galleons. The broken bones of many ships lie on the reef.

Juan Ponce de Leon, the first European known to enter the Gulf, called the end of the keys *Las Tortugas* because his sailors captured 160 tortoises there, plus many manatees and birds. Because the keys lacked fresh water, Americans called the tiny barren islands the Dry Tortugas.[1]

When the British acquired the Floridas in 1763, royal surveyor Gerald deBrahms recognized both the danger and the strategic importance of the Tortugas islands. He proposed a combination lighthouse and fort for each end of the coral reef. His hexagonal wooden tower was to rise 214 feet from the center of a three-story stone fort mounting two dozen cannon. An iron stove at the top would spout "smoak" in the daytime. Rockets would be fired every half hour to guide ships at night. DeBrahm estimated the lighthouses would cut insurance rates in half for ships passing through the Florida Straits. The British never tried to build either tower.

When the United States took legal possession of Florida in 1819, the keys were a haven for wreckers—salvage crews who preyed on ships driven ashore in the unmarked waters. The Key West customs collector estimated that four dozen ships each year, almost a ship a week, splintered their keels on the Florida reef at the height of the cotton trade. The federal government built a lighthouse at the Dry Tortugas soon after gaining possession of the territory in 1819. Even after lighthouses were built, crafty wreckers lured ships ashore by tying lanterns onto the tails of mules and leading them through the sand dunes.[2]

Garden Key Lighthouse

The first lighthouse built on the Dry Tortugas quickly earned a reputation as the least effective on the United States coast, in an American lighthouse system considered by many to be one of the poorest in the world. Until the Loggerhead Key tower was erected nearby in 1858, the Garden Key Lighthouse drew little but complaints from all who sailed by it.[3]

The United States commissioned a survey of the new Florida Territory soon after its cession by Spain. In March 1822 Captain Matthew Perry on USS *Shark* recommended a lighthouse at the Dry Tortugas and at three other Florida locations. The next month the Treasury Department asked Congress for $8,000 to begin construction of the Dry Tortugas station. When no bids for its construction were received, the budget was doubled in 1824.[4]

The project got off to a bad start. The low bidder, Samuel B. Lincoln, sailed from Massachusetts in August 1824, but was lost at sea before arriving at St. Augustine. His company quickly renewed the contract with an extended deadline, and met with the St. Augustine collector's agent to pick a suitable site. Failure of the agent to charter a vessel and a general illness which disabled the entire work force further delayed the job.[5]

There is evidence that a lightship operated at the construction site. A St. Augustine newspaper account reported, "The Light Vessel on the Dry Tortugas has been of the most essential service in warning vessels of approaching danger. Four ships lately have been entirely indebted to the warnings of the bells of the Light Vessels." The old lightship *Aurora Borealis* had left Pensacola around this time, bound for the Chesapeake Bay, and may have been detailed to the Tortugas keys during her passage. The federal government had no lightships officially in operation in the Florida Keys at the time.[6]

Garden Key was chosen because it not only could serve to light the end of the reef but also offered a fine harbor north of the island. Already well behind schedule, the tower was completed in March 1826 and would have been ready for lighting if the appointed keeper had not been more than a thousand miles away.

John R. Flaherty appears to have been the worst sort of political appointee. He insisted on three months' advance pay plus government-provided transportation for his family and household goods from his home near Baltimore. A U.S. revenue cutter dispatched for this sole purpose was unable to carry all Flaherty's baggage. Once at his isolated post, the keeper was unable to manage his food supply. The Dry Tortugas Lighthouse was America's first entirely isolated station, some 60 nautical miles from the nearest supplies. Hungry and broke, keeper Flaherty was forced to beg the Key West customs collector for emergency provisions.

In Washington, the Fifth Auditor of the Treasury, who administered all federal lighthouses, advised the Secretary of the Treasury that unless the government supplied provisions, "it will be absolutely necessary to extinguish the [Dry Tortugas] lights and abandon them." A revenue cutter soon left Charleston with twelve barrels of food.[7]

Finally in operation on July 4, 1826, the lighthouse held its lantern 70 feet above the Gulf Stream, with a circle of 15 lamps and reflectors to provide a "lighthouse of the first magnitude." Sailors were not impressed, however. Flaherty proved to be lazy and incompetent, failing to trim the wicks periodically. The miskept flame deposited a thick coat of whale-oil soot on the lantern glass. After 14 months of almost total isolation and several episodes of near starvation, Flaherty asked for a transfer to some place where groceries could be bought across a counter instead of unloaded over the gunwale of a supply boat. He exchanged duty with Joseph Ximenez, keeper at the Sand Key station.

Inspectors later found the Garden Key station in a state of general disrepair with permanent damage to the lantern glass. A revenue cutter captain reported in 1834 that keepers Alexander Thompson and Richard Watson scrubbed hard but the lantern glass was "opak and cannot be cleaned." All the glass and 13 of the 15 reflectors required replacement.[8]

Congress began wondering if the tower was adequate when the ship *America* wrecked near the lighthouse in 1838. The ship's captain complained, "It was a common remark of all (wreckers excepted) that the light was one of the most miserable they ever beheld. Vessels have been lost in running for it, supposing they could see [the light] before they got ashore." An investigator sent to assess the problem found that a contractor had recently corrected the problem, installing new English plate glass and 21 new lamps and reflectors. He pronounced the light a good one, although he felt it should be raised to 100 feet.[9]

Dissatisfaction continued among mariners. While the light was supposed to be visible 18 miles at sea, one captain charged that he anchored close enough to make out kegs at the base of the tower but could not see the light itself because of a layer of haze at the height of the lantern. The owner of the ship *America* warned his masters that a ship would run aground on the reef before spotting the light. Stephen Pleasonton, Fifth Auditor of the Treasury and Superintendent of Lighthouses, yielded in face of mounting demands and promoted a total of three lighthouses to mark the Tortugas group. When the furor died down, Pleasonton quietly shelved the expensive plan, opting to have lighthouse entrepreneur Winslow Lewis increase the number and size of the reflectors at Garden Key.[10]

When complaints continued to pour in, Pleasonton considered either raising or lowering the light to clear the haze. He wrote to the superintendent at Key West, demanding an explanation as to "the cause of that Light being seen at only a short distance. This is the only Light in the Country that is complained of." In 1846, Winslow Lewis fitted the lighthouse with an entirely new lantern glazed with large panes of French plate glass. The French by this time had established a worldwide reputation for producing the finest lighthouse materials. Parisian lensmaker Henry LePaute claimed that, with his Fresnel lens, the Garden Key Light could be visible 24 miles at sea, using far less oil than the old lamps. In 1847, the privately published *Coast Pilot* warned that the lighthouse at Dry Tortugas could be seen only "when a vessel is on shore and is without a doubt the worst light on the coast."[11]

Tortugas Harbor Lighthouse

A U.S. Navy survey of the coast in 1829 had pointed out that any nation, including an enemy, occupying the Dry Tortugas would control navigation in the Gulf of Mexico. It was almost 20 years later that Fort Jefferson was begun. When the first Army engineers arrived, they were surprised to discover the oil lamps of a lighthouse in the center of the planned powder magazine. Furthermore, the Treasury Department had overlooked the formality of obtaining title to the land. An agreement hammered out between the War and Treasury Departments halted Army plans to raze the tower, and the fort was formed around it.[12]

By this time, cotton from plantations west of the Appalachians drew considerable ship traffic bound for hungry textile mills in New England and Europe. The Coast Survey[13] reported a striking vista from the top of the lighthouse: some 60 ships visible at one time, all heavily freighted, making the turn into the Gulf Stream at the Dry Tortugas. Cotton had grown to be the premier crop of the United States, accounting for more than half the nation's exports by 1860.[14]

In 1851, the Provisional Light-House Board reported that the Garden Key Light fell far short of serving the needs of shipping; the maritime industry recommended replacing it with a tower at least 100 feet tall. Their original plans called for a new tower built within the fort, but a far better site was found farther west on the outermost island in the Tortugas cluster. The Board constructed a taller lighthouse on Loggerhead Key, so named for the loggerhead turtles found there. Upon completion of the Loggerhead Key station, the old Garden Key tower was referred to as the Tortugas Harbor Lighthouse and served only as a guide into the anchorage at the fort. There is convincing evidence that a wooden lighthouse was built on the parade grounds of the fort, some distance from the original brick lighthouse, which was built in an angle of the fort's walls. The tower may have been erected to hold temporarily the first-order lens that was later installed at Loggerhead Key.[15]

The two Dry Tortugas lighthouses were the only Gulf Coast towers which stayed in full operation throughout the Civil War. By the end of the war, leaks began to develop in the lantern at the Tortugas Harbor

Lighthouse. A pressing need to repair war damage at other stations postponed work here. A new lantern eventually arrived at the station, but the Light-House Board asked permission to install it on a new tower "in order that the old, inconvenient and unsightly building may be removed from the parade ground." Before the light was moved, an 1873 hurricane rendered the old tower nearly useless. It was finally razed in 1877. The new hexagonal tower made of boilerplate iron was erected atop a fort staircase and stands today. In about 1912, the station was automated, with tanks of compressed acetylene replacing butts of kerosene to fuel the lights. Within a dozen years, the station was discontinued.[16]

Loggerhead Key Lighthouse

As early as 1838, congressional pressure directed attention to Loggerhead Key as a new lighthouse site for the entrance to the Gulf of Mexico. While Garden Key offered a superior harbor, a light on Loggerhead Key, about three miles west, could steer vessels far clear of the reefs. No work was done until shortly before the Civil War.[17]

In 1855 Army engineer Captain Horatio Wright conducted experiments showing that a 146-foot tower could be built on Loggerhead Key without sinking into the sand. He planned a tower 30 feet in diameter, tapering to 15 feet at the top, with walls 6 feet thick at the base. A wide timber grillage would protect the base from burrowing rats and crabs. He recommended Pensacola or Mobile brick, believing that "they will resist the action of the sea air, whilst many kinds of northern bricks are known to yield." As finally built in 1858, the tower measured 150 feet tall, with a first-order Fresnel lens visible for 20 miles.[18]

In 1868, engineers surmised that wind-driven rain was eroding mortar from between the bricks, but repairs were delayed by a rigid yellow fever quarantine at Fort Jefferson. Problems at this lighthouse received less attention than problems elsewhere in the aftermath of the Civil War. Foul weather caused cracks in the masonry by 1873, when other Southern lighthouses were nearly back to a prewar state. The Light-House Board asked Congress for funds to replace the tower, but emergency repairs proved sufficient for a time. During the rebuilding of the top nine feet of the tower in 1875, the lighthouse was painted with white and black bands to improve its visibility during daylight hours. Shortly afterward, a hurricane did no damage, but the request for a replacement tower was continued. The Board asked for $150,000. Congress offered half that amount.[19]

Facing a funding shortfall, the engineers resorted to ingenuity to save the structure. They again removed the top nine feet of masonry and extended iron rods from the lantern down the entire 150-foot height of the tower. Section by section, workmen chiseled out the masonry, implanted rods, and replaced the bricks. Even when reinforced, the tower

---

Preliminary sketch for a cast-iron lighthouse for Loggerhead Key, which was never constructed.

continued to vibrate like a reed in a heavy blow. The Light-House Board repeated its plea for a new tower and developed a plan for an octagonal, iron-plate tower; however, it was never constructed.

The tower was eventually repainted with its current color scheme, typical of daymark towers surrounded by trees, with the lower third white and the upper two-thirds black. This lighthouse marking the entrance to the Gulf of Mexico became the most powerful in the United States in 1931 when a three-million-candlepower electric light was switched on, about 250 times the intensity of the kerosene lamps it replaced. The lighthouse still serves as an active aid to navigation. Its impressive clamshell lens, replaced with a modern optic, was put on display at the U.S. Coast Guard Aids to Navigation School in Yorktown, Virginia.[20]

Punta Rassa and Charlotte Harbors

Juan Ponce de Leon was the first European known to explore the Gulf of Mexico, landing at Charlotte Harbor on May 23, 1513. He was greeted by a band of hostile Indians who killed one of his crew, beginning more than two centuries of violent competition between the Native Americans and white Europeans. While white settlers eventually conquered both the soil and the inhabitants, Florida's west coast was not an early target of the 19th-century American exodus which flooded the rest of the South with settlers in search of cheap, productive land.

In the 1840s, when many of the feared Seminoles were driven westward, migration began in earnest on this coast. Towns grew up at Fort Dade (now Tampa), on "Sanybell" Island, and in the Cedar Keys. Growth was slow, with maritime improvements primarily in support of the area's lucrative cattle exports to Havana.[21]

Sanibel Island Lighthouse

There was no seacoast beacon anywhere on Florida's west coast in 1833 when "residents of Sanybell Island" first petitioned for a light to mark the port of Punta Rassa. They hoped a light serving the coasting trade would also attract ships and settlers to the tiny port, affording some protection from the constant threat of Indian attack. Commercial interests in Key West also claimed that a light there would be in the best interests of shipping, serving as a seacoast marker on the New Orleans route. At the time, the Florida Territory lacked the political clout in Washington to succeed in appeals for lighthouses. The Sanibel settlement literally died out within five years because of disease and other hardships.[22]

Shortly after the Civil War, the port of Punta Rassa boomed for cattlemen, with almost 16,000 head exported to Cuba alone in 1871, and a like number shipped to domestic ports. While traffic was limited to shallow-draft vessels, almost a ship a day sailed from the port, and traffic seemed to increase by the month. The Light-House Board was struggling with rebuilding the Southern lighthouse system at the time and did not encourage new projects. It was not until 1878 that the Board

Soon after automation in 1949, the Coast Guard turned the Sanibel Island Lighthouse grounds over to the U.S. Department of Interior to become part of the J.N. "Ding" Darling National Wildlife Refuge. The keeper's quarters, now used for housing by the city of Sanibel, are said to be the oldest buildings on Sanibel Island. (Photo by David Cipra, 1994)

asked for $40,000 for an iron skeleton tower at Sanibel Island to guide ships toward Tampa's lighthouse. Sanibel Island was the first landfall for ships rounding the Tortugas, some 120 miles to the south.[23]

Congress authorized funds in 1880, but only half the amount required for the station. The Light-House Board refused to begin work with insufficient funds, fearing that running out of money would only cause complications and increase overall expenses. By the next year, the estimate for the work had risen to $50,000. The additional money was made available in 1882.[24]

Work on the foundation began in March 1884, with metalwork prefabricated in Northern ironworks. Before the parts could be landed, the ship carrying parts for both Sanibel and Cape San Blas wrecked and sank about two miles off Sanibel Island. Two lighthouse tenders and the work crew from the island salvaged every piece of iron, except for two small brackets which were duplicated by a New Orleans foundry.

The tower was completed without further delay, and was first lit by keeper Dudley Richardson on August 20, 1884. The third-order Fresnel lens was held 98 feet above sea level, visible almost 16 miles. The iron tower was based on a model used throughout the Gulf, with three identical towers built in Florida, one in Louisiana, and another in Texas.[25]

Henry Shannahan served at the station longer than any other keeper, from 1888 to about 1913. The last keeper, Bob England, departed for the mainland on April 19, 1949, when the station was automated. The light station has been battered by heavy seas and vicious storms for more than a century, but it still stands as the centerpiece of the island.[26]

Gasparilla Island Lighthouse

Boca Grande, the "big mouth" of Charlotte Harbor, was charted by the Coast Survey in 1859. With 15 feet of depth on the bar and 24 feet in the bay, the harbor held great promise as a port, had the Civil War not delayed Southern commercial development. In 1887 the Light-House Board was informed that the terminus of the Florida Southern Railroad had been established at Punta Gorda, at the head of navigation in the bay. Promoters expected steamship lines to connect with the railroad.[27]

The port grew as expected and established a respectable business exporting large quantities of phosphate, at a time when fertilizer ingredients were in high demand worldwide. In 1888 the Light-House Board asked for $35,000 for a lighthouse to mark Boca Grande and the

Restored and relit by a local citizens group, the Gasparilla Island Light Station is now managed by the Florida Park Service as part of Barrier Islands Geo Park. (Photo by David Cipra, 1994)

shoals which ran to seaward off Gasparilla and Lacosta Islands. An interior lighthouse was planned for the center of Charlotte Harbor.[28]

The Gasparilla Island Lighthouse was completed in September 1890 with two nearly identical, square, "vernacular" dwellings on iron screwpiles. The keeper's quarters held the lighthouse lantern centered on its hip roof, and the other served as the assistant keeper's quarters. The wood lighthouse held a third-and-one-half-order lens 44 feet above sea level, first lit December 31, 1890, by keeper Francis McNulty. The mariner aboard ship saw a white light, interrupted by red flashes, distinguishing this light from the one at Sanibel Island.[29]

In the 1960s the Coast Guard automated the light and locked up the station. Weather and vandals took a toll on the structure until local citizens asked for custody. The Gasparilla Island Conservation and Improvement Association took control of the station in 1972 and lived up to its name. Financed in part by a state grant, restoration was completed in November 1986; the Coast Guard loaned an antique Fresnel lens for the lantern.[30]

Charlotte Harbor Lighthouse

Calusa Indians first settled the keys off Charlotte Harbor. Through a sequence of Spanish and English mispronunciations, the bay received its name from these Native Americans.

A sister lighthouse to the one at Gasparilla Island was built at the same time in the center of Charlotte Harbor, about eight and a half miles eastward. Atop pilings in 10 feet of water, the tower was lit in September 1890 by keeper John Watkins. This tiny harbor lighthouse, holding a fifth-order red lens, was visible only 11 miles. The square, white, story-and-a-half dwelling showed the light at 36 feet above sea level.[31]

The Charlotte Harbor station, like the one at Gasparilla Island, was never seriously threatened by the elements. It was automated with an acetylene light by 1916 and was replaced by a wood beacon in 1943.[32]

Boca Grande (Rear Range) Lighthouse

The United States lighthouse establishment built only one lighthouse on the Gulf Coast which was designed from the start to show an unattended light produced by electricity. The keepers of the nearby Gasparilla Island station were responsible for replacing burned-out bulbs. Until this time, keepers had been assigned to all other lighthouses to tend lamps using whale or vegetable oil, liquefied lard, or kerosene.

The Boca Grande Rear Range Lighthouse was built to replace locally built, lit beacons maintained by the Boca Grande Corporation during winter and spring months as a guide into the local yacht basin. The hexagonal, white skeleton tower was completed in 1932. The tower

The last conventional lighthouse erected on the Gulf Coast, the Boca Grande Rear Range tower is still an active aid to navigation.[33] (Photo by David Cipra, 1994)

showed a red aeronautical beacon 105 feet above the water. The parabolic reflector, visible only to seaward, formed a range with a small light offshore.

From Egmont to the Cedar Keys

The Florida peninsula's most impressive watercourse, Tampa Bay, was recognized early as an important resource. Egmont Key, at the outer entrance to the harbor, is a boomerang-shaped strip of sand less than two miles long. The bay's only lighthouse was placed here. Just to the north lies Anclote Key, a former pirate hangout which showed early promise as a railhead and port.

Egmont Key Lighthouse

The town of Tampa became a relatively busy seaport in the 1830s, despite the sparse population of the region. The Army had occupied the

---

area as early as 1823 during the Seminole Indian Wars. As marine traffic increased, so did complaints of ship captains grounding on the bay's barrier keys. Tampa citizens petitioned for a lighthouse to mark Egmont Key early in the 1830s. Shippers in Key West joined their request at about the same time, asking for a lighthouse there to mark the main sea route to New Orleans and Mobile. The Florida coast juts slightly outward at Tampa Bay, presenting an opportunity for a seamark to guide mariners northward toward very rich cotton country. An 1837 survey by the U.S. Treasury endorsed a lighthouse there because "Eggmont is the point which all vessels endeavor to make when bound to St. Marks, Apalachicola or St. Joseph's." Not until the Florida State Legislature petitioned Congress in December 1846 was $10,000 granted for a lighthouse at Egmont Key.[34]

Francis A. Gibbons of Baltimore received the Egmont Key contract on July 24, 1847; construction began shortly afterward. The contract called for a relatively minor harbor light atop a brick tower only 40 feet high, and specified that the octagonal lantern be glazed with plate glass from Paris, in recognition of French leadership in lighthouse technology. The two-room keeper's dwelling measured only 680 square feet, about half again as large as a two-car garage. The St. Marks customs collector insisted on a foundation of driven pilings, even though frugal Stephen Pleasonton, Fifth Auditor of the Treasury and Superintendent of Lights, believed "that no better foundation could be found than dry shells and sand." Pleasonton relented. Within two years, the investment would save the tower.[35]

The lighthouse was built in 1848, the year the Army released 160 acres of Fort Dade, which became the present downtown Tampa. By contract, the light was to shine by January 1, 1848, but Gibbons' supply ship grounded on Orange Key, and the master jettisoned almost half the bricks to refloat the ship. Construction stopped after only 20 feet of masonry had been laid. The keeper found no bricks available in Tampa, delaying delivery by five months. When it was completed, the Egmont Key Lighthouse was the mariner's only signal over the 400 nautical miles between the Dry Tortugas and St. Marks.[36]

Despite obvious danger and isolation, the keeper and assistant received the lowest pay on the Gulf of Mexico—$400 and $200 each per year. A rapid succession of keepers—7 in its first 11 years—testified to dissatisfaction with this meager compensation.[37]

The first keeper, Sherrod Edwards, soon got his feet wet. A hurricane on September 23, 1848, drove a 15-foot tide over the island. According to local legend, Edwards and his family rode out the storm in a little boat lashed to a stubby cabbage palm, although records indicate the island was under six feet of water. They rowed ashore and quit soon afterward. The storm left the tower in serious danger of toppling.

Egmont Key Lighthouse as it appeared in Frank Leslie's Illustrated Newspaper *during the Civil War.*

Pleasonton could hardly believe the foundation could fail, writing, "The tower, tho' it may have careened, has hardly fallen down, as piles were used for its construction." Lightning opened cracks in the masonry by 1851 and erosion attacked the foundation. Repairs would wait for the Light-House Board to take charge of American aids to navigation in 1852.[38]

A pad of concrete laid to 10 feet around the base in 1854 proved to be a temporary solution. In 1856 the Board asked for $16,000 to replace the tower with one twice as tall. The new tower was completed in late 1857, holding a modern, third-order Fresnel lens 86 feet above sea level. For a year, the Egmont Key tower held the highest light on the Gulf of Mexico.[39]

In 1861, keeper George V. Rickard found himself working for two lighthouse superintendents who were at opposite ends of the state and on opposite sides of a war. Patrolling Union gunboats supported the United States collector at Key West. A small contingent of soldiers at the key backed the authority of the Confederate States collector at St. Marks. Rickard sided with the South and set out to deceive the enemy blockaders. He followed instructions to continue the light for the Yankee visitors and "to keep up such relations with the fleet as would induce them to allow him to remain in charge until such time as the property could be safely removed" from the grasp of Union predators.

As soon as Union ships patrolled some distance offshore, Rickard went into action and at the same time ended his employment. On August 23, 1861, he carefully dismantled and crated the lens. Virtually everything not permanently installed was carted to Tampa. Only the brick tower, six panes of glass and eight iron tower steps greeted the blockaders when they returned. Fearing a Union raid on Tampa, the collector paid Rickard to bury the lens in a secret location "in the vicinity

The lantern at Egmont Key Lighthouse was removed in the early 1960s to accommodate a modern optic. (Photo courtesy of U.S. Coast Guard Historian's Office)

of Tampa" and to ship easily moved materials by rail 50 miles north to Brooksville. When Federals landed at Tampa in May 1864, they found little to capture.

Federals took over the station after Confederates evacuated Egmont Key, using the island as a refugee and prisoner camp. On the tower a light of some sort aided the blockading fleet. The station was thoroughly renovated and a fourth-order lens permanently re-exhibited on June 2, 1866, by William S. Spencer. He was summarily released when he refused to sign an oath of allegiance to the United States.[40]

A red sector was added to the lens in 1893 and, because the colored glass reduced the light's intensity, the lens was upgraded to third-order. Until around this time, the island's principal residents had been lighthouse keepers, with occasional encampments of soldiers during the Seminole and Civil Wars. During the Spanish-American War, the federal government erected more than 70 buildings on Egmont Key. A Navy wireless telegraph station was in place by 1905, using the lighthouse tower to support the antenna. By World War I, a town had grown, bringing electricity, telephones, and a real theater to the island.[41]

The Egmont station holds a record of some sort for the most creative fog signal. Most stations sounded discordant bells, gongs, or steam whistles. According to the 1907 *Light List*, Egmont Key keeper Charles Moore welcomed sailors to Florida's Gulf Coast by blowing a melodious "conch shell, in answer to signals from passing vessels."[42]

By the end of World War II, the proud old lady of Egmont Key was decapitated. The century-old iron lantern and classical Fresnel lens were replaced by a mundane aeronautical beacon. Looking more like an incinerator chimney, the Egmont Key lighthouse was automated in 1989, the last manned lighthouse in the State of Florida.[43]

Anclote Key Lighthouse

The Anclote Keys lie at the north end of Tampa Bay's barrier islands, about three miles off the current city of Anclote. It was from a base on these keys that a small navy of some 400 pirates is said to have hunted booty in early 1682. They relocated northward in mid-year, wresting Fort San Marcos de Appalachee from 45 Spanish defenders.[44]

The 1851 report of the Provisional Light-House Board recommended a lighthouse on the keys, among dozens of other Gulf locations. The Treasury Department acquired the property for a lighthouse reservation in 1866. Almost 20 years later Congress authorized just $17,500 for an iron skeleton tower identical to the one just built at Sanibel Island to the south. When the Board complained that a tower would cost twice that amount, another $17,500 was added in 1886.[45]

The square, iron skeleton tower, placed on the south end of the most southerly key, was designed to allow hurricane winds to blow through the spidery legs. Manufactured in northern ironworks and shipped to the site, it arrived in June 1887. Landing materials on the beach took more than a month. The prefabricated kit was bolted together in less than three months and held a third-order lens, flashing a red light every 30 seconds, 96 feet above ground and 102 feet above sea level. Keeper James Gardner lit it on September 15, 1887. The nearby Egmont Key Lighthouse showed a fixed white light. Painted dark brown, the Anclote tower also stood out among the short trees as a daytime beacon.[46]

In September 1938 most of the 177 acres of lighthouse property had been transferred to the U.S. Biological Survey. The light station was discontinued on November 5, 1952; the remaining property was declared excess to Coast Guard needs in 1954. The lighthouse now watches over the Anclote National Wildlife Refuge.[47]

Cedar Keys (Sea Horse Key) Lighthouse

Just south of the Suwanee River, off one of the least-populated areas of Florida's coast, the Cedar Keys lay directly on the course from Tampa Bay to St. Marks. As early as 1837, federal buoys marked the anchorage behind the keys, serving troop transports engaged in the Seminole War. The buoys were swept away in the 1843 hurricane which destroyed St. Marks and were thought not important enough to replace, since the Seminole wars had been declared a victory and the Army abandoned Cedar Keys. The Florida Legislative Council in 1839 recommended that Congress authorize a lighthouse at the Suwanee River. They hoped the addition of a lighthouse would help develop the port and that settlers drawn to share in the new prosperity would help drive Indians from the coast.[48]

By 1840 the town of Cedar Key had developed, based on the manufacture of pencils from the islets' namesake scrub growth. During

Shown here in 1893, the Sea Horse Key lighthouse was designed in Miami by U.S. Army Lieutenant of Engineers George G. Meade, who would later gain fame at Gettysburg. (Photo courtesy of U.S. Coast Guard Historian's Office)

Florida's West Coast: Dry Tortugas to Cedar Keys

the war with Mexico, General Zachary Taylor predicted the importance of the keys, asking that they be set aside as a military reservation, and "the outer key of the group [Sea Horse Key] the Government should retain, as on it no doubt will be erected ... a light house for the benefit of vessels trading to the Suwanee River." Speculation over a railroad connection to Fernandina on the Atlantic coast intensified interest in the port. A U.S. Coast Survey report in 1850 seems to have provided the stimulus for a lighthouse there.[49]

In September 1850, two months after President Taylor's death, Congress appropriated $8,000 for the lighthouse, but the funds proved to be insufficient for the works. An additional $4,000 was approved in 1852 and plans were prepared. Materials were assembled in Philadelphia and shipped to the site in March 1854. On the evening of August 1, 1854, Keeper William Wilson touched the first match to the wicks.[50]

The brick dwelling, surmounted by a short octagonal tower and lantern, was erected atop "The Mound," a 45-foot sand bank on Sea Horse Key. The light was held 75 feet above sea level, about 18 feet above the roof of the dwelling. Its beam was visible 15 miles to sea on a clear day.[51]

The Confederate States customs collector at St. Marks removed the lens and all supplies by August 1861. The Florida Railroad had already commandeered the station's sperm oil, presumably to keep it out of the hands of Union raiders. Keeper William M. Fields was kept on as caretaker until blockaders took control of the area. A force of Florida troops armed with three cannon was stationed on the island to protect blockade runners using the anchorage. When the USS *Hatteras* arrived in January 1862, only 22 soldiers remained on the island. They poled away in flat-bottomed boats, but neglected to take along oars. Once they were in deep water, the tide carried them further as *Hatteras* closed in for the capture. The Union later used the key as a staging point for the unsuccessful drive to Tallahassee. N.J. Collier was appointed keeper, and the light was re-exhibited on August 23, 1866.[52]

The population on the Cedar Keys fell to only 1,500 by 1890, reflecting a dramatic drop in goods passing through the port. Timber resources dwindled; the oyster beds were exhausted. The only trade still flourishing was the shipment of arms to Cuban revolutionaries. The Cedar Keys station finally went dark in 1915. In 1929, the Cedar Keys National Wildlife Refuge was created nearby. The lighthouse property became part of the refuge in 1936.

Lucky students from the University of Florida now live and learn in the old station while conducting marine biology research. The lighthouse on Sea Horse Key is the oldest still standing on Florida's west coast.[53]

In addition to being an active aid to navigation, the St. Marks Light Station serves as the local headquarters of the Coast Guard Auxiliary, who provide rescue services and boating classes in the area, and is a featured stop on the walking tour of the St. Marks National Wildlife Refuge. (Photo by David L. Cipra, 1994)

Chapter 4

West Florida

St. Marks River to Pensacola Bay

The lands once known as West Florida extended from the St. Marks River to either the Perdido River or Louisiana's Lake Pontchartrain, depending on the national allegiance of the person recording the history. Multiple transfers of this territory between the colonial powers—Spain, France, and England—left the western boundary in much doubt. For a few months in 1810 and 1811, the Republic of West Florida declared freedom from Spanish rule and flew the Gulf's first Lone Star flag. It was not until the War of 1812 that the U.S. Congress proclaimed harbors west of the Perdido to be part of the 1803 Louisiana Purchase and thereby United States ports. Georgians considered the eastern portion of West Florida much like an extension of their own state until the Spanish ceded both the Floridas in 1819, relenting to increasing hostility among residents of North, Central, and South America.

West Florida ports had long been the outlet for much of the goods produced in western Georgia and the Mississippi Territory. Settlers there had put up with high tariffs, poorly managed ports, and corrupt colonial officials for many years and welcomed the acquisition of the Territory of Florida.[1]

The various colonial powers erected at least one, and perhaps two or more, lighthouses along this part of the Gulf of Mexico. The British marked the mouth of Mobile Bay some time after 1683; an American surveyor guessed that a moldering Spanish tower at St. Marks had been used as a lighthouse between its construction date and 1799. The British also occupied small forts at St. Marks, Pensacola, and St. George Island, but they left no records of aids to navigation. The 1820s eviction of the inland native populations opened vast acreage for the migration of planters from depleted farms on the eastern seaboard. Commodities traders followed the population shift, and lighthouses soon marked their ports.[2]

St. Marks to Apalachicola Bay

Nowhere else in the South are the effects of the pre-Civil War cotton trade more evident than at the boom-or-bust ports of St. Marks and Apalachicola. Now not much more than fishing villages and resorts, the ports once commanded the attention and filled the purses of cotton merchants in New York, Liverpool, and Le Havre. From the 1830s to secession, cotton from Florida, Alabama, and Georgia was shipped in massive bulk on rafts, steamboats, and infant railroads to these Gulf ports.

While St. Marks grew steadily as a cotton port, a commercial land venture at Apalachicola fairly exploded, backed by land speculators and bankrolled by freed-up federal cash in the early 1830s. The Apalachicola River drains a considerable portion of rich cotton lands in Georgia and Alabama. Linked to plantations by crude dirt roads, river steamers carried millions of quarter-ton cotton bales downstream for export to hungry European and New England textile mills.

Apalachee Bay, St. George Sound, and Apalachicola Bay provided nesting places for small fleets of shallow-draft cotton freighters. A series of barrier islands protected Apalachicola's sound from hostile weather and at the same time provided several sites for lighthouses to mark the harbors.[3]

St. Marks Lighthouse

The Florida Gulf Coast makes a hard turn to starboard at one of the state's oldest settlements, St. Marks. Originally, the settlement had a hybrid Spanish-Indian name, San Marcos de Apalachee. Stories of Apalachian gold lured Ferdinand DeSoto and other Spaniards to the bay.

DeSoto passed through Apalachee in 1539 and left banners streaming from the oak trees on the St. Marks River as signals for the fleet he knew would someday follow. The Spanish established a weakly garrisoned fort at San Marcos and provided a few navigation aids. Spanish supply ships frequented the port to transport foodstuffs to hungry colonists in Havana. Pirates sought out Spanish sails along the trade route.

In about 1679 the commandant at San Marcos de Apalachee ordered a "watch tower-beacon" to be erected at the river's mouth, manned by two soldiers and two Indians, but only during the summer when piracy was at its height. In 1722 Charlevoix sailed Apalachee Bay, recording in his journal, "All night we perceived fires on the continent ... we perceived the balizes, or sea marks, which the Spaniards directed us to follow." The fires were probably open campfires at Indian settlements. The seamarks were certainly wood stakes the Spanish drove into the shallow oyster banks. Had a real lighthouse been present, Charlevoix would surely have used the French term "pharos" instead of "balize."[4]

Eventually, the Spanish erected a stone tower just below the fort, but it is not known whether signal lights were shown from its summit. British cartographer Gerald de Brahms called the tower a "lookout castle" in 1763. He recorded its measurements as 45 feet high and 12 feet square at the base. It stood adjacent to the Spanish quarry from which the stone was cut. Musket loopholes pierced the two-foot-thick walls. Even if the tower was never used to signal ships, its primary purpose must have been for security. In an official U.S. government survey of West Florida in 1799, Andrew Ellicott recorded evidence that the Spanish displayed a light in the tower. "For what purpose this tower was erected appears to be uncertain," Ellicott wrote. "On the top there appears to be a light-house, but from the condition of the bay, being so shoal and full of oyster banks, as to render it useless to shipping, it appears to have been unnecessary." If the tower was used as a lighthouse and was built before the fort, it was the first lighthouse in the New World.

The probable location of what may have been America's first lighthouse is now called Gibb's Island on the west side of the river, three-quarters of a mile south of the fort. The last remnants of the tower were leveled by a gale in 1851.[5]

As planters poured across the Appalachian Mountains into fertile western Georgia and Alabama, cotton blossomed as an export. Towns such as St. Marks flourished with trade. Florida Governor William P. DuVal and Delegate Joseph M. White convinced the federal government in 1828 to set aside $6,000 for a light tower at Apalachee Bay. The army received funds the same year to begin clearing river obstructions. At first, the lighthouse was to be built on Southwest Cape on a spot still known as Lighthouse Point. The Pensacola customs collector visited the river's mouth and decided on "Oscilla Point," the current lighthouse site, which provided pilots a better guide for entering the Spanish Hole anchorage. When no bidders applied for the contract, the cash offering was doubled, drawing a bid of $11,400 from lighthouse magnate Winslow Lewis. Contract cosigners Benjamin Beal and Jairus Thayer actually built the tower.[6]

Local historians hold that the original tower was built of stone from the old Spanish bomb-proof at Fort San Marcos. The contract specifically called for brick, but it is possible some local stone was used in the foundation of the original or later lighthouses. The current keeper's dwelling, built in 1854 with walls four and one-half feet thick, certainly contains rough Florida limestone. The dwelling stone may have come from the station's 1844 breakwater which, before it was destroyed in 1851, measured 10 feet high, 6 feet thick, and 160 feet in length.

The local St. Marks superintendent of lights refused to accept the first tower, charging the builders with deliberate fraud. Arbitrators found hollow walls instead of solid brick, as called for in the contract. The second St. Marks tower, rebuilt at no cost to the government by Lewis' partner, master mason Calvin Knowlton, was completed on January 29, 1830. Samuel Cosby had been formally appointed as keeper on January 18th. After a few months, large cracks began appearing in the tower. In

June 1831 the local collector was commended for saving the tower by cinching it back together with iron hoops, like a huge brick barrel. He surmised that a poor foundation was allowing the tower to settle unevenly.[7]

St. Marks continued to grow gradually. By 1835 Florida's first railroad was complete, connecting the port to Tallahassee's plantations. By this time the federal government had begun dredging a 17-mile, $28,000 channel through the oyster bars from St. Marks to deep water.

While the collector's iron bands had corrected the symptoms of deterioration, they provided no cure. By 1838 the tower was in serious danger from the instability of the isle on which it was built. A Navy inspector claimed the station was "in a most wretched condition and ought to be rebuilt immediately." The 73-foot tower was found to be built on a sand bank deposited over soft organic soils, which the sea now washed away.[8]

A decade after the contractor was paid, the government felt he was still responsible for ensuring the foundation. In 1842 Lewis was pressured into tearing the tower down and building a third time on a solid footing of pilings. The final St. Marks lighthouse was completed April 21, 1842. It stood 65 feet tall and showed the original chandelier of 15 lamps and reflectors. This lighthouse, too, was built with hollow walls, but by this time the practice was sanctioned by the federal government.[9]

While hostile Indians never presented a direct threat to the station, keeper Benjamin Metcalf asked for armed guards in 1836, or at least a schooner he could anchor in the bay to shelter his family. The St. Marks collector hired two guards, drawing a reprimand from Washington and orders to send the keeper back to work, adding, "If he declines, you will temporarily charge some other person with that duty." Only mosquitoes and Union raiders ever attacked the St. Marks station.[10]

A hurricane on September 13, 1843, demolished nearly every structure below the town of St. Marks, leaving only the lighthouse and keeper's dwelling, which was heavily damaged. The keeper and his family survived by clinging to the attic floor, but about 15 other island residents disappeared. Two hundred houses upriver in Port Leon were leveled and the wooden railroad to Tallahassee was torn up. Local stone was used to build a sturdy breakwater around the reservation.[11]

Another hurricane in 1851 virtually leveled the city of St. Marks, destroying also the Spanish fort and lookout tower. Damage was so extensive at the mouth of the river that the U.S. Coast Survey insisted the station would wash away unless better protection could be provided. In 1854 the Light House Board recommended a new tower at a more protected site. A new breakwater was built instead, and the tower foundation was underpinned without incident. Stone from the old breakwater was used to erect the still-existing keeper's house.[12]

The 1842 St. Marks Lighthouse tower with 1867 lantern, shown here in 1893, survives as the second-oldest lighthouse standing on the Gulf of Mexico and the oldest still in use. (Photo courtesy of U.S. Coast Guard Historian's Office)

By 1860 St. Marks had recovered from those devastating hurricanes to regain its position as the port for the Tallahassee area. About 30 million pounds of cotton moved across its wharves that year, up from only 21 million in 1852. The Confederate States customs collector had made sure every removable item was carefully crated and taken to safety before hostile forces met at the mouth of the St. Marks River. Opposing forces took turns abusing the abandoned station. Occupying Confederate troops turned the lighthouse station into a small fortress. They perforated the massive stone walls of the keeper's dwelling for rifle ports, erected a battery near the tower, and dug breastworks around the buildings. The lighthouse itself became a Confederate lookout and signal tower.[13]

Gunners on USS *Tahoma* and USS *Somerset* bombarded the battery for 40 minutes on June 15, 1862, but there is no evidence that their shots hit the tower. When the Confederates withdrew, Union sailors landed to burn the keeper's dwelling, which the soldiers had used as a barracks. Another Union raiding party torched the wood steps in the tower on July 12, 1863, to prevent enemy lookouts from reaching the top. The fire was so intense it cracked and glazed most of the interior brickwork to 30 feet high and buckled the iron plates of the lantern floor. When troops landed at the lighthouse to march on Tallahassee in

March 1865, they found that retreating pickets had drilled holes into the foundation and set off three charges. The first blasted a hole one-third of the tower's circumference and eight feet high. The second and third explosions took out only half the thickness of the tower walls to about six feet in height. The shocks cracked the upper 12 feet of the lighthouse and blew out the lantern glass.[14]

Remarkably, there was enough left to salvage. The lighthouse district engineer described the tower as "one of the most solid structures on this coast, which alone could have prevented its destruction, every conceivable agency to effect it having been applied." The repairs were finished between September and December 1866 using materials left over from work at St. George and Dog Islands. A new fourth-order Fresnel lens was supplied and first lit on January 8, 1867, by keeper David M. Kennedy.[15]

Land in front of the station had been slowly disappearing for decades; after the war the Light-House Board contended that the station would succumb to the next major hurricane. The theory was proven false in 1874. A hurricane tide on September 18 and 19 pressed into the bowl-shaped bay until the floor of the keeper's dwelling flooded. The keepers, with several women and children, took refuge in the tower, which stood fast. Structural weaknesses in the tower forced the Board to again remove the lantern and rebuild the top in 1883. In the process, the tower height was increased by 10 feet to its present height.[16]

Proposed Southwest Cape Lighthouse

The tip of Apalachee Bay's Southwest Cape has carried the name Lighthouse Point since at least 1858, even though, according to federal records, a lighthouse never stood there. The point had been the top choice among mariners for the St. Marks Lighthouse in 1828. White sand bluffs earned this place the name Bald Point on sailors' charts.[17]

The captain of the U.S. Revenue Cutter *Taney* recommended a lighthouse on the cape in 1834, instead of the one proposed for Dog Island to the west. Petitions the same year from local merchants and mariners pleaded with Congress for a light on "South Cape Promontory," claiming it the first landfall for vessels headed to either St. Marks or Apalachicola. Petitioners persisted until 1854, when Congress authorized $15,000 for a lighthouse. The Light-House Board tried to purchase land for the station, but a clear title was unobtainable.[18]

The Board mentioned Southwest Cape for the last time in its 1857 annual report to Congress, continually complaining about its inability to obtain a clear title to the land. The U.S. Attorney General refused to accept sale papers submitted in 1859; the Civil War soon intervened. Curiously, the Board's engineer secretary pressed for the acquisition of the property in 1877, referring to instructions he had found dating to

December 10, 1856. The only evidence of his success is an empty file folder in the National Archives which once held title papers dated January 9, 1879.

In 1858 the U.S. Coast Survey published its first chart of Apalachee Bay with Lighthouse Point prominently, permanently, and improperly designated. The spot has never been within sight of a federal lighthouse.[19]

Cape St. George Lighthouse

In the 1830s Apalachicola Bay was the only harbor for the export of cotton from eastern Alabama and western Georgia. By 1836 the town of Apalachicola had become the third largest cotton port in the United States. The Apalachicola River extends some 300 miles to Columbus, Georgia, at the head of steam navigation and in the middle of some of the richest cotton land in the world. Nearby St. Joseph's and St. Marks tried to siphon off some of the cotton trade by building railroads to the interior, but Apalachicola wharves continued to be piled high with bales. The territorial legislative council lobbied for a lighthouse to mark Apalachicola Bay beginning on November 11, 1829.

Apalachicola was incorporated as a town in 1831, and in March of that year Congress appropriated $11,800 for a lighthouse on the extreme west end of St. George Island to mark the bay's primary entrance. A clouded title delayed the start of construction; not until March 29, 1833, were 10 acres of land deeded for a consideration of $52. A last-minute proposal to place the lighthouse on the south cape of the island did not reach the Apalachicola collector until after he had acquired property on the west end of the island. Congress had by this time allotted a total of $10,700 for dredges to open up the harbor. Winslow Lewis, builder of the nearby St. Marks Lighthouse, won the St. George Island Lighthouse contract, bidding $9,484. Before the end of the year, he completed a 75-foot tower holding 11 lamps.[20]

By the time the lamps were lit, the lighthouse was already deemed insufficient. Trade at Apalachicola had mushroomed way beyond expectations. Local businessmen complained in 1834 that so much cotton was to be shipped to Liverpool alone that only deep-draft vessels could handle the tonnage. These ships could not cross the shallow bar at the Apalachicola's west entrance. A harbor light on Dog Island later served oceangoing ships seeking the anchorage there.[21]

Vessel masters and cotton agents agreed that the St. George Island Light was inadequate, but for a different reason. Because most ships approached from due east, they would run hard aground on the island's southern cape before the lighthouse could be seen over the sand dunes. They recommended the station be moved to the elbow of the island, about two and a half miles to the southeast. More than a dozen years would pass before their demands were met.[22]

Under an 1841 appropriation, Edward Bowden of Franklin County, Florida, erected a new tower in 1848 at a cost of $6,700. He was the only Floridian to receive contracts to build Florida lighthouses. The lamps, reflectors, and even the brick from the original tower were used at the new site. The station was now officially the Cape St. George Lighthouse. Keeper Francis Lee lit it for the first time on November 16, 1848. A severe gale on August 22-23, 1851, destroyed this tower as well as those at Cape San Blas, Dog Island, and St. Joseph Bay. The cities of Apalachicola and St. Marks were leveled.[23]

The third tower built at the Cape St. George Light Station in 1852 and photographed circa 1859. (Photo courtesy of U.S. Coast Guard Historian's Office)

On December 10, 1851, a contract was signed to build St. George Island's third lighthouse, with Emerson and Adams bidding $6,398. The old tower was again broken up, this time to build a new keeper's quarters. The new tower was to be built on a foundation of pilings, instead of simply laying the first course of bricks atop the bare sand, as was done with the first tower. Finished in 1852, the Cape St. George Lighthouse was eminently successful and stands today as the second-oldest lighthouse on Florida's Gulf Coast.[24]

The Cape St. George Lighthouse 1852 tower as it appeared in 1947. More recently, the tower has been severely undermined by erosion. (Photo courtesy of U.S. Coast Guard Historian's Office)

The Confederate superintendent of lights at Apalachicola hired George Robinson in July 1861 to remove and protect public property at the station, including the Fresnel lens. Keeper Braddock Williams was kept on as caretaker until May 20, 1862, when it was obvious that Apalachicola's barrier islands would be in Union control for the rest of the war. By March 1862 all items had been properly crated and shipped well inland to prevent their capture. Blockaders repeatedly visited the tower to spy on any fortifications or troop concentrations at Apalachicola. Refugees and Union sailors frequented the place. Several panes of lantern glass were shot out, and the dwelling was stripped of every piece of wood. Two walls of the brick keeper's quarters required rebuilding, but the tower needed only minor repairs. The first U.S. Light-House Board engineers to arrive found keeper Williams still at his post. A new keeper, James Reilly, re-exhibited the light on August 1, 1866. Williams received an appointment to tend the Cape San Blas Lighthouse and later returned to Cape St. George, where he died in a fall from the lantern.[25]

The Light-House Board blamed war damage for a "dark angle" in the lens in 1888. The next year, a new lens was installed. The lighthouse received routine repairs through the next century. The property was occupied by the U.S. Army as a coastal lookout station in World War II and has since been unmanned. The lighthouse was active until 1994, when severe erosion undermining the tower caused it to be declared structurally unsound.[26]

Dog Island Lighthouse

Apalachicola's Middle Pass is bounded by St. George Island on the west and Dog Island on the east. It leads into St. George Sound through a relatively young channel, not appearing on charts until after the War of 1812. The government marked the pass with a lighthouse on Dog Island in 1838. East Pass, near South Cape on Apalachee Bay, was to have been marked by a light as early as the 1820s, but that station was never built. The Dog Island Lighthouse served as a guide for ocean sailors into a snug harbor 20 feet deep. While some five fathoms of water lay between the anchorage and Southwest Cape, a shallow oyster bar known as the "Bulkhead" extended from St. George Island to the main shore, preventing all but flatboats and fishing smacks from reaching Apalachicola. The Bulkhead was to have been breached in 1836, but army engineers opted to deepen and straighten the West Pass channel instead.[27]

Congress responded to local lighthouse promoters with an appropriation of $10,000 in March 1837. Winslow Lewis won the contract on May 6, 1838, and completed a 50-foot brick tower, first lit by keeper Jacob D. Meyers on March 1, 1839. Inasmuch as the fixed lights Lewis built at Cape St. George and St. Marks were so close, he configured the Dog Island Light to flash every sixty seconds.[28]

The 1843 storm which did so much damage at St. Marks, St. Joseph's, and Apalachicola was no problem at the Dog Island station; it had been destroyed the year before. A hurricane on October 5, 1842, washed out about a third of the foundation. The tower walls caved in for 30 feet around its circumference and to almost half its height. A maze of cracks, the tower canted almost two feet out of plumb. The brick keeper's house vanished, along with the several occupants. The Fifth Auditor came to "the determination to build a frame tower ... which would not cost half as much as brick." The keeper shored up the teetering tower long enough for the replacement to be built.[29]

Lewis cleared himself of Congressional charges of shoddy workmanship, but only on technicalities in the contract. He received the contract to rebuild. While Lewis wanted to put up a brick tower, his estimate was exorbitant in the government's eyes. The Treasury Department had become convinced that wood lighthouses were best suited to the dangerous climate. The timber-frame replacement Lewis built in 1843 cost only $4,100, including salvaging the lantern and apparatus from the teetering brick tower. The light was displayed 40 feet above ground, and a broad black band five feet from the top helped distinguish the Dog Island Light from the white tower on Cape St. George. Pleasonton tried to force Lewis to erect this tower gratis, but later authorized payment when he claimed bankruptcy. Winslow Lewis' dominance of America's lighthouse construction and illumination appears to have ended on the sands of Dog Island.[30]

The wood tower met the same end as its predecessor. The massive hurricane of August 23-24, 1851, flattened just about everything in the region. A third Dog Island Lighthouse went up. It was also 40 feet tall and was built of brick with a new lantern, lamps, and reflectors, showing a flash every 3 minutes. A Fresnel lens was installed in 1856, showing a flash every 60 seconds, 48 feet above sea level.[31]

Union sailors vandalized the tower shortly after Apalachicola's Confederate superintendent of lights removed and safeguarded government property in the summer of 1861. The Confederate caretaker reported that the enemy shot out one pane of lantern glass and burned some portions of the dwelling and tower. Dog Island became a fleet-coaling station and resort. Blockade-weary Union sailors "rusticated" at the station, fishing and swimming off its beaches and using both the dwelling and lighthouse as smoking lounges. In January 1863 the dwelling burned to the screwpiles and the tower steps were damaged by fires set "accidentally" by the Northerners. After the war, the victors implied the damage was dealt by rebel forces, reporting, "All the destroying influences seem to have been at work at this station." A new fourth-order lens, flashing red and white, was rekindled on August 4, 1866, by temporary keeper Charles Thompson.[32]

The Dog Island Light Station was washed away in a storm in 1873 and was never replaced. (Photo courtesy of U.S. Coast Guard Historian's Office)

By 1868 a new keeper's dwelling was erected on a nearby sand hill, 15 feet above sea level. According to the Light-House Board engineer, it would provide a "secure refuge to the keepers and their families in case of loss of the tower." Erosion had undermined the lighthouse, and the engineer stated, "There is no hope of its outliving the first hurricane that may sweep over this island." He recommended a more prominent tower near the new dwelling.[33]

Four years later, the dwelling itself became the lighthouse. Engineers had surrounded the tower with a three-foot layer of concrete but a gale thoroughly broke it up. Now tilting over, the lighthouse was abandoned in 1872 and its lantern was perched atop the reinforced dwelling. The

Light-House Board felt "the light is safe for some time to come" but still sought funds to relocate it.[34]

"Some time to come" soon came. The brick tower disappeared in a storm on September 18, 1873. The dwelling and lantern were washed off the island but somehow the keeper and his assistant survived. Congress appropriated $20,000 to rebuild the station, but the post-war cotton trade recovered slowly. The funds were never used. St. George Sound no longer warranted two lighthouses. What brought a new lighthouse effort to this part of the sound was the depletion of northern forests. A new light for Middle Pass was placed on the mainland at the mouth of the Crooked River to serve a thriving timber trade.[35]

Crooked River Lighthouse

The South's robust pre-war economy took time to rebound. While the cotton ports recovered slowly over the next four decades, the southern lumber trade picked up quickly in the early 1870s. Florida's extensive pine forests became an important national asset.

Apalachicola and a smaller port at Crooked River, just north of Dog Island, garnered a large percentage of this trade. A lighthouse was again thought necessary. Congressional committees reported favorably on a lighthouse to mark the Middle Pass, and $40,000 became available for a new Dog Island Lighthouse.[36]

The Light-House Board considered a short hexagonal screwpile structure in the shallows behind Dog Island, but finally opted for a tall tower on the mainland. In 1888 the Light-House Board asked that the appropriation be shifted to allow construction at the mouth of Crooked River.[37]

Problems in gaining title to the selected site, followed by a fire which destroyed purchase documents, delayed commencement until January 1895. The square skeleton tower at Crooked River was completed in August and first lit October 28, 1895. The fourth-order lens showed a flash twice every 10 seconds. In 1902 the tower was given its current color scheme to contrast with the surrounding pine forest—its lower half white and upper half a dark red. The Crooked River Lighthouse continues to guide vessels in the area.[38]

Cape San Blas and St. Joseph Bay

A narrow hook of land whose name honors Saint Blassus, the patron saint of wool-combers, forms one of Florida's finest harbors, St. Joseph Bay. At the same time, it presents one of the most treacherous shoals in the Gulf.

The excellent shelter was recognized early by European explorers. The French established the earthen Fort Crevecoeur on the north shore of the bay in 1718 but abandoned it after Spain voiced objections. By

The construction gang poses on the Crooked River Lighthouse on the day the ironwork was completed in 1895. (Photo courtesy of U.S. Coast Guard Historian's Office)

the time the United States government arrived in Florida, many of its citizens had already settled on St. Joseph Bay, alongside the resident Spanish and Indian populations.

When the U.S. Navy began planning a naval station on the Gulf Coast in the early 1820s, St. Joseph Bay was considered to surpass Pensacola as a harbor. Had the citizens of Pensacola not slandered the harbor and the unhealthiness of its climate, the present Navy facilities at Pensacola might have instead lined St. Joseph's shore.

By 1835 federal banking tactics had shifted large sums of money to state banks, making funds available to real estate speculators. The founders and backers of St. Joseph resorted to sly manoeuvres. They built a railroad from the bay to the Apalachicola River, diverting cotton shipments from the established port to the east.

The boom town at St. Joseph was a miracle of expansion. Townsmen soon boasted exports of 60 million pounds per year and a population of 4,000. According to reports from rival Apalachicola, the bay of St. Joseph also harbored rows of saloons, gambling houses, and bordellos.

St. Joseph Bay Lighthouse

Revenue Service Captain Henry D. Hunter was detailed in 1834 to search for the best Florida lighthouse sites. He identified St. Joseph Bay as an excellent safe harbor for coasting vessels, but added, "there is no trade of any kind in this bay." He recommended a lighthouse at Cape San Blas to mark a shoal running 20 miles offshore, endangering vessels bound for Mobile and New Orleans. In 1836, the year the town of St. Joseph was founded, the Florida Legislative Council petitioned the U.S. Treasury for lighthouses at both the cape and the entrance to the bay. The next year Congress offered funds, but only to mark the harbor. On May 26, 1838, a $10,000 contract went to Winslow Lewis, by now the country's premier lighthouse builder.[39]

Shortly before the new year, Ephraim Andrews received the appointment to tend the bay's first lighthouse. The government accepted the lighthouse from the contractor on January 4, 1839. Andrews remained at the station until it was discontinued in 1847. Located just inside the extreme tip of the peninsula to mark the harbor entrance, it was only 50 feet tall but had a powerful beam from 15 lamps in 16-inch reflectors.[40]

The town of St. Joseph busted almost as quickly as it had boomed. Three events in short succession reduced the population to zero, with the exception of the lighthouse keeper and a few scavengers. First, the great economic Panic of 1837 tightened the investment cash supply. Depression in England had slashed cotton prices, bankrupting such ventures as the railroad to the Apalachicola River. Next, an 1841 yellow fever epidemic wiped out virtually the entire town population. The final blow came two years later, when a killer hurricane left what remained of the town a pile of splinters. For decades thereafter few vessels came to this harbor by choice.

In 1842 the Treasury Department sought congressional permission to discontinue the lighthouse "in consequence of the abandonment of the Town of St. Joseph as a place of trade." It was not until 1847, when the Cape San Blas Lighthouse was approved for the elbow of the cape, that the St. Joseph Bay Light went dark. Apalachicola's chamber of commerce had endorsed a lighthouse at the south tip of the cape to mark the route between their port and Mobile.[41]

The iron lantern and some building materials were transferred to the new site on Cape San Blas. The abandoned St. Joseph tower was heavily damaged in the hurricane of 1851, although enough was left to serve as a daymark throughout the Civil War. The foundation was clearly visible as late as World War II.[42]

After the Civil War the Light-House Board asked for $20,000 to re-establish the St. Joseph Bay station. While both houses of Congress reported favorably, funds were too tight and the harbor too insignificant. The bay entrance remained unmarked until after the turn of the century. For the next 30 years, the Board touted the virtues of the bay, but did not win congressional approval until the estimate for rebuilding fell to only $15,000. Finally, Congress relented.[43]

The original reservation just inside the tip of the peninsula was considered suitable even though the shoreline had eroded. Lighthouse engineers reconsidered and, as they did at Crooked River, decided in 1901 on a new location on the main shore.[44]

The new station was a square wooden dwelling on piers, with a stubby tower centered atop the hip roof. A small lens-lantern showed from August 1, 1902, until March 3, 1903, when the third- order lens arrived for installation. The first keeper was Charles Lupton, assisted by his wife Minnie. The couple spent 26 years at the St. Joseph Bay Lighthouse.[45]

In 1960 a tall, antenna-like tower replaced the lighthouse. The Coast Guard transferred all but a quarter acre of the property to the Bureau of Land Management. The 1902 lighthouse still stands under private ownership.[46]

Cape San Blas Lighthouse

Long before Europeans arrived on the Gulf of Mexico, Cape San Blas was an exposed sand bank extending well to seaward. Currents removed all but an itinerant shoal, which became known as the "Hatteras of the Gulf" because of the many shipwrecks there. Early Spanish explorers had documented the dangerous shallows.

Just as the shoals posed a danger to ships, the cape itself proved to be no safer for lighthouses. Attempts to light Cape San Blas constitute perhaps the lighthouse service's most consistent string of failures. Five towers were erected. Four of these were attacked by erosion as the shoreline receded.

The Florida Legislative Council recommended a light to mark the cape and its bay in 1836. A Revenue Cutter Service officer had charted the sand reef, insisting that a lighthouse "will be of essential importance to vessels engaged in the coasting trade." Unfortunately, an economic panic forced severe cutbacks in federal projects. All new lighthouse proposals were to be investigated by a senior naval officer. The official verdict regarding this station was, "A light-house at Cape St. Blas is, I believe, a useless expenditure." It would be 10 years before the national depression ended.[47]

Florida legislators and the citizens of Apalachicola continued to press Congress for a light at the south point of the cape. Ship captains added to the clamor, and in 1847 Congress finally authorized $8,000 for a lighthouse, on the condition that the St. Joseph Bay Lighthouse be extinguished before construction started.[48]

The Apalachicola customs collector visited the cape and chose a site two miles inland from the southern tip, a plot he was certain would not be inundated. Local experts petitioned him for a seacoast light of at least 90 feet, to be seen 20 miles to sea and well beyond the shoal. Edward Bowden of Franklin County, Florida, won the construction contract, which called for salvaging the brick from the St. Joseph Point tower, about 15 miles northward. While the tower was to be completed by March 1, 1848, it was delayed until April 25, 1848, when Winslow

Lewis finally delivered the revolving apparatus. Francis Arran was appointed the first keeper.[49]

The 65-foot tower was much shorter than the seacoast light mariners had demanded. During this era, the Treasury Department considered a tower of 65 feet to be of the first class. Lewis supplied a revolving chandelier similar to the one at Pensacola, displaying five lamps per face, but with alternating red-and-white flashes.[50]

Three years later, on August 23-24, 1851, the tower collapsed in a terrific gale which also destroyed the Dog Island, Cape St. George, and St. Joseph's Bay Lighthouses, plus the old Spanish tower at St. Marks. Congress was slow authorizing a replacement, waiting until the Light-House Board was formed before making $12,000 available to rebuild. An inspector was charged with examining the site and overseeing the laying of the foundation on a safe spot.[51]

An unusual plan for this tower was proposed by lighthouse engineer Captain Danville Leadbetter, who became known for creative architecture. It called for a tall brick tower bulging outward at the bottom like a champagne bottle to enclose an octagonal keeper's dwelling. The massive structure, 90 feet tall and using 160,000 bricks, was to be raised on iron screwpile stilts. The Light-House Board returned plans for a more conventional conical tower.[52]

Yellow fever epidemics and delays in receiving the lantern and Fresnel lens set the project back at least two years. Having hoped for completion in the spring of 1853, the Light-House Board reported that as of October 1855 the masonry was at last complete and the lantern ready to install. The new keeper, Joseph Ridlin, transferred from the Dog Island station and was on duty in November 1855.[53]

Just ten months later in the gale of August 30, 1856, the Cape San Blas Lighthouse was again flattened. Hurricane waves beat against the floor of the keeper's dwelling, raised on 8-foot piles, 14 feet above high tide. "A lagoon now occupies the site of the lighthouse," the Light-House Board succinctly reported, requesting more funds to mark the cape. Congress appropriated another $20,000 in March 1857 for a third attempt at lighting the cape. While this tower lasted far longer than its predecessors, it was to meet the same fate. Construction crews were harassed and delayed by hurricanes. The tower was completed and its new third-order lens lit May 1, 1859, by Keeper John Price. The revolving lens flashed 96 feet above sea level and was visible 16 miles to sea.[54]

The Confederate lighthouse superintendent had the lens and most of the clockwork apparatus removed before the Union fleet arrived. In early July 1861 the crates of lighthouse property were moved far inland to protect them from the enemy. Blockaders visited the island several times to break up the salt works at the tower, smashing the boilers, and burning all associated buildings. It appears the keeper's dwelling and

The fourth tower erected at the Cape St. Blas station lasted considerably longer than its predecessors (1859-1882). (Photo courtesy of U.S. Coast Guard Historian's Office)

the interior of the tower were torched at this time by either a Union landing party or by retreating salt-makers. A local myth that the lens now in use was damaged by Confederate Minié balls is a fabrication. The Light-House Board shipped in a new lens and revolving apparatus, and the tower was lit on July 15, 1866, by renovation foreman Simeon Russel. The station was turned over to its permanent keeper, Joseph Lewcraft, on July 24.[55]

The keeper received a new house in 1870, set 400 yards inshore from the tower. By this time, erosion had cut away enough of the beach that rough seas often washed against the brick base. Twelve years later, erosion laid the foundation bare and high tides lapped at the tower. When heavy weather prevented the keeper from reaching the light, he was instructed to hoist a lantern on a 90-foot pole about 100 yards inshore of the lighthouse.[56]

Wave and current action finally undermined the concrete foundation; workers removed the lens and revolving apparatus. On July 3, 1882, the tower toppled into the Gulf. A year later the beach had receded to the steps of the keeper's dwelling. A more permanent sixth-order lens was displayed from a new pole located farther inland to escape the sea. The Light-House Board hoped an iron skeleton tower would fare better on the fickle sands. These kit lighthouses could at least be dismantled quickly and moved to safer locations. The Board received $35,000 for the new tower in 1883.[57]

The materials did not even arrive at the site before they went to the bottom of the Gulf. The ship carrying both the San Blas and Sanibel Island towers wrecked off Florida's west coast. Most materials were salvaged, and the tower was completed in February 1885. The old third-order revolving lens was relit on June 30. The 98-foot tower was thought to be safe at 1,500 feet from the shoreline and a mile or so from the original site. In only three years, the distance from the tower to the Gulf was cut to 200 feet, and the Board reported the loose sand "will mostly be washed away in the next four months." The answer was to again rebuild, but not on the cape.[58]

Blacks Island was chosen as the new site, lying inside St. Joseph Bay almost two miles from the Gulf and about four miles north of the original Cape San Blas Lighthouse site. Certainly this would be a safe spot. Plans were prepared to elevate the tower 25 feet to clear the trees on the cape. While preparations were under way at the island, a hurricane in 1894 swept away the keeper's dwelling and enough beach sand that the tower now waded in the surf on its stilt-like legs. Keeper William M. Quinn lost all his personal possessions, valued at $124.75. Extinguished by the storm, the light was rekindled.[59]

The Cape San Blas Light was temporarily discontinued on April 13, 1896, as the tower was prepared for dismantling and reassembly inside the cape. Money ran out before the end of the month and work came to a halt. Most of the Blacks Island foundation was by this time finished, and the two dwellings were about half finished. The lens was put back in the old tower until new funding was available.[60]

After a healthy bite of humble pie, the Light-House Board concluded that a site on the cape could indeed be a safe one. The works on Blacks Island were abandoned. Congress authorized $15,000 in 1900 for a move to an ideal site available just over a mile northwest of the station. Suddenly, the beach started building up out from shore. The proposed move now looked unnecessary, and the light remained at the old site.[61]

Hurricanes in 1915 and 1916 stripped away all the new sand. The lighthouse was cut off by 200 yards of water. A new site was acquired

The fifth tower at Cape San Blas, built in 1885, was designed so that it could be dismantled and moved to a new location when threatened by the eroding shoreline. Note the height of the entrance door to keep it above the waterline should the area become inundated. (Photo by David L. Cipra, 1994)

640 yards inland; tower disassembly was completed by mid-1918. The tower was re-erected and on January 22, 1919, was first lit at its present location.

Seventy years and one day later, the light station was discontinued.[62]

Pensacola Lighthouse

Pensacola was one of the first points on the Gulf of Mexico chosen for a colonial settlement. The fact that it was the finest harbor on the Gulf of Mexico could not save it from being considered a port of only military and political significance during colonial occupation. Unlike

New Orleans, St. Marks, Apalachicola, and Mobile, Pensacola lacked river connections with the interior and was not an early commercial success.

The transportation deficiency produced an ironic result. Although little merchandise arrived from inland markets, there were no major rivers sending silt to the mouth of the bay. The bar there would admit the largest colonial sailing vessels, while vast river highways elsewhere on the Gulf suffered from shallow entrances.

There is no proof that colonial powers established aids to navigation at Pensacola. The British erected a lookout tower on Gage Hill in about 1772, and it almost certainly served as a daymark for approaching ships, as did lookouts in other British colonies. Soldiers may have also hoisted a lantern or fired rockets as signals at night.

As Pensacola was the deepest bay on the Gulf Coast, a light was suggested early in 1822, just before the naval base was planned. The lightship *Aurora Borealis* was transferred from the Mississippi River to Pensacola when Louisiana's first coastal lighthouse was completed. By July 1, 1823, the ship anchored just inside the bay's mouth but soon shifted to calmer waters off old Fort Barrancas. Her light proved to be insufficient; the local customs collector Alexander Scott asked permission to raise a simple tripod of pine logs on the bluff, on which a ship's lantern could be hoisted. *Aurora Borealis* stayed on station until the lighthouse was lit up, and was then transferred to the Chesapeake Bay as a relief lightship.[63]

Congress had provided $6,000 to mark the harbor in March 1823; the collector was directed to find "the most suitable scite." Winslow Lewis, his construction gang already busy at the Mississippi River, won the contract with a bid of $5,725. The lighthouse was first lit up on December 20, 1824. Ten lamps mounted in two opposing banks revolved to show a white flash every minute. The 45-foot tower was located on Cemetery Hill, a 40-foot sand bluff about halfway between Fort Barrancas and the current tower. Its lamps were held 85 feet above the bay, making the Pensacola tower the tallest lighthouse on the Gulf until the Egmont Key Light was rebuilt in 1857. Jeremiah Ingraham accepted the job as first keeper, despite petitions in favor of Pensacola's former Spanish *alcalde* (mayor). Ingraham served until his death in September 1840, and was succeeded by his wife Michaela, who remained on duty until January 1855.[64]

Even the coming of the railroad age did not raise Pensacola to commercial standing on the Gulf. A railroad venture to link Pensacola to the rich cotton lands near Montgomery went bankrupt in the Panic of 1837. The line was completed shortly after the port was blockaded by the U.S. Navy. If cotton moved down this line to Pensacola during the war, it was never sent to sea through the port.

Pensacola's maritime interests gave the new lighthouse glowing reviews, but opinions soon changed. Shippers and naval officers began complaining the light was too dim, poorly located and, although the highest on the Gulf, too short. One 1838 report recommended a lighthouse on the west angle of Fort Pickens and relocation of the old lighthouse to Fort Barrancas. The Provisional Light-House Board and the naval station commandant recommended a first-class seacoast light to allow cruisers of all classes to enter the port at night. One of the first actions of the Board in 1852 was to request $30,000 for a new tower.[65]

The current Pensacola Lighthouse was erected in 1858 at a total cost of $45,988.82. Almost 160 feet tall, the tower showed a first-order Fresnel lens 191 feet above sea level. The tower was lit on November 1, 1858, by keeper Joseph F. Palmes. During construction, a first-order Fresnel lens was apparently shown from the old tower.[66]

Two years after its establishment, the Pensacola Lighthouse became the property of the State of Florida and then the Confederate States Light House Establishment. Palmes submitted his resignation from U.S. service on February 1, 1861, and was replaced by a Mr. Glass. The Pensacola Lighthouse was the first to be extinguished on the Gulf Coast. On the evening of April 12, 1861, gunfire was heard from Santa Rosa Island, signaling the landing of Union reinforcements for Fort Pickens. Confederates knew a landing would occur and at 9 p.m. doused the light in the Pensacola tower to hinder the amphibious maneuvers.[67]

While Confederate forces are sometimes blamed for damaging the tower, it was actually Union artillerymen who bounced solid shot off the masonry on several occasions while firing on Confederate positions. Shrapnel can still be found on the station's grounds. The "Light House Batteries" were favorite targets of Union artillery at Fort Pickens. In November 1861 rifled guns in bastions C and D were trained almost exclusively on the Light House Batteries. Other Union gunners also fired on the bay's most prominent landmark. Only a half dozen rounds actually struck the tower, and none pierced beyond the external wall.[68]

The same Union artillery prevented destruction of the tower in March 1862. Withdrawing Confederates were ordered to leave the enemy nothing of value and started burning the naval yard and all other Confederate government property. A cavalry detachment was headed toward the lighthouse when Union cannon fire stopped them short.[69]

At the urging of Rear Admiral David G. Farragut, lighthouse engineer Max Bonzano installed a captured fourth-order lens, which was first lit on December 20, 1862. Light-House Board records show that the original first-order lens was recovered after the war in the Navy Yard, but it seems to have disappeared, probably sent to New York by the Navy. The clockworks were recovered at Montgomery, Alabama. General repairs lasted until 1870, but a new first-order lens arrived for

The current Pensacola Lighthouse was erected in 1858 at a total cost of $45,988.82. (National Archives photo #26-LG-37-26)

lighting on April 1, 1869. It was probably during these renovations that the upper two thirds of the tower were coal-tarred and the lower third whitewashed to contrast with the background of dark pine trees.[70]

Robert McCormack was appointed to tend the light on February 13, 1863, starting a long list of short-termed keepers. In the 23 years after its relighting, 13 keepers were removed from duty or summarily quit. A few lasted less than two months.[71]

Lightning struck the tower twice, in 1874 and 1875, because of a faulty lightning rod. Each time, the shocks melted fixtures in the tower and blasted masonry from the attached covered walkway. Civil War shellings, compounded by notorious Gulf weather, were blamed for numerous cracks noticed just under the lantern in 1878. The brick was repointed with mortar top to bottom and the lantern glass replaced.[72]

On August 31, 1885, Pensacola was shaken by a rare earthquake. "It lasted between three and four minutes," the keeper wrote, "and was accompanied by a rumbling, as if people were ascending the steps making as much noise as possible." The station's clock pendulum stopped, marking the time at precisely 9:07 a.m.[73]

Stories abound that the Pensacola station is home to ghosts, perhaps those of the original keepers. Stories of supernatural occurrences are said to date from 1840, the year Jeremiah Ingraham died. In 1977 a Coast Guard keeper reported hearing a rustling outside a tower window. Peering into the darkness, he saw an elderly lady in a rocking chair, floating some 120 feet above the ground. In another incident, a visitor reported hearing footsteps on the porch and then a loud crash in the living room of the quarters. He left the bedroom to investigate, finding a chair upset. When he returned to the bedroom, only a belt was missing from a pair of pants he had draped over a chair. Loud footsteps have often been heard coming from the iron staircase of the locked and empty tower.

The tower still sends its beacon to sea. It is no longer tended by earthly keepers. The grounds of the Pensacola Light Station are open to the public within the Pensacola Naval Air Station.[74]

Chapter 5

Mobile Bay (Alabama)

Sand Island to Choctaw Point

Alabama may appear to have a very minor ocean frontage, but no other Gulf Coast state can claim a bay equal to Mobile Bay. Fed by the extensive and easily navigable Mobile and Tombigbee River watersheds, the bay was the first important commercial harbor of the Gulf of Mexico.

The earliest European explorers expressed delight with Mobile Bay. Discovered by the Spanish in 1519, its harbor was immediately recognized for its excellence. The low coast offered so few distinguishing features, however, that it was not rediscovered for almost 40 years. The 1699 French settlement of Mauvilla, near the present city of Mobile, was an early colonial capital and trading center. Even earlier came Fort Cadillac and its busy port on Dauphin Island, claimed by today's islanders to be the first French capital of the Louisiana colony.

French, Spanish, English, and two American flags have flown over the bay's settlements, garrisons, and forts. Although the United States had little legal authority for claiming this part of West Florida, Congress on July 22, 1813, "captured" Mobile, declaring it the port of entry for all waterways between the Mobile and Mississippi Rivers. The action led to the ousting of the weak Spanish garrison, serving notice to the English that they could not take the Gulf Coast unchallenged. The U.S. military had already planted the Stars and Stripes at various locations during a War of 1812 invasion of the Spanish territory, making their way as far east as the Florida Peninsula. Andrew Jackson built a rough fort at Mobile Point, already the site of Alabama's first lighthouse, and possibly the site of the first lighthouse on the Gulf of Mexico.

Rivers at the head of Mobile Bay constitute the second-largest marine highway in the eastern United States, eclipsed only by the vast extent of the Mississippi. During the greatest economic expansion in U.S. history, few roads and almost no railroads existed in this basin. Much of the richest cotton land which spawned the rising prosperity of America from 1820 to 1860 was accessible only by riverboat and the port of Mobile. Alabama's first steamboats operated on these rivers in 1818, a year before statehood was achieved.

Mobile enjoyed explosive growth as Alabama's port. Between 1820 and 1850 the population grew from 1,500 to about 30,000, only 10 percent of which was made up of northerners muscling in on cotton profits. By 1850 Alabama had surpassed Mississippi as the leading cotton producer, and all but one percent of Mobile's exports were fluffy, white gold. Mobile won the attention of the federal government as a world-class port, receiving both channel improvements and aids to navigation.

Mobile Bay's entrance lights

While almost invisible without aids to navigation, Mobile Bay's mouth is not particularly hazardous. A long, deep, and fair channel leads from just off Sand Island to an excellent anchorage behind Mobile Point. The lower half of the bay naturally accommodates seagoing ships. Mobile Point, defended by Fort Morgan, stands close by the best channel, which lies only a hundred yards offshore.

Some time after 1763, the British built a crude lighthouse on Mobile Point, probably constructed of native wood. The tower was not long-lived. The Spanish, who ousted the redcoats in 1780, did not try to maintain it.[1]

Mobile Point Lighthouse

Mobile Bay is guarded on the west by a shield of islands and shallow passages. On the east, the narrow mouth is formed by Mobile Point, a sand strip fortified before the U.S. Congress annexed West Florida. The takeover was legalized in 1821, when Spain ceded the Florida territories to the United States. Even before the treaty was ratified, Congress moved quickly to establish control over the region by authorizing the construction of Fort Morgan on the point. Recognizing its commercial potential, Congress also endorsed a lighthouse or lightship to mark the port.[2]

The proposal came in 1820 when the infant United States lighthouse establishment experimented with floating lights. A lightship was thought to be ideally suited to Mobile Bay. When America's first lightship on the East Coast (at Willoughby Spit, Virginia) turned out to be an expensive misadventure, the government decided not to duplicate the fiasco at Mobile.[3]

The U.S. collector of customs chose a sand bar 1,100 yards west of Mobile Point as the lighthouse site. Since period charts show only open water due west of the point, it must be assumed he selected Sand Island, a half mile west and almost three miles south of the fort. Further investigation showed that the island was unsuitable. The lighthouse would instead be built on the grounds of the fort.[4]

Plans for a simple brick tower were modified when the Treasury Department became cautious about encroaching on the military's domain. To ensure that the tower would not interfere with defense of the port, the commanding officer was granted full control over lighthouse operations in peacetime and "authority to demolish it ... in time of war." The lighthouse keeper would live within the fort and be subject to martial law. A last-minute design change made the Mobile Point tower the first fortified lighthouse built by the United States. The usual spiraled tower stairs were interrupted by two stout floors, each offering 10 loopholes through which soldiers could fire muskets at attackers "to answer the dual purpose of a block house and a light house." The foundation was to extend well beyond the tower walls to accommodate a battery of artillery. The Treasury Department soon found these arrangements to be inconvenient. They were eventually fatal.[5]

The Mobile Point Lighthouse cost the taxpayer more than similar stations would cost for several decades. On November 7, 1821, the contract was signed by a four-man Boston consortium for the sizable sum of $9,995. Evidence of the importance of the tower was the cost of illuminating fixtures. At $1,600, the lamps and reflectors cost more than double those of other towers.[6]

In its first 13 years of service, the Mobile Point Light station was an almost constant problem. The 40-foot tower was completed some four months before the Mobile customs collector could find a suitable keeper. In May 1822 Stephen Pleasonton, Fifth Auditor of the U.S. Treasury and Superintendent of Lights, suggested that the commander of the fort assign a soldier to tend the light, with a compensation of $15 per month. The light atop the tower was finally displayed for the first time on September 29.

When the tall Sand Island seacoast light was built offshore in 1858, Mobile Point was downgraded to a harbor light with the smallest available lens. Range lights guided ships through the shoals to the anchorage. (Photo courtesy of U.S. Coast Guard Historian's Office)

Mariners continually complained about the poor quality of the light. The Mobile collector allowed the lighthouse to run out of oil a year after its commissioning, waiting for the supply ship to arrive from Boston rather than buying a small cask locally. Mismanagement by the soldiers forced the hiring of a permanent civilian keeper within a few years, but martial law did not suit him well. Constant harassment from the fort's officers caused a return to military lighthouse tending, this time by the new fort commander, Major Thomas Belton.[7]

As Mobile grew toward status as a premier international port, mariners pressed the government for a real landfall light. Elevated 55 feet above sea level, the Mobile Point Light was visible only 10 miles in the clearest weather. The Mobile bar lay eight miles offshore, where ships could run aground before lookouts aloft could spot the beam. In 1835 Belton suggested erecting a new, 100-foot lighthouse around the old one, salvaging the original staircase and fitting the lantern with one of the lenses recently perfected in France. Instead, the Fifth Auditor accepted a thriftier proposal from Boston lighthouse entrepreneur Winslow Lewis to improve the chandelier of lamps. Lewis claimed his new light would be visible 30 miles to sea, ignorant of the fact that the curvature of the Earth would prevent the light from reaching out more than 17 miles.[8]

He made a greater mistake in not notifying the government when he changed the characteristics of the light. Originally a fixed light showing a steady beam, Mobile Point received a new, revolving chandelier, showing a flashing light like the one at Pensacola, only 45 miles away. Mariners usually received published notices of such changes, but learned of this one by accident. One captain left Mobile seeing a fixed light and, returning 40 days later to a flashing light, he passed it by, not recognizing it. Another believed he was off Pensacola and did not recognize the error until four days later off Louisiana.[9]

Lewis countered his detractors, claiming the Mobile Light to be more powerful than its Florida neighbor and, more importantly, timed to flash at a different rate. "To mistake one for the other," he claimed, "would be like taking a star for the moon." Threats prompted Pleasonton to quickly prepare a contract for converting the light back to a fixed beam. Suddenly, captains in Mobile reversed course, endorsing the flashing light. The contract proposal was withdrawn a few days before it was to have been signed.[10]

Soon after Lewis improved the light, Army keepers earned a reputation for providing a poor light. A new fort commander had been assigned and chose to live several days distant from his duties. Sailors often found the light extinguished all night. Retired ship captain Elias Morris became the new civilian keeper and he too charged the Army with harassment. Soldiers refused him access to the tower, except at night. Morris lived in a hovel far across the sand dunes while ample quarters at the fort stood unoccupied. The Treasury Department negotiated a settlement directly with the Secretary of War, who overruled the Fort Morgan commander.[11]

The lighthouse was fitted up with larger reflectors in March 1851 and received an iron lantern originally cast for a lighthouse in North Carolina. In an attempt to distinguish it from the white light atop the Pensacola tower, colored filters were added at this time to give the light a pale plum tinge. By the time the Light-House Board was formed in 1852, Mobile Point Light was considered to be the finest on the Gulf, even if visible a paltry 12 miles. The new Board insisted on a light elevated 125 feet, fitted with the most advanced optics from France, to better serve what was by then one of the premier ports in the nation. Sand Island, three miles to seaward and the site of a secondary lighthouse since 1838, would become the site for Mobile Bay's entrance light. When the tall seacoast light was built offshore in 1858, Mobile Point was downgraded to a harbor light with the smallest available lens. Range lights guided ships through the shoals to the anchorage.[12]

The Confederate States customs collector at Mobile sent a message to the U.S. lighthouse inspector at Mobile on January 21, 1861: "In the name of the Sovereign State of Alabama, I take possession of the several light houses within the state." In June 1861 the new Confederate States Light House Bureau ordered all lighthouses dismantled. The Mobile Point apparatus and supplies were crated for storage in the customhouse and were later shipped to Montgomery for safekeeping.[13]

Three years later, the blockhouse/lighthouse met its predicted end, demolished by artillery. Confederate forces at Fort Morgan had established a battery at the tower, including a "hot shot" furnace which turned cannonballs red hot to set attacking vessels afire. When Farragut's fleet ran past the fort at Mobile Point, Union gunners bombarded the dangerous Light House Battery, riddling the tower with holes. Confederate artillerymen quickly deserted the battery when brickbats rained down from the tottering old lighthouse. In the following weeks, artillery caused additional damage. Besieging U.S. Army forces sent shells over the fort and into the tower, blasting away nearly its entire east face. With Sand Island mined earlier in the war, Mobile Bay's entrance fell dark.[14]

For a short time, the station was relit as the primary bay light. A wooden beam-and-brace tower, prefabricated in New Orleans and topped by a tiny sixth-order lens, was erected on the ruins of the fort's southwest bastion. In 1866, Congress allocated $20,000 for rebuilding.[15]

It was not until 1872 that a stubby, 30-foot, boiler-plate iron tower went up, showing a red fourth-order lens 50 feet above sea level. Similar to the one built later at Garden Key in the Dry Tortugas, the tower was

The State of Alabama renovated the iron Mobile Point Lighthouse to display it with many other artifacts of war and peace at the Fort Morgan State Historic Site. Note that interior metal plates are missing. (Photo by David L. Cipra, 1994)

first lit February 15, 1873. This tower was sold to a salvage firm in 1966, but has since been returned to the fort.

The final Mobile Point Light was erected in 1966, an antenna-like tower holding a rotating aeronautical beacon 125 feet high. This ungainly tower is heir to its far more elegant ancestors as Mobile Bay's primary seacoast light.[16]

Sand Island Lighthouse

Sand Island lies almost three miles off Mobile Point and was the nearest spot of dry land to the Mobile Bay bar when the United States took control over Alabama in 1819. The island has earned a dubious reputation as fickle and itinerant—eroding, shifting, dividing, and eventually disappearing altogether.

U.S. Treasury Department officials, convinced that the light from Mobile Point somehow arched over the horizon making it visible 30 miles, originally believed a light on Sand Island could never be of any value. A tall iron spindle, visible an advertised six miles to sea, marked the island in 1830.[17]

Years of mariners' complaints and an endorsement from a special U.S. Navy board of commissioners convinced Congress that a new $10,000 lighthouse was needed. The Fifth Auditor tried to block construction by proposing improvements to the old Mobile Point Light, but marine interests silenced his objections.[18]

The nation's leading lighthouse builder, Winslow Lewis of Boston, received the contract on January 1, 1838; his construction crew built the tower for $8,899. At 55 feet, the light was as high above the water as the one on the main shore but, having smaller and one third fewer lamps, was not visible as far off the coast. Mobile Point remained the seacoast light, while the more strategically placed Sand Island Light was rated second-class.[19]

The tower was actually erected on the eastern shore of Dry Shoal which had, in some former age, been part of a more massive Sand Island, some 400 acres in extent and including what is now Petit Bois Island. Even before foundation piles went down, the government should have recognized the problems it would face in taming the vagabond island. The Mobile collector had the original contract modified to stipulate that a ring of piles be driven around the station and filled with sand to form a dry spot in any weather. The government accepted the lighthouse by mid-April 1838; it was first lit up by keeper John McCloud. Only a month later, the Mobile collector feared the foundation was in serious danger and asked for funds to save the tower. The Revenue Cutter Service officer who had selected the site later admitted, "I have known the dwelling and tower to be surrounded by water, near a foot deep, for weeks."[20]

Chronic erosion plagued all three Sand Island lighthouses. By 1848, the Coast Survey reported that about 100 yards of the eastern shore had disappeared. A few years later, they confirmed that the eastern edge of almost every island from St. Marks to the Mississippi River appeared to be wearing away, while the western shores did not. The lighthouse was again in peril. In 1849, Pleasonton agreed to fund an emergency measure "which appears to be calculated to support the tower."[21]

The Provisional Light-House Board recognized the importance of showing the bay's landfall light as far to sea as possible. In 1851 they recommended a tower no shorter than 150 feet, triple the height of the original Sand Island light, displaying a first-order Fresnel lens. The Board asked Congress for $35,000 to begin construction. Alabama's first tall tower was completed on November 1, 1858, by Army Engineer Danville Leadbetter. The final plan raised the height to about 200 feet, making the Sand Island tower the tallest lighthouse ever built on the Gulf Coast, and perhaps the tallest purely masonry building ever attempted in the South.[22]

In the first months of the Civil War, Confederate authorities dismantled the nine-foot-tall lens and moved it to safety, first at Mobile and later at Montgomery. The lens was discovered there in 1865 by Federal lighthouse agent George Burns and was shipped by rail to Pensacola for return to the station. The tower was used repeatedly by lookouts as Union naval forces spied on the strength of the three local forts. Union blockaders reached their peak of effectiveness in the last months of 1862 and apparently felt they exercised full control over the island. Local Lighthouse Engineer Max F. Bonzano moved quickly, if prematurely, to re-establish the light. Under the protection of gunboats, he lofted a captured, fourth-order lens on December 20, 1862, and claimed he could install a first-order revolving lens soon afterward.[23]

Activity on the island provoked an attack by Confederate troops. A small Confederate force under Lieutenant John W. Glenn rowed from Fort Gaines on January 31 to conduct reconnaissance near Sand Island. As the USS *Pembina* weighed anchor to challenge him, Glenn landed at the island and torched five frame buildings near the tower. A few shots from *Pembina* forced a retreat. Glenn vowed to return to the island and "at such a time as I shall judge expedient, I will tumble the Light House down in their teeth." He made good his threat on February 23, but almost lost his own teeth, not to mention his life. That morning, he "commenced sapping the Light House" with 70 pounds of gunpowder buried 10 feet under the base. At 3 p.m. he lit the fuse, but it burned too quickly. Before he could make his escape, a shower of bricks threw him to the ground. A mass of masonry weighing several tons fell six inches from him. "Nothing remains but a narrow shred [of brickwork] about fifty feet high and from one to five feet wide," he reported, adding, "The first storm we have will blow that down." By sad coincidence, his report on the assault was addressed to Confederate States Brigadier General Danville Leadbetter, the U.S. Light-House Board engineer who had built the magnificent tower on Sand Island only a few years before.[24]

The Navy planned to build a platform on the jagged rim of the tower walls to serve as a signal post for the blockading fleet and later for the passing of the fort at Mobile Point. Shortly after Admiral Farragut entered Mobile Bay, a fourth-order lens elevated only 48 feet above sea level again marked Sand Island, this time atop a substantial but temporary wood tower adjacent to the ruins. Bonzano asked Washington for the original tower plans so he could rebuild. Exigencies of war postponed any work.[25]

When hostilities ended, the U.S. Light-House Board quickly asked for a permanent lighthouse on Sand Island, but it took eight years to replace the temporary beacon erected during the war. The new, 132-foot tower was completed in 1873 using a popular1870s design, and placed 670 feet to the northwest of the old site. The Sand Island Lighthouse which stands today is the last classic brick lighthouse built for a U.S. port on the Gulf of Mexico.[26]

The new site was no safer than the original. Erosion continued unchecked on the eastern shore. Within a decade, the remains of the second (1858) tower were awash, and by 1884 the Light-House Board considered retreating to a site further west. A series of jetties, breakwaters, and other erosion-control ventures proved to be expensive and inadequate. On the tower's 15th anniversary, the Gulf had advanced to only 10 feet from its foundation.[27]

Brush and stone jetties were tossed aside by storms. In 1894 water enveloped the foundation. The elevated walkway which connected the

A series of jetties, breakwaters, and other erosion-control devices proved to be expensive and inadequate in saving the land around Sand Island Lighthouse. (Photo courtesy of U.S. Coast Guard Historian's Office)

tower door to the island was repeatedly damaged. The Light-House Board again suggested yielding to nature by abandoning the structure in favor of a portable wooden lighthouse. Instead, they tried one more trick. Since Sand Island insisted on a westward trek, the Board created an artificial island using a small mountain of stone.[28]

The first 1,600 tons of granite, placed in 1889, were quickly dislodged by heavy weather. The tower's condition became precarious. Another 6,548 tons laid in 1899-1900 held fast for a half dozen years. A terse telegram in 1906 described a disaster: "Sand Island light out. Island washed away. Dwelling gone. Keepers not to be found." Assistant keeper

Sand Island Lighthouse in 1963, before the keeper's quarters was gone and water lapped closer to the base of the tower. (Photo courtesy of U.S. Coast Guard Historian's Office)

Andrew Hansen and his wife occupied the dwelling at the time. The Board testified at a Congressional hearing the next year that "Sand Island was completely carried away; but that tower stood on its little mound of rip-rap." The nearest dry land was now a quarter mile away.[29]

More rocks were dumped. In 1907, 525 tons of ballast rock were laid, with another 1,687 tons in 1913. All were dispersed in stormy surf. Six hundred blocks of granite weighing from 2,000 to 3,000 pounds each were arranged in 1914 like so many patio bricks, with 1,000 tons of smaller rock for an underlayer. The current continued to scour away the sand beneath the rip-rap. During World War I, 2,700 tons of stone weighing from one to four tons each were set in place, followed by 1,900 tons in 1923. Sand Island was now a manmade lump of stone on the seabed. The tower, which had cost $175,000 to build in 1873, cost another $100,000 to save in its first half century.[30]

The Sand Island Lighthouse has since survived unaided by man. The station was automated shortly after World War II and is no longer active. Its lens has been on display at the Fort Morgan Museum since 1972. On a clear day the tower breaks the monotony of the horizon when viewed from the fort bastions. Sand Island Lighthouse has earned its place on the National Register of Historic Places.[31]

Mobile Bay's interior lights

Mobile Bay presents a fine sheet of water for the skilled inshore pilot. The first European explorers found an excellent anchorage inside Mobile Point, welcoming the largest of trading ships. The upper bay was too shallow for ocean cruisers, but early sailing luggers and eventually steam barges were widely available to move cargoes between the anchorage and settlements to the north.

French colonial authorities established a small inland port at Choctaw, in what is now southern Mobile, with the harbor for large ships at Pelican Bay south of Dauphin Island. Intended to rule the Louisiana colony, this capital was quickly moved to Fort Cadillac on Dauphin Island when it became obvious that the mouth of the Mobile River was at best marginally accessible. The Dauphin Island port was obliterated by a 1719 hurricane.

The shallow channel from the anchorages to Mobile was marked in the early 1800s by stakes pounded into the soft bottom and by copper-clad wooden buoys made from barrels and logs. Federally funded channel dredging from 1826 to 1857 allowed small freighters drawing no more than 10 feet to approach city wharves. It was not until the mid-1880s that a real ship channel was opened to the city from Mobile Point, with the first true transoceanic steamship docking in Mobile in 1888.

Choctaw Point Lighthouse

Between 1826 and 1829, John Grant of Pascagoula dredged the Choctaw Pass and part of the Pinto Island Pass near Mobile under a federal contract at a cost of $30,000. The crude Baltimore Dredge he had invented cut a six-foot channel about eight feet wide, barely enough to float flatboats laden with cotton bales. This minor success was, however, enough for Congress to appropriate $10,000 for a lighthouse on Choctaw Point in 1830.[32]

The Mobile collector of customs dutifully selected a site which best marked the new channels. Unfortunately the ideal location was in water deeper than the channel itself. Given the construction technology of the 1830s, building there would be difficult. Furthermore, Congress had specified that the light be on Choctaw Point, regardless of the demands of navigators. The station was built on the mainland by Winslow Lewis in late 1830 for the sum of $6,500. The tower was first lit in January 1831 by Sterling Thrower.[33]

The brick tower was positioned on mucky soil only inches above high tide and held its 11 lamps 43 feet above the bay. It was useless from its date of lighting, since vessels could not steer on it by day or night. Most ships continued to anchor in deep water at least halfway down the bay, where the light was not visible from the tallest masthead. Even luggers and barges came to anchor at the Dog River bar at night, following stakes and buoys to town at dawn. An inspector in 1834 was equally unimpressed by keeper Thrower, who did not even present himself for the visit but had left the station in a general state of disrepair, with a hired man or slave in charge. Thrower was tossed out of office.[34]

In its 1849 chartings of Mobile Bay, the U.S. Coast Survey recommended abandoning the station and replacing it with well-placed beacons along the recently improved channel to Mobile. The lighthouse stayed active, however; there is some evidence that private concerns erected small lit beacons to make up for the government's inattention to their needs.[35]

The Light-House Board, formed in 1852, quickly recognized marshy Choctaw Point as a poor location. After expensive renovations and fruitless site protection in 1858, a hurricane the next year devastated the station. The Board sought approval for a replacement screwpile tower, located close enough to the channel that a sailor could actually steer by it. The Civil War interrupted these plans.[36]

For much of the station's history, women served as keepers. The widowed Carmelite Philibert took over from her husband in August 1842. Serving about ten years, she had a longer tenure than any other keeper. At about the time Alabama joined the Confederacy, Elizabeth Michold received the appointment.

To protect Mobile at all costs, Confederates scuttled "stone vessels," flatboats, scows, and steamers in the channel below Mobile, marking them with an array of beacons understood only by local pilots. These stake lights were tended at first by locals known as the Stake Rangers. The Confederate States Navy later took over the lights with oil donated under duress by the Confederate States customs collector. The Choctaw Point tower became the southern terminus of a breastwork which extended to the city of Mobile.[37]

Choctaw Point Lighthouse employed what appears to have been the last Confederate States lighthouse keeper anywhere in the South. Keeper Elizabeth Michold tended the light until November 3, 1862, when the lens and all supplies were carted off to Mobile for safekeeping. Note the old-style lantern and vent. (Photo courtesy of U.S. Coast Guard Historian's Office)

Historians disagree on the fate of the tower. When Mobile surrendered, the district lighthouse engineer tersely described the lighthouse as a "former structure entirely destroyed." Some feel the bricks were used in Mobile's fortifications or to fill channel obstructions. Some of the masonry may have been used in the building of Battery Gladden, five-eighths of a mile to the east. Photographs believed to have been taken in the 1890s, however, show the tower still standing its full height. Regardless, lighthouse remnants remained visible until at least 1917 at the corner of Conception and Tennessee Streets.[38]

Pre-war plans for a screwpile lighthouse were resurrected in 1870. Confederate forces had created an ideal location for the replacement tower at the tiny oval battery just to the east. The Choctaw Point Lighthouse reservation was later used as a buoy depot and in 1939 became a base for U.S. Coast Guard rescue and aids-to-navigation operations.[39]

Battery Gladden Lighthouse

Once cleared of war debris, the Mobile ship channel invited a resurgence of trade, although it would be decades before Mobile would enjoy the shipping fervor of 1860. Cotton exports never again dominated Mobile Bay's exports, but a brisk lumber trade surged after the Civil War. The City of Mobile almost immediately started buying and improving private wharves which had suffered from neglect during the war. The Corps of Engineers renewed its attempts to dredge a ship channel from the anchorages to Mobile, finally succeeding in the late 1880s.

The Light-House Board erected a few channel lights and in 1870 resumed pre-war plans to build a screwpile lighthouse, replacing the useless Choctaw Point Lighthouse. The new site was an artificial island at Battery Gladden, an ex-Confederate military installation near the south tip of Pinto Island. Where seven heavy guns had once threatened invaders, a lighthouse could guide ships into the rebuilt port.[40]

Since the battery was constructed of broken brick and rubble, driving piles for a foundation was deemed impossible. The Board opted for a site in three feet of water just off the island, at the outer edge of the channel. A boardwalk connected the tower to the old battery, where outbuildings, such as the oil house and the keeper's chicken coop, were located. Within twenty years, the old fortification was nearly washed away by storms.[41]

Because post-war labor costs were much higher in the South, the entire hexagonal, wooden superstructure on screwpiles was prefabricated in the North and shipped to the site. The station was completed and first lit by keeper Levi Mangold on April 8, 1872. A fourth-order lens was fitted with a red sector to mark the turning point in the channel. Two assistant keepers helped tend the chain of channel lights leading to Mobile.[42]

In 1906 the station received equipment to produce and compress acetylene gas from calcium carbide. The gas was used in an experiment with lit buoys. (Gas-powered buoys were so successful they eventually replaced the Battery Gladden Light and many other lighthouses and lightships around the nation.) In 1907 the fourth-order lens was replaced by an acetylene lens-lantern.[43]

With the exception of a fire on the wood-shingle roof in 1879 and a severe gale nine years later, the station served peacefully until March 25, 1913, when it was discontinued. The Corps of Engineers had improved the channel to a point that buoys and other channel markers better served interior shipping. The graying wood superstructure remained on its perch until about 1951 and became known as the Old Channel Daybeacon.[44]

Mobile Bay (Middle Bay) Lighthouse

Starting in 1835, Army engineers tried with mixed results to open a channel from the lower anchorages to the dredged channel at the port of Mobile, hoping to achieve 10 feet of depth and 150 yards of width. Unlit buoys and stakes marked the passage, but not always reliably. After multiple tries over some 40 years, they cut a 13-foot shipping lane. When the dogleg channel was deepened to 17 feet in the 1880s, large steamers could approach Mobile for the first time. The Light-House Board proposed a screwpile lighthouse at the first bend, about midway on the 22-mile course. Since the position also tended to mark the upper reaches of the anchorage just inside the bay, Alabama's first United

Mobile Bay Lighthouse before the lantern was removed in 1905 and replaced with twin lights on an iron post. (Photo courtesy of U.S. Coast Guard Historian's Office)

States lighthouse at Mobile Point was to be discontinued when the new harbor light was completed.[45]

This station was also prefabricated in the North and shipped to Mobile Point in 1885. Screwpiles for the hexagonal structure were sunk with great difficulty in 17 feet of water on the channel's edge. Inclement weather frequently halted work. The superstructure was nearly assembled atop the piles when the foundation suddenly sank into the soft bottom. The building settled seven and one-half feet before workmen could drive wood pilings around the screwpiles to stabilize them. Since the tower remained plumb, it received a fourth-order lens and went into commission on December 1, 1885, at a somewhat shorter focal plane than planned.[46]

The French lens and iron lantern were removed in 1905 and twin lights on an iron post took their place atop the dwelling. Two small red acetylene lights would show from the lighthouse for the next three decades, when a single electric light was installed. The lighthouse was automated in 1915.[47]

Early in World War I, the keeper and his wife received two additions to the crew. The first, a baby, was not unusual for a keeper's family. When the mother was unable to nurse, the second addition arrived. A dairy cow was hoisted onto the lighthouse catwalk and plodded for exercise, protesting loudly, around the wooden gallery.[48]

The station has twice been in danger of being dismantled. The first time it was to be moved to Horn Island Pass, Mississippi, to take the place of a light destroyed in the 1906 hurricane. A small lit beacon was to mark the turn in the Mobile channel. Instead, Horn Island received a new lighthouse. The second threat came in 1967, when the Coast Guard advertised for bids to demolish the rotting building. It had outlived its usefulness and had become too expensive to maintain. Bay-area citizens rescued the lighthouse from the wrecker's ball and cutter's torch. Working with donations and a federal grant, volunteers succeeded in renovating the historic building. The lighthouse is now owned by the Alabama Historical Commission.[49]

Grant's Pass Lighthouse

If you take nature's route from Mobile to Mississippi Sound, you must round Sand Island and expose your beam to Mexican Gulf swells. Captain John Grant of Pascagoula, the "Father of Gulf Coast Transportation," dredged a private channel six feet deep just north of Dauphin Island in 1839, offering packets and mail boats a protected passage into Mississippi Sound. This route also tended to draw vessels conveniently close to the often-ignored port of Pascagoula, encouraging trading and mail deliveries there. Grant, the inventor of one of the first successful dredging machines, had won the federal contract for opening

Union naval officers reported "at Grant's Pass, on the site of the old light-house, an earthwork, very strong, mounting one 100-pounder rifle gun, one 64-pounder rifle gun, two eight-inch siege mortars, two 32-pounders smoothbore." None of these guns saw much action in the war.

up the port of Mobile 10 years before. He also built the first railroad west of the Alleghenies, linking New Orleans with Lake Pontchartrain. Grant's Pass overcame the final obstacle to trade along this part of the Gulf Coast.[50]

Grant marked the new passage with rows of stakes on each side of the channel and eventually with the Gulf's first private lighthouse. At the midpoint of the channel, he charged tolls for the convenience of the passage. Virtually all coastal vessels eagerly paid for the advantage of the shortcut. An attempt to deepen his channel in 1860 was interrupted by the Civil War.[51]

The Light-House Board became interested in Grant's Pass during an engagement at Fort Powell on what had become known as Tower Island. Union ships bombarded the fort for several months and between August 1 and 5, 1864, Confederate forces retreated, blowing up everything at the fort. Whether the private lighthouse of Captain Grant was destroyed at this time or during the bombardment is not recorded. The lighthouse was gone by the time the United States lighthouse engineer arrived.[52]

In 1864 newly appointed and confused Lighthouse Engineer Max F. Bonzano noted the lighthouse on an old chart and wrongly presumed it to be a discontinued Federal aid to navigation. Legalities aside, the U.S. Navy wanted the light re-established. Bonzano prefabricated a 25-foot, open-frame tower to guide gunboats through the pass. By mid-December 1864 he had placed a small captured lens on the tower and transferred two loyal Union keepers from the extinguished Round Island station. Soon after the Confederacy collapsed, Grant asserted the right to maintain and collect tolls on his waterway, but did not evict the Federal lighthouse keepers. The United States maintained the light on the private waterway until August 5, 1866, when extensive repairs would have been required to make it permanent.[53]

The rotting tower stood until at least 1873, when it was described as being ravaged by sea worms. At that time the Light-House Board asked for funds to mark the pass, but only small lit beacons were ever built there by the federal government. The site of Alabama's only private lighthouse, Tower Island, gradually disappeared by 1912 and Grant's Pass shoaled soon afterward. The old lighthouse site is now under a fathom of water near the Dauphin Island causeway. Today markers on the intracoastal waterway guide vessels through Pass Aux Herons.[54]

Chapter 6

Mississippi Sound (Mississippi)

Pascagoula to Proctorsville

For most early sailors, Mississippi Sound existed only to connect the important settlements of Mobile and New Orleans. The sound was too shallow, averaging only 10 feet, and its channel too circuitous for any but the shallowest craft to navigate. Anchorages existed, however, and the French established the capital of the Louisiana colony near Biloxi in 1699. Supply ships laid to at Isle des Vasseaux—Ship Island. For more than a century, this anchorage would be an expedient but poor substitute for moorage at New Orleans wharves, which was not generally possible until the invention of steam tugs to carry deep-draft ships over the bars at the Mississippi River passes.

The Mississippi Gulf Coast has long sold its primary commodities— health and comfort—to vacationers. Cool sea breezes drew the gentry from New Orleans, Mobile, and upstate. When beaches blossomed as watering places in the 1840s, the entire shoreline from Bay St. Louis to Pascagoula seemed to sprout long finger piers, terminating in Victorian gazebos and steamboat landings. Once largely ignored by commercial interests, this coast has since become a haven for the Gulf fishing industry. Gulfport and Pascagoula have become major international seaports with extensive shipyards at the latter.

The sound is protected by a chain of low and sandy barrier islands, many of which received lighthouses through the years.

The approach to New Orleans

Mississippi Sound's first coastal lighthouses were built to mark the anchorages and channels used by seagoing vessels trading to New Orleans. The Cat Island Channel, a favorite harbor for British raiders in the War of 1812, and Pass Christian on the coastal mail route, were the first to receive towers. Under pressure from Mississippi Representative Jefferson Davis (later U.S. Senator, U.S. Secretary of War, and eventually Confederate States President), three more lights were established, at the Chandeleur Islands, Ship Island, and Biloxi. Davis had campaigned for a congressional seat by demanding fortifications and lighthouses on his coast. He protested loudly that New England had an abundance of lighthouses while the Gulf Coast was left in the dark.

Cat Island Lighthouse

Cat Island's western tip marks the approaches to New Orleans, both from seaward and through Mississippi Sound's inside passage. Early French explorers gave the island its name, Isle des Chats. The place was overrun with queer-looking felines wearing masks. We now call them by their Algonquin name—raccoons.

A small garrison settled on the island, lorded over by a sadistic officer named deRoux. His soldiers—torture victims themselves—mutinied, murdered him, and escaped to Mobile. During the British blockade of New Orleans, Cat Island Channel was a primary choke point for intercepting American shipping. It was at Cat Island that the first shots of the Battle of New Orleans were fired in 1815, when Juan Cuevas shot two English soldiers for stealing his cattle as the British prepared for attack. He then refused to guide the British through the marsh to Chalmette.[1]

Opinions differed as to how best to mark the channels in this area. Congress had appropriated $5,000 in 1827 for a lighthouse on Cat Island. Packets cruising between New Orleans and Mobile pressed for a lighthouse at Pass Christian supplemented by a lightship north of Cat Island. The New Orleans customs collector wanted a light only at Pass Christian. Ocean sailors who could find their way past the Chandeleur Islands would be best served by a light marking the Cat Island anchorage. Congress settled the matter by mandating a lighthouse at both spots.[2]

Cuevas sold the narrow sand spit on the western tip of the island to the federal government for the Cat Island Lighthouse reservation. His son Ramond served as keeper from 1834 to 1861, with several gaps. The government recognized the importance of the place, observing "all the commerce of the northern Gulf Coast passes through the channels near Cat island." For reasons not recorded, only a small harbor light was planned for this important location, 30 feet tall with only 10 lamps in small reflectors.[3]

The lighthouse was built by Lazarus Baukens, hired as a "master workman" by prime contractor Winslow Lewis. The station's first keeper, George Riolly of Pass Christian, oversaw construction and formally accepted the tower on June 10, 1831, but the tower was not put to use for several months. The New Orleans collector waited for the normal winter oil delivery from the North, rather than buy a few casks locally.[4]

The tower was identical in almost every respect to the tower built concurrently at Pass Christian. The only difference was that the Cat Island tower had no foundation whatever. "Not even a plank (the bricks being simply laid upon the sand)," reported an outraged inspector in 1846, "upon a neck of land 150 feet wide and 6 feet above the low water mark." Storm-driven waves often spilled over the spit, washing the base of the tower. In 1846 a hurricane cut a boat channel between the

Cat Island, marking the approach to New Orleans, was one of the first sites to receive a lighthouse on the Mississippi Sound. Note the old-style lantern and directional exhaust vent. (Photo courtesy of U.S. Coast Guard Historian's Office)

lighthouse and the remainder of Cat Island. The tower stood only a few feet from the water by 1851.[5]

Another hurricane in 1855 wrecked the dwelling and left the tower in severe peril. The Light-House Board feared the tower would tumble down in the next serious blow. The Board erected a new dwelling above the beach, close to a protective stand of trees. They felt the tower should be relocated there as well and asked for funding to save the station.[6]

Congress supplied the requested $12,000 in 1856, but only a sixth of the funds were spent, apparently for a Fresnel lens which was installed in 1857 and a new lantern put up in 1859. The Board pronounced the station fit for duty in March 1860. A storm on September 15 changed their opinion. The storm destroyed the Bayou St. John Lighthouse, devastated the Cat Island tower, and demolished its new keeper's dwelling. Cuevas escaped with his family just before churning seas inundated the island and killed his herd of 300 cattle. Every wharf on the Mississippi coast was destroyed in the storm.[7]

The Board concluded that only a screwpile structure could survive here and requested $20,000 on October 22, 1860. Although there was certainly not enough time to build a replacement tower before the Civil War, there is some evidence that one was actually built. The Board reported in 1868 that a screwpile lighthouse was burned at the outset of the war, although no construction records of such a tower survive. They may have referred to a new dwelling. A *Harper's Weekly* woodcut of the island shows the brick tower flying a Confederate States flag at the beginning of the war.[8]

The Confederate States Light House Bureau maintained the station until July 1861, when Juan Cuevas and his son received their final pay in Confederate scrip. The U.S. lighthouse engineer in New Orleans reported that the old brick tower with its new lantern survived the war, if only barely. The tower balanced precariously on only a third of its foundation. Two gaping holes in the masonry reached 12 feet in height.[9]

The tottering remnant was still of use after the war. Its lantern serves today on the Tchefuncte River Lighthouse. The old brick was moved to protect the station at St. Joseph Island, where it sank into the muck. Wartime funding for restoring southern lights was insufficient for the complete rebuilding task at Cat Island. Congress appropriated $15,000 in 1869, but only a small portion was spent before the remainder lapsed into the surplus fund.[10]

A new screwpile lighthouse was finally under construction in July 1871, when a yellow fever epidemic "prostrated many of the laborers and seriously retarded the work." Sidney Wilkinson received the appointment as keeper in September and lit the lamp for the first time December 15, 1871. A fixed fifth-order lens was elevated 45 feet above high tides, half again the height of the original brick lighthouse. Still, Cat Island showed only a harbor light for the smallest vessels. New Orleans-bound ships all used the Mississippi River passes. Only small coasters dared to run the Rigolets bayou.[11]

Slow but steady erosion continued at the station. Rip-rap placed around the screwpiles in 1900 stabilized the site and eventually the station stood safely offshore. As the number of vessels using this approach to New Orleans and the sound decreased, the station lost its impact on trade. Acetylene channel markers on pilings replaced the lighthouse; it was discontinued on September 22, 1937.[12]

During World War II, the "island of cats" served as an army boot camp where the gripes of dog-faced soldiers about lousy chow were heard only by the wind. Hundreds of recruits were issued khaki leashes at the Cat Island War Dog Reception and Training Center. The land and graying lighthouse were transferred to the War Assets Administration in November 1948 with the lighthouse "in general disrepair."[13]

The Chandeleur Island station was the first in the Gulf of Mexico to be captured and relit by Union forces. (Photo courtesy of U.S. Coast Guard Historian's Office)

Chandeleur Island Lighthouse

The Chandeleur Islands were named by the French for their date of discovery, February 2, 1700—the day of the Blessing of Candles. The actual blessing may be that Yankees did not make the discovery on Ground Hog's Day and so name the island. The islands appear on charts as a crescent moon in the final phase, a sandy arc extending north and south, bulging eastward at the center. The southern tip of the chain showed the course to the mouths of the Mississippi River. Behind the northernmost island lay a vast anchorage on the track to New Orleans via Mississippi Sound.

Chandeleur Sound was dreaded for the hardness of its shoals, but the sizable Naso Roads anchorage offered the depth and breadth to hold a small navy. This fact was proven when the British anchored 50 troop transports and men-of-war in preparation for the planned taking of New Orleans in 1815.[14]

The 1847 appropriation for a lighthouse specified a tower for the South Chandeleur Island, intended to guide ships southward toward the Mississippi River passes. By the time the tower was built, weather had combined the north and south islands into one and a more useful site at the northern tip was preferred, serving to guide ships sailing the parallels toward either the river or the Rigolets. At first, the Treasury Department considered an experimental iron lighthouse for the Chandeleurs. Biloxi's iron tower was also in the planning stages at this time. The site was considered too exposed and the plan reverted to basic brick, surrounded by an artificially raised island of sand and shell. The station was completed in March 1848.[15]

The first keeper, George H. A. Frombling, received an appointment in February and a removal notice in April. The 55-foot tower did not last long, either. A hurricane in August 1852 obliterated the entire work. The elderly keeper, Alexander Lea, and his family survived by clinging to a fragment of the dwelling roof and beaching on a sand hill a mile away. They subsisted for days on what scraps they could comb from the beach. The lighthouse was leveled and in its place stood a broad lagoon 10 feet deep. The new tower approved in 1853 would have been in operation in April 1854, if not for the worst yellow fever epidemic in New Orleans history. In November 1855 Benjamin F. Midgett took over as the first keeper of the second lighthouse. The new tower held a modern, fourth-order French lens 50 feet above sea level.[16]

The Chandeleur Island station was the first in the Gulf of Mexico to be captured and relit by Union forces. Only two others, both on Lake Pontchartrain, were later seized intact. A landing party from USS *Massachusetts* removed the lens and apparatus on July 9, 1861. The ship returned on September 13 to reinstall the fixtures as an aid to the blockading fleet. Purposely misinformed fishermen spread the word that the blockaders had fortified the island with nine batteries. Sailors from USS *Massachusetts* and USS *Preble* manned the lighthouse until a civilian keeper could be appointed.[17]

In September 1863 the commander of USS *Kanawha* reported strange happenings at the station. A blockade runner stood at anchor under the light, apparently kept advised of the Union movements by flag signals from lighthouse windows. Incumbent keeper John H. Elder found himself in a Union stockade. He returned to the post after signing an oath of allegiance and swearing he had never supported the rebel cause.[18]

By 1891 the ocean began making inroads on the tower's foundation. A heap of oyster shells dumped around the base proved to be a flimsy barrier to the hurricane of October 1, 1893, which undermined one side of the tower, allowing it to tilt over several feet. Sixteen-foot tides completely carried away all outbuildings at the station. Winds measured at 100 miles per hour dashed waves against the tower, at times washing over the lantern. Only the aged assistant keeper, Patrick Melheran, was on board at the time. Trapped in the tower for three days without water or food, he stoically kept the beacon lit for sailors desperate to escape the storm. The tower careened so badly that rescuers reached the keeper by scaling the outside of the tower.[19]

Congress soon funded a replacement. Separate contracts were let under the $35,000 appropriation. The first, in August 1895, was for fabricating the metalwork. The second, in September, provided for erection. The final Chandeleur Island Lighthouse was one of five iron skeleton towers built at about this time on the Gulf Coast. It rose 102 feet above sea level, more than twice the height of its predecessor. Thorwald Hansen was named the first keeper.[20]

The third-order lens was put to use for the first time in the second Chandeleur Lighthouse on October 31, 1896. The station is shown here in 1965, one year before automation. (Photo courtesy of U.S. Coast Guard Historian's Office)

During prohibition days a second war was fought between blockade evaders and a Union fleet. A small navy of "rum runners" often anchored behind the lighthouse to await shiploads of illicit liquor for the thirsty New Orleans market. Many a case was tossed overboard by smugglers as Coast Guard blockaders raided the harbor, making beachcombing more interesting for the keepers.[21]

In 1966 all 1,920 acres of Chandeleur Island were reported surplus by the Coast Guard and were turned over to the Bureau of Land Management. The area is now a national wildlife refuge, but the automated light is still active. The unusual "clamshell" third-and-a-half-order Fresnel lens is a featured attraction at the New Orleans Maritime Museum.[22]

Ship Island Lighthouse

The original French name Isle des Vasseaux is evidence that early explorers considered this spot a fine anchorage for the largest craft. While the Cat and Chandeleur Islands also served colonial mariners with harbors, Ship Island became a small colony in itself. Inbound ships loaded with immigrants, slaves, and manufactured supplies landed there for the Louisiana colony. They loaded sugar, indigo, timber, and other products for European and Caribbean markets.

In the 1840s Mississippians lobbied for a naval facility at the island, extolling its advantages over Pensacola. Requests to fortify the island also failed repeatedly, as Army engineers argued that an enemy could choose from too many other passes to invade Mississippi Sound.[23]

Congress ordered a formal survey of the barrier islands. Representative Jefferson Davis published an address in 1846 claiming that the U.S. Coast Survey would soon confirm his opinion that Ship Island should be the state's first naval and military complex, and that "further it will lead to the speedy establishment of the necessary lights along the Coast and upon its adjacent islands." He also went on record against the proliferation of lighthouses on the East Coast. Lights were so plentiful in New England that mariners often became bewildered. After Davis was elected to the U.S. Senate in 1847, the Light-House Board received $12,000 for a light at Ship Island as well as funds for towers at Chandeleur Island and Biloxi. Rumors that the government was considering an iron lighthouse worried Davis, but the Fifth Auditor assured him a substantial brick tower was in store.[24]

Though all of Ship Island had been declared a federal reservation in 1847, a Spanish land grant delayed the start of lighthouse construction until 1853. A 45-foot brick tower was completed by November 1853 and was lit on Christmas Day. The tower originally held old-style reflectors, which were replaced in 1856 with a fourth-order Fresnel lens held 51 feet above the Gulf.[25]

Ship Island was to become the site of a major Army installation. The incomplete works near the light station were seized by a small Confederate force and named Fort Twiggs on January 13, 1861, four days after Mississippi declared its sovereignty. The light went out on July 7. At the same time the occupying force was increased to 140 troops backed by eight heavy cannon.[26]

Commander Melancton Smith, commanding USS *Massachusetts*, reported that on September 15, 1861, Confederate soldiers "destroyed the lighthouse by burning the interior and breaking the plate glass of the lantern," adding that their hasty departure was "undoubtedly accelerated by a message sent from my rifled gun." Actually, most of the enemy had already evacuated, warned of the enemy's approach by a lookout in the lighthouse. Confederate soldiers under Lieutenant John

The first keeper at Ship Island Light, Edward Havens, died after less than two years on duty and was succeeded by his widow, Mary, who served three years. (Photo courtesy of U.S. Coast Guard Historian's Office)

G. Devereux stayed behind to destroy everything of use to the Yankees. They packed the base of the lighthouse with scrap lumber and tossed in a firebrand, "having previously taken down the Fresnal [sic] lamp, which was carefully boxed up and brought away."[27]

Jefferson Davis, now President of the Confederate States, finally got his wish for a military/naval complex on Ship Island. Nearly 2,000 Union soldiers landed in December 1861 to establish Fort Massachusetts, nicknamed after the Union flagship. As temporary headquarters for the Gulf Blockading Squadron, the harbor bristled with masts. This hub of activity required the services of a light, and the lighthouse engineer from New Orleans installed a captured fourth-order lens on the evening of November 14, 1862, tended by temporary keeper John C. Goodwin. Tower repairs were extensive. Workers cinched the fire-cracked masonry together like a barrel using iron hoops. Assisting were a dozen recently freed slaves, nicknamed "contrabands," paid $6 a month, plus rations, a shirt, a pair of pants, and an army blanket. A mast from a seized Confederate schooner served as the newel post for the staircase. A fire raft sent downriver during the U.S. attack on New Orleans provided rough lumber. The old lantern was useless. The one salvaged from the wreck of the Bayou St. John Lighthouse was found in a Confederate warehouse on Lake Pontchartrain and was hoisted onto the Ship Island tower. Just as Confederate authorities had denied the light to their enemies, blinders in the lantern blocked the Ship Island Light from showing to the north, where Confederate raiders still operated in Mississippi Sound.[28]

In 1886 every building at the station was condemned as unsafe. A new square, open-frame lighthouse tower of 12-by-12 hand-hewn timbers replaced the old brick tower and was lit with the old lens on September 26 of that year. Until it received protective weatherboarding in 1887, the beam-and-brace tower was identical to the one built at Barataria Bay. By 1901 the brick tower had fallen and the rubble was formed into

In 1886, a wooden tower was built to replace the old brick tower at Ship Island. (Photo courtesy of U.S. Coast Guard Historian's Office)

Mississippi Sound

a quoin to curb erosion. More than 1,000 tons of rock were spread around the station in 1906 to keep sand from blowing away.[29]

In later years the station became part of the Ship Island tourist attraction. More than 8,000 sightseers visited the lighthouse in 1938 alone, and the numbers grew steadily after World War II. In June 1972 campers accidentally set the wood tower afire, and it burned to the ground. A slender steel skeleton tower erected in 1971 stands now.[30]

The Inside Passage

The Mississippi coastline offered unique protection for sloops, shallops, and small steamers bound between New Orleans and Mobile. The string of barrier islands cut the force of all but the strongest of southern gales, and its channel, although winding, allowed an ample depth for the shallow-draft vessels which could least afford to travel the outside route.

Early French explorers of Louisiana and West Florida sought the elusive mouth of the Mississippi River, but soon turned to Mississippi Sound for its easier access to New Orleans. A large portion of the cotton shipped from Mobile to Europe was actually taken through the quiet waters of the sound to New Orleans and often to New York before crossing the Atlantic Ocean. The completion of a rail line from Mobile to New Orleans in 1870 diverted passengers to the overland route, but Mississippi Sound continued to carry most of the freight.

Pass Christian Lighthouse

Andrew Jackson raised the U.S. flag over Pass Christian in January 1811 as he marched eastward through Spanish West Florida. He demonstrated that Spain could not deny the American claim to this territory.

Pass Christian takes its name from the nearby channel discovered by Christian l'Andier. In 1829 Congress authorized a lighthouse there where the channel passed close by the beach, and $500 for buoys to mark the outer turns.[31]

An Army engineer advised against the expenditure, arguing the pass carried "only five feet water at common tides, and at low water no vessels may pass through it." Packet and mail steamer skippers disagreed, however, and pressed for a guide through the tricky passage. By this time, the Mississippi and Alabama cotton trade was booming, and the Mississippi Gulf Coast drew steamboats loaded with vacationers.[32]

The building contract for Pass Christian was combined with that of Cat Island to the southwest and was won by Winslow Lewis for $9,283. The selected keeper, Roger A. Hiern, also supervised construction. His family name is still applied to a main street in town. The lighthouse was of the smallest class built by the government at the time. The 10 lamps

Pass Christian and Cat Island Lighthouse were both built by Winslow Lewis using identical plans. Wire running down the side of the tower to the ground served as a lightning rod. (Photo courtesy of U.S. Coast Guard Historian's Office)

were held only about 30 feet from the ground and 42 feet above sea level.[33]

Hiern accepted this post on July 1, 1831, but the station was not put to use for almost six months. The U.S. surveyor at Port Pontchartrain complained that the government had not supplied oil for the lamps. Meanwhile, the Pass Christian waterway was lit before a lighthouse was in operation. The captain of the mail steamer on the New Orleans-to-Mobile run paid Hiern $.50 per night to keep a pinewood fire blazing on the beach.[34]

This light was a family station for the next 30 years. Roger Hiern was relieved by Finsley B. Hiern in 1839, who served until Miss C.A. Hiern was appointed in 1844. She was employed by the United States, and then the Confederate States lighthouse services. Another woman who sought the job claimed that the last of the Hiern family and her companion were "two old maids, have no families and contribute nothing to the stranger, neighbor or society. The citizens think there should be a change. The [light]house is in a dilapidated condition." Miss Hiern continued in the job until the light was extinguished on about July 7, 1861. Three other women were appointed keepers here: Mary J. Reynolds, who had been the prewar keeper at Biloxi; Sally A. Dear; and Alice S. Butterworth.[35]

Pass Christian experienced a building boom in the 1850s which drew even more passenger steamers but also interfered with their navigation. The cupola on a store alongside the lighthouse now blocked the beacon. In 1859 the Light-House Board proposed to move the light farther down the beach. By this time the tower and dwelling were dilapidated. A lantern was already being fabricated in a northern foundry for a new lighthouse. The local engineer was unable to sell the old real estate for a price high enough to buy a new site, so he proposed raising the height of the lantern above the nearby building by erecting a "parapet wall" atop the masonry. The new lantern was altered so long bolts would extend through the wall extension into the original brickwork. The new lantern was shipped to Mobile Point, but the war intervened. It was captured after the war.[36]

When the Confederate superintendent of lights at Shieldsboro failed to have the lens removed in July 1861, town citizens hid it in the city. U.S. authorities recovered the lens in June 1865. The station was overhauled for relighting on August 15, 1866, by keeper C. S. Johnson. Engineer Max Bonzano intended to raise the building according to the 1859 plan but increased the height by only two feet and added a cornice to receive the lantern shipped before the war.[37]

In 1878 the Light-House Board announced it would execute the 1859 plan to clear the tops of trees and houses. They reversed course and the station was discontinued, being "of so little benefit to navigation or commerce." The station went dark on October 1, 1882.[38]

Congress considered punitive legislation to force re-establishment of the light, which members argued had been created by Congress and discontinued without its permission. Masters plying the sound petitioned for the bill and the proposed $6,000 appropriation. The measure failed 41 to 55. Pass Christian no longer rated a lighthouse. Buoys and beacons thereafter marked the channel. The Pass Christian city hall now occupies the site of the first lighthouse on the Mississippi mainland.[39]

Round Island Lighthouse

Pascagoula's Isle Ronde was so named by French explorer d'Iberville "on account of its form." Charts of the time depicted the island almost exactly the same shape as it appears today—an elongated teardrop. From the deck of a ship, however, it looks like a black bubble on the horizon, its dark pine trees rising high above the sound. The island lies on the most direct route through Mississippi Sound and as a bonus leads the mariner from Horn Island Pass to Pascagoula, three miles northward. Congress granted $7,000 in 1831 for a lighthouse to guide mail vessels and other traffic past shoals near St. Joseph Island, off Pascagoula. Since there was no such place, the Treasury Department built the lighthouse on Round Island.[40]

The original low bidder defaulted on the contract, causing a one-year delay. The station was eventually built by Bostonian Marshall Lincoln for $5,895. His 45-foot brick tower was fitted with 11 lamps, 48 feet above sea level. The first keeper, Curtis Lewis, took up his post in February 1833.[41]

In September 1849 when keeper Samuel Childress tried to report aboard, he faced a threat quite different from the hurricanes, disease, and isolation he expected. The island had become Sherwood Forest for about 400 adventurers intent on freeing Cuba from Spanish colonialism. A presidential order invoked the first United States blockade of its own soil to prevent arms and provisions from reaching a ragtag army. Childress was ignorant of the political excitement when he loaded a boat in Pascagoula with barrels of salt pork, beans, and other supplies. Armed sailors intercepted his schooner, taking him and his two sons prisoner. They proclaimed his boat a prize of war and seized his old scatter-gun. A copy of his official appointment as a lighthouse keeper proved to be evidence enough of his innocence. He was allowed to pass. The mercenaries eventually dispersed after causing considerable damage to the Round Island Light Station.[42]

When the Light-House Board took over the service in 1852, they considered the tower poorly placed and improperly protected from erosion. The foundation had been laid at sea level with only 26 feet of sand between it and the shoreline. Pilings placed around the grounds provided only a temporary solution. In 1854 the Board complained the light was "exhibited from an old and badly built tower," exposed to easterly storms. An 1856 appropriation of $8,000 allowed rebuilding about 500 feet to the northwest on a more suitable part of the island. A fifth-order Fresnel lens was temporarily placed in the old tower that year. The present Round Island Lighthouse was erected in 1859, 50 feet tall with a more-powerful fourth-order lens. Dredging had produced a channel to Pascagoula, and a companion harbor light already stood on the east branch of the Pascagoula River.[43]

The Confederate States inspector at Mobile removed the lens early in the Civil War and stored it at Montgomery. The island became a terminal for blockade runners and a haven for northern refugees during the war. On March 10, 1865, James Duggan lit up the fourth-order lens in response to U.S. Navy requests.[44]

The island has been pummeled by several hurricanes, but its sheltered location has prevented serious damage. A September 15, 1860, gale dealt the worst damage. Keeper S. Fischer, with his wife and six children, huddled in the top of the tower as waves rolled across the island. For two days they awaited rescue without food or water. All they

The present Round Island Lighthouse was erected in 1859. Shown here in 1892, the tower survived many hurricanes before and after this date. Note oil house to left of tower. (Photo courtesy of U.S. Coast Guard Historian's Office)

owned was lost. Every building on the island except the tower completely vanished. The 1906 hurricane which killed five people at other lighthouses also threatened keeper Thorwald Hansen on Round Island. Breakers crashed against the lighthouse, reaching halfway up the tower in the storm.[45]

The Coast Guard automated the station in 1944, 111 years after its first lighting. It was discontinued within two years. The City of Pascagoula sought ownership in 1985 and successfully nominated the site to the National Register of Historic Places. Slow erosion has since etched away the beach, and vandals have partly dismantled the tower and brick oil house, making renovation plans more difficult.[46]

Biloxi Lighthouse

Early Biloxi imported shipments of weary humans and exported refreshed, healthy vacationers, a trade at which it excels today. The upper classes from New Orleans and Mobile flocked to Mississippi's coast to escape heat, mosquitoes, and worse, the dreaded swamp vapors thought to spread yellow fever. It was otherwise not a commercial port, lacking the requisite transportation to interior cotton fields.

In 1848 the town received one of three lighthouses sponsored by Representative Jefferson Davis. The Treasury Department's Fifth Auditor, Stephen Pleasonton, began an experiment at Biloxi that would revolutionize lighthouse building in America. He explained to the New Orleans collector, "I intend to put a Cast Iron Light House at Biloxi ... and this will prove the utility which they may be of." The 45-foot tower was made of metal plates bolted around a brick liner. The masonry was added for strength, rust-proofing, and insulation from the subtropical heat. Already convinced that a new iron age had dawned for lighthouses in the tropics, Pleasonton welcomed Southern congressmen eager to view the tower construction at a Baltimore foundry.[47]

The British had recently built three iron lighthouses for export to tropical colonies. American civil engineer I. W. P. Lewis, nephew of Winslow Lewis, visited the inventor in 1844 and introduced a modified plan to the United States. Iron lighthouses offered durability and portability at a reasonable cost. They went up quickly, even in remote locations. The Biloxi tower is the only one of the four built on the Gulf Coast which has remained in place. The others were all easily relocated.[48]

The Murray and Hazlehurst Vulcan Works outbid a Mobile foundry and provided the ironwork and erected the tower at Biloxi in April 1848. The station was considered an important one and was soon upgraded from nine small reflectors to 14 large, 21 1/2-inch reflectors. Originally, the tower was to have been placed on Deer Island to mark the harbor in Biloxi Bay. The New Orleans collector convinced Pleasonton to place it inside the village of Biloxi as a guide for the increasing coastal traffic of mail boats, as well as passenger steamers visiting Mississippi Sound's spas.[49]

Marcellus J. Howard became the first keeper on April 4, 1848. The tower was completed by May 11, 1848. With the exception of his six-year tenure and a one-year stint by Perry Younghans, the Biloxi Lighthouse was tended by women for its first 81 years. The first was the widow Mary J. Reynolds, who also tended a large flock of orphaned relatives. She kept the light from as early as January 1854 to June 18, 1861, when Mayor James Fewell, head of the Biloxi Home Guards,

The first sailors steered their course to and from Biloxi by a huge magnolia tree which stood behind the future site of the lighthouse. Shown here in 1959, the 1848 Biloxi lighthouse stands on the median strip of U.S. Highway 90. (Photo courtesy of U.S. Coast Guard Historian's Office)

ordered the light extinguished and the lens stored in the city. Reynolds tended the Pass Christian Lighthouse after the war. When keeper Perry Younghans died on November 6, 1867, his widow Maria was appointed in his place. She tended the light 51 years, retiring with an immaculate record and earning a commendation for courage as "the plucky woman in charge of the light" in the hurricane of 1893. Her daughter Miranda took over in 1918 and retired in 1929 at age 76.[50]

The Light-House Board in 1854 was unhappy with the tower's location at the edge of a sand bank only 29 feet from shore. Instead of moving the tower back 100 yards as one inspector proposed, they poured a concrete seawall faced with hardened brick in 1854. This action probably saved the tower from disaster during the hurricane of August 1860, which destroyed two other nearby stations and nearly every structure on the Mississippi coast. Keeper Reynolds braved the storm and kept a good light continuously. "I ascended the tower at and after the last destructive storm," she wrote, "when man stood appalled at the danger I encountered."[51]

During the Civil War, the Home Guards manned a battery of four cannons at the lighthouse. Union gunboats taunted them but were unable to draw fire. They did not know that only one gun was in working order. Another was beyond repair and two more were "Quaker cannon"— pine logs painted black. A landing party dismantled the works without more than verbal protests from local citizens. The lighthouse lens was secreted in a Biloxi house and was recovered in 1865.[52]

Post-war renovations took only a month. In the 1860 storm a portion of the retaining wall had collapsed, allowing seas to undermine the foundation. During the entire war, the tower was canted over several feet. The U.S. lighthouse engineer applied an experimental remedy. His crew simply excavated under the opposite side of the foundation and the tower rocked back into position under its own massive weight. A solid-brick tower would probably have succumbed to the stress. Perry Younghans lit up the tower's fifth-order lens on November 16, 1866.[53]

In 1867 Biloxi's white tower was one of several iron lighthouses to be smeared with sticky, black coal tar as a rust retardant. This color choice started a persistent myth that the tower was painted black to mourn Abraham Lincoln's death. The tower was repainted white in 1869, since the dark color made it difficult to distinguish in the daytime from surrounding trees.[54]

Erosion cut away the beach and broke up the seawall, as well as several replacement walls made of wood pilings. Hundreds of tons of rock rip-rap were laid in 1902, 1907, and 1927. The lighthouse was electrified in 1929 and was in the same year turned over to the final keeper, William B. Thompson. The City of Biloxi now owns and operates the iron sentinel as a private aid to navigation. She stands guard between the east- and west-bound lanes of U.S. Highway 90 as the centerpiece of the city. Still in use as a private aid to navigation, Biloxi Lighthouse is the first of many iron lighthouses erected in the United States.[55]

East Pascagoula River Lighthouse

Although many colonial powers have occupied the mouths of the Pascagoula River, Americans owned its watershed at the end of the Revolutionary War. The lone-star flag of the Republic of West Florida flew there in 1810-1811, followed quickly by the Stars and Stripes. Soon the coasts of what are now Mississippi and Alabama were claimed to be part of the Louisiana Purchase. On January 4, 1811, Louisiana territorial governor William C. C. Claiborne reported, "the flag of the United States has been reared at . . . the mouth of Pascagoula."[56]

The shallow river bar prevented the entrance of any but the smallest craft, although anchorages in Mississippi Sound sheltered small ocean freighters. Congress funded dredging in 1827, but the task was not attempted until 1835. The channel was only 5 feet deep and 45 feet wide at the eastern branch, but was deemed sufficient for vessels using the river. Congress appropriated $3,500 for a harbor light in 1850, but an inspection of the port confirmed previous opinions. Captain John Grant, a "man of the river," had tried dredging at his own expense and agreed that a lighthouse would be of little use. He had recently opened a private channel from the sound to Mobile Bay and erected his own Grant's Pass Lighthouse there.[57]

In 1853 the U.S. Coast Survey offered a different view of the river. Lieutenant Benjamin F. Sands recommended a small-class lighthouse or beacon at Spanish Point, now an industrial complex. Despite the shallow entrance, "the river has now a large and increasing trade in lumber," he reported, and could easily become a cotton port. All that was needed was a safe harbor for seagoing ships. Nature obliged with a storm in October that year. Hurricane tides raced through shallow Horn Island Pass, scouring out shoals and knolls and creating a ship channel for Pascagoula. By the autumn of 1854 the Light-House Board had signed a contract with John Lowry for a combination brick lighthouse and keeper's dwelling. The lighthouse was completed by the end of the year. The first keeper was a woman, Celestine Dupont, who tended one of the first two French Fresnel lenses on the Gulf Coast.[58]

There are no records of the lens being removed during the Civil War. The Confederate superintendent at Shieldsboro had formed up a company of soldiers and ignored orders from Richmond to safeguard the lenses. The station was listed as "dilapidated" after the war. Repairs amounted to a whopping $22,000, more than four times the original cost of the station only a dozen years before. While the building sat idle, local health authorities used it as a smallpox hospital. The fifth-order lens was re-exhibited by Charles Kennedy on April 20, 1868, from a square tower over the south end of the dwelling roof.[59]

Dredging in 1888 reshaped the river channel, rendering the lighthouse less useful but drawing a large number of ships to load timber for export. The government established range lights in 1889 and added an assistant keeper to the station to tend them.[60]

The October 1, 1893, storm which destroyed the Chandeleur Island Lighthouse swamped Spanish Point. Portions of the tower were rebuilt at a cost of $30,000. The entire station was flattened in the hurricane of September 27, 1906. The three keepers at Pascagoula survived, although with great personal property losses. The East Pascagoula Lighthouse was

The East Pascagoula Lighthouse in 1892, 14 years before it was flattened in a hurricane which killed five keepers and family members at nearby lighthouses. Note piping from roof to cistern. (Photo courtesy of U.S. Coast Guard Historian's Office)

never rebuilt. The lighthouse property at Spanish Point was sold to Jackson County and the City of Pascagoula on May 17, 1957.[61]

Horn Island Lighthouse

A dropped French powder horn put Isle a Corne on charts in 1699. Almost two centuries later, as Pascagoula's lumber trade flourished, Horn Island received the first new lighthouse erected after the Civil War.

Most coastwise vessels preferred the safer and shorter toll channel at Grant's Pass because winter "norther" storms often pushed the water out of Mobile Bay and Mississippi Sound, leaving that pass almost dry. Vessels were forced out into the Gulf, rounding Sand Island. A light on Horn Island, sailors thought, would make their stormy voyage a bit less dangerous. In 1851 Mobile Collector John Walker suggested that the appropriation for the Ship Island Lighthouse would be better used to mark the Horn Island Pass.[62]

Three buoys were set in the channel that year by the Coast Survey, and in 1856 the Light-House Board placed an unlit beacon on the east end of the island in an attempt to satisfy the needs of packets and cotton steamers struggling into Mississippi Sound. By the end of the Civil War, northern forests were grossly depleted, and the demand for southern yellow pine resulted in increasing volumes of timber shipped down the Pascagoula River. Dredging had increased the depth of the river's mouth to 10 feet; Horn Island Pass allowed ships drawing 14 feet to anchor in safety.[63]

The government proposed an entrance light made of local brick which was available in excellent quality and great quantity. A more expensive screwpile structure was selected, however, with a dwelling topped by a lantern. While the site was elevated more than that of the lighthouse at Ship island, surveys showed the island unsuitable for a brick tower. The surveys were correct and the decision was fortunate. Horn Island, like so many of its neighboring sand bars, was a piece of real estate on the move. Lighthouses were built on, or moved to, five locations at Horn Island Pass.[64]

A Baltimore company supplied the ironwork for the first lighthouse. The station's fourth-order lens was first exhibited June 30, 1874—the first new lighthouse site on the Gulf Coast since the start of the Civil War. The revolving lens showed a red flash every 60 seconds to distinguish it from other lights nearby. The first keeper, Valentine B. McArthur, was removed for incompetence after only two months on the job. His replacement was war hero Martin Freeman, who remained at the post about 20 years. Freeman was a local fisherman when Federal blockaders captured him. He became one of the most important figures in the Civil War, serving as the pilot guiding Admiral David Farragut's fleet through the torpedo fields at Mobile Bay. He passed the forts riding the top of the flagship's mainmast as enemy shells whistled past. Once the fleet was inside the harbor, he was seriously wounded when a torpedo he was removing exploded. Freeman's gallantry earned him the Medal of Honor, as well as a job as lighthouse keeper.[65]

By 1880 the Gulf shoreline had worn away so badly that the Light-House Board created a futile system of jetties to slow the erosion of Horn Island. Within a few months, however, the tower was dismantled and moved 300 feet to the north. It now stood inside Mississippi Sound. The island increased its rate of northward creep. Only a year later, the tower was again in the Gulf of Mexico. Since the screwpiles had been turned 25 feet into the sand, the station was considered safe, 110 feet offshore in 7 feet of water.[66]

While the foundation appeared to be sound, the station was no longer as functional. Iron tension rods strengthening the pilings did not stop the structure from shaking so hard in gales that the revolving lens often stopped. A new station was built in 1887 about a mile away on what was thought the safest part of the island. Stripped of everything worth salvaging, the old building remained for years as a daymark. It was totally destroyed in the hurricane of 1893.[67]

Front Elevation.

Front elevation drawing for the proposed Horn Island Lighthouse dated 1886 (above) and the completed structure in 1892 (below). Note the cistern on front porch. (Drawing and photo courtesy of National Archives)

The new lighthouse was a substantial structure. The lantern from the old station rested atop a one-and-a-half-story, three-bedroom dwelling. This tower too was soon endangered by the forces of erosion. Instead of using breakwaters, jetties, or rip-rap, the Light-House Board solved the problem with barbed wire. Cattle, which the keeper believed were attracted like insects to the light, had been overrunning the station and consuming the sparse sea grasses that had been holding the loose sand in place. Still, erosion continued. In 1900 the tower was dismantled for another move, 253 feet north. Reassembled on high wood pilings in two feet of water, it was once again in Mississippi Sound.[68]

Disaster struck in the hurricane of 1906. The whole east end of the island washed away. No trace of a lighthouse remained. The bodies of keeper Charles Johnsson and his wife and daughter were never found. Where a lighthouse once stood, a channel allowed boats drawing six feet to pass. Horn Island was abandoned as a lighthouse site.[69]

At this time, the Light-House Board proposed tearing down the obsolete Mobile Bay Lighthouse and moving it to Horn Island. Congress instead provided $10,000 for a new building. The station was completed and lit on March 15, 1908. It rested on wood pilings across Horn Island Pass, just off Petit Bois (locally pronounced "petty-boy") Island. From that time on, the station was referred to as the Petit Bois Island Lighthouse and was considered Pascagoula's landfall light.[70]

The new site was in 21 feet of water alongside the dredged channel. The foundation was never again in danger of being undermined. In fact, by 1951 when the station was automated, the water depth had actually decreased to 13 feet. In 1961 the Coast Guard built range lights to mark the pass and discontinued the lighthouse.[71]

Merrill's Shell Bank Lighthouse

Merrill's Shell Bank lies a few miles due south of Pass Christian, at the "Tail of the Square Handkerchief Shoal." Buoys guided vessels through the pass after 1829. In 1847 America's first iron lightship was anchored there to mark Pass Marianne, named for Marianne l'Andier, a sibling of Pass Christian's namesake.

Technology caught up with the expensive rusting lightship. The Light-House Board asked Congress for permission to replace it with a more-maintainable screwpile lighthouse in 1857, but funds were withheld. The Board offered conclusive proof that most shallow-water lightship stations could be replaced with screwpile lighthouses and in 1859 received broad authority to do so. Every lightship in the Gulf was retired or relocated soon afterward.

The station built at Merrill's Shell Bank was a typical square wood dwelling on five piles, surmounted by an iron lantern. It was completed and lit August 10, 1860, apparently with a temporary lens. Keeper James

In 1860 a screwpile lighthouse replaced the expensive rusting lightship marking Merrill's Shell Bank. A second tower, built to replace the first which had burned to its foundation in 1893, is shown here in 1944. (Photo courtesy of U.S. Coast Guard Historian's Office)

Carver and his assistant, "French Charley" Briois, served until Confederate authorities removed the fourth-order lens in July 1861.[72]

The U.S. lighthouse engineer found the station "in measurably good condition" in 1862 and installed a temporary sixth-order lens on November 19, at the urging of General Benjamin Butler. In May 1863 keeper James Burroughs was arrested for supplying the enemy, caching almost a quarter ton of bacon at the lighthouse. His assistant keeper was fired at the same time for chronic insobriety. The original fourth-order lens was captured at Bay St. Louis in March 1863. It was repaired and replaced in 1866, "the wants of navigation of the locality rendering the change advisable."[73]

In June 1880 the building's shake roof caught fire from stovepipe sparks, but simply replacing the burned portions with more wood failed to solve the problem. On September 6, 1883, the entire station burned to the screwpiles. It took only 44 days to completely rebuild the superstructure for lighting on November 20. The new station was roofed with fireproof slate.[74]

This tower survived the severe hurricanes of 1893 and 1906 with only superficial damage. In 1893 water washed over the gallery surrounding the dwelling, 15 feet above normal tides. The lighthouse was automated in 1932 and discontinued in 1945. The spot is now marked by the Square Handkerchief Shoal Light, mounted on wood piles.[75]

St. Joseph Island Lighthouse

St. Joseph Island, originally called Half Moon Island, once marked the western extremity of Mississippi Sound. Low, marshy, and often submerged in storms, the site met every requirement for a lighthouse engineering disaster. An army engineer proposed a boat with a light at its masthead for St. Joseph Island in 1829. He felt a lighthouse could never be built there. The recommendation was ignored.[76]

In 1837 when the railroad boom was heard on the Gulf Coast, a rail line was to connect Mobile to a proposed port at Bay St. Louis, known then as Shieldsboro. Congress appropriated $12,000 for a lighthouse near the railroad's western depot. On the recommendation of a cautious naval inspector, funds sat idle for a decade waiting for the speculative venture to mature or fail. The latter occurred. The Panic of 1837 bankrupted the railroad. Before the 10-year depression eased, the appropriation was transferred to place a lighthouse or lightship at Merrill's Shell Bank.[77]

By 1851 local steamship lines established a day beacon on St. Joseph Island as a guide between Mississippi Sound and Lake Borgne. Also in that year the Mobile customs collector pressed the Provisional Light-House Board for a revolving light 20 feet above the water. The Board obtained funds in 1854, but the property was mired in real estate negotiations for two years. Thinking it had obtained a clear title, the Board raised a lighthouse but, while the station was ready, the land it rested on was not. In 1859, before it could be occupied, the tower was sinking into the mud. The U.S. Attorney took over the entire 200-acre island through condemnation proceedings in 1860. Finally, the tower was lit up on January 1, 1861. Nine days later, Mississippi seceded from the Union. A more violent land dispute ensued. Keeper Walter D. Reding continued on the Confederate States Light House Bureau payroll until June 30. The station's lens was moved to Bay St. Louis and recovered there by U.S. soldiers in late 1862.[78]

St. Joseph Island was ravaged only by nature during the war. Renovations were complete on April 10, 1865, when the station was placed back in operation. The wood dwelling had once stood on brick columns which, by the time of its relighting, had sunk unevenly several feet into the muck. The low island was often entirely under water. Even the best soil there was as much liquid as solid, "into which a pole can easily be thrust to a depth of twenty feet," the Light-House Board reported.[79]

Timbers under the foundation, renewed in 1864, were worm-ridden in only three years. The station balanced on only three of its nine brick support piers. The keeper shoved timbers under the rest of the building to save it from total collapse. The Board presumed the foundation would rot away every two years and recommended an iron screwpile structure in the water alongside the channel. A shoal of sand 800 yards south would provide an excellent new site.[80]

Congress would not agree to fund a new station. Using general repair funds, Engineer Max Bonzano hastily prepared a new foundation 25 feet from the old building. Piles were driven 60 feet. To protect the wood against boring worms, the soil was excavated to encase the piles in brick and concrete. The move was just in time. The structure stood fast as the gale of September 1868 carried away every outbuilding and the wharf.[81]

In ten years the foundation was again failing. A poorly designed breakwater let waves sweep between the pilings and under the tower. Ballast rock and brick from the old Cat Island tower sank into the mud, and the masonry around the pilings broke apart. Still, engineers hoped the station could be saved. Site protection continued until 1886, when the Light-House Board flatly gave up.[82]

The St. Joseph Island Lighthouse had been plagued by problems from the start; it was finally "impractical to rebuild or save the station." The building was condemned in August 1888 and keeper Robert Dimitry moved to Bay St. Louis, tending an eight-day kerosene light from a boat.[83]

All this effort had been expended to display a relatively minor channel light. The fifth-order lens was never visible more than 11 miles. A new lighthouse established on September 1, 1889, in Lake Borgne replaced the St. Joseph Island Lighthouse. The abandoned building survived until the 1893 hurricane entirely washed it away. Submerged pilings now mark the ruins on charts.[84]

Lake Borgne Lighthouse

The replacement for the St. Joseph Island Lighthouse was situated a few miles to the west on Lower Point Clear. While the official name of the station was the Lake Borgne Lighthouse, locals continued to call it the St. Joe Light for decades. The Light-House Board asked for $20,000 to erect a lighthouse there in 1878, but funds were not available until they agreed to abandon the incredible misadventure at St. Joseph Island.

The chosen site was a broad marshland, but it served vessel traffic well, being only 500 yards from Grande Pass, leading into Lake Borgne. Long screwpiles held the square, seven-room wood dwelling high above the water. A lantern was mounted at the south end of the roof, housing a fifth-order lens 42 feet above sea level. The first keeper, Henry Wilkinson, lit the lamps on September 1, 1889.[85]

The hurricane of October 1, 1893, demolished the old St. Joseph Island Lighthouse and dealt severe damage to its replacement. The metal roof flew into the swamps and was never found. The hurricane of September 10, 1906, effectively destroyed the station. This time the roof landed in the marshes a half mile away, and wind and rain left the building's interior a shambles. Keeper John A. Munch was able to show a light during and after the storm. Temporary repairs kept the station in operation until Congress appropriated $7,000 for a new superstructure in 1908. Construction started on June 21 with completion by the end of September. For three years the new tower displayed a weak acetylene light usually reserved for minor channel beacons. The lens-lantern was replaced by a fifth-order Fresnel lens and oil light in 1911, mounted in a circular lantern.[86]

The lighthouse was discontinued in 1937; the heavily vandalized property was offered to the Federal Works Agency ten years later as surplus property. Lighthouse Bayou is still prominently marked on charts.[87]

Proctorsville Lighthouse

Transportation speculators went almost wild in the 1830s, building railroads to and from almost every obscure corner of the country. One such outpost was Proctor's Plantation at the southern extreme of Lake Borgne, which by 1840 became the terminus of the Mexican and Gulf Railroad. The investors originally announced plans to extend the rails all the way to Malheureux Point near Cat Island. There deep-draft ships would tie up directly to a rail wharf at the first deep-water railroad port on the Gulf of Mexico. An immense port was fantasized, with thousands of tons of cargo zipping the 18 miles to and from New Orleans at fully 12 miles per hour! The expansion was never realized.[88]

When the first section of track was laid, the railroad company pressed for a light to mark its triumph. An impressed U.S. Congress dug into federal coffers in 1848, withdrawing $500 to build the tiny "Proctorsville Bug Light." A puzzled and naive Fifth Auditor asked the New Orleans collector, "What is meant by a *Bug Light*? I do not exactly comprehend." Obviously, Pleasonton had no idea just how much attention a light could draw above Louisiana's swamps. The result was a contraption similar to beacon lights built elsewhere along the Gulf Coast, as well as on old lightships. A little square lantern slid up and down like a guillotine between two upright timbers, hoisted each night by the president of the rail company, W. Alex Gordon. It held only one lamp in a small reflector, equivalent in power to sparks from a steamer's stack.[89]

More brilliant illumination was provided, even if only briefly, on November 24, 1853, when the structure burned to the ground. A temporary beacon light replaced it, strung up 35 feet above water on a pole, tended by Cary Watkins.[90]

A real lighthouse followed, displayed for the first time on August 17, 1858. The lighthouse was patterned on plans for the Bayou St. John Lighthouse. Like its model, this square dwelling on screwpiles was completely demolished in a hurricane on August 10-11, 1860, and was never rebuilt. Keeper Charles Combret "drowned in endeavoring to save the premises & property." The Light-House Board asked for permission to rebuild the station out of general repair funds, but the U.S. Treasury Secretary decided, "where a light house is destroyed by the Act of God, the Board has no power to renew the light."[91]

Meanwhile, rail operations resumed; by 1867 the railroad company raised an iron beacon. Federal funds were available to erect an insufficient lit beacon, but port activity declined for all but a few fishermen. In 1871 the site was described as "formerly the terminus" of the railroad. Some railroad track survives. The old site of Proctorsville is now the town of Yscloski.[92]

Chapter 7

Louisiana's Lake Country

The Rigolets

The crooked bayou known as the Rigolets (pronounced *RIG*-o-leez) is Lake Pontchartrain's main outlet to Mississippi Sound. It connected New Orleans lakefront ports to the anchorages of Cat, Ship, and Chandeleur Islands. The French first explored this waterway, naming it "Pass á Guyon" on their earliest charts. The name Rigolets originally belonged to a waterway inside islets off the Pearl River, called "les Rigolets ou passant les chaloupes" (channels for ships' boats).

The Rigolets allowed colonial New Orleans to be a port, as well as an outpost guarding access to the vast center of what is now the continental United States. The Mississippi River's swift and turbulent currents effectively prevented sailing ships from ascending the 100 miles to New Orleans. Crews fought the current by hauling against trees on the banks, a labor which often took a month or more. To avoid the expense and lost time, ships gathered in Mississippi Sound and transferred passengers and cargoes to small luggers for a few hours' sail to a landing.

Once through the Rigolets, the boats crossed Lake Pontchartrain and entered Bayou St. John, about five miles from the city. Other ports were later opened at the Port Pontchartrain railhead and on the New Canal.

During the War of 1812, the U.S. Navy established small fortifications at the Rigolets. One was at the mouth and the other halfway up the channel, near the future sites of the East Rigolets and West Rigolets Lighthouses. The forts mounted no more than 10 cannon and were quickly subdued by lightly armed British barges.

The Rigolets became less important to seaborne commerce when the invention of steam tugs let ships ascend the river in a matter of days and when jetties allowed deep-draft ships to enter the river passes.

Federal lights were authorized to mark the Rigolets as early as 1826, but only $600 was made available at that time for three tiny lights to mark forts in the area. The sum was hardly enough to hang steamer lanterns from posts.

East Rigolets Lighthouse

With towers already under construction in Mississippi Sound to mark the approaches to the Rigolets, Congress authorized a lighthouse at the east end of the Rigolets in 1831. The President had vetoed an appropriation bill the previous year.[1]

Construction was delayed almost two more years when the New Orleans lighthouse superintendent failed to select a proper site. He finally settled on an island directly across from the west mouth of the Pearl River on what has always been officially called Rabbit Island. As long as the lighthouse was active, the government called the place Pleasonton's Island, honoring Stephen S. Pleasonton, Fifth Auditor of the Treasury and administrator of the nation's lighthouses.[2]

Marshall Lincoln built the 45-foot tower, as well as the one on Round Island off Pascagoula. The tower was due for completion by December 15, 1833, but the contractor arrived to begin construction two days after that date. Although most government records claim the tower was built in 1833, it is unlikely it went up in only two weeks. The lantern held a revolving chandelier of 10 lamps, tended the first seven years by Isaac H. Smith.[3]

The East Rigolets tower was not well built and was poorly maintained. An inspector in 1846 found it built directly on the soft alluvial soil, yet somehow perfectly plumb without the benefit of a foundation. Nor were keepers held in high esteem. The station's second keeper was fired for drunkenness. His successor allowed the station to fall into near ruin. The tower door disappeared, windows were broken out, and bricks fell from the tower. In the period from 1840 to 1844 five keepers held the post, averaging only a year each on the job.[4]

In 1839 the local collector removed the revolving apparatus at the East Rigolets Light so that it showed a fixed light 60 feet above sea level. The Light House Board installed a fourth-order Fresnel lens and modern lantern in 1857.[5] (Photo courtesy of U.S. Coast Guard Historian's Office)

The East Rigolets station received relatively little damage during the Civil War. The lens was taken to the Shieldsboro home of the Confederate States customs collector in the sloop *Henry Larnes*. Union forces recovered it by September 1862 and shipped it to New Orleans. The tower was relit on November 21, although renovations were not completed for more than three years. A new, larger lantern was added in 1866, requiring the rebuilding of the top four feet of the tower.[6]

The station was discontinued on May 25, 1874, "it being no longer required for purposes of navigation." A railroad line had spanned the Rigolets, connecting New Orleans, Mobile, and points between. Passenger steamers ceased operations and freight traffic diminished. The keeper was transferred to the newly built Horn Island station; for four years the East Rigolets tower stood idle. By 1878 fishermen and barge operators pressed for relighting. Citing the obvious, the Light-House Board claimed, "It is difficult to find this entrance at night." They asked Congress for $6,000 to re-establish the station, but it was never recommissioned.[7]

In 1883 the State of Louisiana asked to use the property as a quarantine station. Ironically, Light-House Board transfer documents referred to the location as "Rabid Island." The last mention of the tower in Lighthouse Service records was in 1923, when the site was sold to Jahncke Service, Inc.[8]

West Rigolets Lighthouse

In 1826 Congress allotted $200 for a lighthouse at the Petite Coquilles, just inside Lake Pontchartrain. The appropriation would hardly pay for a cypress log pounded into the shell islands, let alone a ship's lantern. A real lighthouse was recommended in 1832 to mark Fort Pike at the west end of the Rigolets, but the government felt the East Rigolets tower adequate to serve the needs of navigators in the area. During its 1850s efforts to create a true system of lighthouses, the Light-House Board suggested a screwpile harbor light 1,200 feet west of Fort Pike as a guide to vessels entering the Rigolets from the lake. At the same time, they proposed rebuilding four of the five existing lake lights. The square dwelling erected at West Rigolets held a lantern centered on its hipped roof, elevated only 30 feet above the lake but visible 10 miles. The station was completed in 1855.[9]

During the Civil War the lens and supplies were left in the charge of Confederate States keeper James Cain after the light was extinguished on July 6, 1861. When a lighthouse engineer was appointed at New Orleans late in 1862, this light received a high priority. A temporary ship's lantern showed from the lighthouse in late November in support of U.S. Navy operations in the lake. The Federal engineer reconsidered the installation of the original fifth-order lens after an attack on the keeper. The second night Thomas Harrison was on the job, he was found shot on the wharf. He is the only keeper known to be killed at his post during the hostilities. The lighthouse engineer could not determine "if he was shot by rebels, contraband Negroes [escaped slaves] or some of our own soldiers. Nearby Fort Pike had recently been occupied by Union soldiers." The station was fully renovated and a fifth-order lens was shown the next year by John M. Read. He remained on duty 36 years and was succeeded by his widow, Anna.[10]

Hurricanes through the years troubled the West Rigolets station, although it was never in serious jeopardy. A storm in 1868 caused $5,000 in damage, the original cost of the station. A gale the next year dealt $6,000 in damages. In 1917 the station was raised six feet and placed on ferro-cement columns after the shoreline finally encroached.[11]

In 1945 an electric 200mm lens was established nearby. The lighthouse was discontinued and left to rot.[12]

Tending the West Rigolets Light was generally uneventful; however, keeper Charles W. Heartt found some excitement in a 1922 adventure. In July that year, he rescued two drowning fishermen who were thrown into the water when a tarpon leapt into their boat. (Photo courtesy of U.S. Coast Guard Historian's Office)

Lake Pontchartrain

Once inside Lake Pontchartrain, the mariner looks over a seemingly peaceful sheet of water 26 miles broad and 42 miles long. Its depth, however, averages only about 14 feet, and the lake kicks up violently in storms. A boat drawing one fathom or so can pound to pieces on the bottom in a five-foot chop.

The lake is actually a wide spot in a bayou which was once the easternmost pass of the Mississippi River. Only traces of this bayou are visible above Lake Maurepas. The lake's north shore is high and sandy. The south shore is made up of marshy river deposits and, of course, New Orleans, the commercial capital of the South since before the U.S. Constitution was written.

In colonial and territorial days all but a few vessels made directly for Bayou St. John, where the federal government built the first lighthouse ever erected in a United States territory. Colonial governments erected a light of some sort at the bayou, but the beacon is virtually undocumented. The bayou connected the lake to New Orleans through a canal and provided the quickest access to the city. In the 1830s a second canal and a railroad were established between the city and the lake, drawing traffic away from the natural bayou. The ports became worthy of their own lighthouses.

Lights were also placed at the Tchefuncte River on the northwest shore and at Pass Manchac, leading to Lake Maurepas and rich plantations in the interior. Once lighthouses marked Bayou Bonfouca and the Amite River, a sailor could find hardly a spot on the lakes where a lighthouse was not visible.

Bayou St. John Lighthouse

The French choice for the capital of Louisiana was based on transportation and domination. A city at New Orleans, the site of an ancient Indian portage between the river and Lake Pontchartrain, would guard two-thirds of the North American continent. It was also approachable through the natural waterway named Bayou St. John. Choctaws called it Tchoupic-hatcha, translating very roughly into "river of stench," named after the inedible bowfins which abounded there.

Colonial governors built small forts at the swampy bayou mouth and appear to have marked the spot with a small lit beacon, probably shown over Fort St. John. In 1727 an attempt to link the bayou and the river with a canal failed. Another try in 1794 by Baron de Carondelet was more successful. The five-mile waterway was dug and cleared by as many as 150 slaves volunteered by local planters. By the end of 1796 schooners were able to sail through the lake and moor in the canal basin at New Orleans. The waterway was cleared of logs and debris each year by slaves and criminals condemned to hard labor.[13]

In 1807 Congress authorized spending $25,000 to lengthen and improve the Canal de Carondelet and to deepen the river at New Orleans. The next year the master and wardens of the Port of New Orleans recommended that two ship lanterns be hoisted over the fort, or a lighthouse built if the expense was not too great. At the time the low lake shoreline was entirely devoid of buildings or other landmarks.

Congress allowed $2,000 for the light. Treasury Secretary Albert Gallatin suggested "a mere open frame, 20 or 30 feet high, with a ladder & hanging lantern."[14]

The first lighthouse the United States built outside the 13 former English colonies was completed at Bayou St. John on August 5, 1811. In December an agreement was struck with Lieutenant Sands, commanding the fort, to tend the light for $15 per month. He served as keeper until 1820, when the crew of the local revenue cutter took over. When the cutter was withdrawn in 1821, Pierre Brousseau became the first civilian keeper.[15]

The octagonal wood tower was built offshore on an artificial shell island contained by timber pilings. The lantern, 28 feet above the water, held a sperm-oil lamp, even though most U.S. lighthouses used candles until the invention of the Argand Lamp in 1812. Within two years the original lamp became untenable and was replaced by a common street lamp from New Orleans. The U.S. surveyor at Port Pontchartrain complained often about the quality of lighthouses and was especially critical of the one at Bayou St. John. He claimed the glow of candles through ship portholes were a better guide to the bayou.[16]

Bayou St. John became a watery playground for those New Orleans residents who could not afford the trip to the lake's north-shore health resorts or the Mississippi coast's healthier climate. On hot summer days the cool waters of the lake invited many a bather. The swimming was considered best around the lighthouse.

Although harbor and road improvements continued at the bayou, only a small fishing village developed. Cargo vessels preferred the superior facilities at Port Pontchartrain and New Canal.[17]

In 1837 a new channel was opened at the mouth of Bayou St. John, increasing the natural five-foot depth. The navigation company granted a site for a new lighthouse and, although the importance of the waterway continued to dwindle, a new lighthouse was authorized. That fall the original lighthouse was swept away by a storm.[18]

A contract was let in May 1838, and a new tower was completed within a few months, although it was not fitted out with lamps until the following March. The first keeper was John Clement. This station was a real lighthouse, advertised to carry nine lamps 48 feet above sea level, glowing a soft, pale red.[19]

When the Light-House Board was placed in control of aids to navigation in 1852, they considered this and its sister Port Pontchartrain and New Canal Lighthouses to be wholly worthless. The New Orleans superintendent agreed, calling all three towers "shamefully built and the public completely cheated." The sagging Bayou St. John tower was strengthened in 1854, but its future was hopeless. A new screwpile

Keeper A. B. Shelby took his post at the new Bayou St. John Lighthouse in 1856. The small sixth-order harbor lens was centered atop a square dwelling, 39 feet above the lake.[20] (Photo courtesy U.S. Coast Guard Historian's Office)

lighthouse was prefabricated for $6,000 in 1855, but work on the bayou entrance delayed erection until the next year.

This tower was damaged beyond repair in a hurricane on September 11-12, 1860. Salvable portions were stored in a makeshift warehouse until 1862, when Union forces entered New Orleans. A steamer lantern was shown on December 1, 1863, from an enclosed wooden tripod on the lakeshore. The lens and apparatus were placed elsewhere in support of the war effort. The original lantern was stripped from the ruins of the tower and mounted on the Ship Island Lighthouse in Mississippi Sound. Occupying troops destroyed everything else but the iron piles.[21]

A permanent replacement was erected on the original screwpiles; its sixth-order lens, again 39 feet above the lake, was first lit in March 1869. This beacon-light did not double as a keeper's dwelling. Keeper Robert Gage reached the tower in heavy weather by wading from his quarters ashore across a rotten plank walk owned by the canal company. Within a year the Light-House Board recommended raising the platform on which the beacon was built at least nine feet to place it above hurricane tides.

The prominence of the bayou continued to decrease, however, in favor of better ports nearby. Rail connections with Mobile and the Mississippi Gulf Coast siphoned off all the passenger trade and much of the freight. Virtually all commercial traffic in the lake ended after the turn of the century. Only small beacons have since been shown at Bayou St. John.[22]

Port Pontchartrain Lighthouse

Milneburg's Port Pontchartrain was the lake's first artificial harbor. Alexander Milne and a group of investors were empowered to open a turnpike road from New Orleans, and a decade later formed a company to build the first steam railroad west of the Allegheny Mountains. The novelty and efficiency of overland rail travel soon drew freight and passengers away from old Bayou St. John. Steamboat lines connected to the lake's north shore to mail ports everywhere on the Gulf Coast.

The railroad company did not ask the government to build them a lighthouse. In fact, when the Treasury Department proposed a tower, the company argued against it. By 1832 they had fashioned Louisiana's only private lighthouse, which looked more like a guillotine from the French Revolution. The square lantern was hoisted between two channels to a height of 50 feet.

Congress appropriated $5,000 for a replacement in 1834, and the government announced plans to replace the 50-foot tower with a puny 20-footer. The rail company preferred to sell the government its tower. The project stalled for several years.[23]

In 1836 U.S. Port Surveyor John Bingey urged the Treasury Department to build a real lighthouse. Four steamers, five sailing vessels, and a number of lives had been lost off the port for want of a good light. The local customs collector blamed the situation on deficient funding from Congress. Meanwhile, the railroad company maintained its own light.[24]

Congress in 1837 overwhelmed the Treasury Department with $25,000 for a lighthouse and other aids to navigation at Port Pontchartrain. Contracting problems delayed completion of the tower until February 1839. The light was built for only $4,400—well within the original 1834 appropriation limits. Even with additional buoys and beacons, the total expenditure was only $5,647.50.[25]

The octagonal wood tower was identical in all respects to those at Bayou St. John and New Canal, except that its chandelier revolved to show a flashing light. It measured 28 feet in height atop the pilings and 18 feet in diameter. The first keeper, Benjamin J. Shane, received his appointment on February 15, 1839, two days after the lighthouse was completed.[26]

By the 1850s Milneburg had drawn traffic away from ports as far as Mobile. The Coast Survey reported more than a half million tons of cargo passing across Port Pontchartrain wharves each year. Since there was no natural harbor at Milneburg, the port literally shut down in the stormy winter months, at a time when freight shipments peaked. Congress voted $25,000 in 1852 for harbor protection and $6,000 for a new lighthouse in 1854. Engineer Captain Danville Leadbetter proposed a substantial brick tower on the mucky lake bottom, even though other lake lights at the time were to be erected atop screwpiles.[27]

The lighthouse was begun in October 1855 on a broad concrete pad atop pilings and was completed by the end of the year. The apparatus from the original tower was placed in the new tower and was replaced in 1857 by a Fresnel lens of the fifth order.[28]

Only one keeper stayed at his post on the Gulf Coast for the duration of the Civil War. Charles Fagot, the former Federal keeper, served under the Confederate States government until New Orleans fell to Admiral Farragut. Confederates failed to extinguish his light when they evacuated the city. He was retained by the Light-House Board, even when the light was briefly blacked out in mid-1863. The 1839 tower was taken down in 1864, "a weather-boarded, eight-sided truncated pyramid of very ugly shape; its removal has very much improved the general

The 1855 Port Pontchartrain Lighthouse was the only brick tower ever built on a submarine foundation in the Gulf. (Photo courtesy of U.S. Coast Guard Historian's Office)

The top of the Port Pontchartrain Lighthouse was flared out in 1880 in order to accommodate a new lantern. Shown here in 1994, the lighthouse is inactive and privately owned. (Photo by David L. Cipra, 1994)

appearance of the station." The old wood went into a new walkway over the lake to the railroad pier.[29]

Masons flared out the top of the brick tower, raising it seven feet, to install a new lantern in 1880. The focal plane of the lens was now 42 feet above the lake. By this time, rail service was available to points east of New Orleans and the port fell idle.

For the last 48 years of this tower's service, the keepers were women. Ellen Wilson served as keeper from April 1882 to about 1895, when she was relieved by Margaret R. Norvell, widow of the Head of Passes keeper. Norvell was publicly recognized for hosting some 200 storm refugees during the 1903 "Cheniere Caminada" hurricane. Every building in the vicinity was damaged. She was transferred to New Canal in 1924, and Mrs. W. E. Coteron was keeper until the light was discontinued and turned over to the New Orleans Levee Board on May 29, 1929. The lighthouse was once 2,100 feet offshore, but landfill projects have surrounded it with dry land.[30]

New Canal Lighthouse

A few miles west of Bayou St. John, a private company excavated a toll canal to connect Lake Pontchartrain with New Orleans. It was creatively named "New Canal" to differentiate it from the old Canal de Carondelet and Bayou St. John. It was a significant improvement over the shallow, winding bayou; shippers could avoid the cargo handling required at the Port Pontchartrain rail depot. The waterway extended to near the Union Station, about five and a half miles from the lake.

Before the canal was complete, Congress authorized $25,000 in 1837 to mark the entrance and approaches. By September 1837 the New Orleans collector had fixed a site for the lighthouse and keeper's dwelling. The tower was identical to its two south-shore companions and was built by Francis D. Gott of New Orleans for $4,500. The cypress tower was completed in February 1839. The nearly simultaneous construction of the three towers was entirely a coincidence; each site happened to be in need of a lighthouse at the same time.[31]

The New Canal station was at several times under the care of a woman keeper and is an example of how the lighthouse establishment took care of its keepers' families and capitalized on the experience of the keepers' wives. Lighthouse wives usually assisted their husbands and learned the family trade. They often took over when widowed. At New Canal, Elizabeth Beattie received an appointment on January 2, 1847, after her husband Thomas, the station's first keeper, died. In 1850, Jane O'Driscoll also replaced her deceased husband as keeper. Mary F. Campbell relieved her husband in 1870 and held the post until Caroline Riddle took over in about 1895. Riddle was in turn relieved in 1924 by Maggie Norvell, another lighthouse keeper's widow.[32]

By 1843 the tower's lower timbers had rotted, allowing the structure to cant over. In 1853 the Light-House Board renewed the foundation piles, hoping they would hold until a replacement could be built. The new tower went up in May 1855, a square wood dwelling on screwpiles, holding an iron lantern atop the hipped roof. The fixed fifth-order lens was shown 33 feet above the lake by keeper Israel Brull. The original lighthouse stood on pilings which had decayed so much that the tower tilted toward the lake and was in danger of collapsing.[33]

The lighthouse was active well into the Civil War. Confederate States Collector Frank Hatch reported the light in nightly operation as late as the autumn of 1861; it probably continued until the fall of New Orleans in 1862. Union forces took the city and the lake's south shore in April 1862. Operations against Confederate forces on the north shore were usually staged from Navy gunboats; the New Canal Light was important to these strikes. The light was re-established by the end of September 1862, with the pre-war keeper, William A. Waldo, reappointed on December 15.[34]

In 1881 the Light-House Board considered discontinuing the station. Changes in the mouth of the canal rendered the location ineffective. "The light is not of much use," the Board reported, "but it is more important than the Bayou St. John light." The light was not high enough to clear the top of the nearby yacht club to the northwest. Instead, a two-story superstructure was mounted on the original iron piles in 1890. The old squat building was sold for scrap but the new lighthouse remains, unaged by a century of torturous weather. The structure held the light 49 feet above the lake, a 16-foot increase in elevation, and was first lit June 2, 1890, by Mary F. Campbell.[35]

The New Canal keepers were not immune to danger. A hurricane in September 1915 heavily damaged the station with winds estimated at 130 miles per hour. Keeper Caroline Riddle was commended for heroism in showing the light through the storm. The barometer fell to 28.11 inches, setting a U.S. record, and Lake Pontchartrain rose so high it topped the levees and flooded parts of New Orleans. Riddle was forced to douse the main light and hang a small lantern in the rocking tower. Keeper Maggie Norvell helped 200 victims ashore from an excursion boat fire in 1926, treating each of them until they could be evacuated. A Navy pilot who crashed into the lake near the station owed his life to Norvell, who rowed out to his sinking biplane in a two-hour rescue.[36]

Hurricane damage in 1926 convinced engineers to raise the tower on new concrete piers. The light's elevation was increased to 52 feet above the water. Once 1,000 feet offshore, the station soon stood at the edge of the levee. Landfill projects created what is now the Lakefront Park, with the lighthouse its most prominent feature. In 1936 the

Still very much active as a Coast Guard rescue station, the New Canal Lighthouse was one of the last manned lighthouses in the United States.[37] (Photo by David L. Cipra, 1994)

breakwater around the station was filled in, placing the lighthouse on dry land for the first time.

Tchefuncte River Lighthouse

At Madisonville, just above the mouth of the Tchefuncte River, a few tiny American gunboats were built to face 50 British men-of-war in the War of 1812. The little fleet hardly sounded a gun before being soundly trounced before the Battle of New Orleans. The boatyards flourished in the decades to come, as did health resorts and ozone spas which attracted steam ferries filled with New Orleans residents.

Congress authorized a lighthouse for the mouth of the river in 1834, the same year as Port Pontchartrain's, but construction was delayed almost three years by a clouded land title. On July 17, 1837, a contract was signed with Jonathan Alston of New Orleans to build a 30-foot tower of "hard-burnt lake brick," probably from Bayou Bonfouca, topped by a wrought-iron lantern. He served until his death in December 1845. The New Orleans customs collector forgot to contract for lamps or reflectors, delaying the lighting of the tower until near the end of 1838. Winslow Lewis supplied the illuminating apparatus, which was identical to that at Pass Manchac, only a few miles away. Benjamin Thurston was nominated as its first keeper in November 1837.[38]

The Tchefuncte River tower was the only Lake Pontchartrain lighthouse not rebuilt when the Light House Board assumed command. The old reflector system was replaced by a Fresnel lens in 1857, elevating the focal plane about four feet. (Photo courtesy of U.S. Coast Guard Historian's Office)

The brick tower was at least badly scorched in the Civil War; possibly an attempt was made to blow it up. A post-war pencil sketch shows a large hole broken out of the tower. The damage was so great that the lighthouse could not be saved, although many bricks were recycled. The lighthouse engineer tore down and completely rebuilt the tower on its old foundation. Work started in early 1867 and ended almost a year later. The lantern in use today was transferred from the destroyed Cat Island station. The first post-war keeper was William A. Stewart, who was commended for "coolness, courage and good conduct" while piloting USS *Richmond* past the guns of Fort Morgan in August 1864.[39]

The Tchefuncte River Lighthouse was unmanned in World War II, but is still very much active on the west side of the river's mouth.

The old tower having been damaged in the Civil War, the new tower at Tchefuncte River was 10 feet taller than its predecessor. Note the oil house to left of tower and what was probably a bell tower to right. (Photo courtesy of U.S. Coast Guard Historian's Office)

Bayou Bonfouca Lighthouse

Bonfouca is a "Franglicized" Choctaw Indian word meaning "bayou residents." The bayou was short but deep and lay just inside Lake Pontchartrain at the western edge of Spanish West Florida. Historians believe the oldest settlement on the north shore of the lake was established there, founded by at least 1725, four years after New Orleans. A small Spanish garrison maintained control over the town until 1807, when U.S. claims to West Florida became more vocal. The settlement was located about six miles from the lake on the site of the present city of Slidell, at the junction of Bayou Liberty. The town was locally well known for cattle exports but even more for an excellent "hard-burnt lake brick" which was apparently used in several Louisiana lighthouses as well as many fine New Orleans buildings. Boatyards at the bayou catered to the lake trade. At the time the lighthouse was authorized, 18 lake schooners were on the ways to carry bricks to New Orleans.[40]

The Louisiana General Assembly petitioned for a lighthouse at the bayou in 1840 and 1841, but it was a letter from the New Orleans postmaster that caught the attention of Congress. A bill to fund the lighthouse foundered in a congressional committee in 1844 when no one in Washington could locate the place on a map. It passed in 1847, with only $3,000 made available for a minor harbor light. The Treasury Department instructed the New Orleans collector to pattern the structure after the wood lighthouse just completed at Pass Manchac. Designer George Bowditch drew up plans for a shorter tower. "As it is not necessary to see this light more than five miles," he explained, "I have drawn the house but one story." The light was obviously never intended as more than a guide into the bayou, although it was advertised as a guide between the Rigolets and other lake lights.[41]

The construction contract was won with a bid of $2,975 by the newly formed company of Joseph M. Howell and Moses Coats of New Orleans. The two-room dwelling was raised on a five-foot brick foundation wall. A central, 9-foot chamber between the rooms served as the base for the tower, which extended 12 feet from the roof. The lantern was likewise tiny, only three feet in diameter and six feet tall. It was designed to hold only four small lamps 39 feet above sea level.[42]

Bonfouca Light was completed by early March 1848, and was briefly tended by keeper John Wadsworth. Within a year, Vincenzo Scorza took over the post and served until his capture by Confederate forces in 1862. The following decade proved to be an economic heyday for local commerce. When the lighthouse was destroyed by fire in 1862, trade fell dramatically and never rebounded as it did at most other Southern ports.[43]

Confederate soldiers retreated to the north shore of Lake Pontchartrain after the Union captured New Orleans in April 1862. In May or June they burned the lighthouse and took Scorza prisoner, even though he was a Confederate States employee at the time. He escaped from Camp Moore and reported to the United States collector at New Orleans. The New Orleans lighthouse engineer recommended that the lighthouse not be rebuilt. The bayou carried only three feet of water at the entrance; the light was useless to vessels transiting the lake. "It is difficult to conceive the motive which could have led to the placing of a lighthouse at this point," complained Max Bonzano, "when Point aux Herbes . . . remains to the present without a dumb beacon."[44]

In 1868 the Light-House Board agreed to a successor site at Point Aux Herbes, directly across the lake. While this choice served traffic between the south shore and the Rigolets, it doomed Bonfouca to be a secondary port. Thereafter not more than a small lit beacon was used at the bayou.

Point Aux Herbes Lighthouse

The first anchorage used by European explorers in Lake Pontchartrain was the lee of Point Aux Herbes, a few miles inside the Rigolets, on the south shore. Bienville's expedition came immediately to anchor there with a small group of boats in 1699 and named the point for its tall grasses, or possibly the seaweed which fouled his anchors in the shallows.

The point was marked by a lighthouse in 1875. By law, the lighthouse replaced the lighthouse burned during the Civil War at Bayou Bonfouca. In reality, it served a whole new purpose, guiding vessels between the Rigolets and lakeshore ports.[45]

The Light-House Board had just entered the final stages of purchasing a reservation at Point Aux Herbes when the 1869 appropriation lapsed into the surplus fund. The $8,000 was reappropriated in 1871, surveys were prepared, and negotiations for land resumed. Title claims delayed the start of construction until February 1875.[46]

Local engineers had considerable experience with lighthouses disappearing into Louisiana's alluvial soil. They opted for a foundation on a small scale similar to the massive base of the Southwest Pass tower on the Mississippi River delta. The 28-foot-square, straw-colored building was to rest on 8-foot brick piers, 4 feet square, resting on a 30-inch-thick slab of concrete and timber. The spongy soil was deemed unsuitable for pilings. A square dwelling with a lantern centered on top was built; the light was first exhibited August 1, 1875, with a red, fifth-order lens.[47]

Much of the reservation was sold at auction to the New Orleans Pontchartrain Bridge Company in 1928. The station was discontinued just after World War II; vandals burned the superstructure in the 1950s. The remains of the foundation are still visible from the northbound lanes of Interstate 10 as they leave the south shore of the lake.[49]

While the Point Aux Herbes Light Station was protected by the mainland from dangerous southerly storms, it was fully exposed to wave action from every other direction. Gales in 1888 and 1890 washed away all but the lighthouse itself. At least five breakwaters were built to protect the site, reinforced by thousands of tons of rock.[48] (Photo courtesy of U.S. Coast Guard Historian's Office)

Lake Maurepas and the Manchac

The natural flow of the Mississippi River into Lake Pontchartrain is through ancient Bayou Manchac and Lake Maurepas. Still sparsely settled, the lake is ringed by thick cypress swamp, yielding timber uniquely resistant to rotting.

Maurepas is connected to Lake Pontchartrain by Pass Manchac, a narrow watercourse not unlike the Rigolets. At the lake's western end lies the Amite River. Its lower reaches were once named Bayuk Massaic, a Choctaw term for a waterway providing a rear entrance. The Manchac offered a "back door" into the strategic Mississippi River just below Baton Rouge. For that reason General Andrew Jackson obstructed it in the War of 1812, believing the British would try reaching the river through the lakes. In 1826 this easternmost branch of the Mississippi River Delta was blocked by levees to protect sugar and cotton plantations from the annual spring floods. These crops, plus the valuable cypress timber from the Maurepas shoreline, drew a flourishing, shallow-draft trade.[50]

Pass Manchac Lighthouse

Pass Manchac was one of the sites included in the system of five Lake Pontchartrain lights conceived by the New Orleans customs collector. In 1837, $6,000 became available to build a lighthouse guiding vessels to the narrow pass. Francis D. Gott of New Orleans built the tower of brick on the same generic plan as the Tchefuncte River Lighthouse. The first keeper, Isaac Zachary, was appointed on January 16, 1839.[51]

In only three years the tower required rebuilding. The bricks had been laid in "mud mortar" instead of lime and sand. Rain and lake waves quickly disintegrated the tower's base until a large hole formed. Because the 1842 rebuilding contract amounted to only $1,630, it is obvious that most of the old bricks were recycled. The lake's shore soon encroached on this tower too, covering the floor with 20 inches of water. The Fifth Auditor recommended a wood lighthouse on piers on the south side of the pass, but the new one was built adjacent to the original two foundations.[52]

The third Pass Manchac tower was completed in February 1846 on a design credited to George Bowditch. His plan was probably patterned after one Winslow Lewis had sketched a few years earlier for the Fifth Auditor. The 38-by-19-foot, two-story Victorian dwelling was built of local cypress and held a cupola 8 feet in diameter jutting 5 feet from the center of the roof ridge. Keeper Isaac Zachary showed a red light from the lantern, about 36 feet above the level of the lake. This tower served as a rough model for those built a few years later at Bayou Bonfouca and at the South Pass of the Mississippi River.[53]

This lighthouse was no safer than its predecessors. Breakwaters failed to hold back the lake; even before the building was complete it began to tilt toward the lake. The contractor was held liable for the failure and rebuilt the foundation. In 1855 the Light-House Board asked for $10,000 to rebuild 200 feet northwest of the first three towers on a site "seldom overflowed." They considered a cheap screwpile structure, but opted for a combination brick dwelling and tower. The fourth tower's brick foundation wall was to be three feet thick and eight feet high, laid atop a timber grillage. The light was elevated 45 feet above the lake on the only cylindrical brick tower built on the Gulf. The lighthouse was completed in 1857 and used the old reflector lights for illumination. The Board supplied a fourth-order lens, first exhibited in February 1859 by Bartholomew Settson. Confederate authorities removed the lens on September 18, 1861, and stored it at the New Canal station. Federal occupying forces captured it there.[54]

The top of the tower sustained heavy damage "by the occupation of it by troops, rebel and national" during the war. A description of required repairs implies that a charge went off in the lantern. The four-inch-thick, granite lantern deck was shattered; the lantern required replacement. Engineer Max Bonzano reported, "As might be expected, there was all possible damage done, such as carrying away doors, windows, breaking the lantern glass by making a target of it." He supplied a fifth-order lens; the brick keeper's quarters received new woodwork. Repairs took less than two months, completed in mid-January 1867. Levi Wells took over as keeper. In 1868, Anthony Succow received the appointment. He was relieved by his wife Mary in 1873, who served until 1909, when she was relieved by her son Hugo.[55]

The station was automated in 1941, and its last keeper, Louis Barbier, was placed in charge of a nearby light attendant station. A small electrified lens was mounted on the lantern gallery. In 1952 the antebellum dwelling was razed to prevent vagrants from living there. The tower now stands alone where Pass Manchac empties into Lake Pontchartrain.[56]

Amite River Lighthouse

The lower reaches of what we now call the Amite River are actually the remains of old Bayou Manchac. This bayou originally connected Lake Maurepas to the Mississippi River below Baton Rouge. The name Amite is a colonial derivative of the Choctaw word Hamitta, which means "young," as opposed to the ancient trace of the Mississippi River flowing through Bayou Manchac. The Amite flowed into the Manchac about 32 miles upriver from Lake Maurepas and was itself navigable several miles.

The relatively high ground along the Amite proved ideal for early sugar cane planting; it later yielded cotton. By 1803 the Spanish trading settlement of Galvis-Town grew at the mouth of the Amite with about

28 families nearby. A dozen Spaniards and a few bad cannon guarded the junction.

Bayou Manchac was almost dry at low water. In the War of 1812 it was entirely blocked above the Amite by General Andrew Jackson's men to prevent the British from reaching the Mississippi above New Orleans. In 1826 a levee across the Manchac erased almost all traces of the original bayou. Its lower portion took on the name of the tributary.[57]

The Light-House Board received $6,000 to mark the Amite River in 1856. They purchased a Fresnel lens but could not acquire land for the station. The funds reverted to the surplus fund in 1859. A new lighthouse at the Amite fell far behind other priorities until well after the Civil War.[58]

When the lighthouse system along the southern coast was back to its pre-war state, the Board again asked for funds to light the Amite. In 1880 Congress offered only $3,000 for the purpose. A minimal station was erected after some difficulty and lit for the first time on May 1, 1882. Just after completion, the entire structure settled two and a half feet into the cypress bog. It was raised and the pile foundation improved.

The Amite River station can just barely be considered a lighthouse. There was a light and there was a house. The keeper hoisted a small "Western River Lantern" on a mast over the dwelling roof, 45 feet above the lake. The station was replaced in 1934 by an automated acetylene lamp.[59]

Chapter 8

America's Marine Highway: Delta to Natchez (Louisiana)

Mississippi Delta

European explorers had never seen anything like the Mississippi River's crowfoot delta. They expected two or three mouths to the river, but not a dozen or so, extending 50 miles inland.

An estimated 500 million tons of soil wash down the river each year, although the amount was probably much less before farm machinery caused large-scale erosion. The turbid river slows upon reaching the Gulf, the suspended silt settles, and the delta builds ever farther to sea.

Nouvelle Orleans, the future economic capital of the South, was an Indian portage and the first dry land Europeans found, more than 100 miles upriver.

When the Spanish first discovered the delta, calling it Cabo de Lodo, or "Muddy Cape," they did not recognize its strategic importance. The Mississippi River drains a watershed equal in size to the whole continent of Europe (not counting Russia and Scandinavia). Navigable rivers totaling 14,500 miles connect almost half the continental United States to the sea. The Mississippi Delta has been viewed as a chokepoint which controls the interior of North America.

After the Spanish discovered the mouth, the French started their explorations in the north near the Mississippi's head of navigation. They moved quickly to colonize the river and stop the English from moving west of the Appalachian Mountains. La Salle planted a marker or *balize* at one river pass in 1682 but could not relocate it a year later. Navigators of the time lacked accurate chronometers to determine their longitude, forcing a heavy reliance on sailing due east or west along measurable latitudes. La Salle, sailing through the Gulf, miscalculated the delta and sailed too far south, landing in Texas near Matagorda Bay, almost 400 miles to the west.

The French called the Mississippi the Rivière Colbert, La Louisiane, and St. Louis. Eventually they adapted the northern Algonquin term for "big water," Mes-cheseepik. Chesapeake Bay was Anglicized from the same roots. The term "Father of Waters" appears to be an invention of white settlers, and has no roots in Indian or colonial lore.

The eastern passes of the river delta, although they did not offer any greater depth of water, were considered the primary entrances. This was due in part to the practice of approaching from due east, roughly following the 30th parallel. Shortly after the French colonial capital moved to New Orleans in 1721-23, Adrien de Pauger, the king's architect, planned a fort and lighthouse for La Balize at the Northeast Pass. Just when this lighthouse was built, if at all, is unknown. In 1767 the new Spanish owners of Louisiana reported a wooden, pyramidal lighthouse in use.

The U.S. government placed lights at all three major passes between 1817 and 1831, as each entrance gained or lost favor in tandem with silting or deepening.

The invention of the steam-powered tug by the 1820s gave the river mouth greater importance. Until that time a skipper could expect to be stranded on the bar for a week or more, hoping for a southerly sea to bounce his hull into deeper water inside the river. He then faced as much as six weeks of warping upriver by securing lines to trees on the bank and hauling constantly against the swirling current. The more economical alternative was to anchor in Mississippi Sound and transship cargoes and passengers on shallow-draft luggers running to Bayou St. John and New Orleans. Powered tugs reduced the river voyage to New Orleans to a week or less.

Steam power also allowed cheap transportation to America's western frontier for the first time. In a period when virtually no roads crossed the Appalachian Mountains, rafts and keel-boats traveled only downriver, carting furs and crops to New Orleans for export. Steamers later plowed over the sandbars and tamed the current to carry manufactured luxuries, mail, and settlers far into the interior.

At about the same time, planters abandoned the overworked soils of the Atlantic Coast. Soldiers forced Indians from their homelands, opening up half the continent to new settlement. This population explosion brought on a corresponding increase in traffic through the port of New Orleans. In the 1830s the Gulf's watershed started bankrolling the nation's economy.

La Balize

Louisiana's first navigation marker was a wood beacon displaying the French coat of arms, erected in 1682 by René Robert Cavalier, Sieur de la Salle. He discovered the river mouth not by sailing the Gulf of Mexico, but by drifting downriver from the northern French colony.

Before 1699 the French built a rude little fort in marshes along the most important pass. It became known as La Balize, or "the Seamark." Just how early a light was shown on its lookout tower to guide ships into port is unknown. In 1721 engineer Adrien de Pauger built a 62-foot

La Balize a year after the U.S. acquired Louisiana in 1803.

unlit tower. Two years later he drew up plans for a crescent-shaped fort on Isle Toulouse, enclosing a hexagonal, two-story lighthouse. The plan was never executed.[1]

Although it is commonly accepted that La Balize was located a few miles from the mouth of Northeast Pass, early maps of the river are distorted, and the location may have actually been what we now know as South Pass. The soil near the river mouths was soon considered unacceptable for such construction, and La Balize was moved upstream to near Head of Passes.

Occupying French and Spanish authorities built several blockhouses and watchtowers. Their occupants probably showed at least small ship's lanterns or fired signal rockets, and certainly flew large banners to beckon ships. In the 1740s all traces of human habitation were erased by gales. In the process the isle of San Carlos suddenly surfaced and became the site of the new Balize. Spanish governor Don Antonio E. Ullola reported dredging a new river channel using harrows and "near the new canal there has been built a pyramid, using to build it posts 40 yards tall. This pyramid will be used as a *pharos* [lighthouse] and I do not doubt that, in fair weather it will be seen by vessels from a distance of four to five leagues [eight to 10 miles] at sea." The tower was complete in about 1767. On October 7-10, 1778, a hurricane cleared the marshes of all artificial structures.[2]

A lookout built shortly afterward was replaced in 1794 by a tall blockhouse garrisoned by Spanish soldiers and pilots. By the time the United States acquired Louisiana in 1803, this tower was rotted and often flooded. The first United States official to report from the new Louisiana Territory pressed the Treasury Secretary for a lighthouse downriver from the Balize. When William C. C. Claiborne assumed governorship, he asked Secretary of State James Madison to urge Congress for funds to mark the river.[3]

The U.S. Congress authorized $25,000 to repair the dilapidated Spanish tower and fit it with a light, inasmuch as chronic problems were delaying the building of the Frank's Island Lighthouse nearby. Meanwhile pilots hoisted a broad flag above the blockhouse when a sail broke the horizon. In 1817 the New Orleans customs collector installed a temporary light in the tower, tended by Captain Gardner, the local customs boarding officer. In October 1818 Gardner was formally appointed the full-time keeper. The light went out in March 1821 upon the arrival of the lightship *Aurora Borealis*.[4]

By mid-century the Northeast Pass had shoaled to uselessness, and the entire Balize settlement and its pilot-town were abandoned. In the 1865 hurricane every vestige of civilization at La Balize was obliterated, with the exception of an iron marker over a child's grave.

Frank's Island Lighthouse

The United States bought New Orleans and the Louisiana Territory in 1803 to ensure control over the Mississippi River and its watershed. The government lost no time in providing for a lighthouse to mark the mouth of the river. Only three months after the purchase was completed, Congress authorized $25,000, the largest amount appropriated for a lighthouse to that date. Unforeseen circumstances delayed its lighting for two decades.

Few Americans had ever seen the river. Fewer still could comprehend how a tall structure could be balanced on bottomless depths of alluvial muck. The government's official architect proposed a monumental stone tower which would not have looked out of place among ancient Greek temples or the finest palaces of Europe.

Before any lighthouse was built, the importance of the river shifted from national security to economic expansion: New Orleans blossomed from not much more than a permanent encampment to "the southern metropolis"; Americans poured into the new commercial capital; the first steamboat revolutionized travel in the interior; the War of 1812 came to a close at a New Orleans battlefield. The father-son designers of the proposed Mississippi River Light each died of yellow fever before their lighthouse marked the river.

The local collector, Hore Brouza Trist, warned strongly in 1804 against the attempted erection of a brick or stone tower, arguing that materials would have to be shipped from Havana, or even beyond, and that a foundation could never be laid in the muddy delta for a lighthouse patterned after those built on the rocky cliffs of New England. Instead, he proposed a practical, lightweight tower of hewn cypress timbers, measuring 40 feet square and between 80 and 100 feet tall. The open framework of posts and beams would let hurricane winds whistle through without toppling the tower. Trist actually argued against a lighthouse of any kind. He felt a floating beacon would be more satisfactory, but he received no support. Had a lightship been provided, it would have been the first in the United States.[5]

A respected New Orleans architect drew up plans for the serviceable wooden tower. Treasury Secretary Albert Gallatin consulted his close friend Benjamin H. Latrobe, designer of the United States Capitol and recognized as the father of American architecture. Latrobe designed a magnificent Gothic Revival edifice, surrounded by an ornate Doric customs complex. The selected site was on Northeast Pass, a musket shot or two from La Balize.[6]

Advertisements for bids, published in May 1807, drew no takers. The elegant tower was far too complex and was simply not feasible from an engineering standpoint. The advertisement described the structure in such excruciating detail that it repulsed the few contractors who could understand the design. The foundation was entirely experimental, consisting of inverted arches, flying buttresses, and intricate radial walls. The *pharos* enclosed a grand marble staircase and was enveloped by a majestic circular dwelling with stone colonnade and piazza. This royal palace would be surrounded by alligators, snakes, and clouds of mosquitoes on a mud bank inelegantly named "Frank's Island." Finally, Robert Alexander of Washington, D.C., agreed to attempt the construction. As conflict with England increased, the Mississippi River lighthouse was placed on long-term hold.[7]

General Andrew Jackson's defeat of the British, upriver on the Chalmette plain, brought New Orleans into the national limelight. By 1816 the lighthouse saga resumed with an entirely new cast. Trist had died of yellow fever, a new commissioner in the Treasury Department now administered the lighthouse system, and Latrobe's son Henry moved to New Orleans to simplify his father's plan.

On November 7, 1816, Henry Latrobe drew up a blueprint for a lighthouse based on his father's plan. He eliminated most of the pretentious federal complex but retained the circular dwelling, stone piazza, and unusual foundation of inverted arches. Bidders still ignored the contract, even when tempted by a fattened $55,000 budget. Finally the Treasury Department's commissioner of revenue goaded his old friend, Winslow Lewis, into taking the job. Lewis was a Boston ropemaker, inventor, and chandler who supplied inferior patented reflector-lamps and sperm oil to light stations on the Atlantic coast. The lighthouse at Frank's Island would be the first of more than 80 he would build for the United States.[8]

Lewis was wisely cautious on his first and most demanding construction venture. He insisted on three provisions for the contract. First, he would attempt the experimental foundation only if he would be exonerated if it failed. Second, he insisted that the government

Winslow Lewis knew from the start that the 8,000-ton tower for Frank's Island would fail. "Some of the items in this stupendous fabric were: 1,100,000 bricks, 1,000 tons rubble stone, 200 tons hammered stone, and 800 tons timber," he later wrote. *"The stone piazza around the building cost $8,000 in Boston." All these materials were to be heaped one atop the other, resting on centuries-old river deposits.[9] Drawing courtesy of National Archives.*

designate an official inspector to supervise construction and ensure he followed the obtuse plans exactly. Finally, he would accept no less than an astounding $79,000 for the whole work, paid in installments. No other lighthouse would cost this much for many decades to follow.

Lewis purchased materials in February 1818 and prepared a work site on the island. By the end of the year the brickwork rose from the island. Within a few months of the expected completion, the first cracks appeared. On January 31, 1819, one side of the foundation suddenly settled, only eight days from the tower's completion. The masonry was a spiderweb of cracks. Columns toppled onto the mud. The U.S. attorney general ruled that Lewis should be paid $85,507.56 for his work and materials, since he had faithfully followed the government's plan, however absurd. Lewis received payment on June 15, 1820; Latrobe died of yellow fever on September 3. Washington now owned a pile of ornate rubble a few yards from land's end. Lewis offered to rescue the endeavor, rebuilding the tower on a foundation of his own design and with his personal guarantee of success. A tower serving the needs of navigators, if not Washington architects, would cost only $9,750. The old tower was taken down and the materials saved for later use.[10]

The Frank's Island Lighthouse was completed and lit in March 1823, releasing the lightship *Aurora Borealis* to duty at Pensacola. Its 30 lamps were elevated 82 feet above sea level, making it the tallest and most powerful lighthouse on the Gulf Coast until 1858. Lewis claimed the power of the lamps made the light visible 27 miles; however, a lookout aloft at 55 feet can see an 82-foot-high light no more than 19 miles.[11]

Northeast Pass had served as the primary entrance to the river for more than a century, but almost as soon as it was properly marked, it fell out of favor with mariners. By 1829 ships sailing the parallels sighted the light and hove-to until daylight, when they made for the deeper Southwest Pass. In 1831, with river traffic rapidly increasing, the government built shorter entrance lights at both the Southwest and South Passes. Each was built by Winslow Lewis.[12]

The Frank's Island Lighthouse guided mariners to the Mississippi River passes until 1856, when nearby Pass a l'Outre received an iron tower. The government had learned a lesson perhaps worth the $95,257.56 investment. Winslow Lewis and company could build lighthouses. Lewis went on to be the premier lighthouse builder in America and perhaps in the world. His lighthouses were based on the basic instinct and common sense of a master mason. During an 1842 congressional investigation, Lewis observed, "So much for engineering and architectural science in building lighthouses." He was precisely correct. His tower at Frank's Island is the first and oldest lighthouse still standing on the Gulf of Mexico. After sinking some 20 feet, it remains almost perfectly erect. Frank's Island disappeared some 130 years after the lighthouse was built. As Blind Bay formed, cane breaks gave way to estuaries. The lighthouse now stands in at least a fathom of water.

Pass a l'Outre Lighthouse

The waterway we now call Pass a l'Outre (literally, "the pass beyond") was originally named Passe a la Loutre ("otter pass") by French explorers. Otters abounded there, sought by trappers because a pelt brought $5 American at the territorial capital of New Orleans.

In 1852 the new Light-House Board decided to discontinue the Gulf's first coastal lighthouse at Frank's Island, as the Northeast Pass was shoaling badly, in favor of a tower at the mouth of nearby Pass a l'Outre, which tended to deepen. Before the 1850s Pass a l'Outre seldom offered the sailor more than six feet of water. Even fishermen shunned the pass. By 1854, however, one could suddenly float three times that depth without the aid of persistent steam tugs. While established steamer lines preferred the Southwest Pass because they had depots there, New York's cotton-laden steamships and those bound for the Panama isthmus now sought the straight and deep Pass a l'Outre. The young pass also seemed more stable than the older Southwest Pass, where mysterious "mud lumps" suddenly arose from the river bottom to block the channel.[13]

Rather than build a costly new tower, the Board chose to take down the iron Head of Passes Lighthouse and reassemble it at Pass a l'Outre. The tall tower had been useless where the passes converged; a small beacon would be more helpful. Congress authorized $6,000 in 1852 to accomplish the move, the erection of a little beacon at Head of Passes, and the purchase of new Fresnel lenses for each station. Reconstruction was delayed almost four years by title disputes, state politics, and annual yellow fever epidemics. On December 16, 1855, Engineer Captain Danville Leadbetter proclaimed the tower ready for lighting by John Lory, the former keeper at Frank's Island. The new revolving Fresnel lens fit well enough into the lantern, but the iron floor could not bear the weight of the clockwork machinery. It was mounted outside on the lantern gallery.[14]

When the Pass a l'Outre Lighthouse was discontinued in 1930, its light was less than three-quarters of its original height above sea level because of settling into the Mississippi River mud. (Ca. 1893 National Archives photo #26-LG-37-17C)

America's Marine Highway: Delta to Natchez

Before the Confederate States government issued its general order to remove property from all lighthouses, Union blockaders sealed off the Mississippi River and visited all its lighthouses. On June 23, 1861, a lieutenant from the commerce raider CSS *Sumter* stove in the oil casks to prevent the enemy from capturing the 120 gallons of irreplaceable sperm oil stored at Pass a l'Outre. *Sumter's* captain was Raphael Semmes, former U.S. Light-House Board Naval Secretary and former chief of the Confederate States Light House Bureau. He hoped a gale would force the Federal blockading fleet aground, allowing his escape from the river.[15]

When *Sumter* crewmen returned on July 11, they found the lens gone. A crew from USS *Brooklyn* had captured all lighthouse materials the day before, leaving, of course, very proper receipts for the valuable property.[16]

Unlike their Confederate counterparts, Union sailors treated captured lenses rather roughly. The Pass a l'Outre lens arrived at New Orleans in a "deplorable condition." Virtually every prism was cracked, chipped or loosened from its mountings. Shipboard stowage had twisted the heavy brass lens frames.[17]

Max Bonzano, the U.S. Light-House Board engineer in New Orleans, readied the station for lighting on April 20, 1863, by C. Woltze, four months after most other river lights were in operation. Repairs included an entirely new keeper's dwelling to replace the one burned by Confederates on January 1, 1862, and a thick coat of coal tar on the tower to retard rust. The cast-iron tower received a new brick liner with braces to stabilize the staircase, because a man ascending the stairs could cause tower vibrations so strong that the lens stopped rotating.[18]

The new dwelling went up on nine brick piers, but it soon settled. By 1868 the keeper's house had sunk three feet. The tower too suddenly descended, possibly from the added weight of the new brick. Originally eight feet above ground, the floor was soon inundated by high tides. In 1876 engineers raised the tower floor five feet and enlarged the doorway to let water-sodden keeper James Broe enter without holding his breath. In another ten years, the tower had settled a total of 15 feet, showing a light only 62 feet above sea level. Once the tallest tower on the Gulf west of Matagorda Bay, the Pass a l'Outre Lighthouse was in 1877 shorter than its little neighbor at Southwest Pass.[19]

By 1888 the youthful Pass a l'Outre had matured. It shoaled to only seven feet of water and suffered from the mud lump problems chronic at its older sibling, Southwest Pass. Vessel traffic quickly fell off. The station became known as the loneliest on the coast. In 1902 a red third-order lens replaced the original, reducing the visibility to only 12 miles. Pass a l'Outre was now a harbor light for fishing smacks. The station was maintained only to guide small vessels approaching from the east in their search for deep water at South and Southwest Passes.[20]

Before the light was discontinued in 1930, the tower was painted with black and white spiral bands, the only corkscrew color scheme on the Gulf. After the light station was decommissioned, the Coast Guard established a lookout and small base at the station to spot rum-runners during prohibition. In 1934 the State of Louisiana insisted on reclaiming the incredible sinking tower for state use as a wildlife preserve. The spiral bands lasted until the 1950s, replaced gradually by rust and graffiti.[21]

South Pass Lighthouse

The middle toe of the Mississippi River's crow-foot delta represents the South Pass. La Salle may have planted his marker there in 1682. Even though South Pass was the preferred entrance to the river as early as 1720, the French instead fortified and lit Northeast Pass with a tower at La Balize to satisfy the needs of parallel navigation.

A federal survey of the passes in 1829 established South Pass as the secondary choice for freighters. Southwest Pass offered a greater depth over the bar. Vessels laid off the lighthouse at Frank's Island and made for South Pass after dawn. If the depth there prevented entry, they continued west to take on a pilot at Southwest Pass. The surveyor's observations led to an appropriation of $40,000 for a single lighthouse at South Pass and twin towers at Southwest Pass.[22]

An army engineer designed a 100-foot, octagonal lighthouse for South Pass, but the Fifth Auditor relied on advice from his old friend Winslow Lewis: "A Light in a Lighthouse of sixty-five or seventy feet can be seen at a greater distance than one in a house of greater elevation." Experience convinced Lewis that a layer of haze at about 80 feet blocked tall lights. The former ship captain received the contract, bidding only $19,150, half the appropriation, for the two stations combined. He offered a plan to distinguish the two towers, both day and night, while dispensing with the expense of two lighthouses at Southwest Pass.[23]

Because the three delta sites were close together, light characteristics and tower colors would distinguish the lighthouses. The South Pass station showed a revolving light and was painted white with a horizontal black band about halfway up the tower. The Southwest Pass tower showed a fixed main light and three smaller lights below the lantern. Black vertical stripes marked the tower. The old Frank's Island tower remained all-white, showing a single fixed light.[24]

Often referred to as the South Point or Gordon's Island Light, the South Pass tower held 14 lamps, lit for the first time on May 15, 1832, by keeper Henry Heistand. Seven lamps were arranged on each face of the revolving chandelier. The light gained a reputation as the best on the Gulf. The tower was located on Gordon's Island, named for the customs collector at New Orleans. Lewis created a retaining wall on the

The 1848 South Pass Lighthouse was very similar to the Victorian structure built at Pass Manchac, but on a larger scale. (Photo courtesy of U.S. Coast Guard Historian's Office)

island and filled it in to elevate the tower base about 15 feet above the Gulf, giving the light an elevation of 80 feet above sea level. Only six months after completion, the river channel was shifting and washed away. Waves crashed completely over the island in violent storms, threatening to "sweep the whole establishment off," according to the federal surveyor at New Orleans.[25]

His prediction proved accurate. The dwelling was wrenched from its foundation by logs swept downriver in December 1839. The collector reported that the lighthouse could not be saved. A storm on December 30, 1841, erased every sign of the station. A storm was also raised in

---

The 54-foot South Pass East Jetty Light worked in conjunction with a smaller tower on the west jetty. Note the bell which served as the fog signal. (1937 photo courtesy of U.S. Coast Guard Historian's Office)

Washington, D.C., where one Congressman charged Lewis with building a shoddy tower on a foundation of old flatboat planks. Lewis countered by stating that he had shipped pilings and a pile driver to the site, only to be forced by Collector Martin Gordon to "float" the tower on a horizontal grillage of squared timbers. Lewis claimed that, had he not been prohibited from driving piles in compliance with the original contract, the lighthouse would have stood fast even if all land had been washed away for two miles around.[26]

A replacement tower went up in June 1842 across the river, again built by Lewis. The illuminating apparatus was identical to the original, but the tower itself was built of weatherboarded timbers. The timber-frame construction would facilitate moving the tower if erosion threatened again. The octagonal tower was also painted with a broad black band. Mariners considered the light a good one, even though it was elevated only 40 feet.

In only five years the wood tower had decayed beyond hope. The New Orleans collector asked for a 60-foot iron lighthouse, but the Fifth Auditor proposed a wooden, 54-foot octagonal tower on the original site, surrounded by a substantial 40-by-30-foot dwelling. It was completed in 1848.[27]

The Light-House Board intended to discontinue the light as soon as they completed a first-class iron skeleton tower at Southwest Pass, which was authorized in 1857. South Pass had shoaled to only six feet by this time, and the light there was almost useless, except to guide ships onward to Southwest Pass. By the time the Southwest Pass tower was completed, jetties deepened South Pass and it became the primary entrance to the river.[28]

In 1951 the Coast Guard removed the first-order revolving lens from the South Pass Lighthouse and replaced it with an aeronautical parabolic reflector light (DCB 2-24). The station was automated that year and is still in service.[33] Note the screen around the lantern to protect it from birds. (1945 photo courtesy of U.S. Coast Guard Historian's Office)

Keeper James Fisher worried about his livelihood in June 1861. The crew of CSS *Sumter* had paid him a visit earlier in the month, removing the lens. In a letter to Confederate States Collector Frank Hatch, he inquired, "As our light has been extinguished and the lamps and oil taken to the Head of Passes, I wish to know how this will affect me." The reply was decisive. Hatch discharged all keepers on July 6, 1861.[29]

The tower was refitted with a third-order revolving lens on September 21, 1862, after U.S. forces captured the lighthouse materials in New Orleans. A few years later a lighter, fourth-order lantern was installed atop the decomposing tower. By 1867, the Light-House Board considered South Pass vital and asked that a tall iron tower be built immediately after the Southwest Pass tower was completed.[30]

Not until the late 1870s was the request approved by Congress. Captain James Eads had built experimental jetties at the river pass, channeling the water through a narrow opening at the bar and forcing a natural hydraulic excavation. The silt was carried out to deep water and the pass soon deepened to 28 feet. For the first time, the largest steamers could enter the river unaided by tugs. When word of this phenomenal success reached Washington, Congress granted $50,000 for a new tower.[31]

The 105-foot, hexagonal, iron skeleton tower went up in 1881 using materials salvaged from the construction disaster at Trinity Shoal. Meanwhile the jetties themselves offered a platform for small lens-lanterns. A 54-foot wood tower on piles marked the east jetty with a fifth-order lens in 1890, paired with a smaller tower on the west jetty.[32]

On April 8, 1923, East Jetty keeper I. C. M. Erickson started to row across the river to start up the fog signal. He returned via Mexico. An outbound freighter picked him up 15 miles offshore and radioed, "Is very tired. Will deliver to American Consul in Tampico." A year later, on April 14, Erickson again set out on the same task. This time, he never returned. The East Jetty station was automated a few years later.[34]

Southwest Pass Lighthouse

The early history of the Southwest Pass Lighthouse is similar to that of South Pass. Twin towers were recommended here to distinguish the station from South Pass. A single tower 65 feet tall was actually built, identical in form to the one at South Pass. Winslow Lewis completed the tower on April 18, 1832; it was lit by Captain Thomas S. Easton. On the seaward side, three openings were left in the tower walls 40 feet above the base to display three reflector lamps from each window. Unfortunately, the design prevented the ventilation of the lower lamps. Greasy whale-oil soot rose up the tower every night to coat the lantern glass.[35]

Only six months after the tower was built, it was endangered by erosion. Within two years, the station was plagued by high water. The keeper built a useless driftwood breakwater and filled it in to protect his home, but this had little effect. An inspector in 1834 wrote, "The keeper reports that where they had the cooking apparatus eighteen months since, there are now twenty feet of water and he has been obliged to break away the walls of his dwelling house to allow the water to escape." The base of the tower was awash and in jeopardy.[36]

Soon after the second tower at Southwest Pass was built, one side of the tower settled and the tower tilted to the westward, almost five feet out of plumb. The settling quickly stopped and the tower showed no signs of strain. The lighthouse had been built on a manmade bank of sand and clay, enclosed by posts and planks. The building in the foreground probably served as a summer kitchen. (Photo courtesy of U.S. Coast Guard Historian's Office)

In April 1837 the oil-delivery contractor reported the base of the tower was standing in 10 feet of water. Within a few months, the lighthouse fell into the river. The keeper, however, continued to aid mariners by displaying a lantern from a tall post. The keeper's dwelling was less than regal: "a hut of boards some eight or ten feet square, by six or seven feet in height for himself and assistant."[37]

Congress in 1838 approved a new tower almost identical to the original. Two box-bay windows were set 25 feet below the lantern. When viewed from the best channel, these lamps formed a perfect triangle with the main light. A total of 29 lamps were shown, 6 of them in the two windows. The vertical stripes of the original tower were duplicated on the new one.[38]

For the first time a delta lighthouse was to be built by someone other than Winslow Lewis, although not without his influence. The Treasury awarded the contract to Leonard Hammond and Allen Dexter of Massachusetts, for completion on June 1, 1839. Because Winslow Lewis's lighthouse efforts had failed so miserably, the government appointed a presumably neutral civil engineer to supervise construction— Winslow's nephew, Isaiah W. P. Lewis. He delayed the completion by at least six months, harassing the contractors until they walked off the job. Modifications he made to the foundation caused its failure after only 20 feet of brick were laid. The Fifth Auditor removed I. W. P. Lewis and left the contractor to resume construction on a plan developed by Winslow Lewis.[39]

Soon after it was built, the Southwest Pass tower settled and tilted; by 1849 the entire island had sunk so much that the tower stood in a foot of water. A lightweight cypress tower was recommended as a replacement, elevated 70 feet to reach above the river fog. This tower was never built.[40]

The Light-House Board was not impressed with the leaning tower of Southwest Pass. They received $45,000 in 1855 for a first-class iron skeleton tower. They ordered the basic metalwork but felt they needed another $70,000 to start the construction. Congress supplied full funding on March 3, 1861, too late for reasonable action.[41]

Keeper Manuel Moreno was on board only a few months before he found himself in the Confederate States lighthouse service. Although the Confederacy was in no position to respond, he complained about the station being continuously under water. Both the dwelling and tower floors were flooded a foot deep; floating logs often rammed the structures during the spring flood. On March 31, 1861, two weeks before Fort Sumter was fired on, Moreno pleaded for information. He knew a crisis was developing outside his tiny domain and the only news came from tugboat crews and pilots. "I am in this deserted place, ignorant of what is transpiring out of it," he wrote. "We ought to have about six muskets

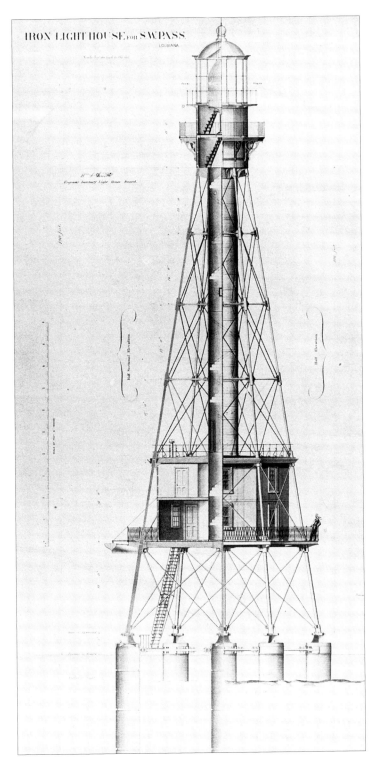

Drawing for the iron lighthouse to be built at Southwest Pass, begun in 1870 and first lit in 1873. (Photo of drawing courtesy of U.S. Coast Guard Historian's Office)

Southwest Pass Lighthouse in 1945. (Photo courtesy of U.S. Coast Guard Historian's Office)

& a few pistols, and powder & balls, so as to be ready at all times to resist attack." When the Federal blockading fleet arrived off the delta in May, Moreno blocked the seaward portions of the lantern, showing the lens for only friendly vessels upriver.

Blockaders thwarted Confederate government attempts to protect the Fresnel lens. Moreno reported on July 5, 1861, that 34 armed men from the USS *Powhatan* visited the station and by noon had stolen the lens. "I hope that our salary will not be discontinued," he pleaded. He and all other local keepers were discharged the next day. Lighthouse property elsewhere was quickly removed by Confederate agents to prevent Union predators from capturing Confederate property.[42]

Southwest Pass received the U.S. government's attention even before New Orleans was taken. A temporary fifth-order light was established soon after the U.S. fleet took possession of the pass. By this time, the tower floor was almost four feet under water, forcing the keeper to wade chest-deep to reach the stairs.[43]

A fourth-order lens was placed in the old tower in 1863, showing 70 feet above sea level. At the same time, the Light-House Board asked Congress to reappropriate the prewar funds for a new tower. In 1867 Congress offered $108,000; however, the estimated cost had risen to $150,000.[44]

After more than a year of preparations, a massive foundation was under way in 1870. The 185 pilings, four feet apart, were driven 33 feet deep, with concrete forced in and around them as far as possible. To the top six feet of the pilings were fastened horizontal timbers, covered with more concrete, a floor of three-inch planks and then two more layers of timbers, with concrete forced between them and layered to four feet above the wood. All this work had been done below the high tide line. The foundation reached to only 18 inches above low water.

Fabricated in Ohio, the iron superstructure consisted of eight cast-iron columns tied together by wrought-iron rods. The second series of columns enclosed a two-story iron keeper's dwelling. This creation of the industrial age was completed and the first-order lens first lit on July 1, 1873, 128 feet above sea level and a half mile from the old tower.[45]

Lighthouse engineers were awestruck by damage caused by a fire on May 22, 1894. The dwelling was completely gutted; when the fire reached the stair cylinder, the chimney effect created a giant blowtorch. The iron stairs melted completely, the lantern was entirely consumed, and the whole central cylinder required replacement. Lighthouse engineers guessed that if oil had been stored in the tower the whole lighthouse would have become a puddle of molten iron.[46]

A light was established on the east jetty in 1929, although this station's primary mission then was as a fog signal. In 1953 the Southwest Pass Jetty Lighthouse was upgraded to serve as the entrance light and to mark jetty extensions. Modern aids to navigation, such as radio-beacons, had made lighthouses obsolete by this time. In 1965 the jetty light was replaced by what looks more like an oil rig, a "Texas Tower" on tall stilts nearer the end of the jetties.[47]

Head of Passes Lighthouse

The Mississippi River begins its fragmentation into the passes at Deer Island, 108 miles below New Orleans and about a dozen miles from the many mouths. The Head of Passes is the Greenwich Meridian of the Mississippi River. River charts measure all distances "AHOP" (Above Head Of Passes) because the delta continues to extend annually into the Gulf. The first French outpost was built a mile or two below Head of Passes, probably on the South Pass. It was soon shifted to Northeast Pass at La Balize.

A U.S. government light of some sort was in operation on Deer Island as early as 1836. That year David B. Ahern was employed, probably as a lamplighter. The Treasury Department received funds for a real lighthouse in September 1850, at the urging of the Louisiana State Legislature, and let a contract eleven months later for an iron tower patterned after the one at Biloxi. Completed in 1852, the first Head of Passes Lighthouse was scheduled to be dismantled only two years later.[48]

The light was designed to show above the springtime river fog. At 67 feet in height, it was two feet taller than the lights at the primary river mouths, yet on the clearest days was invisible from salt water. The light was also useless to river navigation. Ships could not steer for it in the winding river. The fog was often so thick that none but lookouts manning the tallest masts could possibly take a fix on the light.[49]

There is some indication that the Head of Passes Lighthouse may have been the only one ever imported into the United States. The final bidder, John J. McCaughan of Mississippi City, submitted plans for a

The Southwest Pass Jetty Light tower supports an aircraft-style beacon, 80 feet above sea level, visible some 24 miles. (1966 photo courtesy of U.S. Coast Guard Historian's Office)

　　　　　　　　　　　　America's Marine Highway: Delta to Natchez

sample British-export lighthouse erected at Barbados. The Fifth Auditor immediately rejected the plans because of the thinness of the iron plate near the base, but did not restrict McCaughan from ordering thicker stock from a British foundry. McCaughan erected the Head of Passes Lighthouse in the winter of 1851-1852.[50]

The Light-House Board received $6,000 in 1853 to establish a small beacon at the Head of Passes and to move the iron tower to Pass a l'Outre. Carpenters added a simple dormer window to the keeper's dwelling house at Head of Passes, showing three reflectors upriver. A quarter-fraction of a sixth-order Fresnel lens replaced the reflectors in 1854. A lens showing over a wider angle may have been installed by 1860.[51]

At the outbreak of the Civil War, the tiny station was a hub of activity. Confederate ships anchored there to wait for breaks in the Union blockade. Union ships probed cautiously upriver to test Confederate forces. The station also became a lighthouse depot of sorts. Commander Raphael Semmes, former head of the Confederate States Lighthouse Bureau, raided stations at the passes and stored lighthouse property at the Head of Passes Lighthouse until it could be shipped to New Orleans. After Confederates burned the dwelling, the U.S. Navy established a battery there inside the station's levee to prevent blockade-running.[52]

A temporary, sixth-order lens in a brass housing showed from a timber tripod in January 1863. By April the original foundation received a new wooden lighthouse with a fifth-order lens. The Civil War keeper for the Union was James Fisher, the former keeper at South Pass. A depot built on the grounds supported repairs to stations along the entire Gulf of Mexico. By this time the neglected levee had washed away and was rebuilt. Annual spring floods still drove huge trees into the station with enough force to smash brick piers supporting the gallery. The keeper, recently widowed Jessie Fisher, was summarily fired in 1866 for not lofting the trees back into the swirling current. A year later a male keeper was retained, and logs continued to bash against the dwelling foundation. A log shield was built around the station in 1867. Eventually a gale broke up the protection and erosion threatened. The building was retired about 200 feet from the river in early 1872.[53]

When jetties were built northward from Deer Island, pier lights replaced the lighthouse. From 1888 Head of Passes was considered a light attendant station, servicing minor river lights.[54]

Natchez Lighthouse

When a light goes out during the night, the keeper is certain to be disciplined. An outage of a few days would outrage ship masters and lead to a new keeper's appointment. The Natchez Lighthouse was extinguished for almost five years and no one cared.

In the late 1820s Natchez was America's most inland seaport, 300 miles from salt water. It was also the terminus for America's Natchez Trace, the first road into the western frontier. Oceangoing steamers frequently ran this far upriver; the city's wharves bustled with international activity. The port received the second lighthouse ever built by the United States on the Mississippi River and the only one built above the river's delta.

In 1826 Congress appropriated only $1,500 for the lighthouse. Fifth Auditor Stephen Pleasonton asked the Natchez customs collector if a 35-foot brick tower could be built for such an amount. The negative reply soon came, and he advised Congress that even though the land would be donated, the only interested builder wanted $3,426 for the work.[55]

Natchez architect Andrew Brown received the contract in March 1827, after Congress increased the appropriation. He finished the tower in December on a bluff overlooking the river. The site was on the city commons at the foot of what is now High Street. Joseph Bowman received the appointment as keeper of the tower, but not of the light. The lighthouse sat idle for more than six months because the government forgot to arrange for lamps and reflectors. Winslow Lewis provided his patented apparatus; on July 1, 1828, the lighthouse was finally finished.[56]

The Natchez Light played an uncertain role in river navigation. From atop the bluff it was visible 12 miles north or south, the distance to the next river bends. Riverboats could hardly steer a course by it, however. One 1835 traveler commented, "Were a good telescope placed in its lantern it would make a fine observatory. Now, it is merely a standing monument."[57]

The station was hardly mentioned in federal documents from its completion until 1836. A U.S. customs collector was appointed for Natchez that summer; the old superintendent of lights suddenly refused to pay the keeper. Apparently no one in Washington thought to transfer lighthouse supervision to the new collector. A full year later Pleasonton asked him why the keeper had not been paid for the past 12 months, nor any oil bought for the lamps. Six months later, when the collector had not replied, he asked the Secretary of the Treasury to appoint a new superintendent of lights for Natchez. The tower sat idle for four more years, but drew no complaints from river pilots.[58]

The situation was not resolved until June 1841, when a newly appointed Natchez collector asked what he should do with the ruins of the old brick tower. A tornado on May 7, 1840, had blown it down; townspeople started to complain about the eyesore in the center of town. Pleasonton admitted that the light had not been in use "for some time past," although he could not guess just how long.

The rubble was sold to the highest bidder.[59]

Chapter 9

Bayou Country (Louisiana and Texas)

Barataria and Timbalier Bays

At Barataria Bay the mud of the relatively young Mississippi Delta gives way to sandy beaches and older alluvial deposits. Wide, twisting bayous lead far inland from the bay and in colonial days connected with the river, at least during the spring floods. These uninhabited, shallow waterways and their circuitous access to New Orleans spawned early commercial enterprise that the United States was reluctant to support with navigation aids.

Baratarians of old are best known through the exploits of Jean Lafitte. Pirate, patriot, or privateer (depending on your point of view), Lafitte amassed great wealth and stature, not to mention a heavily armed colony of almost 1,000 of his kind on Grand Terre Island, across from the current city of Grand Isle. Loot from victim ships was smuggled to New Orleans through Bayou Barataria until 1819, when revenue cutters and naval ships encouraged his removal to Galveston. The Spanish governors of Louisiana operated a lookout tower on Grand Terre Island with the garrison watching for pirates and smugglers.[1]

Just to the west are Timbalier Bay, which offered shelter to the smaller fishing vessels, and Isle Dernier or Last Island, where resort hotels and gambling houses served the New Orleans elite until August 10, 1856.[2]

Barataria Bay Lighthouse

Even after organized smuggling ended, Barataria Bay's route to the Mississippi was of considerable importance. Remembering the English movement through swamplands toward New Orleans in the War of 1812, the government began building Fort Livingston near old Fort Lafitte in 1835. Resorts flourished then as today, although they offered fewer pleasures than Lafitte's establishments. Steamboats and luggers made regular trips through the marshlands to landings near New Orleans.[3]

The Provisional Light-House Board recommended a first-class lighthouse to mark this important bay, but later settled for a smaller fourth-order light. The Coast Survey in 1853 documented severe erosion on Grand Terre Island and recommended the lighthouse be placed instead on Grand Isle, which showed signs of increasing in size. Because the government already owned the land around the fort, Grand Terre was selected as the lighthouse site.[4]

The lighthouse was erected in 1857 by Army Captain Danville Leadbetter, district lighthouse engineer, at a cost of $10,000. The construction delay was probably due to this lighthouse being built in conjunction with those at Sabine Pass, Timbalier Bay, and Aransas Pass, which followed the same basic plan. The first keeper, Nicholas Johnson, was nominated for the post in June 1857. Problems in shipping the lens to the station caused a seven-month delay in lighting.[5]

The octagonal brick tower held a fourth-order lens 60 feet above sea level, showing 270 degrees. Only two years after its lighting on October 1, 1859, the station was discontinued as an unnecessary expense.[6]

Fort Livingston, although still incomplete, was occupied during the Civil War by Union troops. Troop transports heading west to the Texas campaigns often loaded their human and other cargoes here; the fort became a center of operations. In March 1864 the army commander asked the Light-House Board to exhibit a light from the tower. The station was refurbished that year and on January 10, 1865, keeper Jacob Brankhorst was placed in charge. Originally left a natural brick color, the tower was also painted white.[7]

The disastrous hurricane of October 1, 1893, "almost totally wrecked" the station. Of the approximately 1,500 local inhabitants, more than half died or disappeared in the storm. The Light-House Board proposed rebuilding on the cover face of the crumbling fort. A square, timber-frame tower was begun in January 1897 and completed on March 13. The 66-foot tower displayed a fourth-order lens 77 feet above sea level.[8]

Just after World War II the station was automated with a 200mm lens. Coast Guardsmen from the Grand Isle Station tend the electric light.[9]

Timbalier Bay Lighthouse

Timbalier Bay (in French, "kettledrummer") was for decades marked on private charts as impossible to navigate. The first U.S. Coast Survey excursions into the bay found 10 feet of water at Grand Pass and enough water for steamers to ply Bayou Lafourche, an ancient Mississippi River pass. They recommended a lighthouse to guide vessels to the rich cotton and sugar plantations inland.[10]

At the same time that Congress authorized the Barataria Lighthouse, $15,000 was approved for a light at Timbalier Bay. The stations were built concurrently. Keeper Elijah Chester was nominated in June 1857.[11]

The army asked the Light-House Board to reestablish the light in 1864, but the local engineer could not fill the order. While the light

At the outbreak of World War II the Coast Guard stationed lookouts at the Timbalier Lighthouse as enemy U-boats prowled the Louisiana coast. By 1950 the tower was abandoned for the last time and left as a daymark.[12] Note the two cisterns on the lower deck with downspouts from the roof. (1945 photo courtesy of U.S. Coast Guard Historian's Office)

would have supported troop movements to Texas, other wartime repairs were considered more pressing. The Navy recovered the lens in a somewhat dilapidated condition from a Confederate warehouse in St. Martinsville on June 21, 1865. The station was refurbished in September 1865 and turned over to keeper Thomas C. Barton.[13]

Erosion at the east end of Timbalier Island threatened the station in the summer of 1866. Barton was ready to abandon his post when "ugly, threatening weather" hit on July 12. Two brick piers of the dwelling gallery washed away; Barton reported, "for the past twenty four hours the sea[s] have been breaking against the Dwelling." The tower was surrounded by three feet of water. Knowing he could not survive a hurricane on the lonely bank, Barton promptly resigned. On February 20, the local engineer removed the lens and placed it in the keeper's dwelling for safekeeping, then displayed a temporary light from the dwelling roof.[14]

One month later the entire station was annihilated. The new keepers tried to tend the temporary light in the dwelling house until it was also demolished by gale-driven seas. Barely escaping with their lives, they clung to an iron can buoy, bobbing about in the storm for several days. The old station site was now covered by enough water to float a small schooner.[15]

The Light-House Board immediately proposed a replacement. The third-order iron skeleton tower would be sheltered from the open sea by the shoals of Timbalier Island. The Board petitioned a resistant Congress for years before enough funds were available to begin work. The tower was finally lit on January 26, 1875. The revolving second-order lens, 111 feet above sea level, showed a fixed white light with a red flash every minute.[16]

In 1881 the lens refused to rotate as the tower tilted out of plumb. Nine iron leg sockets were cracked and were repaired by banding with wrought iron collars. The lens was leveled and the tower was coal-tarred as a rust preventive and to keep the old leaded paint from entering the station's drinking water.[17]

Again in 1894 the lens stopped because of canting of the tower. This time the problem was fatal. A new channel was forming at the base of the tower, with the tidal wash scouring sand from around the screwpiles. The damaged lens was saved, but the tower continued to heel over. A lighthouse tender was unable to approach close enough to try dismantling the ironwork. The tower slowly twisted downward and then crashed into the bay. A lens-lantern showed from the keeper's dwelling until a replacement tower was built in 1917.[18]

The third Timbalier Lighthouse was decommissioned three times. The white square dwelling surmounted by a lantern was completed in 1917 on 25 iron-encased wood pilings. Even this substantial foundation could not resist the forces of nature. A hurricane on August 24, 1926, barreled out of the southeast, moving directly over Timbalier Bay and tipping the lighthouse toward the northwest. Some 500 tons of riprap were placed around the foundation piles the next year, only to be washed out in 1931.[19]

Because a deep hole was forming under the tower, a buoy was recommended to replace the lighthouse. The station was discontinued in 1934, but was reactivated after only a few months. The Timbalier Lighthouse was automated in 1939 and left unmanned.

Ship Shoal Lighthouse

Isle Dernier, also called Last Island and Isle de Vin, was known as the watering place of the aristocratic South. A massive, two-story hotel and dozens of other vacation structures satisfied the recreational needs and urges of those rich enough to escape the yellow fever and summer discomforts of New Orleans.

Located about four miles off Raccoon Point on the Louisiana coast, the island would be the southernmost extent of the state if not for the

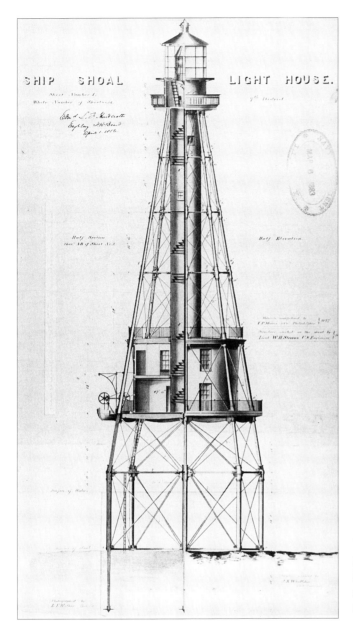

SHIP SHOAL LIGHT HOUSE.

The plan for Ship Shoal Lighthouse was based on the offshore screwpiles built along the Florida Keys.

burgeoning Mississippi River delta. Exposed as it was to the healthy Gulf breezes, Isle Dernier was also naked to the full fury of its hurricanes. On August 10, 1856, at the height of the vacation season, human life on the island was wiped out. More than 200 vacationers drowned in the cataclysm. Only a few brick foundation piers broke the surface; the only survivor was one terrified cow.[20]

Eight days later Congress appropriated more than $39,000 for a lighthouse at Ship Shoal, at an even more exposed location 12 miles

---

The Ship Shoal Lighthouse was assembled in a Philadelphia foundry before being shipped to and erected at Ship Shoal. Note the screen to protect the lantern from birds; the station's boat is rigged out to the left. (Photo courtesy of U.S. Coast Guard Historian's Office)

southeastward. The shoal lay on the heavily traveled route between Galveston and the Mississippi River delta.[21]

The shoal had been well known for decades. The Louisiana Legislature petitioned Congress for a lighthouse at Isle Dernier in 1848, but instead assigned a lightship to mark Ship Shoal. The Provisional Light-House Board of 1851 felt that a real lighthouse would best serve the needs of commerce. The Ship Shoal station was at the top of their prioritized list of new works in Louisiana. In 1852 the Board asked Congress for $20,000 for a first-class iron skeleton tower to replace the inadequate and inefficient lightship. The Coast Survey had begun to chart the Louisiana coast and was charged with selecting a site.[22]

The lightship anchorage was confirmed as the best spot for the new tower. A light on the alternate spot at Raccoon Point could serve only small vessels hugging the shoreline. A light on Isle Dernier would serve only the resort itself.[23]

An iron skeleton structure modeled on the successful Florida Reef lighthouses was recommended, to be placed on 30-foot screwpiles sunk 15 feet into the seabed. The original $20,000 appropriation was supplemented by $30,000, but even this sum was considered insufficient. A total of $103,179.16 was spent on erecting the lighthouse.[24]

The tower was constructed twice. In January 1858 the Philadelphia contractor erected the entire structure at the foundry before loading it on a ship. It took almost two years to put the tower up at Ship Shoal. The second-order Fresnel lens was elevated 110 feet above sea level.[25]

Confederate authorities removed the lens, apparatus, and plate lantern glass with great difficulty. Four times Union blockaders turned back Confederate expeditions, but never themselves tried to capture the disputed property. The materials were taken to Berwick City in October 1861 for storage in the customhouse. They were later transferred inland to St. Martinsville and seized there by Union forces in 1865.[26]

Ship Shoal Light was considered vital to Union operations in Texas. The U.S. commander asked that the light be restored in 1864 when Federals were moving to retake Galveston. Before the original lens was captured, the Light-House Board ordered a new second-order revolving lens from France. Keeper Charles J. Lottman lit up the lamps on November 1, 1864.[27]

The lighthouse inspector at New Orleans became aware of health problems at Ship Shoal in 1866. Several keepers at the light had become paralyzed; with the news spreading widely ashore, replacement keepers were impossible to hire. Rain, the only drinking water available so far offshore, was washing lead into the cisterns from the red-lead paint used on the tower as a rust preventive. The toxic coating was removed from this and all other iron lighthouses in the fall. By December the poison was stripped away and the Ship Shoal tower blackened with coal-tar.[28]

A severe hurricane in 1867 drove "pyramidal seas" against the tower, causing "such vibrations that the oil was thrown out of the reservoirs, and all efforts to relight the lamps were unavailing for six hours." As the sea floor was scoured from under the tower, the lighthouse began leaning several degrees toward the northeast. The local engineer poured concrete around the screwpiles; sand soon built up around the tower legs.[29]

By 1873 additional riprap placed around the foundation was carried away by wave action. Three shiploads of granite blocks were delivered to the Pensacola depot in 1875 but were not set in place at Ship Shoal until 1896. When the station was automated in 1929, the tower was found to be listing about 20 degrees from perpendicular.[30]

The Ship Shoal Lighthouse was briefly manned as a Coast Guard lookout in World War II and was permanently discontinued in 1965.

Atchafalaya and Vermilion Bays

The Atchafalaya and Vermilion Bays, roughly separated by Marsh Island, lead to the heart of Louisiana's plantation country. Until railroads became a more effective form of transportation to export markets, sugar, cotton, and other crops were floated down bayous and through the bays to await ships in the Gulf.

Some of the earliest settlers were Germans—"Deutsch" in their own tongue and "Teche" in Cajun. Bayou Teche was a prime waterway and became a port of entry complete with customs officers soon after the Louisiana Purchase. When Americans first arrived, Atchafalaya Bay was considered to be the wide mouth of Bayou Teche. It was navigable in the daytime only, for the channel was narrow, shallow, and crooked. Since the 1850s the lower reaches of the bayou have been considered part of the Atchafalaya River.

Lighthouses marking this low marshy coast were generally useless until technology allowed screwpile construction close to ship channels and far from dry land. Louisiana's second coastal lighthouse was built at Point Defer in 1827 to mark what was considered the mouth of Bayou Teche. Located too far from deep water, this lighthouse (and the companion lightship built later) was replaced by a screwpile lighthouse in 1858.[31]

The southwest pass of Vermilion Bay was the site of an even more useless lighthouse, completed in 1841. With a controlling depth of only four feet, this pass was suitable for little more than rowboats. Vermilion Bay itself ranged in depth from four to nine feet, although the Vermilion River was navigable by shallow-draft steamers for 80 miles.[32]

Point Defer Lighthouse

Atchafalaya Bay is formed on the southwest by Marsh Island and on the southeast by Point Defer, now called Point Au Fer. An extensive shoal or bar stretches westward about 15 miles from the point. A rather unscientific survey of the territory in 1806 showed Point Defer as the mouth of Bayou Teche, although the actual mouth is about 14 miles north.[33]

The surveyor, architecture student Louis deMunn, reported the Teche channel to be narrow and its navigation tedious. Vessels could carry about eight feet of water up to New Iberia, but beyond that town, trees hanging low over the water restricted passage to pirogues (dugout canoes). A lighthouse to mark such a limited resource was considered a waste of money.[34]

By 1825 enough trade passed through Atchafalaya Bay to interest Congress in commissioning a survey to report on the need and site for a lighthouse. Since the bay was too shallow to navigate at night, no lighthouse at the actual mouth of the Teche could serve the purpose. Instead, a station was built at the last dry point of land on Point Defer. This tower was intended to guide vessels to the bay's wide mouth, which they would then enter after dawn. Stakes and buoys were set in the bay to mark the winding channel to the Teche.[35]

This isolated and mysterious country did not invite the attention of northern lighthouse builders. Congress appropriated $10,000 in 1825, but no bidders applied for the contract, even when $4,000 sweetened the deal the next year. One builder from Boston made an offer but later refused to sign the contract. The government prodded lighthouse entrepreneur Winslow Lewis to bid, but he cautiously declined the offer. Eighteen months after the original funding, James B. Gill and Hersey Stowell of Boston finally took the contract for the lighthouse, dwelling, and installation of the lighting apparatus.[36]

Even with a contractor finally in hand, the project suffered further setbacks. When Gill failed to show up at the construction site by November 15, 1826, his work force dispersed. Disputes over the site selection, illnesses among the workers, and other roadblocks delayed the construction. On September 20, 1827, the Treasury Department pressured Gill to turn the first spade of soil on Point Defer. Keeper John Stine had been appointed about seven months before. The lighthouse was completed around the end of the year.[37]

The lighthouse tower stood on a low sandy bank about 5 feet above high tide, with the light held 70 feet above sea level. At this elevation, the 15 lamps were visible only a dozen miles in the best weather. The light therefore could be seen from neither the mouth of the Teche nor the channel into the bay. In 1842 an Army engineer recommended rebuilding at least five miles west of the station on screwpiles "invented recently in England." The Treasury Department asked Congress for funds to place a lightship or screwpile lighthouse at Point Defer in 1845, but no appropriation resulted in that tight budget year.[38]

By 1846 the foundation on Point Defer began giving way. An inspector reported the tower three feet out of plumb. One side of the timber grillage under the tower had rotted, allowing that side of the tower to settle. He described the foundation as "simply eight stakes placed on the surface of the ground, each 11 or 12 inches square." He recommended placing new timbers for those that had rotted, or removing the timbers from the other side.[39]

The tower was hardly a proper mark for ships entering the bay, being out of sight of a vessel aground at the bar. On December 29, 1848, a lightship was sent to mark the actual channel into Atchafalaya Bay, and was anchored near the end of the reef for about 11 years. [40]

The Light-House Board was disappointed with the entire system of lights in the area but was undecided as to what action to take. In 1855 they considered abandoning the lighthouse on Point Defer when the new Shell Keys Light was completed off Marsh Island. The next year they proposed keeping the lighthouse and doing away with the Atchafalaya Lightship. The matter was settled in 1857 when a small screwpile lighthouse was authorized near the end of the reef to replace both the lightship and the Point Defer Lighthouse. Before the Southwest Reef Light was completed, the old tower temporarily received the fourth-order Fresnel lens and lantern destined for Southwest Reef. [41]

The Point Defer station was discontinued and replaced by the Southwest Reef Lighthouse on September 1, 1859. Keeper George Wright was transferred to the new station. Military authorities asked the Light-House Board to rekindle the light in 1864, but there is no evidence any action was taken. [42]

Local fishermen in the late 1980s circulated rumors that the ruins of the old lighthouse, cistern, and dwelling recently exposed by a storm were an old pirate fort. Treasure hunters have removed some interesting artifacts, but nothing of real value. [43]

Southwest Reef Lighthouse

The dark red iron lighthouse at Southwest Reef was completed in 1859 under a special appropriation to replace expensive and inefficient lightships with screwpile lighthouses. The station had little time to show rust before the Civil War broke out. [44]

Instead of the usual iron skeleton tower or wood dwelling atop upright piles, lighthouse engineers designed a plan for a square pyramid fully enclosed in iron boilerplate. Only one other lighthouse, at Calcasieu River, was built on this design. The location did not indicate a tall tower, but its exposure to the fury of hurricanes called for more endurance than a fragile wooden structure. A proposal for a conical iron tower like the one at Biloxi met with little favor in Washington. [45]

Drawings were complete in mid-1858, but a mild economic recession caused a moratorium on lighthouse building. Established on September 1, 1859, the tower showed a fourth-order red Fresnel lens 49 feet above sea level. [46]

Confederates saved everything of value at the station in October 1861, but heavily vandalized the remaining property. In 1865, a U.S. Navy party captured the lens, lamps, and lantern glass unbroken but in a "neglected condition" at St. Martinsville. Federal authorities pressed for reestablishment of the light at Point Defer in 1864, but instead the Southwest Reef Lighthouse was renovated and relit. The tower received repairs in July and August 1865 for relighting on its sixth birthday.[47]

Toxic leaded paint was scraped from the lighthouse in 1866 after keepers at nearby Ship Shoal suffered from lead poisoning and paralysis. The Southwest Reef tower, already resembling a Franklin stove, was smeared with black coal tar to retard rust. The resulting oven effect must have made the tower unbearably hot under the baking summer sun.[48]

In October 1867 an unusually severe hurricane drove through Atchafalaya Bay. High seas totally demolished the nearby Shell Keys Lighthouse; if not for a stroke of luck, the Southwest Reef tower would have met the same end. Waves stove in the iron floor of the dwelling, ruining almost everything inside. The crew was tossed around the inside of the quaking tower. Seas beating against the iron skin tore the entire walkway from around the tower. The Light-House Board reported "it is probable that but for the timely breaking off of the gallery, the entire light-house would have been destroyed." The screwpiles, bent and twisted, were straightened and leveled. Diagonal braces, originally planned but never installed, were added to fortify the tower legs against winds and seas.[49]

Heavy weather still threatened. High tides pushed by southeast gales regularly pounded against the tower floor, 11 feet above normal high tide. The Board considered removing the iron plating from the bottom story, which would have left the keepers homeless. Instead, $10,000 was spent in 1875 on raising the structure 10 feet on additional iron columns secured by diagonal braces. A fog-signal tower was attached on a base of screwpiles.[50]

The station was rendered ineffective by a new channel cut through the shoal just before World War I. Replaced by the Point Au Fer Reef Lighthouse on March 30, 1916, the old iron tower sat idle until the 1980s, when it was moved ashore. Owned by the town of Berwick, it is intended to serve as a centerpiece for a town park.[51]

Point Au Fer Reef Lighthouse

By the Civil War, Point Au Fer became the official name for the original Point Defer. Where the newly dredged channel to the Atchafalaya River cut through the long Point Au Fer Reef, the government built a lighthouse in 1916. A dredging spoil bank known as Eugene Island, immediately adjacent to the channel, was selected.

Half the $50,000 appropriation was intended for buoys and markers along the channel; the rest was dedicated to the lighthouse. The tower was raised on iron-encased pilings 17 feet above high water. The fourth-

After WWII the Coast Guard manned the Point Au Fer Station primarily as a rescue unit until its decommissioning in 1976. Note oil house and cisterns. (Photo courtesy of U.S. Coast Guard Historian's Office)

order lens was held 54 feet above sea level, about the height of the original light.[52]

The first keeper, E. L. Rollingson, was appointed in May 1916 and drowned three months later. Between 1918 and the end of World War II, only three keepers cared for the station.[53]

Vermilion Bay Lighthouse

One of America's more fruitless lighthouse adventures was at the extreme western tip of Marsh Island, marking the southwest pass of Vermilion Bay. The reasons for choosing this spot are not well documented. All but the smallest fishing smacks sailed to the Vermilion River through Atchafalaya Bay.

Someone must have realized the limitations of this pass, for Congress provided only $5,000 in 1837 to construct a beacon. The Treasury Department, however, pressed for an additional $8,000 to fund a real lighthouse. Congress agreed to the proposal; a construction contract resulted. Construction at Vermilion Bay was scheduled to follow the completion of the Southwest Pass Lighthouse on the Mississippi River. When the contractors walked off the job there, the Vermilion project suffered a delay of almost two years.[54]

Once the works resumed, the grounds were filled in with four feet of soil contained by pilings, raising the site to two feet above spring tides. The lighthouse was completed in May 1840, but could not be immediately lit. Oil arrived on February 6, 1841, and keeper Alexander Kinns lit the lamps on that date. To distinguish the tower from the nearby Point Defer Lighthouse, it showed a revolving apparatus. Kinns lost his job by the end of the year after a dispute with the local revenue officer. A rapid succession of keepers followed. With only one exception, the average tenure for a keeper was a single year from 1841 to the station's decommissioning in 1855.[55]

The Treasury Department recommended discontinuing the lighthouse in August 1854. The U.S. Coast Survey was charged with inspecting the site to confirm this opinion, and in January 1855 it reported finding less than a fathom of water in the pass. Keeper John Shaw admitted that only three vessels each year entered Vermilion Bay through this pass, and then only in the winter to visit two plantations upriver. In effect, he resigned. The Light-House Board discontinued the station on June 1, 1855. A coast light had by this time been planned for the nearby Shell Keys, a few miles south of Marsh Island. By 1876 no trace of the station existed.[56]

Shell Keys Lighthouse

A lighthouse stood at Shell Keys for eight years, half of them in darkness.

The iron skeleton tower took the place of the Vermilion Bay Lighthouse and the Atchafalaya Lightship. Congress authorized $30,000 in 1854 for the substantial tower, which was the second tall iron tower built on the Gulf Coast and the first of its kind to be destroyed by the elements. The Light-House Board had prepared plans for a 100-foot, third-order brick tower, but the law specifically required an iron skeleton on screwpiles.[57]

The hexagonal red tower was completed and lit on June 1, 1859, three months before its neighbor at Southwest Reef. The 80-ton tower was fabricated and erected by J. M. Poole & Co. of Wilmington, Delaware, at a cost of $11,675. The site was the highest land available in the keys, standing 10 feet above high water. A third-order Fresnel lens was shown about 81 feet above sea level.[58]

Confederate authorities extinguished the light in the fall of 1861 to deprive Union blockaders of its aid. They removed the lens, lamps, and lantern glass for storage at St. Martinsville, where Federal sailors seized them on June 21, 1865. Engineer M. F. Bonzano reestablished the light on September 1.[59]

Only two years later, on October 5 or 6, 1867, a hurricane sheared off the legs of the tower and the ironwork toppled. The only keeper on

---

board was Seth Jones. His body was never found. The lighthouse tender *Geranium* located twisted pieces of the roof and some braces. The site of the tower was under four feet of water.[60]

Congress in 1869 answered Light-House Board requests for a new tower with an appropriation of $60,000. Unable to divert attention from other post-war reconstruction, the Board allowed the money to lapse into the surplus fund.[61]

Salt mines discovered on Petit Anse Island 10 years later prompted another plan to rebuild, but no lighthouse was ever constructed in this area again. An attempt to erect a tower to the south on Trinity Shoal ended in disaster in 1873.

The Shell Keys are now part of a national wildlife refuge.

Trinity Shoal Lighthouse

Trinity Shoal was discovered at about the time the Shell Keys Lighthouse was destroyed. It lay almost exactly on the track of vessels bound between Galveston and the Mississippi River via Ship Shoal. The shoal was made up of 15 miles of hard sand bottom 20 miles offshore. About half its length was covered by less than 12 feet of water, with the highest part of the shoal barely breaking the surface.[62]

A substantial iron skeleton tower similar to the one destroyed at Shell Keys was produced in northern foundries in 1872 for the full $60,000 appropriation, but construction was delayed a year for lack of an additional $44,000 to erect the structure. This delay proved fatal for the lighthouse, if not for the workmen on site.[63]

Turbulent weather was a constant enemy. Construction started at the beginning of the hurricane season in June 1873. By October only a 100-foot-square platform to house the workers was completed. Storms several times threatened to destroy this work; on one occasion the pile driver was nearly lost. Support ships often put to sea to avoid being dashed against the shoal.

The worst weather struck in mid-November. The tender *Guthrie*, carrying most of the lighthouse parts, pounded hard on Trinity Shoal and put to sea with her hull badly damaged. The holds flooded faster than pumps could empty them. The schooner drifted back over the shallows, where she was beaten to splinters. Remarkably, the crew of the tender *Pharos* rescued all hands. The Trinity Shoal Lighthouse now lay on the bottom of the Gulf.

The storm reached its height three days later. Waves peaked at nearly the height of the work platform, 15 feet above water. The platform gave way, dumping the superintendent, 16 workers, and the *Guthrie*'s captain into the stormy sea. They clung to floating timbers as long as three hours before the *Pharos* crew could rescue them all.[64]

Turbulent weather prevented the Trinity Shoal Lighthouse from ever being completed. (Photo of drawing courtesy of U.S. Coast Guard Historian's Office)

A hired cotton barge salvaged some materials; they were later used to build the South Pass Lighthouse in the Mississippi River delta. The Trinity Shoal Lighthouse site had deepened from 14 feet to 24 feet of water during the gale. Had the tower been built on schedule a year earlier, it would probably not have survived the storm. Having spent $97,000 on the effort, the Light-House Board concluded that only a lightship could ever serve mariners at this spot.[65]

Oyster Bayou Lighthouse

A harbor light was built in 1904 at Oyster Bayou, which connects the eastern end of Atchafalaya Bay to the Gulf. Some 300 small vessels

Laundry day at the Oyster Bayou Lighthouse before automation in 1947. (1945 photo courtesy of U.S. Coast Guard Historian's Office)

ran the pass with cargoes of oysters bound for packers in Morgan City. Southerly gales often banked up six or seven feet of water, completely inundating the surrounding marsh grass and hiding the bayou entrance. Lacking any landmark to spot the bayou, vessels sometimes sailed five or more miles past before realizing their mistake. Retracing that distance could be deadly when racing a storm to reach port.[66]

The Light-House Board received $5,000 in 1902 for a small wooden lighthouse to be built on short pilings. All four bids were rejected as excessive and the Board chose to hire day labor to complete the station. A storm beached the ship carrying materials to the site; most of the cargo was lost. This delayed the project start several months and caused a cost overrun. New materials soon arrived and work started in May 1903.[67]

By the end of the year funds ran out; a temporary red lens- lantern was shown from the lighthouse gallery. The station was completed in

1904 with a fifth-order red Fresnel lens held 47 feet above sea level, visible eight miles. The first keeper was Robert G. Miller.[68]

Automated in 1947, the square wood structure still stands. In 1975 the lantern was removed and a small wood structure of piles served as the aid to navigation.[69]

Sabine Pass Lighthouse

The Calcasieu and Sabine Rivers empty directly into the Gulf of Mexico. Because their mouths were shallow and because only negligible cargoes were available upstream, neither gained much favor among early navigators. Even technology came slowly to this part of Louisiana. Not until the SS *Velocipede* ascended the Sabine in 1837 did steamship travel commence. The Calcasieu River was largely ignored until it provided Galveston's lumber supply after the Civil War.

The Sabine River was officially recognized in 1821 as the western boundary of the Louisiana Purchase. Many geologists agree that it is also the western edge of the ancient Mississippi River delta.

The Sabine Pass Light Station was designed and built by Captain Leadbetter, later a Confederate States general. It stands today in testimony to his architectural creativity. Instead of balancing the tower atop a simple ring of pilings, he added eight fin-like buttresses to spread the tower's weight over the soft soil. The result looks much like an antique brick rocket aimed at the stars.[70] (Ca.1951 photo courtesy of U.S. Coast Guard Historian's Office)

Until the Republic of Texas gained its independence in 1836, the Americans showed little interest in the river. The Texas President reserved more than 20,000 acres for Fort Sabine on the Louisiana side of the river mouth in 1838. Sabine's commercial importance became apparent a decade later, after Texas achieved statehood. A tiny corner of the military property would later become the lighthouse reservation.

Louisiana's legislature joined citizens of Texas in petitioning Congress for a lighthouse at the Sabine in 1848. Congress answered with a $7,500 appropriation the next year. A Navy commander was dispatched to survey the river mouth and recommend a lighthouse site. His negative report postponed construction: "The coast is so free from danger in that vicinity, the place itself so easy of access, and the business done there so inconsiderable ... a lighthouse is not necessary there at this time."[70]

The Provisional Light-House Board disagreed entirely in 1851, recommending a first-class seacoast light and a fat budget of $30,000. Pressured by the Texas membership, Congress provided the funds, subject to a U.S. Coast Survey of the pass. The surveyors chose a spot on the Texas side of the river, two and a half miles from the mouth. Army engineer Danville Leadbetter rejected the location and instead obtained Brandt Point in Louisiana from the military reservation.[71]

Galveston's lighthouse inspector, Navy Lieutenant Montgomery Hunt, fired a broadside at the Sabine plans in 1853. The Bolivar Point Lighthouse, marking the largest port in Texas, was suffering from chronic delays, while the insignificant ports on the Sabine were scheduled to receive a lighthouse of double the cost in less time. "Money should not be thrown away upon such an unimportant place," wrote Hunt. "Five thousand dollars would build as good a light as is required there for the next twenty years."[72]

The tower was built on a mud bank only three feet above high tide. The third-order lens showed a steady white light interrupted by a flash, 85 feet above sea level. The lamps were lit in March or April of 1857. The Sabine tower is usually considered to be a sister to the Aransas Pass, Timbalier, and Barataria towers, even though it was raised 25 feet higher.[74]

The light was extinguished on the morning of August 17, 1861, by order of Confederate authorities in Sabine. The following January the lamps, lens, and clockwork were dismantled and crated for storage. Keeper Gowan W. Plummer and his assistant received Confederate States pay as caretakers until September 1862, when they stole away to Maine. There they applied to the U.S. government for pay during their service in the Confederacy, reasoning that they were caring for Federal property as well. The request was quickly denied.[75]

The lighthouse was the scene for several bloody Civil War skirmishes. Union Navy landing parties often used the tower to spy on enemy defenses and gunboats. Twice in April 1863, landing parties were ambushed and repulsed by Confederates. An abortive large-scale attack on Sabine in September ended in a sharp skirmish at the lighthouse during which 50 were killed and 200 wounded. It appears that portions of the lens may have fallen into Union hands in 1863. Occupying soldiers located remaining pieces in September 1865. The lighthouse received minor renovations after the war; the original lens was restored to use on December 23.[76]

A severe storm in June 1886 whipped up an eight-foot tide which surrounded the tower with five feet of water. Every building except the lighthouse was washed away. A hurricane in 1915 forced the keepers to turn the revolving lens by hand when tower vibrations put the clockwork out of order.[77]

The lighthouse was discontinued in 1952 and retained by the Coast Guard for two years until arrangements could be made for proper transfer to the State of Louisiana for use as part of a wildlife refuge. In 1986 the property was transferred into private ownership.[78]

Sabine Bank Lighthouse

The Sabine River between Louisiana and Texas saw a dramatic increase in traffic in the 1890s, when jetties succeeded in scouring out the shallow entrance. Until this time goods were generally transshipped by rail or lugger to Galveston Bay for export.

English-style lantern apparatus for a third-order lens before being shipped to Texas for use in the Sabine Bank Lighthouse. Note the diagonal astragals. (National Archives photo #26-LG-38-27)

The Sabine Bank Lighthouse during assembly at a Detroit, Michigan, foundry. (National Archives photo #26-LG-38-25)

In 1898 the Light-House Board requested $80,000 for a lighthouse on Sabine Bank, a shoal about 17 miles offshore. Congress authorized a lighthouse not to exceed $50,000, but did not fund the project until the next year.[79]

The contracting advertisement allowed bidders flexibility in recommending the type of construction. Those proposing a caisson foundation bid the lowest; the Gulf Coast soon received its only "Texas sparkplug on a tin can."[80]

The Sabine Bank Lighthouse was the first ever attempted by the United States in open water. The foundation was created by building a

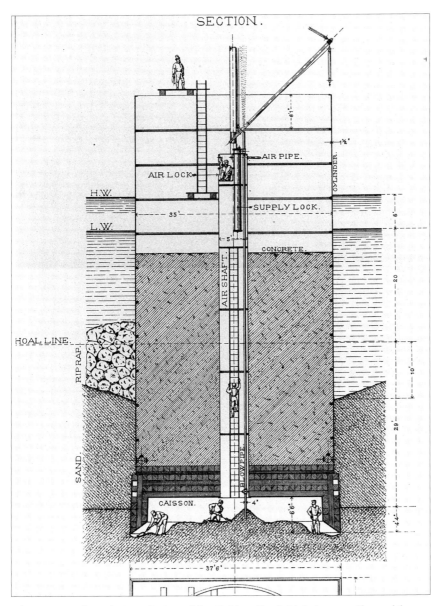

SECTION.

AIR PIPE.

AIR LOCK

CYLINDER.

H.W.

35'

SUPPLY LOCK.

L.W.

5'

CONCRETE.

AIR SHAFT.

HOAL LINE.

RIP RAP.

SAND.

BLOWPIPE

CAISSON.

4'

6'6"

37'6'

The caisson foundation designed for Sabine Bank Lighthouse allowed for building the lighthouse in much deeper water and provided a more secure foundation than that of a screwpile. (Drawing courtesy of U.S. Coast Guard Historian's Office)

floating cylinder with its lower rim a cutting edge. The tube was ballasted and sunk atop the bank as more sections were added on top. Workmen entered a pressurized chamber and shoveled out the seabed under the cutting edge. The caisson slowly settled downward to a solid footing. Concrete was then forced into the void, plugging the base.[81]

Still an active aid to navigation in 1996, the Sabine Bank Lighthouse is one of 11 American caisson lighthouses installed by pneumatic means. Shown here in 1945. (Photo courtesy of U.S. Coast Guard Historian's Office.)

This design allowed the tower to be secured in much deeper water than a screwpile lighthouse. The water depth on the bank was 20 feet. The base was topped with a circular iron tower holding a third-order lens 72 feet above sea level. It was first lit on March 15, 1906.[82]

The 1915 hurricane which tormented the Sabine Pass and Calcasieu stations cast heavy seas against the Sabine Bank tower. Waves stripped the hatches off the gallery level, stove in the storm shutters, and tore most of the iron gallery from the tower. Several iron plates covering the second story were torn free or loosened. The keepers maintained the light during the storm and for days afterward. They finally were forced ashore by thirst; the water tanks had been washed away in the storm.[83]

The lighthouse was reported dark only one more time in its history. One morning in 1924 the pilot light for the acetylene lamp was found to be extinguished. Attendants from the Sabine Pass station found a small port opened and a small hawk trapped in the lens room.

The lighthouse was automated in 1923 when an acetylene lantern replaced the lens. The lens is now on display in a Port Arthur museum.[84]

Calcasieu River Lighthouse

The Calcasieu River lies in Louisiana about 35 miles from the Texas border. The river's name comes from the Atakapa Indian term meaning "crying eagle." Southern bald eagles can still be found there.

In its flurry of recommendations for establishing a true system of lighthouses, the Light-House Board in 1854 insisted that a light was needed to mark the river mouth. The official Coast Survey report disagreed: "The houses mark the entrance sufficiently well for the small craft that can cross the bar, and from a commercial point of view it is of little importance." All money appropriated for the lighthouse was carried into the surplus in 1857.[85]

By 1860, however, interest resumed in lighting the Calcasieu. In June Congress appropriated $7,500 for a small lighthouse; the Board tried repeatedly to buy land at the selected site. War intervened before work could begin.[86]

Union gunboats frequented the river, foraging for pork, mutton, and beef to feed the blockading fleet. After the war, even with only a fathom of water on the bar, a lively lumber trade developed between the river and Galveston. Several petitions were circulated in 1868 to light the river entrance; local interests established a private light on a post.

When coal and sulfur were discovered upriver in about 1870, Congress granted $20,000 to erect a lighthouse. The Board apparently dusted off the original pre-war plans, identical to the 1859 Southwest Reef station. A tower was prefabricated in the North to hold a light 50 feet above sea level on a screwpile foundation. The tower was to be sheathed in boilerplate iron.[87]

Renewed efforts to obtain title to land stretched out so long that the remaining funds were carried into the surplus. In 1876 the Light-House Board abandoned the site when changes in the channel made land already owned by the government available.[88]

The Calcasieu River Lighthouse was quickly built after the reinstatement of funds. Keeper Charles F. Crossman first lit the lamps in the fourth-order lens on the evening of December 9, 1876. Crossman, then age 50, held his post well into the 20th Century.[89]

The area was visited by several severe hurricanes. In 1886 and again in 1915 all outbuildings were carried completely away while the

The 1876 Calcasieu River Lighthouse as depicted in a Harper's *illustration.*

lighthouse stood fast. In the hurricane of October 1919, several neighbor families took refuge in the tower.[90]

There were calm nights, too. One night in 1922 keeper William Hill reported the lantern buzzing with insects of every type. So thick were the bugs on the lantern glass, he doubted the light could be seen from the mouth of the river three miles away. Smaller insects made their way through the screens and caused constant flare-ups in the lamps. Even constant tending could not produce a good light.[91]

A new channel was cut through the marsh to Lake Charles just before World War II, its path running directly through the lighthouse reservation. The tower was dismantled easily, but the screwpile foundation had to be blasted out. Small beacons in the new channel replaced the lighthouse.

Galveston Bay (Texas)

Galveston Bay

Galveston Bay is Port Texas. From the beginning, this 30-mile-square body of water (although not all navigable) was the primary outlet for Texas crops and the arrival point for most of its citizens.

Shallow and speckled with islets, the bay is home to wildlife of all kinds. John James Audubon was amazed by the wildfowl during his visit in the 1830s to the bay's islets and shoals. The many birds were also hazards to the mariner.

The need for a seacoast light at Galveston was obvious. The port attracted major shipping lines from Liverpool and Le Havre, with cotton the primary export. The Coast Survey recommended lighthouses at three strategic spots inside the bay to mark dangerous shallows. With the exception of color and lens size, all three were identical when built in 1854. Two marking dangerous shoals were painted white and red, holding small sixth-order lenses. The third, marking the entrance to the San Jacinto River, was painted all white and held a larger fifth-order lens. All were completed at about the same time as the Bolivar Point entrance lighthouse.

They encompassed all the navigable part of the bay. Mariners could sail to almost every point, always in sight of one or more lighthouses. Only one other lighthouse was ever deemed necessary for the bay; it was placed at Galveston's Fort Point.

Bolivar Point Lighthouse

The Republic of Texas announced its intention to erect a $7,000 lighthouse at Galveston in 1845, a few months before achieving statehood. It was never built. The U.S. government announced similar plans as the war with Mexico drew attention to the newly added state. In March 1847, $15,000 was appropriated.[1]

Fort Point on Galveston Island, ceded by Texas as a military reservation, was the predicted site, but local shippers quickly pointed to Bolivar Point across the entrance as the ideal location. A light there could guide ships through the narrow channel almost on a single bearing, while a lighthouse at Galveston would serve only as a landfall light.[2]

Several unexpected problems delayed construction for almost five years. The owner claimed his land's value to be equal to township lots rather than open farmland, and demanded as much as $9,000, depending on the acreage desired. The local customs collector did not dispute the claim and recommended increased funding of $5,000 to cover the added cost. Congress agreed to the relocation but did not approve the extra funds. In the following two years, negotiations for a two-acre plot brought the price down to $1,000.[3]

The Texas legislature added to the delay by neglecting to cede jurisdiction over the land until 1851—a failure that would plague lighthouse construction across the state. At one point Galveston Collector William R. Smith publicly accused the governor and his aides of deliberately sabotaging the lighthouse. The attorney general in particular delayed matters, spending much of his time promoting his railroad enterprises. As a result the unspent money lapsed into the surplus fund; Congress was forced to reappropriate the next year.[4]

The government became impatient to establish a light of any sort at Galveston, the busiest port in Texas and one of the three busiest on the Gulf. In 1851 the Provisional Light-House Board had identified Galveston as the most important light yet to be built on the Gulf. Because preliminaries had faltered, a lightship was placed at the Galveston bar in 1849.[5]

Once real estate issues were settled, the Treasury Department issued plans for an iron lighthouse on Bolivar Point. The tower was fabricated and erected by Murray & Hazlehurst of Baltimore, builders of the 1848 iron Biloxi Lighthouse. The identical Bolivar Point and Matagorda Island Lighthouses were combined into the same $24,000 contract.[6]

Construction started at Bolivar Point in February 1852 and was completed by October, only a few months after the Light-House Board was formed to modernize America's lighthouse system. One of its first acts was to ensure that America's lighthouses received modern Fresnel lenses. The Bolivar Point Lighthouse was finished, however, and illuminated with reflectors before the first lenses arrived from France. The reflectors were put up by Christmas Day and a light was shown shortly afterward.[7]

Complaints about the inadequacy of this light were first heard only a few months after its lighting. In 1853 Navy Lieutenant Montgomery Hunt, assigned as lighthouse engineer for the Galveston district, claimed the port deserved a lighthouse visible more than 14 miles offshore. He argued loudly that the Sabine Pass Lighthouse then under construction was a waste of government funds, and that $10,000 should be diverted to raising the Bolivar Point Lighthouse by at least 25 feet and improving it with a Fresnel lens.[8]

The third-order lens at the 1872 Bolivar Point Lighthouse stood 117 feet above sea level. A new revolving lens with kerosene lamps was placed in the lantern in 1881 after the old one was rated deficient in clarity. (Photo courtesy of U.S. Coast Guard Historian's Office)

Four years later his recommendations were followed. Engineers assembled materials in 1857 to elevate the lantern using 25 feet of new iron sections. The extensions also flared outward enough to receive a larger lantern which would hold the tower's new third-order lens 100 feet above sea level. The work was completed by the spring of 1858.[9]

When the Confederate States Light House Bureau in Richmond issued orders to remove and safeguard lighthouse property, the Galveston superintendent of lights took the orders more literally than any of his counterparts. The entire lighthouse was dismantled, plate by plate, and lowered by block and tackle to the ground. The brick liner was taken down, and even the granite foundation stones disappeared. Buoys from Galveston Bay were moved to Confederate forts, where they served as water tanks.[10]

The iron components of the lighthouse were never found. The Light-House Board assumed they had been used in support of the South's war effort inasmuch as iron became a precious metal during the war. Needs could not be met by industry, imports, or high prices. Prices before the war averaged about $25 per ton; by 1865 they had risen to $1,500 per ton, when any iron could be found. Early in the war Texas outfitted steamers as gunboats, protecting the pilothouses with plates of iron about the same thickness as the lighthouse skin.[11]

A temporary wood tower 34 feet tall was completed on August 5, 1865, near the old Bolivar Point foundation, holding its light 40 feet above sea level. A new lightship was added in 1869 to replace range beacons destroyed in a storm. Congress authorized $40,000 in 1870 for rebuilding the tower, but yellow fever epidemics and a quarantine of the coast between Galveston and New Orleans prevented any prompt attempts at construction.[12]

The new tower was under way by the end of 1871. The Light-House Board chose to recast a tower from the original plans, but preferred a new site to complement the range lights. When the landowner refused to sell at a reasonable price, engineer Max Bonzano laid a new foundation on the original reservation. The new tower was fabricated in New York City and shipped to the site. Work paused in August 1872 when funds ran out; the tower's lighting was delayed until November 19, 1872. [13]

The Great Hurricane of 1900, which virtually leveled the city of Galveston, furiously pounded the Bolivar tower. Swaying and moaning in the screaming wind, the tower became a refuge for all who could reach its iron door and stairs.[14]

Passengers from a stranded train were among the first to wade to the tower when tides covered Bolivar Point a foot or more deep. In all 125 terrified neighbors and travelers huddled on the iron stairs throughout the storm. Trapped by swirling waters, they were without fresh water. Keeper Harry C. Claiborne held a bucket against the wind from the gallery of the tower, 117 feet above the normal sea, but he caught only salt water even at that height. When the winds and tides subsided, the lighthouse was surrounded by dozens of bloated bodies. Claiborne fed and clothed the survivors, exhausting his month's supply of food at the station.[15]

Calamity struck again in 1915. Claiborne reported the water higher and the wind stronger than in the 1900 hurricane. Practically every family on the point headed immediately for the lighthouse. Sixty people sheltered in the tower, which shook like a reed. Water rose neck-deep at the bottom of the tower and tore open the iron door. Assistant keeper J. P. Brooks, tethered by a rope so his body could be hauled back in, struggled to the door and secured it against the flood. When the lens clockwork was put out of commission by the swaying of the tower, the keepers turned the lens by hand. Soon tower convulsions made it impossible to rotate the lens. Waves destroyed the brick oil house, carrying away the entire supply of oil. The quantity kept in the tower lasted two more days and then the tower went dark.[16]

The lighthouse was downgraded and held a second-order lens when the Galveston Jetty Lighthouse became the bay's landfall light in 1918. The Bolivar Point Lighthouse was discontinued in 1933 and is now privately owned.[17]

Galveston Bay

The construction of the Galveston Jetty Lighthouse took longer than any other lighthouse construction on the Gulf. (Photo courtesy of U.S. Coast Guard Historian's Office)

The tower was built of concrete plastered around corrugated expanded steel reinforcements. The Galveston Jetty Lighthouse was the only one constructed in this manner on the Gulf. The red and white flashing light was elevated 91 feet above sea level.[18] (Photo courtesy of U.S. Coast Guard Historian's Office)

Galveston Jetty Lighthouse

The only lighthouse on the Gulf Coast to take advantage of 20th-century skyscraper technology was under construction for almost two decades.

Although Galveston Bay had always been the state's busiest port, the largest steamships were unable to enter the shallow mouth. Jetties opened Galveston Bay to vessels with the deepest draft by concentrating the flow of water and hydraulically flushing sand from the bottom. Jetty construction started in the 1880s and continued for decades as the heavy stones sank into the sand.

When engineers saw some progress in the jetties, the Light-House Board asked Congress for $35,000 to build a jetty lighthouse in 1894. In October 1897 a temporary light was in place at the end of the jetties. The Board drew up plans for a standard iron-pile foundation with a relatively fragile wood dwelling on top. The 1900 hurricane led them to reconsider. Tens of thousands of homes were wrecked and 6,000 people killed or missing at Galveston. The original design was scrapped in favor of a ferro-cement castle atop an I-beam framework driven into the jetty rocks.[19]

Work started in 1905 when it appeared the jetties were nearing completion. This took longer than any other lighthouse construction on the Gulf. Inflation, changes in jetty plans, weather, and war pushed the completion date to late 1918.[20]

The first pilings were twisted and bent in a 1911 hurricane, forcing the crew to start over. Four years later in August 1915, the structural steel for the tower was nearly in place when another hurricane struck, bending the substructure and damaging the superstructure. The lens, stored ashore, was also damaged. During the entire construction period, the tower's blueprints underwent almost constant change to strengthen the structure.[21]

When the station was ready for lighting in June 1918, military authorities ordered a port blackout to avoid aiding German U-boats. The lamps were first lit by keeper George W. Bardwell on November 12, 1918, the day after the World War I armistice was signed.[22]

After all the difficulties and plan revisions, the Galveston Jetty Lighthouse suffered little from subsequent storms. The tower was automated in 1973 because safety hazards threatened the keepers. The ties holding the 10-inch iron piles had rusted through, and the concrete base for the support beams had become cracked.[23]

Redfish Bar Lighthouse

Galveston Bay is pinched at the center by Edwards and Smith Points, with Redfish Bar forming a barrier across the bay between them. By

The Redfish Bar Cut Lighthouse, shown here in 1909, served from 1900 until 1936, when it was dismantled and replaced with channel lights on pilings. (Photo courtesy of U.S. Coast Guard Historian's Office)

1851 private traders had erected a beacon light 18 feet above the water to mark the deepest passage over the bar. Vessels paid an annual subscription to keep the light.[24]

The Coast Survey in 1851 recommended an iron screwpile lighthouse near the private light, warning that a competent engineer should be sent to test whether the soft sands would hold such a foundation. If not, a lightship should be stationed there. Congress had already appropriated $5,000 the year before for a lighthouse, subject to the Coast Survey recommendation.[25]

Civil engineer Isaiah W. P. Lewis, nephew of lighthouse builder Winslow Lewis, was selected to design and build the Redfish Bar and two other bay lights. He had visited England a few years earlier to study screwpile lighthouse techniques in use there since the 1830s. Before construction began, the Light-House Board took control and the plans were redrawn significantly. The final design was a simple, four-room, square dwelling atop five screwpiles.[26]

Just before the Redfish Bar Lighthouse was finished, the local lighthouse inspector complained that the screwpiles were too short to protect the station from high waves. Since he had not recognized this problem early enough in assembly, the Light-House Board was forced to accept the structure on February 9, 1854. Keeper John W. Lytle took charge on that date. The dwelling was painted white with red horizontal stripes and held a cheap, pressed-glass lens 35 feet above sea level. A sixth-order lens and a new lantern were mounted in late 1856.[27]

After the Civil War, all that remained was the set of screwpiles. Evidence indicated that Confederates had burned the station. A work force arrived to rebuild the lighthouse in July 1867. While a new lantern was being shipped from the North, workers showed a temporary light starting in May 1868. In November a permanent sixth-order Fresnel lens was installed in the tower.[28]

A ship channel breached Redfish Bar in the 1880s and 1890s; the lighthouse served only to mark the spot where the channel was not. In 1895 the Board asked Congress for $8,000 to build a more substantial structure on the edge of the new waterway. The old lighthouse was by this time decayed so badly that it could not endure a move to a new foundation.[29]

The Redfish Bar Cut Lighthouse went into service on March 20, 1900, with a fifth-order lens held 39 feet above the bay. A lens-lantern placed on the old lighthouse guided schooners able to navigate the old channel.[30]

In the 1900 hurricane the new lighthouse narrowly escaped destruction. A large steamer broke free from its moorings in Galveston and drifted over Redfish Bar just a few feet from the lighthouse. The station was relatively undamaged in this storm, but in the 1915 hurricane the cistern platform was torn from under the dwelling and much of the siding was carried away by the wind. The lighthouse was dismantled in 1936 in favor of cheaper and more effective channel lights on pilings.[31]

Halfmoon Shoal Lighthouse

About ten miles south of Redfish Bar, halfway between Pelican Island and Dollar Point, lies Halfmoon Reef. The Coast Survey report of 1851 recommended a small lightship for the spot, stating that the bottom could not hold a screwpile lighthouse foundation. This opinion was reversed a year later when an extremely low tide exposed the shell reef for a closer inspection.[32]

The Halfmoon Shoal Lighthouse was built concurrently with those at Redfish Bar and Clopper's Bar. The dwelling was painted white with red corners and held a sixth-order lens 35 feet above Galveston Bay. Gilbert Bray was named the first keeper.[33]

The extent of Civil War damage is not accurately recorded. The station was the last to be repaired inside the bay, other works taking a higher priority. It would have been fully renovated in September 1869 had a steamer not rammed the substructure, bending several screwpiles.[34]

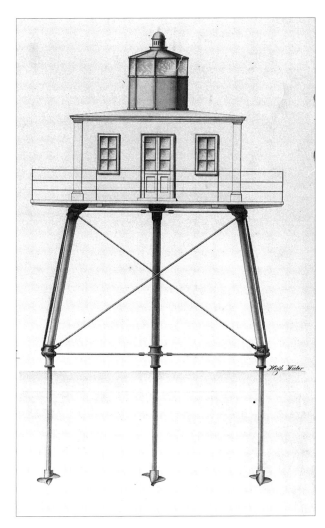

Drawing of screwpile lighthouse design used for three locations in Galveston Bay: Halfmoon Shoal, Redfish Bar, and Clopper's Bar. (Courtesy National Archives)

On the night of September 8, 1900, a hurricane drove several ships hard against the moored British freighter *Kendall Castle*. A nudge from the Norwegian freighter *Gyller* sent the *Castle* on a wild ride to Texas City, 10 miles away. The ship passed directly over the Halfmoon Shoal Lighthouse, pounding it into the sand. Keeper Charles K. Bowen was never found. His father, wife, and daughter ashore were listed among Galveston's 6,000 killed or missing.[35]

In 1902 the Light-House Board placed a lens-lantern on pilings 50 yards from the old lighthouse site.[36]

Clopper's Bar Lighthouse

The San Jacinto River was bounded by a bar carrying only five and a half feet of water until "The Big Ditch" to Houston was dredged. One of the three Galveston Bay lighthouses built in 1854 marked the deepest natural channel over Clopper's Bar, about halfway between Morgan's Point and Cedar Creek. Identical to the Redfish Bar and Halfmoon Shoal Lighthouses, the dwelling mounted on screwpiles was painted all white and held a fifth-order lens. The first keeper was John Alfsson.[37]

The lighthouse was untouched by either adversary in the Civil War. A coat of paint was all that was needed to restore the station to good order.

Channel improvements in 1880 rendered the lighthouse useless to navigation. It was discontinued April 1, 1880. The lighthouse was listed as a daymark as late as 1888.[38]

Fort Point Lighthouse

One of the first acts of the Republic of Texas was to set aside certain lands for defense. The reservation on Galveston Island became known as Fort Point and was located a short distance from the fort originally occupied by pirate Jean Lafitte. As a condition of annexation, Texas ceded the hook-shaped and swampy land to the U.S. government in 1845.

By the 1850s private interests had established beacons of some sort on Galveston pierheads. The first federal lighthouse at Galveston was authorized for Fort Point in 1878 on the old 1836 military reservation. Unfortunately, nothing was left of the real estate. The shoreline had moved so far westward that the selected lighthouse site was under 15 feet of water. Screwpiles were not long enough to take a good bite in the sand.[39]

Local pilots advised the lighthouse engineer that a light would better serve their needs if placed near the end of the breakwater and jetty extending northward from the island wharves. In 1880 the Board acquired for $1 a 10-acre submarine plot two miles south of the Bolivar Point Lighthouse and about 1,000 yards off the breakwater. The Fort Point Lighthouse was delayed in construction for a year and was first lit on August 15, 1882, by keeper Emilius Gerhardt.[40]

The fourth-order lens had three red sectors to show the location of the jetty, wharves, and turning buoy. The light was extinguished in the summer of 1898 because of a Spanish-American War prohibition on nighttime navigation and was permanently discontinued on July 31, 1909. The adoption of acetylene as a lamp fuel had made lit buoys and beacons possible. The station remained as a fog signal until December 1950. The Army Corps of Engineers took it over in 1954.[41]

Brazos River Lighthouse

Just outside Galveston Bay, about 50 miles down the coast, the Brazos River drains an incredible expanse of Texas from near the Oklahoma border to the Gulf. As early as 1834 a small steamboat carried freight and passengers between the mouth and San Felipe de Austin, 150 miles upriver. No waterway other than the Mississippi River and possibly the Alabama and Tombigbee allowed travel so far into the interior.

The land served by the Brazos was soon heavily settled by Americans and became some of the richest farm and ranch land in the Republic of Texas. After statehood the Light-House Board recommended a lighthouse there, receiving funding in 1859. No action was taken; the funds were declared surplus in 1861.[42]

By 1893 dredging and jetties had improved the river to the degree that Congress asked the Board to recommend a lighting system for the harbor. The Board requested $40,000 to erect a lighthouse and $10,000 for jetty markers and a fog signal.[43]

In 1894 the government acquired a small plot only 300 feet square through condemnation proceedings. Construction began the next year. The square, iron skeleton tower was to be identical to others built in Louisiana and Florida. First lit May 30, 1896, by keeper Thomas H. Jenks, the tower held a third-and-a-half-order revolving lens 99 feet above sea level.[44]

During the 1900 hurricane the Brazos River tower suffered little damage, although the jetty light and fog signal building were destroyed. (National Archives photo #26-LG-34-51)

Lighthouses, Lightships, and the Gulf of Mexico

In 1915 the tower shook so hard in a hurricane that the revolving mechanism was put out of order. The lens, weighing many hundreds of pounds, floated in a bath of mercury to allow frictionless movement. More than a gallon of the toxic liquid metal splashed out of the reservoir and spattered onto the floor. The keepers turned the light by hand for two nights.[45]

In 1967 a chemical company bought the land and tore down the lighthouse after the optic was transferred to another tower. The lens is on display today in the Brazoria County Historical Museum; the lantern is on display outside.[46]

Chapter 11

Lower Texas Coast

Most of the 400-mile arc of Texas coastline is protected by sandy barrier islands and peninsulas running close in to shore. Bolivar Point and Galveston Island are the easternmost while Padre Island extends farthest south. The bays behind the isles offer a natural waterway interrupted only occasionally by sand bars. In 1845 Texan Sam Houston recommended to Congress that canals be dug through the sand bars, forming an intracoastal waterway from the Sabine to the Rio Grande. Extensions through the Louisiana marshes would connect almost the entire Gulf Coast. A century later the federal government completed the Intracoastal Waterway almost exactly according to his plan.

Matagorda, San Jose, and Padre Islands are the longest of the Texas barrier islands. Gaps between them, called passes, afford access to Matagorda, Corpus Christi, and Brazos Santiago Bays. The Treasury Department contracted for lighthouses at all three passes during the time the Light-House Board was being formed. The towers originally received outmoded reflector lamps, but by 1858 the Light-House Board upgraded them with Fresnel lenses.

Matagorda Bay

Perhaps Matagorda Bay's most celebrated visitor was Rene Robert Cavelier, Sieur de La Salle, who, in trying to find a navigation marker he left at the Mississippi River, landed instead in Texas, only to be murdered by his own men.

The bay mouth is formed by the Matagorda Peninsula on the north and Matagorda Island on the south. The entrance offered a tricky channel to early pilots, with sharp turns and shifting sand bars. Five or six light stations, depending on how you count, were established at or in the bay. The primary light was an iron tower south of the entrance. Screwpile lighthouses marked shoals just inside the entrance; two more lighthouses were placed inside the bay to serve local navigation.

Matagorda Island Lighthouse

Before Texas statehood, a safe entrance into Pass Cavallo depended on the pilots' beacons on the beach and the survival of a lone tree on Matagorda Island. Sailing instructions for 1841 told visiting ships to line up the beacons with the tree to clear the bar. Passing the shoals inside the entrance was another matter. The Republic of Texas proposed a lighthouse at the pass, but deferred action when statehood was at hand. The U.S. government set a buoy in the entrance in 1847, the year Congress authorized $15,000 for a lighthouse on Matagorda Island.[1]

After more than a year of disputes over ownership of land on the north point of the island, the government acquired five acres in December 1848. The State of Texas dragged its bootheels so long on ceding jurisdiction that the Galveston customs collector openly accused Governor Peter H. Bell of personally sabotaging the lighthouse project. A hot public debate ended in November 1851 when the state approved federal land ownership.[2]

Murray & Hazlehurst Vulcan Works of Baltimore completed the tower after several months of delays. Keeper James Cummings lit the lamps for the first time on December 21, 1852. The tower was identical to the one at Bolivar Point; the two were included in the same $24,000 construction contract. The skin of iron plate was lined with brick for added strength, insulation, and rust prevention. The lantern held a chandelier of 14 metallic reflectors 79 feet above sea level. Two years after its construction, the Light-House Board authorized its first paint job of red, white, and black horizontal bands.[3]

A terrific hurricane blew through the area in September 1854. Every wharf in Matagorda Bay was carried completely away, and the town of Matagorda disappeared. Pass Cavallo did not suffer at all from the storm. The hurricane forced a high tide through the narrow mouth with such force that the channel was straightened and deepened by at least two feet. The gale damaged the lighthouse apparatus and convinced the Light-House Board to move the keeper's dwelling to higher ground.[4]

The Board also recommended raising the lantern 24 feet and replacing the outdated reflectors with a Fresnel lens. Before the reconstruction, the Board flirted with the idea of moving the lighthouse away from the eroding beach. Negotiations with the landowner failed; work to elevate the tower began on the old site in the summer of 1858.[5]

The Confederate States customs collector at LaSalle reported in November 1861 that he had removed and crated the lens and revolving machinery from the Matagorda tower and would soon ship them to Victoria or Texana. A Union agent recovered the lens shortly after the war. The lighthouse station was taken over by troops under General John B. Magruder, commander of the District of Texas, who had a battery of four guns installed around what became a lookout tower. On December 25, 1862, Magruder issued orders to blow up the lighthouse. The explosion heavily damaged the foundation and several iron plates, but the lighthouse withstood the shock. By the time the Federal lighthouse engineer arrived to reestablish the light, the tower was canting slightly because of erosion at the base. The Light-House Board was forced to dismantle and relocate it. The tower materials were stored on the highest

Built of cast-iron plate, the Matagorda Island Lighthouse was dismantled after the Civil War because of erosion at its base; it was re-erected at a new site in 1873. (Photo courtesy of U.S. Coast Guard Historian's Office)

part of the island until 1873. A wood tower holding a revolving fifth-order lens served shipping from October 16, 1865, until the old tower could be rebuilt.[6]

The State of Texas provided a new site almost two miles further inland. Oxcarts and drovers assembled at the island in late 1870 to move the iron plates from storage. Before erection could start, a yellow fever epidemic quarantined the workers. Work stopped again on July 31, 1872, when funds ran out only a few days before completion of the

---

brick and concrete foundation. When new money was available in March the next year, work resumed. The tower was finally finished and lit on September 1, 1873, with its original third-order flashing lens.[7]

A hurricane in August 1886 violently shook the tower. The tide rose 11 feet and stood 4 feet deep around the tower, destroying all but the tower and the main keeper's dwelling. The tower swayed so wildly that a piece of the lens shook free and shattered on the lantern deck. All supplies, tools, and fresh water were lost. The keepers had to travel three miles to the nearest well.[8]

In contrast, an October night in 1918 was so calm that all that could be heard was the buzzing of insects—billions of them. "It was calm and not a bit of air," the keeper reported. "The bugs got so thick around the lantern that they obscured the light. I had to shovel the bugs up in the lantern as well as on the lantern gallery, by the shovelful."[9]

The Matagorda Island Lighthouse was automated in 1956 when electricity reached the station. The Coast Guard replaced the lens in 1977. The original lens is displayed in the Calhoun County Historical Museum in Port Lavaca.[10]

Swash Channel Lighthouse

Once ships negotiated the breakers on Matagorda's bar, they needed help fighting the currents in the dogleg channel leading to the bay. As late as World War I, there were no licensed pilots to take ships through the pass. In good weather the keeper of the local Coast Guard station, when signaled, would serve as a pilot.

In 1855 the Secretary of the Treasury asked the Coast Survey to comment on lights in the area. They recommended a lighthouse to mark the Swash Channel, which cut between the shoreline and submerged sand bars near Alligator Head. The Light-House Board built a small, hexagonal, screwpile lighthouse in 1858, modeled after one erected at Wades Point, North Carolina. It was identical to the one built nearby at Halfmoon Reef. The lantern-on-dwelling was 30 feet square, holding a fifth-order lens 38 feet above sea level.[11]

At the end of the Civil War the lighthouse engineer found only the seven iron screwpiles standing. The lens was located in 1866. Since the tower was an interior navigation light, the Light-House Board focused its attention on more important works. The $15,000 appropriated for a replacement station was allowed to lapse into the surplus fund in 1869.[12]

A screwpile lighthouse was planned for the Swash Channel in 1871, but instead the Board built two lights, known as the East Shoal and West Shoal Lighthouses, or collectively as the Decros Point Light Station. They also served to replace the Saluria Lighthouse.[13]

Saluria Lighthouse

Saluria Bayou (officially McHenry Bayou) lies just inside Pass Cavallo, on the south side. In 1858 a tiny lighthouse marked a shallow channel dredged by the State of Texas to connect Matagorda and Esprito Santo Bays. The small town of Saluria was a busy port in the 1850s. The bayou carried 10 feet of water and provided a harbor for barges and bay boats. Mail landed there for ports as far away as Corpus Christi. Saluria was also home to the local U.S. customs collector, making it the port of entry for the surrounding waterways.[14]

Congress voted only $500 to mark this place. For that sum the Light-House Board bought a 2,500-square-foot bit of swamp and erected a simple but effective wooden lighthouse. Twelve feet square at the base, the open timber-frame tower measured only 34 feet from the ground to the lantern ventilator. Even the lantern was made of wood instead of the usual iron or copper. In July 1858 a sixth-order lens was illuminated.[15]

The Saluria Lighthouse was kept in operation by Confederate forces longer than any other in Texas. Every other lighthouse was extinguished by July 1861 in response to the Union blockade. The Saluria station was put out briefly, but was relit to support interior travel through the bayou. The light was shaded on the seaward side to prevent its targetting by Union gunboats. This station was active until at least the end of November 1861. No Texas lighthouse dispatches were received after that time in the Light House Bureau office in Richmond.[16]

Withdrawing Confederates torched the tower on their expedition to blow up the Matagorda Lighthouse. There was not enough left to rebuild after the war. The Light-House Board reported, "There seems to be no pressing necessity for its immediate construction." The East Shoal and West Shoal Lighthouses built in 1872 served to mark the bayou.[17]

East and West Shoal Lighthouses

The only twin lighthouses built on the Gulf of Mexico marked shoals on the edges of the Pass Cavallo channel. The East and West Shoal Lighthouses were eventually built to fulfill the functions of both the Swash Channel and Saluria stations, which had been burned during the Civil War.

The Light-House Board had hoped to erect inexpensive and easily tended range lights to mark the entrance. Congress supplied $15,000 for the lights, but the landowner on Matagorda Peninsula repeatedly refused to sell. The Board then considered a structure alongside the channel, but a closer examination showed that a pair of screwpile lighthouses would serve multiple purposes. Twin towers would provide range lights, obstruction markers, and a guide to the Saluria harbor.[18]

The stations were completed in March 1872. The West Shoal Lighthouse, nearest the Gulf, showed a white light. The East Shoal held a red light.[19]

Three years later, in the second-worst lighthouse disaster in the Gulf, both stations and their keepers were swept away. Rampaging breakers crashed through Pass Cavallo on September 17, 1875, leaving nothing behind but twisted screwpiles. Keeper John S. Hicks and assistant Jacob Hall were lost at West Shoal. Keeper Thomas H. Mayne and assistant Edward Finck, Jr., were drowned at East Shoal. Present charts still show submerged ruins at the lighthouse sites.[20]

The range lights originally planned for Decros Point eventually replaced the two lighthouses.

Halfmoon Reef Lighthouse

Halfmoon Reef is the shoal which separates Matagorda and Palacios Bays. It was marked by a hexagonal screwpile lighthouse in 1858. This structure is the only surviving wood lighthouse in Texas, although it is now high and dry in Port Lavaca.[21]

The customs collector at Saluria recommended the lighthouse in 1853 to support the brisk trade inside the bay. Local petitions reinforced his opinion. Congress funded the project the next year; the Coast Survey selected the ideal site in 1855. Construction started during the winter working season; the lighthouse was completed in June. At first it held only a hand lantern 40 feet above the bay. Soon mariners complained that this tiny light was invisible between the sand dunes on Matagorda Peninsula. As they sailed along, the light seemed to wink on and off and could be mistaken for the Matagorda Lighthouse. To correct the problem, a red sixth-order lens replaced the small lantern.[22]

The Halfmoon Reef Lighthouse was damaged only by the elements during the Civil War. Confederate authorities removed the lens for storage in November 1861. Federal agents recovered it in May 1866. Although easily repaired, the station lay dormant until February 20, 1868. Coastal lighthouses and those marking critical ports took precedence over those serving strictly internal navigation.[23]

The lighthouse was discontinued on November 15, 1886, when bay traffic was considered too light to justify the cost. Railroads had satisfied most transportation needs in the area. Shipping increased by the turn of the century; in 1902 the Light-House Board decided to revamp and relight that station. Although the station is often listed as being rebuilt that year, repairs consisted mostly of replacing much of the woodwork and renewing the roof. The lantern received a new, red, fourth-order lens visible 11 miles, almost double the distance of the original sixth-order.[24]

In 1935 the light was downgraded to an eight-day lantern. The keepers moved ashore and tended the lighthouse and channel lights in the new Intracoastal Waterway. The Coast Guard sold the property; the new owner barged the lighthouse ashore in 1942. The tower was restored as a Scouting project and now is located next to the Chamber of Commerce building in Port Lavaca.[25]

Aransas and Corpus Christi Bays

It is generally accepted that Alvarez Alonzo Pineda discovered Corpus Christi Bay in 1519. Because the discovery took place on the Roman Catholic festival day of Corpus Christi, Pineda chose to honor the bay with this name. Aransas Pass provides an entrance into the 30-mile-long and 15-mile-wide bay. The inlet had a shallow bar of about six feet, but once inside, mariners could find between 10 and 20 feet of water in the bay.[26]

Aransas Pass Lighthouse

While Pass Cavallo may have been the earliest preferred route to Corpus Christi, Aransas Pass was the more direct. The passage was well known for its fickle shoals, shifting channel, and breaking surf.

Congress appropriated $12,500 for a lighthouse in 1851, to be built on a site selected by the Coast Survey. Just before the Light-House Board was established, civil engineer I. W. P. Lewis drew up initial plans for a 65-foot screwpile lighthouse surmounted by a rugged iron dwelling at the top.[27]

The Coast Survey had begun charting the Texas coast by 1851 and recommended a lightship of 40 tons, claiming, "a light-house cannot be built at this place in a suitable location with any certainty of its standing five years." St. Joseph and Mustang Islands were prone to shifting wildly during storms; the marshy island behind the pass was too far north to align with the charted channel.[28]

In the meantime the new Light-House Board ordered a new survey of the pass. By 1853 the crooked channel had straightened out and had shifted measurably southward, aligning perfectly with Low Island. The local engineer modified and resubmitted the Lewis plans to the Light-House Board, where the engineer secretary summarily rejected them.[29]

He ordered new plans to be prepared from scratch. The new plan called for a rather conventional, round brick tower 50 feet tall, 5 feet of which would be under water. Even this design was discarded in favor of a new approach taken by Army Captain Danville Leadbetter in New Orleans. His octagonal brick towers were also built at three Louisiana locations.[30]

The 50-foot Aransas Pass Lighthouse was completed in 1855 on borrowed funds. As engineering and real estate negotiations dragged

---

on, the Light-House Board diverted the original appropriation elsewhere rather than let it lapse into the surplus. Money intended for a New York beacon later found its way to the Texas project. Auditors apparently never caught on.[31]

The Confederate customs collector at Saluria removed the lens and lamps in November 1861, although local legends dispute this documented fact. The lens was not buried in the local marshes by withdrawing Confederates. The materials were carried to Indianola on Matagorda Bay. George Brundreth was paid $5.00 for cartage on November 19, 1861. A U.S. Treasury special agent at Indianola reported finding a fourth-order fixed lens in May 1866 "in pieces but capable of repair in New Orleans." The lens was in good order by October. It was common practice to return lenses to their original stations, although exigencies of war may have diverted them to other uses. Surviving documents are inconclusive.[32]

The tower itself did not survive the war unscarred. The first mischief-makers were Union blockaders. The ship's gunners from the USS *Arthur* fired on it but missed. The USS *Monongahela* fired seven rounds at the tower over two months. It did not take long before Confederate authorities complained that the lighthouse "furnishes the enemy with many advantages." On Christmas Day General John B. Magruder directed

The former Port Aransas Lighthouse has been renovated and relit as a private aid to navigation and called the Lydia Ann Channel Light. (Photo courtesy of U.S. Coast Guard Historian's Office)

Lower Texas Coast

troops to explode two kegs of powder in the tower. The order was carried out by Captain Benjamin Neal shortly afterward. The top 20 feet of brickwork were split open by the blast. The lantern was damaged somewhat but was saved.[33]

Restorations began in 1866 and continued during the winter— the ideal Gulf Coast working season, free of tropical hurricanes and pesky mosquitoes. The work crew assembled on February 1, 1867, only to be belted by a "Texas Blue Norther." Winds turned the water to an icy froth. "The cold was so intense that fish, thrown ashore by hundreds, were frozen," the Light-House Board reported, "and birds of all sorts sought refuge in the tower and camp of the workmen, where they perished in large numbers." The tower was relit on April 15 after only two and a half months of work.[34]

The station suffered heavily in the hurricane of 1916. The keeper's dwelling and all outbuildings were carried away, leaving the tower standing alone. The keeper received a commendation for keeping the light shining while the station buildings around him were obliterated. A new dwelling was finished just in time for the 1919 hurricane to roll through, although the station received little damage.[35]

A major channel shift in 1952 reduced the need for a lighthouse. The station was now a mile from the entrance. A light placed on the roof of the nearby Coast Guard station replaced it. The property is now privately owned. The Fresnel lens installed or reinstalled in 1867 is on display in the Port Aransas Civic Center.[36]

Corpus Christi Lighthouse

One of America's least-known lighthouses was in commission briefly on the bluff now occupied by Corpus Christi's financial district. The lighthouse was originally located on a 50-by-150-foot residential lot at the corner of Broadway and Buffalo streets.[37]

Citizens of Corpus Christi, led by the mayor, who had dredged a channel to the city's wharves, had petitioned for the light. In 1856 Congress appropriated $5,000 for the station.[38]

A one-and-a-half-story building of "concrete brick" was completed in December 1858 and was scheduled for lighting on January 1. The lantern at the north end of the building showed a sixth-order Fresnel lens 38 feet above the ground and 72 feet above the bay.[39]

The station was in use only a few months. The Light-House Board resolved on September 15, 1859, to discontinue the light. Exterior walls had suddenly started bulging outward, breaking free of the partition walls. The lighthouse engineer was baffled by the local "shell-crete" brick construction, and believed the material could not handle the weight of even a sixth-order lantern. On further examination he discovered that the most damage was to the south end of the building, opposite the tower end. By questioning builders he also discovered that the Texas climate and "gumbo" ground below the building caused the problem. The lighthouse had been built on rain-swollen ground. When the soil baked during an ensuing drought, fissures opened and ripped the lighthouse apart. The next rainy spell again swelled the ground, causing an upheaval and even more damage. Had the foundation included deep pilings, the lighthouse would probably have survived. The Light-House Board considered adding buttresses to press the building back together, but pier lights on the wharves were a cheaper alternative.[40]

The abandoned building became a Confederate arsenal during the Civil War and received the attention of the USS *Arthur* in the attack on Corpus Christi on August 16 and 18, 1862. At least one round struck the lighthouse, but powder stored there did not ignite. Confederates set off a charge under the tower end, knocking the old lantern to the ground. After the Union captured this part of Texas, mischievous boys tried to complete the job with a butter churn filled with gunpowder. Fire spread to the building and the powder stored inside exploded.[41]

In 1870 the U.S. customs collector at Corpus Christi reported the building in total ruins. Only two walls stood to hold up the sagging roof. Children from the neighborhood school often played in the wreck, and he feared for their lives. When the building still stood in 1878, city alderman Dick Jurgan hired a labor gang to pull it down with a rope.[42]

The Brazos Santiago

El Fronton de Santa Ysabel was the site of an early Spanish settlement intended at first to support gold prospecting and later a cattle ranch. When General Zachary Taylor arrived to stage attacks on Mexico, his troops found a ghetto of rude thatch huts covered in malodorous raw cattle hides. Taylor established his main supply camp at Fort Fronton, which he later named Fort Polk.[43]

The Texas Legislature passed a resolution in 1847 calling for a federal lighthouse to mark the Brazos Santiago, the last seaport reached before the Mexican border. A second petition in 1850 resulted in an appropriation of $15,000. The bulk of these funds went to build the seacoast light at Point Isabel.[44]

Point Isabel Lighthouse

The Mexican War drew national attention to the Brazos Santiago as the last American stronghold before the Rio Grande. Once the government approved a lighthouse at the pass, the more difficult task of finding a location came to hand. A Revenue Cutter Service officer believed the main landfall light belonged atop a sand mound on Padre Island, complemented by a portable wood beacon to form a range over the bar. The frugal port collector, John S. Rhea, called the plan impracticable, costing thousands more than necessary and posing the risk of land title fights delaying the works for years. The hard clay bluff at Point Isabel's fort was his preference, to which Texas Senator Sam Houston lent his considerable weight.[45]

He selected a site inside the fort's main bastion, about 25 feet above sea level, and advertised for bids in July 1851. John E. Carey of Brownsville, low bidder at $7,000, received the contract in December. After considerable procrastination, Carey completed the tower early in 1853.[46]

A crew dispatched to install the illuminating apparatus in the new Texas lighthouses from Galveston to the Brazos Santiago finished their work at Point Isabel and Padre Island on March 20, 1853. The tower was designed to hold 15 old-style lamps in 21-inch metallic reflectors 82 feet above the water. The light gained an excellent reputation as easily visible at sea over Padre Island's low sand hills. In 1857 the Light-House Board installed a rotating French Fresnel lens of the third order, making the light visible 16 miles at sea.[47]

Keeper J. H. B. Ham and his family lived for two years in old Army quarters until a keeper's dwelling was built in 1855. Ham's wife Hannah took over as keeper when he died in March 1860. Her boarders, William and James Thwaite, served as assistant keepers until the lighthouse was extinguished in the Civil War. The family stayed at the station as caretakers at least until communications to the Light House Bureau in Richmond were severed in early 1862.[48]

Confederate forces often used the tower to spy on U.S. ship movements offshore and troop landings on Brazos Island. The local military commander, Colonel John S. "Rip" Ford, took possession of the lens and fixtures in 1862 and carted them off to Brownsville. The area around the lighthouse was entrenched and two heavy cannon were mounted.[49]

On May 30, 1863, a force of 87 Union sailors and marines approached the lightly manned Confederate works. To keep the tower out of the hands of the Union invaders, vastly outnumbered Confederate cavalrymen tried to destroy it by setting off a charge of gunpowder. Five months later, Union forces again approached the bluff and Confederates tried again to destroy the lighthouse. This blast blew out the tower door and cracked the brickwork at the top. The brass clockwork for the revolving lens was damaged but repairable.[50]

Repairs were made during the winter of 1865. The original lens was reportedly smashed at Brownsville by frustrated ex-Confederates. A new third-order revolving lens was lit February 22, 1866, by keeper R. Burdeen. When the new screwpile lighthouse was completed at Brazos Santiago in 1878, the work crew was sent to Point Isabel to repair the leaky lantern. Their attempts were to no avail. In 1881 a new, larger

Point Isabel Lighthouse was discontinued in 1905 after the railroads had cut shipping to almost nothing. (National Archives photo #26-LG-37-46B)

lantern was supplied and the top of the tower corbelled outward to receive it.[51]

Retired Fort Polk suddenly attracted attention in 1886 when the rightful landowners stepped forward and sued the lighthouse keeper for trespass. General Taylor had built his fort on private property. The Treasury Department had assumed it was receiving clear title when the War Department transferred the fort to the Treasury in the 1850s.[52]

The Light-House Board balked when asked to buy the property. The option selected was to discontinue the lighthouse and abandon the property in 1887. The new screwpile Brazos Santiago Lighthouse, offering nearly the same range of visibility, would suffice as both the entrance and landfall light.[53]

The public was outraged by the decision. Mariners, politicians, and the press universally and harshly condemned the action. The American Consul at Tampico claimed Brazos Santiago was becoming a "marine graveyard" of wrecked ships. The Galveston *Daily News* pressed for "immediate orders" to relight the tower, reporting that "old seamen and pilots are loud in their denunciation of the action of the government in suspending the light."[54]

Public outcry forced the government to reopen negotiations with the lighthouse owners, who now offered the land and improvements for only $8,000. Congress quickly provided the cash, but Justice Department lawyers just as quickly stepped in to negotiate. After four years of legal opinions and a mountain of paperwork, they allowed the land purchase, but at a reduced price of $5,000.[55]

The government bought a bit less than a half acre of land in the deal; the former keeper, William Egly, returned to duty. He served until the station was permanently closed on August 1, 1905. Railroads had cut shipping to almost nothing. Point Isabel marine interests openly

Lower Texas Coast

After extensive renovations in 1951-52, Point Isabel Lighthouse became a state historic site. (Photo courtesy of U.S. Coast Guard Historian's Office)

charged the railroads with subversion when the barge *Luzon* sank at the rail wharf. The barge blocked the turning basin and effectively shut the port down.[56]

The lighthouse property was sold on January 10, 1928, to J. S. Ford of Brownsville, probably a relative of Colonel Ford, who had removed the lens during the Civil War. After extensive renovations in 1951-52, the lighthouse became a state historic site and the focal point of Point Isabel. This is the only lighthouse on the Gulf Coast maintained especially to attract visitors instead of ships.[57]

Brazos Santiago Lighthouse

The words "lighthouse" and "contraption" hardly seem to fit in the same sentence, but at the Brazos Santiago the U.S. government built a structure that fit both definitions. The Padre Island Beacon resembled a medieval siege tower, or perhaps a torture rack on an oxcart.

*A hexagonal screwpile tower, the Brazos Santiago Lighthouse
was taller than most of its cousins. Extra tiers of ironwork
raised the dwelling and lantern almost twice as high as normal.
The focal plane of the fourth-order lens was 61 feet above sea
level, only 21 feet shorter than the primary seacoast light on
Point Isabel, and visible almost as far to sea.[65] (1926 photo
courtesy of U.S. Coast Guard Historian's Office)*

The beacon marking the Brazos Santiago Pass was set on 5-foot
wheels resting on 19-foot oak "axletrees." Obviously, this tower was
meant to be moved, presumably to form a range with the Point Isabel
Lighthouse as the Brazos Santiago channel made its regular migrations
north and south. The wood structure measured about 30 feet in height
and was fixed on a 15-foot-square platform resting atop the axles. Each
evening the keeper hoisted a square copper lantern between two upright
beams using a block and tackle. The superstructure was typical of hoisting
apparatus used on American and English lightships since at least 1820.[58]

The light was conceived and contracted for by the Fifth Auditor,
before the Light-House Board was formed. Contractor John P.

McDonough of Brownsville completed the mobile light on April 20, 1853, at a cost of only $1,335. Local pilots agreed to tend and position the vehicle, but soon found the task too burdensome. The port collector nominated John Wells as the first regular keeper.[59]

The Light-House Board was unimpressed with the beacon. They claimed the original tower was never really completed and was inadequate for the task. They built a more conventional timber-frame tower in July 1854. This beacon held a real fifth-order lighthouse lens 35 feet above sea level. In only seven years the tower was reportedly decaying, but there was little description of its condition when Confederates burned it to the ground early in the war.[60]

To support U.S. Army operations there, Lighthouse Engineer M. F. Bonzano prefabricated a 34-foot tower at New Orleans and shipped it to the pass in 1864. Instead of erecting it at the original site, he placed it near the Army depot on Brazos Island on the south side of the pass. Lighthouse engineers had asked to relocate the tower there when it was rebuilt in 1854, but legislation stipulated the Padre Island location. Possibly to hide his actions, Bonzano referred to the beacon as the "Brazos Padre Island Light House."[61]

By 1872 the lower portions were so rotted that the Light-House Board felt the structure would be lost in the next storm. Previous gales

Three years after a fire destroyed the superstructure of the Brazos Santiago Lighthouse in 1940, the optic was moved to this nearby Coast Guard station. (1945 photo courtesy of U.S. Coast Guard Historian's Office)

---

had shaken the tower so badly that "lantern glass cracked." The Board recommended a common screwpile lighthouse, estimating $25,000 for its construction.[62]

In a September 1874 hurricane the wood tower indeed failed. The Board reported, "The old wooden tower was completely swept away and everything at the station destroyed." The keeper's wife was in the tower during the storm and was killed when it fell.[63]

The replacement lighthouse progressed slowly. Congress appropriated the full $25,000 six months after the disaster, but the Texas Legislature delayed site acquisition for two years. The state sold the 10-acre underwater plot for $1. It was not until 1878 that metalwork for the substructure was shipped from Philadelphia; the wooden superstructure was framed in Mobile.[64]

The first true lighthouse for Brazos Santiago Pass was completed and lit on March 1, 1879, in shallows in the lee of Padre Island. The Brazos Santiago Lighthouse served as the primary entrance light from 1888 to 1895, and from 1905 onward after the Point Isabel Lighthouse was discontinued. The light was electrified and the station automated in 1939. In 1940 fire destroyed the wood superstructure. The light was moved to the nearby Coast Guard station in 1943.[66]

Chapter 12

Lightships

Floating lights

Few Americans at the time of the Louisiana Purchase had ever seen a floating light and certainly not in American waters. The British had experimented with floating lights as early as 1731. By the end of that century Americans had fitted a few boats with bells and daytime signals and considered the possibility of a lantern and crew on such a vessel.[1]

The first aid to navigation suggested for the Gulf of Mexico was a lightboat. If it had been built in 1804 as contemplated, it would have been America's first. Keeping a fair light in a tower specifically designed for the purpose was hard enough, given the technology of the time. Hoisting a lantern to the masthead of a bobbing sloop and making it visible more than a few miles seemed impossible.

The first U.S. lightships were fishing schooners modified somewhat for riding constantly at anchor. They held lanterns fashioned after proven British designs—a square box which slid up and down between two beams. The very first American lightship was a failure, not from its design but because too much was expected of her. The ship was anchored at Willoughby Spit, Virginia, for only a few months before she was moved to more protected waters inside Chesapeake Bay.

The Gulf received its first lightship a few months later in 1821, when *Aurora Borealis* arrived at the Northeast Pass of the Mississippi River. The ship was later transferred to Pensacola and finally to Virginia. She served as a temporary light at each Gulf location while permanent lighthouses were being built. *Aurora Borealis* ended her days in Virginia as a relief lightship.

More permanent lightship stations were established in the 1840s at Galveston, Merrill's Shell Bank, Ship Shoal, and Atchafalaya Bay, when it was found impossible to mark the spots with lighthouses. Technology eventually caught up with the ships; each was replaced by lights ashore or atop screwpile foundations.

Planning the first lightship

New Orleans Customs Collector Hore Brouza Trist recognized the difficulties in balancing a tall lighthouse on the muddy Mississippi River

---

delta. In 1804 he suggested a floating light in lieu of the Frank's Island Lighthouse. A landlubber, he admitted ignorance of the subject and added, "I can find no person to coincide with me on this opinion." He later changed his position on the matter inasmuch as the only place a light vessel would be safe was inside Balize Bayou, too distant from deep water to be of assistance to the New Orleans-bound mariner.[2]

His idea resurfaced two years later in a letter from the Secretary of the Treasury. Albert Gallatin wrote, "Would not a Hull placed in a bayou of still water, with a lantern at the head of the mast, answer the purpose of a Light House and be a safe and convenient place of residence?" Gallatin also showed his ignorance, asking how a lantern could be possibly suspended from, or fixed at, the masthead and if a crew would be required. Meanwhile plans continued for the magnificent but impossible lighthouse at Frank's Island.[3]

Aurora Borealis

In early 1820 the lighthouse tower began crumbling before it was completed. The government quickly prepared a proposal for a lightship to mark the Mississippi River. Congress authorized a ship not exceeding $15,000 in cost. In June the Fifth Auditor notified the new collector at New Orleans, Beverly Chew, "Instead of a Light House at the Mouth of the Mississippi, it is determined to make trial of a floating light." An advertisement for bids appeared in northeast newspapers a few days following.[4]

Christian Bergh of New York received the first lightship contract awarded by the U.S. government, bidding $6,900. Aurora Borealis was designed to displace 41 tons but was enlarged to 50 tons while still on the drawing boards, driving the cost $1,025.58 higher. Framed in locust and red cedar, the hull was planked with white oak and bolted with iron. A trunk cabin aft accommodated six bunks; a caboose raised forward of the mast served as the galley. Farther forward a "gallows" was framed for a 200-pound fog bell.[5]

A 50-foot mast was originally to carry an octagonal copper lantern fixed at the masthead. The crew was expected to climb the rigging to tend the light. The lantern was to measure three feet in diameter and five feet in height, holding four compass lamps mounted in gimbals to keep them horizontal as the boat tossed about. A Bergh employee suggested modifications based on his experience in building British lightships. A new lantern of wood and copper was substituted, four and a half feet in diameter and four feet tall. This lantern could be raised and lowered between two masts for lighting, trimming, and cleaning. Christened Aurora Borealis (or Northern Lights), the ship served two years at each of two Gulf locations. She was fitted out and ready for sea on November 6, 1820, and arrived at New Orleans in mid-December for duty at the mouth of the Mississippi.[6]

Difficulties in crewing *Aurora Borealis* delayed her use for three months. The advertised salary of $400 per year drew no skipper willing to waste his life bobbing about in the marsh. The sum was only slightly more than the wages of an able seaman.[7]

The Fifth Auditor recommended raising the salary to $500 per year or hiring one of the customs boarding officers as keeper, drawing double pay. This salary was still not enough to attract a skipper. On March 23, 1821, Captain William Cranston accepted the position at $600 per year in addition to his boarding officer salary. The ship went into service anchored at Wallace's Island, near the construction site of the Frank's Island Lighthouse.[8]

When Winslow Lewis offered to rebuild the lighthouse, the Fifth Auditor advised Congress, "The floating light now in use near Frank's Island could be transferred advantageously to the neighborhood of Pensacola." The new lighthouse was completed in March 1823 at about the same time Congress authorized the Pensacola tower.[9]

Aurora Borealis was provisioned and repaired at New Orleans in May and arrived to mark the Pensacola entrance on June 23, 1823. Captain Cranston announced his intent to return to Louisiana and was replaced by crew member John Gates. Gates was then transferred to the Frank's Island Lighthouse as keeper in December 1823, replaced on the ship by Captain John McGregor on the first of December.[10]

The ship was again displaced in 1825 when the Pensacola Lighthouse went into service. She was moored temporarily at a local dock until a new home could be found. In the summer of 1825 *Aurora Borealis* was ordered to Norfolk and designated a relief lightship. The last reference to the ship by name was on March 31, 1837, when the Fifth Auditor asked Congress for $8,000 to repair the decaying hull.[11]

Aurora Borealis was the first lightship traceable from one station to another. Its two predecessors and dozens of following lightships were usually named for the station they held at any particular time, with the name changing as the station changed. Thus lightships would seem to suddenly disappear and new ones appear in lighthouse records, with virtually no way to trace their lineage.

Merrill's Shell Bank Lightship

As early as 1829 government inspectors suggested anchoring a 'light-boat' at the west end of Mississippi Sound, marking the approach to New Orleans. The proposal was, however, for only a small unmanned vessel—an oak and cedar boat costing no more than $1,500. Further examination showed that the Cat Island Lighthouse already approved by Congress would suffice for navigation in the sound. In 1837 Congress approved funds for a lighthouse at nearby St. Joseph Island, but the appropriation was repealed in favor of a brick lighthouse at Merrill's

Merrill's Shell Bank Lightship marked the approach to New Orleans from 1848 until 1860, when she was replaced by a scewpile lighthouse. (Photo courtesy of U.S. Coast Guard Historian's Office)

Shell Bank. An engineer sent to the site reported that a tower could never be built there; the funds were applied to stationing a lightship on the bank.[12]

The Treasury Secretary originally had his eye on the surplus Revenue Cutter *McLane*, a steam-driven engineering failure in the Mexican War. The cutter was laid up at New Orleans awaiting auction. *McLane* was stripped of her power plant and fitted with a makeshift lantern 38 feet above the waterline. She went into service the first week of June 1848.[13]

By 1854 the ship was already showing signs of age. Iron vessels were a novelty in that time; not much was known about preventing rust in the marine environment. *McLane* sprung a leak that year, requiring repairs in Mobile. The Light-House Board approached the Coast Survey asking if the old Revenue Cutter *Legare* was available for transfer to lightship duty. The Coast Survey declined the offer, but it appears they eventually agreed. A log of *Legare's* travels indicates she was converted to a lightship, her last station being "Pass Mary Ann." Pass Marianne is the channel adjacent to Merrill's Shell Bank.[14]

It is possible that a 740-ton Austrian gunboat may also have served as a Merrill's Shell Bank lightship. The only evidence is an annotation on the reverse of a photo taken in 1859 of the former *Legare* at the bank.[15]

Thoroughly rotten by the end of the decade, the lightship went dark on August 1, 1860, when the screwpile Merrill's Shell Bank Lighthouse was commissioned. The Light-House Board advised the local engineer not to "incur any great expense in towing this vessel, as she is worthless." The hulk was stripped, towed to Bay St. Louis, and left there to rot as a derelict. Every fixture of value was taken to Mobile. All supplies were transferred to the new lighthouse.[16]

Already disgraced, the rusting old lady was battered by a hurricane on September 15, 1860. Her moorings parted and the hulk came to ground in the bay. A citizen of Pass Christian wrote to Mississippi Governor Pettus the next spring suggesting the ship be salvaged for the ballast iron the Confederacy needed so badly or possibly for conversion to a gunboat. The ship last served for a few moments as a target for the Mississippi Coast Artillery before settling into the sand for seven decades of rest.[17]

With every piece of iron above water rusted away, the remains were dynamited in 1932 by the Corps of Engineers. Once a guide to safety, it was removed as a hazard to navigation.[18]

Atchafalaya Bay Lightship

The lighthouse at Point Defer being too far from the Atchafalaya Bay channel, a lightship was ordered in 1848 to be placed on the bay entrance about 14 miles west of the Point. Both the Revenue Cutter Service and the Navy inspected the site to identify the best location and to report on the utility of placing a lightship there.[19]

The Atchafalaya Bay Lightship was built in 1849 by H. N. and J.W. Easby of Washington, North Carolina, who also built the Galveston Lightship later in the year. With $12,000 authorized, the vessel was outfitted and ready for duty on May 1, 1849, at a cost of less than $8,000. She was placed on station in August. The first keeper was R. S. Wardle.[20]

Measuring only 72 tons, the ship was sheltered inside the shoal now known as Point Au Fer Reef near the future site of the Southwest Reef Lighthouse. Its single mast held a lantern with 12 wicks 35 feet above the water.[21]

The ship was in a sinking condition by July 1854, requiring a tow to Berwick City for repairs. The Galveston inspector borrowed her that fall in case the rotted Galveston Lightship sank at her moorings. Only a few years later the new Light-House Board recommended replacing all lightships with more economical screwpile lighthouses. The Atchafalaya Lightship was one of the first considered for replacement. Years before, an army engineer had recommended such a structure, but his advice was ignored at the time. In 1855 the Board planned a major screwpile skeleton tower at Shell Keys to the west; another was soon discussed for the southwest tip of Point Au Fer Reef. Together the two lighthouses would replace the ship and save nearly $5,000 a year.[22]

In 1855 a hurricane tore across the Louisiana coast, driving the Atchafalaya and Ship Shoal Lightships from their moorings. They grounded and were "rescued from the perilous situations in which they were found at the subsiding of the gale." The Atchafalaya grounded hard well inside the bay. The ship received extensive repairs and returned to her station in 1856, but only temporarily. When the Southwest Reef Lighthouse was commissioned on September 1, 1859, the Atchafalaya Lightship was "removed from the waters of Louisiana." This apparently meant Louisiana's salty waters, for the old Atchafalaya stayed in Berwick until at least July 16, 1860. At that time the Light-House Board again considered sending her to Galveston for duty. There is no record of the ship being used again. Since no devices were in place to track vessels of the era, her later history is unknown.[23]

Ship Shoal Lightship

The Louisiana Legislature in 1848 called on Congress and the Treasury Department to establish a lighthouse on Last Island, or Isle Dernier. In fewer than four months Congress authorized $15,000 not for a lighthouse tower but for a ship to mark a shoal lying well off the island. A Revenue Cutter captain advised against putting a lightship there, arguing that the Atchafalaya Lightship and the proposed lighthouse at Raccoon Point would serve to guide mariners past Ship Shoal. Somehow a captain of the Texas Navy was able to convince the Fifth Auditor to reconsider. The deciding vote came from the ranking naval officer at New Orleans. He endorsed a light at Ship Shoal to serve both coastal traffic and vessels making for the resorts on Last Island.[24]

The lightship was built at New Bern, North Carolina, after considerable delay. The contractor was unable to obtain materials and took about a year to send her down the ways. Christened *Pleasonton*, after Fifth Auditor Stephen Pleasonton, the ship anchored on station on December 29, 1849.[25]

The ship was fitted with two lanterns, each raised between twin masts. One was elevated 40 feet and the other 30 feet above the waterline. *Pleasonton* was larger than her sister at Atchafalaya Bay, since she was to be anchored in a more dangerous location. Fully fitted out, the ship cost $12,774.67.[26]

As soon as the Light-House Board took charge, it argued for a first-class lighthouse to replace the inefficient lightship. The Coast Survey reported that the ship was well positioned but "the lights can scarcely be seen beyond five or six miles."[27]

Pleasonton was blown hard aground on the Shell Keys west of Atchafalaya Bay during a hurricane in 1855. Repairs uncovered serious decay in the hull plates and fittings. The black hull was coated with red paint with the name Ship Shoal in large letters on each side.[28]

Meanwhile work progressed on the tall iron lighthouse one and a half miles to the south on the shallowest part of Ship Shoal. Once two steamer lanterns could be rigged on the incomplete lighthouse,

Pleasonton sailed to the nearest harbor. In 1860 the lightship was towed to Smith's Point, Virginia, for relief duty.[29]

Trinity Shoal Lightship

The lighthouse building boom of the 1850s was motivated in great part by an effort to replace lightships with more cost-effective screwpile lighthouses. The opposite occurred at Trinity Shoal 20 miles off Marsh Island near Atchafalaya Bay. When attempts to build a screwpile tower ended in near disaster, the Light-House Board chose to establish a lightship to mark the spot.

Lightship *43*, the first composite-hull light vessel built in the United States, was placed on the shoal June 10, 1881. The iron hull was sheathed with yellow pine planks. Shipbuilders of the time felt nothing but natural materials could withstand the fury nature could deal out. The schooner was built 110 feet in length at the waterline. Although lanterns were carried at both masts, only one was shown.[30]

The ship was buffeted by the frequent gales that prevented a lighthouse from being built, but never received any storm damage. Twice storms drove her from her moorings, the crew dropping the spare mushroom anchor to check her drift.[31]

The Light-House Board proposed in 1894 to move the ship to South Pass. Vessel traffic near Trinity Shoal had fallen off drastically. A bell buoy replaced the lightship on August 15, 1894.[32]

South Pass Lightship

Jetties made the South Pass of the Mississippi River so successful that virtually all ships made for it to reach New Orleans. As the jetties extended outward in search of deep water, the entrance bar too moved offshore and farther from the South Pass and East Jetty Lighthouses. Ships approaching the bar in fog could not hear the East Jetty fog signal in time to prevent grounding.[33]

Petitions to Congress in 1882 asked for a lightship with a fog siren to be anchored off the river mouth. The Secretary of the Treasury responded that a lightship "would prove more of an obstruction than a benefit and is therefore not recommended." The Light-House Board caused a reversal 12 years later; the Treasury asked Congress for permission to move Lightship *43* from Trinity Shoal to the pass.[34]

After thorough repairs the ship was anchored in the pass on November 5, 1894. A month later, it was shifted a mile offshore to 72 feet of water.[35]

The South Pass Lightship was active only during the winter months when the warm river waters hitting the chill air created a thick cloak of "sea smoke." The ship withdrew each summer when the weather cleared. Until 1903 only one of the two lights was shown from the mastheads.[36]

Lightship 102, a thoroughly modern ship, arrived at South Pass in 1918. Her fifth-order Fresnel lens was set in a real lantern fixed atop a hollow mast which allowed access during the worst weather. The ship was not rigged for sail. She was propelled by an internal combustion engine burning kerosene, the same fuel used in the lens.[37] (Photo courtesy of U.S. Coast Guard Historian's Office)

By 1901 the hull had rusted badly, requiring extensive repairs. The wood sheathing had protected the iron inner hull for a remarkable 20 maintenance-free years. In 1912 the Light House Establishment began asking for a $125,000 replacement ship; expecting a replacement soon, they asked permission to move the old ship to Southwest Pass. The South Pass had begun shoaling despite the jetties. Lightship *43* was transferred to Southwest Pass, where jetties were affording greater depth.[38]

Even though most traffic now moved through Southwest Pass, the South Pass still accounted for $314 billion in imports and exports in 1914. Congress approved the funds.[39]

The South Pass station was discontinued in 1933. The ship was replaced by more modern and reliable radio beacon service, as well as by buoys sounding bells, gongs, and whistles. Lightship *102* was transferred to New England and used at several stations before her sale in 1963. The ship was last listed as the fishing vessel *Big Dipper* out of Ketchikan, Alaska.[40]

Southwest Pass Lightship

As the South Pass fell out of favor with shipmasters, the Southwest Pass gained the traffic. The pass after 1912 retained its prominence as the preferred entrance to the Mississippi River.

When Lightship *43* arrived at Southwest Pass in 1912, it was known to be nearing the end of its useful life. Congress in 1913 provided $125,000 to replace the ship.[41]

The old vessel, already at its third station, was anchored off the pass in December 1912. She was placed a little more than a mile off the end of the jetties in 100 feet of water. Fog was more prevalent at the Southwest Pass, requiring the ship to remain on station at least nine months of the year.[42]

The replacement ship, Lightship *102*, arrived at Southwest Pass on February 24, 1917; old Lightship *43* was laid up as a relief lightship. The new vessel was about the same size, measuring 101 feet overall, but offered many modern features. The hollow lantern mast allowed the crew to tend the light in virtually any weather. The lantern housed a Fresnel lens instead of the usual reflector system. The fifth-order lens was the only revolving lightship lens on the Gulf. Panels could be removed to show a fixed light during extreme weather.[43]

The lightship at Southwest Pass displayed a Fresnel lens instead of the usual reflector system. (Photo courtesy of U.S. Coast Guard Historian's Office)

Lightship *102* stayed at the Southwest Pass station only a few months. When returned to winter service in late 1918, the ship was placed at the South Pass. Improvements in aids to navigation at the Southwest Pass had reduced its need.

New Orleans Lightship

For the first time in 29 years, a lightship was sent to the Gulf Coast, arriving at New Orleans in March 1965 from Savannah. Lightship *109* was 42 years old at the time.

The ship marked the mouth of the manmade Mississippi River Gulf Outlet, locally nicknamed "Mr. Go." The canal had been in operation since 1963. The Coast Guard had hoped to place a light on common wood pilings, but disputes between shipping and petroleum interests made such a venture risky.

Lightship *109* marked the Mr. Go until October 14, 1971, when a "super-buoy" 50 feet in diameter replaced her. The ship was transferred to Five-Fathom Bank off New Jersey.[44]

The lightship stationed at New Orleans marked the mouth of the manmade Mississippi River Gulf Outlet from 1963 until 1971, when she was replaced by a "super-buoy." (Photo courtesy of U.S. Coast Guard Historian's Office)

Lightships

Galveston Lightship

In 1847 citizens of Galveston, through their Senator Thomas Rusk, petitioned for a screwpile lighthouse "on or near the north breakers at the entrance of the harbor." While the bay's mouth appeared to be wide and deep, a shallow sand bar stretched completely across, leaving only two narrow channels for ships to negotiate.[45]

The Fifth Auditor had received authority to erect a landfall light on Galveston Island. All that would be needed was a small light to mark the main channel. Since the government had never tried screwpile construction in heavy surf, a lightship was a more practical option.

The shipbuilding firm of H. N. and J. W. Easby in Washington, North Carolina, signed the contract for the first Texas lightship on May 19, 1849. This company had completed the Atchafalaya Lightship about three weeks earlier. They had also provided the first ten buoys for the Texas coast a few years before.[46]

Christened *Walton*, the ship was at first anchored about one mile outside the Galveston bar on November 11, 1849. About 90 feet in length and displacing 145 tons, the ship held her single lantern 35 feet above the sea. Constant exposure to pounding waves and the threat of storms carrying the small ship into the breakers soon convinced the local customs collector to move the lightship to calmer water inside the entrance. While this move certainly pleased the crew, mariners were quite unhappy.[47]

The Coast Survey report of 1851 charged that "the lightship at Galveston, in her present position, is of scarcely any use to seagoing vessels . . . anchored nearly three miles inside the bar." The captain of the barque *Montauk* claimed the light was visible only five miles in clear weather and was practically eclipsed by normal haze. A ship approaching at night would be hard aground before the light was visible.[48]

The Bolivar Point Lighthouse was soon completed, however, and the lightship served primarily as a range over the bar and as a guide to the turning points in the channel.

Marine worms thrive in Gulf waters; *Walton's* uncoppered hull was soon honeycombed. When she had been at anchor two and a half years without major repairs, the keeper feared for the ship's safety. In spite of this neglect, the Light-House Board felt the $2,000 required for repairs was excessive; the ship should be anchored in sheltered waters. "She is not worth the expense," the naval secretary wrote. "There can be no economy in repairing such a vessel." In the summer of 1853, the Light-House Board overruled the naval secretary and approved the repairs. The Galveston Lightship spent the summer of 1853 as a floating hospital and quarantine station. Citizens and sailors afflicted with deadly yellow fever were banished to the ship. They had a fifty-fifty chance of living to see shore again.[49]

In 1857 the Light-House Board saw greater economy in replacing the lightship with a series of small range beacons on shore holding sixth-order lenses. Three such lights erected in 1859 indicated the channel and turning points. *Walton* was laid up at a city dock. Again, shippers voiced their objections. Petitions prompted Congress to ask the Board to restore the vessel on station, but the ship was too rotten to anchor even inside the bar. The Board requested $25,000 for a replacement.[50]

Meanwhile local interests established the only private lightship on the Gulf Coast. The City of Galveston chartered the schooner *Excelsior*, fitted her with a lantern of sorts, and placed her at the old lightship position. They also complained loudly that they had asked for a screwpile lighthouse in 1847 and received only a leaky lightship. Now even that was gone. Congress passed a resolution to restore the ship, but this time the ship refused to comply, sinking at the dock. The Light-House Board considered moving the old Atchafalaya Lightship to Galveston, but war settled the question.[51]

Lightship *28*, replaced by a lighthouse in Virginia, was towed to Galveston, arriving for duty in January 1870. During the rebuilding of the Bolivar Point tower, the lightship served as Galveston's entrance light.[52]

In her first year on duty she was blown off station, grounding in the heavy surf north of the channel when the skipper failed to let go the spare mushroom anchor. The ship was quickly returned to duty, but damage was found to be worse than originally thought. Lightship *28* was hauled in 1872 for repairs. The local engineer reported, "She leaks so badly that she cannot be kept afloat." A chartered ship was anchored at the spot, inasmuch as the district did not maintain a relief vessel.[53]

Five years later a cyclone stranded Lightship *28* on Pelican Spit with considerable hull damage. Even after repairs in New Orleans the ship was listed in bad condition.[54]

In the winter of 1880 the ship was "made almost entirely new." The frame, hull, and superstructure were almost totally replaced for a few hundred dollars less than the original $16,000 purchase price. The ship was towed back to Galveston, arriving on March 24, 1881. The ship now held a red light 48 feet above the water, visible 12 miles.[55]

In the great hurricane of 1900 the Galveston Lightship was again torn from her moorings and driven almost halfway up the bay before the crew could make an anchor hold. The anchor windlass was completely destroyed in the fight, the whaleboat wrecked, and one mast lost. The ship returned to station for a few weeks and was towed to New Orleans for refitting, returning to her anchorage on February 2, 1901.[56]

Acetylene buoys replaced the Galveston Lightship on April 23, 1906. The old vessel served at least three more years as a barracks for entrance beacon keepers and was then laid up. The Light-House Board considered transferring the ship to new duty elsewhere, but instead sold her at auction on May 31, 1911, for $312.00, "generally in excellent condition."[57]

Heald Bank Lightship

The last offshore lightship station in the open Gulf was established at Heald Bank in 1905. The bank was discovered in 1884 by Navy Lieutenant E. D. F. Heald, but at that time it posed no great danger for shipping. The bank is located about 28 miles northeast of Galveston, about halfway between the bay and the Sabine River and directly on the fairway of vessels bound between the Tortugas and Galveston. After the turn of the century jetties at Galveston Bay deepened the mouth enough that deep-draft ships frequented the port. With 27 feet of water, the shoal presented a danger to these ships.[58]

It was felt a lightship here would complement the Sabine Bank Lighthouse, built at about the same time on a shallower bank to the

The Heald Bank Lightship was the first modern lightship in the Gulf, powered by a 380-horsepower steam engine as well as by canvas and making greater speed than most lighthouse tenders. The Heald also was built with an iron hull and a high, flaring bow to part the high waves in her exposed position.(Photo courtesy of U.S. Coast Guard Historian's Office)

east. The Sabine Bank station was well along in planning in 1901 when the Light-House Board estimated $90,000 to build Lightship *81*.[59]

The ship was delivered to the inspector at New Orleans in January 1905, but could not be crewed or provisioned because operating funds were lacking. The ship was dry-docked, repainted, and finally sent to her station, mooring at Heald Bank on April 3. The twin lights at her masthead were held 50 feet above the water. The red hull measured 112 feet and displaced 188 tons.[60]

Despite exposure to the full fury of the seas, the Heald Bank Lightship was never heavily damaged by weather at its station. The only storm damage recorded for the ship was dealt by a hurricane which swept through Pensacola in 1926. The ship was moored at the lighthouse docks there and was heavily damaged by repeated banging against the South Pass Lightship.[61]

The Heald Bank Lightship left her station for routine maintenance on July 15, 1936, and never returned. Radio beacon signals from shore stations by this time provided better service to deep-draft vessels endangered by the shoal. A buoy marked the shoal; the ship was reassigned as the Boston Lightship. From 1942 to 1945 old Lightship *81* mounted a three-inch deck gun and joined the war, serving as an "examination ship." The ship returned to lightship duty off Boston but was decommissioned and sold in 1951.[62]

Afterword

For over two centuries ships have struggled to navigate the coral reefs, shifting shoals, unstable islands, and winding bayous of the Gulf Coast. Their captains had a pressing need for navigational markers to find their way along a shoreline bereft of prominent landmarks. The earliest daymarks were small stone or wood pyramids. Later the walls of small forts broke the monotony of a flat horizon. Finally, as commerce with the interior increased, beacons and lightships were placed at strategic locations to mark navigable water. Lighthouse towers were constructed at the entrances to channels and ports, providing guidance to mariners bent on reaching safe anchorages and bustling wharves.

Immediately after the Louisiana Purchase, Congress funded a survey of the Louisiana Territory for lighthouse sites. Aids to navigation were planned and their construction begun on the Gulf Coast to support a burgeoning seaborne commerce. The first steamboat on the Mississippi (1811) opened the heartland of the continent to the Gulf and to the world. Waves of European immigrants settled in the wilderness recently wrested from the Native Americans. The produce of their new farms— particularly cotton—moved to the world market down the Mississippi in a growing fleet of riverboats to Gulf ports for transshipment abroad. Ports handling outbound cotton and inbound consumer goods expanded rapidly. The addition of Florida to the United States in 1819 extended the Gulf Coast all the way to the Florida Keys.

Approximately 55 light stations were established on the Gulf Coast before the Civil War. The soggy terrain and treacherous bottoms, buffeted by heavy winds and periodic hurricanes, challenged the skills of lighthouse designers and builders, as well as of the men and women appointed to keep the lights. The tall rubblestone towers built on solid rock foundations in New England were hopeless as models for Gulf Coast lighthouses, for there was no base to support them. A screwpile foundation, first constructed at Brandywine Shoal on the Delaware Bay in 1850, met the particular needs of the Gulf, for it was relatively inexpensive to build and permitted turbulent water to pass unimpeded through the iron pilings under the structure—its weight distributed over a large area. The first screwpiles on the Gulf were constructed in Galveston Bay in 1854. The installation of Fresnel lenses in the lighthouses starting in the 1850s also greatly improved the efficiency of the lights on the Gulf.

The Civil War temporarily extinguished the lights on the Gulf and the commerce which they served. Lighthouses became Confederate lookout posts and Union targets. Some of them were bombarded—destroyed or badly damaged.

When the war was over and migration and commerce revived, damaged lighthouses were rebuilt. New technologies permitted the construction of strong cast-iron towers. Prefabricated iron-skeleton towers became the ultimate solution to the singular problems of Gulf shore terrain beginning in the 1870s. Even later, the Texas tower, adapted from an offshore oil drilling platform, served locations in deep water and heavy weather.

Of the 90 light and lightship stations built on the Gulf Coast between 1811 and the merging of the U.S. Lighthouse Service into the U.S. Coast Guard in 1939, approximately 48 are still extant (none of the lightships remain at their stations). The others have disappeared from the landscape. Some of the surviving towers still serve as active aids to navigation, although that function is no longer vital as it was before the invention of radio, radar, loran, GPS, and other sophisticated navigational systems. Nevertheless, each lighthouse is a unique landmark in its particular setting, assuring mariners of their location and promising a safe journey to their destination.

To the people who lived around them, lighthouses were a reminder of the interdependence of their lives and the vigilance that guided the traveler safely home. The men and women who tended the lights had a sense of mission that kept them at their posts throughout all the long days and nights, in fair weather or through the wild terror of a hurricane, knowing that the safety of men who braved the sea depended on the light keeper's discipline and devotion.

A lighthouse that no longer beams its light still lifts the heart. We see it today in its peaceful solitude, and our minds drift back to a time when comfort mattered less than courage and determination. The tower is empty, but we sense the keeper on the stairs or in the watchroom and the beam of light reaching into the darkness, making us aware of man's vulnerability and the selfless gift of the stranger who guides him home.

Endnotes

Abbreviations used throughout the endnotes:

CSLHB: Confederate States Light House Bureau, adopted by the C.S. government on April 15, 1861, and gradually fading away to its end in early 1865. Virtually all extant correspondence is attributable to Thomas Martin, chief clerk and later chief of the bureau.

CS Treasury Letters: Treasury Department Collection of Confederate Records, Record Group 365, National Archives.

Collector: U.S. or C.S. Collector of Customs for the port indicated, usually also serving as the Superintendent of Lights for the named collection district (although in the largest ports, this duty was sometimes delegated to a subordinate). Unless indicated, U.S. collector is assumed.

NA: National Archives, U.S. General Services Administration, primarily in Washington, DC, including the Maps and Plans section. Records of the U.S. Coast Guard, U.S. Commerce Department and U.S. Treasury Deparment relating to America's lighthouses are mostly contained in Record Group 26. Information relating to the Confederate States Light House Bureau are contained in Record Group 56, General Records of the Department of the Treasury.

Lighthouse Letters, RG 26, NA: Lighthouse Letters in Record Group 26, consisting of many hundreds of volumes, dating (for the Gulf of Mexico) from 1803 to the present. Most old letters are bound, arranged in strict chronology, while others are arranged chronologically by district. Several volumes are designated by the recipient, such as Letters to the Secretary of the Treasury and Letters to Congress. A fire at the U.S. Department of Commerce in 1931 destroyed many important volumes of these primary references.

ORA: R. N. Scott et al, eds., *The War of the Rebellion: A Compilation of the Official Records of the Union and Confederate Armies*, 128 vols. (Washington, DC: Government Printing Office, 1880-1901). While certainly not rich with lighthouse information, Series I, volumes 1, 6, 9,

14, 26 (part 1), 35 and 48 (part 1) offers a valuable perspective on peripheral events.

ORN: Richard Bush et al, eds., *Official Records of the Union and Confederate Navies in the War of the Rebellion*, 38 vols. (Washington, DC: Government Printing Office, 1894-1927) Series I, volumes 16 through 22. Because lighthouses were relit along the Gulf of Mexico largely to support naval operations, these volumes give an invaluable perspective on aids to navigation during the war. There are many direct references to lighthouses.

Register of Officers: published by the U.S. State Department biennially as the *Register of Officers and Agents of the United States Government.*

RG: Record Group in the National Archives.

USCG: U.S. Coast Guard, responsible for United States lighthouses since 1939. The site files at USCG Headquarters hold much reliable, general information, but all original documents have been donated to the National Archives for improved security and public access. The USCG Seventh (Miami) and Eighth (New Orleans) Districts possess much "local knowledge" but are a limited source of historical information.

USLHB: U.S. Light-House Board, formed in 1852 and disbanded in 1910, directing all lighthouse activities in those years. USLHB annual reports fill the gaps where original engineer and inspector reports have been lost.

USRM and **USRC:** the U.S. Revenue Marine and the cutters under its control. Forerunner of today's U.S. Coast Guard.

Persons cited throughout the notes:

Bonzano, Dr. Maximilian F., acting engineer and inspector for both the Eighth and Ninth Lighthouse Districts, New Orleans, from August 12, 1862, to June 16, 1871, with gaps. Bonzano concurrently held all four positions during the trauma of war and reconstruction.

Lewis, Winslow, of Boston, prime contractor for supplies and patent reflectors during the reign of S.

Pleasonton. In the 1830s he became America's premier lighthouse builder, wielding vast influence over the Fifth Auditor. Fell from grace and was bankrupted in approximately 1842 after Congressional attacks.

Martin, Thomas, chief clerk and later acting chief of the Confederate States Light House Bureau, Montgomery and Richmond, May 1, 1861, to early 1865. He reported to the Bureau 15 days after its conception and served to its end.

Pleasonton, Stephen, Fifth Auditor and Acting Commissioner of the Revenue, U.S. Treasury Department, Washington, DC. He was often referred to as the Superintendent of Lights, although the title did not exist, because his tenure lasted more than 32 years, from 1820 to 1852. Pleasonton reported directly to the Secretary of the Treasury.

Notes to Chapter 1, The Gulf Coast of the United States before the Civil War

[1]George R. Putnam, *Lighthouses and Lightships of the United States* (Boston: Houghton Mifflin Co., 1917), p. 5.

[2]Work Projects Administration, *Texas: A Guide to the Lone Star State* (New York: Books, Inc., 1940), p. 671; Work Projects Administration, *Louisiana: A Guide to the State* (New York: Hastings House, 1941), p. 693.

[3]Work Projects Administration, *Louisiana*, p. 38; Francis Ross Holland, Jr., *America's Lighthouses: Their Illustrated History Since 1716* (Brattleboro, VT: The Stephen Green Press, 1972), p. 190.

[4]Work Projects Administration, *Louisiana*, p. 218.

[5]Ibid. p. 696.

[6]USLHB, *Laws of the United States Relating to the Establishment, Support, and Management of the Light-Houses, Light-Vessels, Monuments, Beacons, Spindles, Buoys, and Public Piers of the United States from August 7, 1789, to March 3, 1855* (Washington, DC: A. O. P. Nicholson, Public Printer, June 30, 1855), p. 37 passim; Talbon Hamlin, *Benjamin Henry Latrobe* (New York: Oxford University Press, 1955).

[7]Clement Eaton, *A History of the Old South* (New York: Macmillan Publishing Co., Inc., 1975), pp. 195-205.

[8]Hamlin, *Latrobe*.

[9]Putnam, *Lighthouses and Lightships,* pp. 113-34, 201-02.

[10]George Weiss, *The Lighthouse Service: Its History, Activities and Organization* (Baltimore: The John Hopkins Press, 1926), pp. 2-4, 33; Putnam, *Lighthouses and Lightships,* pp. 33, 38, 43; USLHB, *Laws,* p. 4; Holland, *America's Lighthouses,* pp. 26-27.

[11]Weiss, *The Lighthouse Service,* pp. 4, 6.

[12]Holland, *America's Lighthouses,* p. 144; U.S. Congress, House, *Message from the President of the United States, Transmitting Copies of Surveys made in Pursuance of Acts of Congress, of 30th April, 1824, and 2d March, 1829.* H. Doc. 7, 21st Cong., 1st sess., 1829, p. 5 passim; U.S. Congress, House, *Letter From the Secretary of the Treasury,* H. Doc. 114, 22d Cong., 1st sess., 1832.

[13]USLHB, *Laws,* p. 68.

[14]George Brown Tindall, *America, A Narrative History* (New York: W. W. Norton & Co., 1984), pp. 433-34.

[15]Eaton, *A History of the Old South,* p. 211.

[16]Work Projects Administration, *Louisiana,* pp. 81-82; U.S. Congress, House, *Letter from the Secretary of the Treasury Transmitting Statements of Contracts authorized by the Treasury Department during the year 1838,* H. Doc. 131, 25th Cong., 3d sess., 1839, pp. 1-5.

[17]F. E. Chadwick, "Aids to Navigation." *Proceedings of the United States Naval Institute* 17, no. 3 (1881):8.

[18]USLHB, *Annual Report to the Secretary of the Treasury, 1855* (Washington, DC: Government Printing Office, 1855), pp. 419-20.

Notes to Chapter 2, The Civil War

A listing of authoritative works on Civil War history could be the subject of a book by itself. An excellent, if biased, description of the maritime and economic importance of the South is contained in Admiral Raphael Semmes, *Memoirs of Service Afloat During the War Between the States.* In addition, various issues of J. D. B. De Bow, *De Bow's Commercial Review,* published at New Orleans and later Charleston, 1853-1862, offer a broad, first-hand description of the South from an economic viewpoint.

[1]Frank Moore, ed., *Rebellion Record: A Diary of American Events* (New York: G. P. Putnam, 1861-1868), 3:28; Martin to Bolling Baker, January 22, 1862, CSLHB, Records of the Department of the Treasury, RG 56, NA; James D. Johnston to C. G. Memminger, October 2, 1861, ibid.; T. Sanford to E. L. Hardy, January 21, 1861, Lighthouse Letters, RG 26, NA; Sanford to R. S. Chapman, January 31, 1861, ibid.

[2]Carol Welles, "Extinguishing the Lights: 1861," *Louisiana History* 19, no. 2 (1978):301.

[3]St. Marks Collector to Martin, August 23, 29, 1861, CSLHB, RG 56, NA; Raphael Semmes to U.S. Treasury Secretary, January 26, 1861, Lighthouse Letters, RG 26, NA; Semmes to Joseph Fry, January 26, 1861, ibid.

[4]Raphael Semmes, *Memoirs of Service Afloat during the War between the States* (Baltimore: Kelly, Piet & Co., 1869), pp. 77-78, 88; Memminger to Jefferson Davis, April 10, 1861, Letters Sent by the C.S. Secretary of the Treasury, C.S. Treasury Letters, p. 39.

[5]Semmes, *Memoirs,* p. 88.

[6]Memminger to Raphael Semmes, April 15, 1861, CSLHB, RG 56, NA; Memminger to Davis, April 16, 19, 1861, C.S. Treasury Letters, pp. 57, 59.

[7]Memminger to Davis, April 16, 1861, C.S. Treasury Letters, p. 57; Memminger to Edward F. Pedgard, ibid.

[8]Memminger to Davis, April 19, July 11, 1861, C.S. Treasury Letters, pp. 59, 319.

[9]Memminger to Martin, May 11, 1861, ibid., p. 79; Memminger to W. G. Dozier, April 30, 1861, ibid.

[10]Pensacola Collector to Martin, December 5, 1861, February 1, 1862, CSLHB, RG 56, NA.

[11]Semmes, Memoirs, pp. 110-11.

[12]Johnson to Sanford, June 25, July 1, 1861, CSLHB, RG 56, NA; Galveston Collector to Martin, July 13, 1861, ibid.; A. B. Noyes, record of property removed from Egmont Key, August 29, 1861, and letter March 13, 1862, ibid; S. S. Selleck to Frank Hatch, October 9, 1861, ibid.; LaSalle to Martin, November 21, 1861, ibid.; Hatch to Martin, November 22, 1861, ibid.; N. Baker to Martin, November 27, 1861, ibid.; James Ferrell to Martin, February 5, 1862, ibid.

[13]Memminger to Davis, September 20, 1861, C.S. Treasury Letters, p. 571; Chief Clerk of C.S. Treasury Department to Martin, September 21, 1861, ibid.

[14]Memminger to Martin, September 30, October 7, 8, 10, 1861, ibid., pp. 599, 619, 626, 636; Martin, circular letter to C.S. Customs Collectors, November 11, 1861, CSLHB, RG 56, NA; Memminger to Martin, April 30, 1862, ibid.

[15]Richard H. Jackson to Lewis G. Arnold, November 25, 1861, ORA, Ser. I, 6:477; Walter K. Schofield Diary, January 1862, quoted in Maxine Turner, Navy Gray: A Story of the Confederate Navy on the Chattahoochee and Apalachicola Rivers (Tuscaloosa: University of Alabama Press, 1988), pp. 42-43, 118, 121; H. H. Bell to Bonzano, September 14, 1863, ORN, Ser. I, 20:587; Bell to W. K. Mayo, September 14, 1863, ibid.; A. F. Crossman to Theodorus Bailey, July 16, 1863, ibid., 17:494-496; Joseph Finegan to S. Cooper June 17, 1862, ORA, Ser. I, 14:41; A. Read to Gideon Welles, April 18, 1863, ORN, Ser. I, 20:147-52; William Griffin to W. R. Scurry, April 8, 1862, ORA, Ser. I, 20:150; Statement of Pilot Crome, October 12, 1863, ORN, Ser. I, 20:623; Bonzano to USLHB, November 14, 1863, Lighthouse Letters, RG 26, NA; LaSalle, Texas, Collector to Martin, July 22, 1861, CSLHB, RG 56, NA; J. W. Kittredge, February 26, 1862, quoted in Francis Ross Holland, Jr., Aransas Pass Light Station, A History (Corpus Christ, TX: By the Author, 1976), pp. 41, 46; James Trather to Wm. W. McKean, December 18, 1861, ORN, Ser. I, 17:6-7.

[16]Mobile Collector, Pay slips for Mobile District, June 11, 1861, October 1, 1862, Receipt for Cartage of Light-house Materials, November 3, 1862, CSLHB, RG 56, NA.

[17]Martin to Memminger, January 25, 1864, ibid.

[18]Memminger to Martin, January 27, February 5, 1864, ibid.; Moone to Memminger, June 19, 1863, ibid.

[19]J. C. Colsson to Martin, March 5, 1864, ibid.; Martin to Colsson, March 22, 1864, ibid.

[20]Colsson to Martin, Receipt for Storage, December 31, 1864, ibid.; Memminger to Martin, October 26, 1863, ibid; Martin to Chief Clerk of C.S. Treasury, October 31, 1863, ibid.

[21]Melancton Smith to Wm. Mervine, July 9, September 13, 1861, ORN, Ser. I, 16:670; New Orleans Daily Picayune, September 20, 1861; New Orleans Commercial Bulletin, September 21, 1861; Manuel Moreno to Hatch, June 22, 1861, in Tom Henderson Wells, The Confederate Navy, A study in organization (Tuscaloose, AL: University of Alabama Press, 1971), pp. 304-305; David D. Porter to Mervine, July 4, 1861, ORN, Ser. I, 16:573; Thomas F. Wade to E. M. Chester, Receipt for Property Removed, July 10, 1861, CSLHB, RG 56, NA; George F. Emmons to McKean, December 18, 1861, ORN, Ser. I, 17:7-8; Bonzano to USLHB, May 18, 1866, Lighthouse Letters, RG 26, NA; USLHB, Annual Report, 1866; Turner, Navy Gray, p. 42; N. Baker to Martin, November 27, 1861, CSLHB, RG 56, NA; Holland, Aransas Pass Light Station, p.47.

[22]George S. Dennison to USLHB, July 5, 1862, Lighthouse Letters, RG 26, NA; William A. Goodwin to USLHB, August 5, 1862, ibid.; USLHB, Annual Report, 1884.

[23]Bonzano to USLHB, August 30, September 22, 29, October 17, 30, November 24, December 1, 1862, January 3, 1863, Lighthouse Letters, RG 26, NA; New Orleans Collector to U.S. Treasury Secretary, May 16, 1863, [extract], ibid.; USLHB to Bonzano, June 4, 1863, ibid.

[24]Bonzano to USLHB, November 24, 1862, October 5, 1868, Letters Sent to USLHB by 8th and 9th District Engineers, New Orleans; Bell, diary, ORN, Ser. I, 19:734; John W. Glenn to Danville Leadbetter, February 24, 1863, Lighthouse Letters, RG 26, NA; Engineer's Register of Light Ships and Light House Tenders, Coast Guard Historian's Office, Washington, DC.

[25]USLHB, Annual Reports, 1859 through 1882.

[26]K. Jack Bauer, A Maritime History of the United States (Columbia: University of South Carolina Press, 1988), pp. 160-77.

[27]Donald Whitnah, ed., Government Agencies (Wesport, CT: Greenwood Press, 1983), pp. 527-29.

Notes to Chapter 3, Florida's West Coast: Dry Tortugas to Cedar Keys

For general information on the Florida peninsula and its maritime heritage, refer to Charlton W. Tebeau, A History of Florida; and compiler of primary documents Clarence Edward Carter, The Territorial Papers of the United States. A large quantity of information was also gathered from publications and collections of libraries, historical societies, and museums from Key West to Cedar Keys.

[1]T. Frederick Davis, "Juan Ponce de Leon's Voyages to Florida," *Florida Historical Society Quarterly*, 14 (1935):1; S. R. Mallory to A. D. Bache, Coast Survey, December 18, 1848, published in U.S. Congress, Senate, *Report of the Secretary of the Treasury, Communicating a report from the Superintendent of the Coast Survey, in relation to the survey of the coast of Florida*, S. Ex. Doc. 30, 30th Cong., 2d sess., 1849, pp. 9-13.

[2]Gerald DeBrahm, *Report of the General Survey in the Southern District of North America* (Columbia: U.S. Car Press, 1971), p. 253; Hans Christian Adamson, *Keepers of the Lights* (New York: Greenburg, 1955), p. 175.

[3]U.S. Congress, House, *Letter from the Secretary of the Treasury, Accompanied by a Report of the Fifth Auditor, upon the Subject of Light-Houses*, H. Doc. 19, 19th Cong., 1st sess., 1825, pp. 5-11.

[4]Matthew C. Perry report to Secretary of Navy, March 28, 1822, published in Clarence Edwin Carter, ed. and comp., *The Territorial Papers of the United States*, vol. 22, *Territory of Florida, 1821-1824* (Washington, DC: Government Printing Office, 1956) p. 388; U.S. Treasury Secretary to Thomas Newton, Jr., April 24, 1822, ibid., 22:41; USLHB, *Laws*, p. 364.

[5]*Letter from the Secretary of the Treasury*, H. Doc. 19, 19th Cong., 1st sess., 1825, pp. 5-11; U.S. Congress, Senate, *Report from the Secretary of the Treasury, Relative to Light Houses and Buoys on the Coast of Florida and Gulf of Mexico*, S. Doc. 17, 18th Cong., 2d sess., 1825, p. 4.

[6]*East Florida Herald*, June 6, 1826, cited in Clarence Edwin Carter, ed. and comp., *The Territorial Papers of the United States*, vol. 23, *Territory of Florida, 1824-1828* (Washington, DC: Government Printing Office, 1958), 583.

[7]Pleasonton to Baltimore Collector, April 6, 1826, Lighthouse Letters, RG 26, NA; Pleasonton to Wilmington [DE] Collector, April 22, 1826, ibid.; William Pinkney to Pleasonton, April 22, 1826, ibid.; Pleasonton to U.S. Treasury Secretary, November 10, 1826, ibid.; Pleasonton to Pinkney, November 11, 14, 1826, ibid.

[8]Key West Collector to Pleasonton, July 4, 1826, Lighthouse Letters, RG 26, NA; Robert Mills, *The American Pharos, or Light-House Guide* (Washington: Thompson & Homans, 1832), p. 89; Pleasonton to S. R. Mallory, June 30, 1846, Lighthouse Letters, RG 26, NA; Alex[ande]r Thompson to H. D. Hun[t]er, May 15, 1834, ibid.

[9]U.S. Congress, Senate, *Report from the Secretary of the Treasury, in compliance with a resolution of the Senate of the 25th instant, transmitting copies of the representations made to him relative to the light-houses of the United States, by the Messrs. Blunt, of New York, &c.*, S. Doc. 138, 25th Cong., 2d sess., 1838, pp. 37-41; Edward Rowe Snow, *Famous Light Houses of America* (New York: Dodd, Mean & Co., 1955), p. 215; Pleasonton to Lewis, June 5, 1838, Lighthouse Letters, RG 26, NA; U.S. Congress, Senate, *Documents on Light-House Establishment of the United States*, S. Doc. 258, 25th Cong., 2d sess., 1838, pp. 16-17; U.S. Congress, House, *Letter from the Secretary of the Treasury, transmitting a report of the Fifth Auditor in relation to the execution of the act of 7th July last, for building light-houses, light-boats, etc.*, H. Doc. 24, 25th Cong., 3d sess., 1838, pp. 113-15.

[10]Pleasonton to Key West Collector, May 13, 1827, Lighthouse Letters, RG 26, NA; *Report from the Secretary of the Treasury*, S. Doc. 138, 25th Cong., 2d sess., 1838, pp. 37-41; Pleasonton to William R. King and Francis O.J. Smith, April 5, 1838, Lighthouse Letters, RG 26, NA; Pleasonton to Howland, April 6, 1838, ibid.

[11]Key West Collector, Annual Statement of Light Houses, 1840, Lighthouse Letters, RG 26, NA; Pleasonton to Adam Gordon, Key West Collector, May 3, 1845, ibid.; Pleasonton to Mallory, June 30, 1846, ibid.; Henry Lepaute to U.S. Senate, May 8, 1840, *Report from the Secretary of the Treasury*, S. Doc. 138, 25th Cong., 2d sess., 1838, p. 2.

[12]General Land Office, report to U.S. Treasury Secretary, August 25, 1847, Lighthouse Site Files, RG 26, NA; Pleasonton to Land Bureau, August 31, 1847, ibid.

[13]The U.S. Coast Survey was a mapping agency started before the War of 1812. Surveys were conducted by naval officers lent to the agency. It became the Coast and Geodetic Survey in 1878.

[14]Mallory to Bache, December 18, 1848, *Report of the Secretary of the Treasury*, S. Ex. Doc. 30, 30th Cong., 2d sess., 1849, p. 2.

[15]*Report of Officers Constituting the Light House Board*, H. Ex. Doc. 55, 32d Cong., 1st sess., 1852; USLHB, *Annual Report, 1855*; Holland, *America's Lighthouses*, p. 134.

[16]USLHB, *Annual Reports*, 1868, 1874 and 1876; U.S. Commerce Department, *Annual Report*, 1913.

[17]USLHB, *Laws*; *Letter from the Secretary of the Treasury*, H. Doc. 24, 25th Cong., 3d sess., 1938, pp. 113-15; USLHB, *Annual Report, 1856*.

[18]National Archives Site Files; *List of Light-Houses, Lighted Beacons and Floating Units of the Atlantic, Gulf and Pacific Coasts of the United States*, USLHB, Treasury Department, 1858. (Publication's name changed slightly throughout its existence. It will hereafter be cited as Light List, with year of publication.)

[19]USLHB, *Annual Report*, 1868, 1869, and 1874.

[20]Ibid., 1876.

[21]Davis, "Ponce de Leon's Voyages," p. 41.

[22]Florida Peninsular Land Company to U.S. Treasury Secretary, December 13, 1833, quoted in Paul Snodgrass, "Beacons of the Sea," *Gulfshore Life* (October 1990):78; Residents of Sanybell, petition to U.S. Treasury Secretary, December 20, 1833, cited in Carter, 24:930;

Residents of Key West, petition to U.S. Congress, ibid, 24:933-34.

[23]U.S. Congress, House, *Report of the Superintendent of the United States Coast Survey*, H. Ex. Doc. 41, 36th Cong., 1st sess., 1859, pp. 323-28; U.S. Congress, Senate, *Memorial of W. H. Gleason, asking that a light-house be constructed at the harbor of Punta Rassa, on Sanibel Island, Florida*, S. Misc. Doc. 106, 42d Cong., 2d sess., 1872; USLHB, *Annual Report*, 1878.

[24]USLHB, *Annual Report*, 1881; *United States Statutes at Large*, 1874-, 22:309.

[25]USLHB, *Annual Report*, *1884*; Secretary of the Interior, *Official Register of the United States, containing a list of Officers and Employés in the Civil, Military, and Naval Service on the First of July, 1885* (Washington, DC: Government Printing Office, 1885), p. 213.

[26]Neil E. Hurley, *Keepers of Florida Lighthouses, 1820-1939* (Alexandria, VA: Historic Lighthouse Publishers, 1990), p. 113; Site Files, U.S. Coast Guard Seventh District, Miami, Florida; Site Files, Coast Guard Headquarters, Washington, DC.

[27]*Report of the Superintendent of The United States Coast Survey*, H. Ex. Doc. 41, 36th Cong., 1st sess., 1859, pp. 323-28; USLHB, *Annual Report, 1887*.

[28]U.S. Congress, Senate, *Report on the Committee of Commerce*, S. Rept. 577, 578, 50th Cong., 1st sess., 1888.

[29]USLHB, *Annual Reports*, 1890 and 1891; Hurley, *Keepers of Florida Lighthouses*, p. 63.

[30]Site Files, U.S. Coast Guard Seventh District, Miami; Lighthouse Database, National Maritime Initiative, U.S. National Park Service, Washington, DC.

[31]Thornton Jenkins to T. W. Osburn, January 16, 1872, Lighthouse Letters, RG 26, NA.

[32]Light Lists, 1916 and 1947.

[33]Site Files, U.S. Coast Guard Seventh District, Miami; Light List, 1932.

[34]Carter, 24:930, 934; Napoleon L. Coste to U.S. Treasury Secretary, July 5, 1837, in U.S. Lighthouse Establishment, *Lighthouse Papers, Compilation of public documents and extracts, 1789-1871* (Washington: Government Printing Office, 1871), p.28; U.S. Congress, Senate, *Resolution of The Legislature of Florida, relative to the erection of a light-house on Egmont Key*, S. Doc. 130, 29th Cong., 2d sess., 1847, p.1; USLHB, *Laws*, p. 131.

[35]U.S. Congress, House, *Letter from the Acting Secretary of the Treasury Transmitting Statements under acts of 21st April, 1808, and 2d March 1909*, H. Ex. Doc. 52, 30th Cong., 1st sess., 1848; Deeds and Contracts, RG 26, NA; Pleasonton to St. Marks Collector, August 10, 1847, Lighthouse Letters, RG 26, NA.

[36]Title Records, Site Files, Coast Guard Headquarters, Washington, DC; Pleasonton to House of Representatives, December 15, 1847, in U.S. Congress, House, *Light-House Establishment*, H. Ex. Doc. 27, 30th Cong., 1st sess., 1848, pp. 9-10; St. Marks Collector to Pleasonton, February 5, April 19, 1848, Lighthouse Letters, RG 26, NA; Pleasonton to St. Marks Collector, February 15, and May 2, 1848, ibid.; Pleasonton to Francis A. Gibbons, February 19, 1848, ibid.

[37]Pleasonton to U.S. Treasury Secretary, July 17, 1848, Lighthouse Letters, RG 26, NA; Hurley, *Keepers of Florida Lighthouses*, p. 57.

[38]U.S. Department of State, *Register of all Officers and Agents, Civil, Military, and Naval, in the Service of the United States, on the Thirtieth September, 1847* (Washington, DC: J. & G. S. Gideon, 1847), p. 126; Sherrod Edwards to Pleasonton, November 20, 1847, Lighthouse Letters, RG 26, NA; St. Marks Collector to Pleasonton, September 25, 1848, ibid.; Pleasonton to St. Marks Collector, December 11, 1848, September 14, November 6, 1850, ibid; Pleasonton to Key West Collector, November 4, December 23, 1851, ibid.

[39]USLHB, *Annual Reports*, 1854-1858; Site Files, Coast Guard Headquarters, Washington, DC; National Archives Site Files; Key West lighthouse engineer to USLHB, February 25, 1857, Lighthouse Letters, RG 26, NA; Light List, 1858.

[40]St. Marks Collector to Martin, August 23, 29, 1861, CSLHB, RG 56, NA; Noyes to George V. Rickard, March 13, 1862, ibid.; Daniel P. Woodbury report, May 12, 1864, ORA, Ser. I, 35:389-90; USLHB, *Annual Report*, 1862; Hurley, *Keepers of Florida Lighthouses*, p. 57.

[41]USLHB, *Annual Reports*, 1894 and 1896; National Archives Site Files.

[42]USLHB, *Annual Report*, 1907.

[43]Lighthouse Keepers and Assistants—Egmont Key, Site Files, Coast Guard Headquarters, Washington, DC; Site Files, U.S. Coast Guard Seventh District, Miami.

[44]Mark F. Boyd, "Fortifications at San Marcos de Apalachie," *Florida Historical Society Quarterly* 15 (July 1936):5.

[45]*Report of Officers Constituting the Light House Board*, in H. Ex. Doc. 55, 32d Cong., 1st sess., 1852; Title Records, Site Files, Coast Guard Headquarters, Washington, DC; National Archives Site Files; USLHB, *Annual Report*, 1885; *Statutes at Large*, 24:224.

[46]USLHB, *Annual Reports*, 1887 and 1888.

[47]U.S. Commerce Department, *Annual Report, 1938*; National Archives Site Files; Title Records, Site Files, Coast Guard Headquarters, Washington, DC.

[48]Augustus Steele to F. H. Gerdes, May 13, 1852, in U.S, Congress, Senate, *Report of the Superintendent of the United States Coast Survey for 1852*, S. Ex. Doc. 58, 32d Cong., 2d sess., 1852, p. 159; Carter, 25:570; ibid, 26:54.

[49]Zachary Taylor to Adjutant General, Headquarters, Army of the South, January 27, 1840, cited in Carter, 26:54; James Alden, May 27, 1850, ibid., 99; Pleasonton to A. Dallas Bache, June 8, 1850, Lighthouse Letters, RG 26, NA.

[50]USLHB, *Laws*; USLHB, *Annual Reports*, 1852 and 1853; Site Files, Coast Guard Headquarters, Washington, DC; Hurley, *Keepers of Florida Lighthouses*, p. 37.

[51]Light List, 1858.

[52]Noyes to Martin, Record of Items Removed From Seahorse [Cedar] Key, August 29, 1861, CSLHB, RG 56, NA; Martin to First Auditor, December 4, 1862, ibid.; William Watson Davis, *The Civil War and Reconstruction in Florida* (New York: Columbia University, 1913), pp. 151-53, 314; National Archives Site Files.

[53]Title Records, Site Files, Coast Guard Headquarters, Washington, DC.

Notes to Chapter 4, West Florida

General historical information on the Florida Panhandle is widely available. This book uses significant material from: Sidney Walter Martin, *Florida during the Territorial Days*; Maxine Turner, *Navy Gray*; and a compiler of primary sources, Clarence Edward Carter, *The Territorial Papers of the United States*, volumes 22-26. Primary sources in the archives of the Pensacola Historical Society contributed to this work.

[1]Charles L. Sullivan, *The Mississippi Gulf Coast* (Northridge, CA: Windsor Publications, 1985), p. 35; Dunbar Rowland, ed., *Official Letter Books of W. C. C. Claiborne*, 6 vols. (Jackson, MS: Mississippi Department of Archives and History, 1917), 5:103.

[2]Peter J. Hamilton, *Colonial Mobile* (Tuscaloosa: University of Alabama, 1976), p. 517; Amy Turner Bushnell, "How to Fight a Pirate: Provincials, Royalists, and the Defense of Minor Ports During the Age of Buccaneers," *Gulf Coast Historical Review* 5, no. 2 (Spring 1990):23; John D. Ware and Robert R. Rea, *George Cault, Surveyor and Cartographer of the Gulf Coast* (Gainesville: University of Florida Press, 1982); Andrew Ellicott, *The Journal of Andrew Ellicott, Late Commissioner on Behalf of the United States, etc.* (Philadelphia: Budd & Hartram, for Thomas Dobson, 1803), p. 239.

[3]Sidney Walter Martin, *Florida during the Territorial Days*, (Athens, GA; University of Georgia Press, 1944), pp. 173-75.

[4]Florida Department of Natural Resources, "San Marcos de Apalache State Historic Site," (Division of Recreation and Parks, n.d.); Bushnell, "How to Fight a Pirate," p. 23; Francois Xavier de Charlevoix, *Journal of a Voyage to North America*, trans. Louise Phelps Kellogg (Chicago: The Caxton Club, 1923), p. 320.

[5]Ware, *George Cault*; Ellicott, *The Journal of Andrew Ellicott*, p. 239; *United States Coast Survey*, S. Ex. Doc. 58, 32d Cong., 2d sess., 1852, pp. 88-90.

[6]Wm. P. DuVal to Joseph M. White, January 10, 1828, cited in Carter, 23:996; White to Levi Woodbury, January 21, 1828, in U.S. Congress, Senate, *Expediency of Deepening Channel, Erecting Light-house, and Establishing Port of Entry, at St. Marks and Removing Obstructions in Apalachicola and Ocilla Rivers in Florida*, S. Doc. 50, 20th Cong., 1st sess., 1828, pp. 1-3; Lighthouse Board, *Laws*; Robert Mitchell to Stephen Pleasonton, October 27, 1828, Lighthouse Site Files, RG 26, NA; Pleasonton to House Commerce Committee, December 19, 1828, Lighthouse Letters, RG 26, NA; U.S. Congress, House, *Light-House Establishment*, H. Rept. 811, 27th Cong., 2d sess., 1842, pp. 31-35; Lighthouse Site Files, RG 26, NA; U.S. Congress, House, *Treasury Statements*, H. Doc. 57, 21st Cong., 1st sess., 1830, pp. 6-7.

[7]U.S. Congress, House, *Letter from the Secretary of the Treasury, transmitting a statement of contracts, &c., made in that department*, H. Doc. 152, 28th Cong., 2d sess., 1845, pp. 8-9; Bonzano to USLHB, October 2, 1866, Lighthouse Letters, RG 26, NA; Pleasonton to Jessie H. Willis, June 2, 1831, ibid.; Lighthouse Site Files, ibid.

[8]Lawrence Rousseau to Woodbury, October 29, 1838, in *Letter from the Secretary of the Treasury*, H. Doc. 24, 25th Cong., 3d sess., pp. 113-15.

[9]Pleasonton to John P. Kennedy, House Commerce Committee, May 13, 1842, in USLHB, *Light House Papers*, p. 314; William H. Ward to Pleasonton, April 30, 1842, in *Light-House Establishment*, H. Rept. 811, 27th Cong., 2d sess., 1842, p. 95; George G. Burns to Bonzano, undated [c. September 1866], Lighthouse Letters, RG 26, NA.

[10]St. Marks Collector to Pleasonton, May 20, 1836, Lighthouse Letters, RG 26, NA; Pleasonton to St. Marks Collector, May 31, 1836, ibid.; Pleasonton to Messrs. Swain and Madden, April 22, 1837, ibid.; Pleasonton to U.S. House of Representatives, March 29, 1844, ibid.

[11]Ware to Pleasonton, September 17, 1843, in U.S. Congress, House, *Report of the Fifth Auditor in Relation to Light-houses*, H. Doc. 38, 28th Cong., 1st sess., 1844, pp. 55-56; *United States Coast Survey*, S. Ex. Doc. 58, 32d Cong., 2d sess., 1852, p. 96; U.S. Congress, House, *Letter From the Secretary of the Treasury transmitting statements relative to public contracts with that department, &c.*, H. Doc. 159, 28th Cong., 1st sess., 1844, pp. 12-13.

[12]USLHB, *Annual Report*, 1854; *United States Coast Survey*, S. Ex. Doc. 58, 32d Cong., 2d sess., 1852, p. 96.

[13]A. B. Noyes to Thomas Martin, March 13, 1862, CSLHB, RG 56, NA; Burns to Bonzano, undated [c. September 1866], Lighthouse Letters, RG 26, NA; Joseph P. Couthouy to Wm. W. McKean, June 7, 1862, ORN, Ser. I, 17:257.

[14]Naval History Division, comp., *Civil War Naval Chronology* (Washington: U.S. Navy Department, 1971), 2:69; Joseph Finegan to S. Cooper, ORA, Ser. I, 14:41; Theodorus Bailey, report, July 30, 1863, in U.S. Navy Department, *Report of the Secretary of the Navy, 1863* (Washington, DC: Government Printing Office, 1863), p. 29; Burns to Bonzano, undated, [c. September 1866], Lighthouse Letters, RG 26, NA; Bonzano to USLHB, October 2, 1866, ibid.

[15]Bonzano to USLHB, October 2, 1866, Lighthouse Letters, RG 26, NA; USLHB to St. Marks Collector, April 16, 1867, ibid.; USLHB, *Annual Report, 1867.*

[16]USLHB, *Annual Reports,* 1872, 1874, and 1883; Light List, 1888.

[17]U.S. Coast Survey, chart, 1858, Records of the Office of the Chief of Engineers, RG 77, NA; Mitchell to Pleasonton, October 27, 1828, Lighthouse Site Files, RG 26, NA.

[18]Willis to Henry D. Hunter, April 24, 1834, Lighthouse Letters, RG 26, NA; Hunter, report, April 30, 1834, ibid.; Pleasonton to Willis, December 22, 1834, ibid.; Merchants, Mariners and others, petition to U.S. Congress, undated [c. April 1834] in Carter, 25:11; Thornton Jenkins to Jackson Morton, March 28, 1855, Lighthouse Letters, RG 26, NA; Hugh Archer to Jenkins, December 3, 1856, ibid.

[19]USLHB, *Annual Reports,* 1857 and 1858; U.S. Treasury Secretary to USLHB, June 4, 1859, Lighthouse Letters, RG 26, NA; Lighthouse Site Files, ibid.; U.S. Coast Survey, chart, 1858, RG 77, NA.

[20]Lighthouse Board, *Laws; Statutes at Large*, April 23, 1830, 4:395, March 2, 1833, 4:664; Lighthouse Site Files, RG 26, NA; Title Records, Site Files, Coast Guard Headquarters, Washington, DC; Pleasonton to Boston Collector, August 7, 1833, Lighthouse Letters, RG 26, NA; Lighthouse Deeds and Contracts, noted in Carter, 24:924; Davis, *Civil War and Reconstruction in Florida*, p. 24.

[21]Merchants, Traders and others, Memorial to Congress, December 9, 1833, in Carter, 24:924.

[22]Masters of Packets Between New York and Apalachicola, petition to Congress, December 1, 1834, in Carter, 25:70; Apalachicola Chamber of Commerce, memorial to Congress, undated [c. December 1842], ibid., 26:584; Pleasonton to Kennedy, January 16, 1843, Lighthouse Letters, RG 26, NA.

[23]Deeds and Contracts, RG 26, NA; Pleasonton to U.S. Congress, December 16, 1847, Lighthouse Letters, ibid.; Pleasonton to U.S. Congress, December 15, 1847, in *Light-House Establishment*, H. Ex. Doc. 27, 30th Cong., 1st sess., 1848, pp. 10-11; Pleasonton to Apalachicola Collector, July 1, 1848, September 12, 1851, Lighthouse Letters, RG 26, NA; Apalachicola Collector to Pleasonton, Jan 2, 1849, ibid.

[24]Deeds and Contracts, RG 26, NA; Pleasonton to U.S. Treasury Secretary, December 11, 1851, Lighthouse Letters, ibid.

[25]Turner, *Navy Gray*, pp. 42-44, 64, 121; N. Baker, receipt, July 6, 1861, CSLHB, RG 56, NA; Baker to Martin, March 12, May 20, 1862, ibid.; George Emmons to McKean, December 18, 1861, *ORN*, Ser. I, 17:7; Bonzano to USLHB, July 24, 1865, May 8, July 19, October 2, 1866, Lighthouse Letters, RG 26, NA; Simeon Russell to Bonzano, July 19, 1866, ibid.; USLHB, *Annual Report*, 1866; Hurley, *Keepers of Florida Lighthouses*, pp. 23, 25; Henry Eagle to Bonzano, July 26, 1866,

Lighthouse Letters, RG 26, NA; USLHB to Bonzano, July 26, November 4, 1866, undated [c. 1866], ibid.

[26]USLHB, *Annual Reports,* 1888 and 1889; Site Files, Coast Guard Headquarters, Washington, DC; Lighthouse Database, National Maritime Initiative, U.S. National Park Service, Washington, DC.

[27]Merchants, Traders and others, memorial to Congress, December 9, 1833, in Carter, 24:924; *Statutes at Large*, July 4, 1836; Edmund M. Blunt and George W. Blunt, *The American Coast Pilot*, (New York, George W. Blunt, 1867); U.S. Congress, Senate, *Report from the Secretary of the Navy, Transmitting, in compliance with a resolution of the Senate, a report of the survey of the coast from Appalachicola Bay to the mouth of the Mississippi River*, S. Rept. 38, 27th Cong., 1st sess., 1841, p. 4.

[28]Lighthouse Board, *Laws*; Deeds and Contracts, RG 26, NA; Pleasonton to Apalachicola Collector, July 23, 1839, Lighthouse Letters, ibid.

[29]Inhabitants of the Territory, petition to Congress, undated [c. January 1844], in Carter, 26:865; Pleasonton to U.S. Treasury Secretary, October 27, 1842, Lighthouse Letters, RG 26, NA; Pleasonton to Winslow Lewis, October 27, 1842, January 30, 1843, ibid.; Pleasonton to New York Collector, November 3, 1842, ibid.; Pleasonton to Apalachicola Collector, November 8, 1842, ibid.

[30]Pleasonton to Lewis, November 10, 16, 1842, Lighthouse Letters, RG 26, NA; Deeds and Contracts, ibid.; Pleasonton to Walter Forward, February 15, 1842, Lighthouse Letters, ibid.; Alexander George Findlay, *Memoir, Descriptive and Explanatory, to Accompany the Charts of the Northern Atlantic Ocean; and Comprising Instructions, General and Particular, for the Navigation of that Sea*, (London: R.L. Laurie, 1845), p. 67; U.S. Treasury, *Estimates of Appropriations*, 1847; Blunt, *The American Coast Pilot, 1847.*

[31]Pleasonton to Apalachicola Collector, September 12, 1851, Lighthouse Letters, RG 26, NA; Deeds and Contracts, ibid.; Light List, 1858.

[32]Baker to George Robinson, July 6, 1861, CSLHB, RG 56, NA; Baker to Martin, November 27, 1861, ibid.; Walter K. Schofield, diary in Turner, *Navy Gray*, pp. 42-44, 121; Bonzano to USLHB, May 8, 1866, Lighthouse Letters, RG 26, NA; Simeon Russel to Bonzano, July 19, 1866, ibid.; Eagle to Bonzano, July 26, 1866, ibid.; USLHB to Bonzano, September 6, 1866, ibid.

[33]Bonzano to USLHB, October 2, 1866, October 5, 1868, Lighthouse Letters, RG 26, NA; USLHB, *Annual Report*, 1868.

[34]USLHB, *Annual Reports,* 1872 and 1873.

[35]Ibid., 1874 and 1875.

[36]House Commerce Committee, report, February 20, 1883, in U.S. Congress, House, *Light-house at Cape San Blas in Florida*, H. Rept. 1973, 47th Cong., 2d sess., 1883, p. 2; USLHB, *Annual Report*, 1888.

[37]Senate Commerce Committee, report, March 15, 1888, in *Report on the Committee of Commerce*, S. Rept. 578, 50th Cong., 1st sess., 1888, pp. 1-2.

[38]USLHB, *Annual Reports*, 1889-1902; Title Records, Site Files, Coast Guard Headquarters, Washington, DC.

[39]Hunter, report, April 23, 1834, Lighthouse Letters, RG 26, NA; Legislative Council of the Florida Territory, resolution, January 11, 1836, in Carter, 25:244; Deeds and Contracts, RG 26, NA.

[40]U.S. State Department, *Register of all Officers and Agents, 1847* ; Light List, 1839; Apalachicola Collector to Pleasonton, Jan 4, 1839, Lighthouse Letters, RG 26, NA.

[41]Pleasonton to Kennedy, December 13, 1842, January 16, 1843, Lighthouse Letters, RG 26, NA; Pleasonton to John C. Spencer, October 30, 1843, ibid.; Lighthouse Board, *Laws*.

[42]Pleasonton to U.S. Congress, December 16, 1847, Lighthouse Letters, RG 26, NA; Deeds and Contracts, ibid.; Site Files, U.S. Coast Guard Eighth District, New Orleans, Louisiana; U.S. Navy Department, *Report of the Secretary of the Navy, 1863*, p. 282.

[43]U.S. Congress, House, *Letter from the Secretary of War in answer to a resolution of the House of the 18th instant, making revised and reduced estimates of appropriations required for harbor and river improvements for the year ending June 30, 1869*, H. Doc. 224, 40th Cong., 2d sess. 1868; *Letters from the Secretary of the Treasury, Transmitting Estimates of Additional Appropriations Required for the Service of the Fiscal Year Ending June 30, 1869, and Previous Years; and also Estimates of Appropriations Required for the Service of the Fiscal Year Ending June 30, 1870*, (Washington, DC: Government Printing Office, 1868); USLHB, *Annual Reports*, 1867, 1888-1898; U.S. Congress, Senate, *Report from the Committee on Commerce*, S. Rept. 1034, 50th Cong., 1st sess., 1888, pp. 1-2; U.S. Congress, House, *Light-House at St. Joseph's Point, Florida, Report from the Committee on Commerce*, H. Rept. 423, 51st Cong., 1st sess, 1890, p. 1.

[44]USLHB, *Annual Reports*, 1899 and 1901.

[45]Ibid., 1902 and 1903; Department of the Interior, *Official Register of the United States, containing a list of the Officers and Employees in the Civil, Military, and Naval Service, together with a List of Vessels Belonging to the United States, July 1, 1903* (Washington, DC: Government Printing Office, 1903), p. 1136.

[46]Site Files, U.S. Coast Guard Eighth District, New Orleans; Title Records, Site Files, Coast Guard Headquarters, Washington, DC.

[47]Hunter, report, April 23, 1834, Lighthouse Letters, RG 26, NA; Legislative Council of the Florida Territory, resolution, January 11, 1836, in Carter, 25:244; Rousseau, report, October 29, 1838, in *Letter from the Secretary of the Treasury*, H. Doc. 24, 25th Cong., 3d sess., pp. 114-15.

[48]Legislative Council of the Territory of Florida, resolution, March 3, 1841, in Carter, 26:586; Apalachicola Chamber of Commerce, memorial to Congress, referred December 28, 1842, ibid., p. 584; Pleasonton to Kennedy, January 16, 1843, Lighthouse Letters, RG 26, NA; Spencer to Commerce Committee, January 10, 1844, in U.S. Congress, House, *Letter from the Secretary of the Treasury, transmitting a report of the Fifth Auditor in relation to the light-houses, &c.*, H. Doc. 62, 28th Cong., 1st sess., 1844, p. 1; Lighthouse Board, *Laws*.

[49]Apalachicola Collector to Pleasonton, May 22, 1847, Lighthouse Site Files, RG 26, NA; Pleasonton to U.S. Congress, December 16, 1847, ibid.; McClintock Young to House of Representatives, March 15, 1848, in *Letter from the Acting Secretary of the Treasury*, H. Ex. Doc. 52, 30th Cong., 1st sess., 1848, p. 7; Deeds and Contracts, RG 26, NA; Pleasonton to Spencer, January 19, 1848, April 3, 1848, Lighthouse Letters, ibid.; Pleasonton to John Davis, Senate Commerce Committee, March 31, 1848, ibid.

[50]Pleasonton to Spencer, June 22, 1848, Lighthouse Letters, RG 26, NA; Light List, 1852.

[51]Pleasonton to Spencer, September 12, 1851, Lighthouse Letters, RG 26, NA; Pleasonton to U.S. Treasury Secretary, December 11, 1851; Lighthouse Board, *Laws*.

[52]Maps and Plans, Cartographic Division, RG 26, NA.

[53]Pensacola *Gazette*, April 21, 1855; USLHB, *Annual Report*, 1855; Hurley, *Keepers of Florida Lighthouses*, p. 25.

[54]USLHB, *Annual Reports*, 1856, 1858, and 1859; U.S. Treasury Department, *Statement of Appropriations and Expenditures For Public Buildings, Rivers and Harbors, Forts, Arsenals, Armories, and Other Public Works, From March 4, 1789 to June 30, 1882* (Washington, DC: Government Printing Office, 1882), p. 363.

[55]Baker to Robinson, July 6, 1861, CSLHB, RG 56, NA; Baker to Martin, November 27, 1861, ibid.; Emmons to McKean, *ORN*, Ser. I, 17:8; G. W. Doty, memorandum, February 5, 1862, ibid., 17:121; Bonzano to USLHB, February 12, May 8, July 19, October 2, 1866, Lighthouse Letters, RG 26, NA; USLHB, *Annual Report*, 1866; Russell to Bonzano, July 19, 1866, Lighthouse Letters, RG 26, NA.

[56]USLHB, *Annual Reports*, 1870, 1878, 1879, and 1882.

[57]Ibid., 1882 and 1883.

[58]Ibid, 1884, 1885, and 1889; Light List, 1888.

[59]USLHB, *Annual Reports*, 1894 and 1895; Lighthouse Site Files, RG 26, NA; Title Records, Site Files, Coast Guard Headquarters, Washington, DC; Maps and Plans, Cartographic Division, RG 26, NA.

[60]USLHB, *Annual Reports*, 1896 and 1898.

[61]Ibid., 1899 and 1900.

[62]Department of Commerce, Lighthouse Service, 1912-1939, *Lighthouse Service Bulletin*, 5 vols. (Washington, DC: Government Printing Office) 1:225, 244, 297, 2:31; 62; Title Records, Site Files, Coast Guard Headquarters, Washington, DC; U.S. Commerce Department, *Annual Reports*, 1918 and 1919; Lighthouse Database, National Park Service.

[63]Pleasonton to Congress, March 12, 1822, Lighthouse Letters, RG 26, NA; Alex[ander] Scott [Sr.], Pensacola Collector, Notices to Mariners, in Pensacola *Floridian*, July 19, 1823, December 13, 1823; Alex[ander] Scott, Jr. to Pleasonton, July 24, 1823, Pensacola Historical Society; Moses Myers to Pleasonton, February 13, 1829, Lighthouse Letters, RG 26, NA; White to U.S. Navy Secretary, November 25, 1825, in Carter, 23:360; Pleasonton to P. A. Wm. Hamilton, November 11, 1824, Lighthouse Letters, RG 26, NA.

[64]U.S. Treasury Department, *Statement of Appropriations and Expenditures*, p. 365; Deeds and Contracts, RG 26, NA; Mayor P. Alba and others, petition to Hamilton, July 1, 1824, National Archives Site Files; Lewis to Pleasonton, December 22, 1835, in *Report from the Secretary of the Treasury*, S. Doc. 138, 25th Cong., 2d sess., 1838, pp. 68-69; Walter McFarland, map drawn June 10, 1861, Pensacola Historical Society; Mills, *The American Pharos*, p. 90; Lighthouse Site Files, RG 26, NA; Pensacola *Gazette*, January 8, 1825.

[65]Hunter, report, April 14, 1834, Lighthouse Letters, RG 26, NA; Rousseau, report, October 29, 1838, in USLHB *Lighthouse Papers*, p. 242; U.S. Lighthouse Board, *Report of Officers Constituting the Light House Board*, H. Ex. Doc. 55, 32d Cong., 1st sess., 1852; U.S. Congress, Senate, *Report of the Secretary of the Treasury on The state of the Finances*, S. Doc. 22, 32d Cong., 2d sess., 1853, p. 97; Jenkins to Congress, February 10, 1853, Lighthouse Letters, RG 26, NA; USLHB, *Annual Report*, 1853.

[66]Light List, 1858; U.S. Treasury Department, *Statement of Appropriations and Expenditures*, p. 365.

[67]Joseph F. Palmes to USLHB, February 1, 1861, Lighthouse Letters, RG 26, NA; A.H. Adams, log entry, April 12, 1861, *ORN*, Ser. I, 4:208; Braxton Bragg to L.P. Walker, April 13, 1861, ibid., 4:135.

[68]Richard H. Jackson to Lewis G. Arnold, November 25, 1861, *ORA*, Ser. I, 6:477; Moore, *Rebellion Record*, 3:91; Bonzano to USLHB, January 30, 1861, Lighthouse Letters, RG 26, NA.

[69]Watson, *The Civil War and Reconstruction in Florida*, p. 165; D. Trenchard to Gideon Welles, May 20, 1862, *ORN*, Ser. I, 18:503-505.

[70]Bonzano to USLHB, October 30, November 1, 1862, July 18, 24, 1865, September 30, October 2, 1866, October 5, 1868, Lighthouse Letters, RG 26, NA; USLHB to Bonzano, July 24, 1865, ibid.; H. H. Bell, diary entry, December 21, 1862, *ORN*, Ser. I, 19:728-734; USLHB, *Annual Report*, 1870; Light List, 1875.

[71]Hurley, *Keepers of Florida Lighthouses*, pp. 77-81; Lighthouse Site Files, RG 26, NA; Pensacola Historical Society.

[72]USLHB, *Annual Reports*, 1874, 1875 and 1878.

[73]Ibid., 1885.

[74]Pensacola *Journal*, February 18, 1978.

Notes to Chapter 5, Mobile Bay (Alabama)

Concise but thorough information on Mobile's bay and rivers is contained in three technical publications of the U.S. Army's Corps of Engineers Mobile District: *Identification and evaluation of Submerged Anomolies, Mobile Harbor* (cited hereafter as *Submerged Anomolies*); *Underwater Archaeological Investigations, Mobile Bay*; and *Cultural Resources Survey of Mobile Harbor* (cited as *Cultural Resources*). Also refer to Peter J. Hamilton, *Colonial Mobile*. Museums and libraries in the city of Mobile and at Fort Morgan also hold a wealth of information.

[1]Hamilton, *Colonial Mobile*, p. 517.

[2]U.S. Army Corps of Engineers, *Identification and Evaluation of Submerged Anomalies, Mobile Harbor, Alabama* (Mobile, AL: Army Corps of Engineers, 1984), p. 26; Lighthouse Board, *Laws*, p. 54.

[3]Pleasonton to Henry Dearborn, June 27, 1820, Lighthouse Letters, RG 26, NA.

[4]Pleasonton to Treasury Secretary, June 19, 1821, ibid.

[5]Ibid.

[6]U.S. Congress, House, *Letter from the Secretary of the Treasury, Transmitting Statements of Payments made at the Treasury during the year 1821*, H. Doc. 48, 17th Cong., 1st sess., 1822; *Light-House Establishment*, H. Rept. 811, 27th Cong., 2d sess., 1842, p. 32.

[7]Pleasonton to Addin Lewis, May 8, 1822, Lighthouse Letters, RG 26, NA; Mobile *Commercial Register*, December 2, 1822; Pleasonton to [unidentified], October 1, 1823, Lighthouse Letters, RG 26, NA; Pleasonton to Addin Lewis, [undated] ibid.; Henry D. Hunter, report, May 1834, ibid.; Pleasonton to Winslow Lewis, April 14, 1835, ibid.

[8]Hunter report, May 1834, Lighthouse Letters, RG 26, NA; Pleasonton to Congress, February 14, 1835, ibid.; U.S. Treasury Department, *Statement of Appropriations and Expenditures*, p. 344; Lighthouse Board, *Laws*, p. 101; Pleasonton to W. Lewis, April 14, 1835, Lighthouse Letters, RG 26, NA; Pleasonton to Thomas S. Belton, May 12, 1835, ibid.; *Light-house Establishment*, S. Doc. 258, 25th Cong., 2d sess., 1837, p. 3.

[9]Except where noted, correspondence related to the Winslow Lewis scandal involving the Mobile Point Lighthouse is collected and in USLHB, *Lighthouse Papers*. Most letters are also found in Lighthouse Letters, RG 26, NA. Edward and G. W. Blunt to Treasury

Secretary, November 30, 1837, *Lighthouse Papers*, p. 100; Pleasonton to Treasury Secretary, January 22, 1838, ibid., p. 110; Blunts to Treasury Secretary, February 22, 1838, ibid., p. 110; Pleasonton to Winslow Lewis, December 15, 1835, ibid., p. 16.

[10]Winslow Lewis to Pleasonton, December 22, 1835, ibid., pp. 16-17; Pleasonton to [unidentified], March 14, 1837, Lighthouse Letters, RG 26, NA; Pleasonton to Winslow Lewis, March 22, 1837, ibid.; Pleasonton to Boston Collector, April 10, 1837, ibid.

[11]Pleasonton to Mobile Collector, December 4, 1838, ibid.; Pleasonton to Secretary of War, April 25, 1839, June 3, 1839, and June 18, 1839, ibid.; Mobile Collector to Pleasonton, April 29, 1839, ibid.

[12]Pleasonton to Winslow Lewis, January 30, February 4, 1850, ibid.; Pleasonton to John Walker, Mobile Collector, February 6, 1850, ibid.; *Report of Officers Constituting the Light House Board*, in U.S. Congress, House, *Cape Vincent Harbor*, H. Ex. Doc. 55, 32d Cong., 2d sess., 1852, pp. 127, 142,; Light List, 1858.

[13]T. Sanford to E.L. Handy, Lighthouse Letters, RG 26, NA; James D. Johnston to Sanford, June 25, 1861, CSLHB, RG 56, NA; Mobile Collector, Pay and Accounts, July 1, 1861, ibid.; J. C. Colsson to Martin, January 5, 1862, ibid.

[14]R.B. Hitchcock to G. V. Fox, February 25, 1863, *ORN*, Ser. I, 19:102; Jenkins to David Farragut, August 5, 1864, ibid., 22:463

[15]USLHB, *Annual Report*, 1864; Bonzano to USLHB, September 30, 1865, Lighthouse Letters, RG 26, NA; U.S. Congress, House, *Letters from the Secretary of the Treasury, tranmitting estimates of Additional appropriations required for the service of the Fiscal Year ending June 30, 1867, and also Estimates of Appropriations Required for the Service of the Fiscal Year ending June 30, 1868*. H. Ex. Doc. 2, 39th Cong., 2d sess., 1866, p. 67.

[16]USLHB, *Annual Reports*, 1872 and 1873; *Mobile Press Register*, July 14, 1991; Light List, 1993.

[17]*Light-house Establishment*, S. Doc. 258, 25th Cong., 2d sess., 1837, p. 3; Winslow Foster, Notice to Mariners in unidentified Mobile newspaper, August 12, 1830, Historic Mobile Preservation Society.

[18]Hunter report, Lighthouse Letters, RG 26, NA; Pleasonton to Winslow Lewis, April 14, 1835, and March 14, 1837, ibid.

[19]Deeds and Contracts, ibid.

[20]Ibid.; *Report of the Commander of USRC Woodbury*, June 23, 1843, Lighthouse Letters, RG 26, NA; Mobile Collector to Pleasonton, April 17, 1838, ibid.

[21]U.S. Congress, Senate, *Report of the Secretary of the Treasury, communicating a report of the Superintendent of the Coast Survey, showing the progress of that work during the year ending November, 1848*, S. Ex. Doc. 1, 30th Cong., 2d sess., 1848, p. 51;

Pleasonton to Walker, September 15, 1849, Lighthouse Letters, RG 26, NA.

[22]Mobile Collector to Provisional Light House Board, October 24, 1851, Lighthouse Letters, RG 26, NA; USLHB, *Annual Report*, 1858.

[23]Johnston to Sanford, June 25, 1861, CSLHB, RG 56, NA; Colsson to Martin, January 5, 1862, ibid.; Bonzano to USLHB, June 28, September 27, 1865, Lighthouse Letters, RG 26, NA; Stephen R. Wise, *Lifeline of the Confederacy* (Columbia: University of South Carolina Press, 1988), p. 83; H. H. Bell, diary, *ORN*, Ser. I, 19:734.

[24]John W. Glen to Danville Leadbetter, February 1 and 24, 1863, Maury Papers, Museum of the City of Mobile, AL.

[25]Farragut to James S. Palmer, July 30, 1864, *ORN*, Ser. I, 21:392; Bonzano to USLHB, August 18 and 26, 1864, Lighthouse Letters, RG 26, NA; Light List, 1865.

[26]*Letters from the Secretary of the Treasury*, H. Ex. Doc. 2, 38th Cong., 2d sess., 1864, p. 67; USLHB, *Annual Report*, 1873; Lighthouse Site Files, RG 26, NA.

[27]USLHB, *Annual Reports*, 1882, 1886, 1888, and 1889; *Statutes at Large*, 25:509.

[28]USLHB, *Annual Reports*, 1892, 1894, 1895, and 1896.

[29]Ibid., 1898, 1899, and 1900; Putnam, *Lighthouses and Lightships*, p. 112; Site Files, Coast Guard Headquarters, Washington, DC; Department of the Interior, *Official Register of the United States, containing a list of the Officers and Employees in the Civil, Military, and Naval Service, July 1, 1905* (Washington, DC: Government Printing Office, 1905), p. 1125.

[30]USLHB, *Annual Report*, 1907; *Annual Report of the Commissioner of Lighthouses to the Secretary of Commerce* (Washington, DC: Government Printing Office, 1914, 1917, 1923).

[31]Light List, 1951.

[32]Tim S. Mistovich and Vernon James Knight, Jr., *Cultural Resources Survey of Mobile Harbor, Alabama* (Mobile: U.S. Army Corps of Engineers, 1983), p. 21; Sullivan, *The Mississippi Gulf Coast*, p. 64; *Light-House Establishment*, H. Rpt. 811, 27th Cong., 2d sess., 1842, p. 32.

[33]Pleasonton to George W. Owen, February 17, 1830, and December 14, 1830, Lighthouse Letters, RG 26, NA; Pleasonton to Winslow Lewis, July 13, 1830, ibid.; Pleasonton to U.S. Treasury Secretary, January 18, 1831, ibid.; Deeds and Contracts, ibid.

[34]Mobile Collector to Provisional Lighthouse Board, October 24, 1851, Lighthouse Letters, ibid; Hunter, report, May 1834, ibid.; U.S. Congress, Senate, *Report of the Superintendent of the Coast Survey showing progress during the year ending November 1849*, S. Ex. Doc. 5, 31st Cong., 1st sess., 1850, pp. 92-93.

[35]*Report of the Superintendent of the Coast Survey*, S. Ex. Doc. 5, 31st Cong., 1st sess., 1850, pp. 92-93; Lighthouse Board, *Laws*, p. 191.

[36]Pleasonton to James Perrine, October 12, 1842, Lighthouse Letters, RG 26, NA; Pay Slips, Mobile District, June 11, 1861, November 11, 1861, and October 1, 1862, CSLHB, RG 56, NA; Receipt for Cartage of Lighthouse Materials, November 3, 1862, ibid.; Lighthouse Board, *Laws*, p. 191; USLHB, *Annual Reports*, 1856, 1860, and 1868; USLHB to 8th District Engineer, August 30, 1860, Lighthouse Letters, RG 26, NA.

[37]Memorandum of G. Forcheimer and P. Helman, [c. January 1864], *ORN*, Ser. I, 18:63; Report of a refugee, June 7, 1862, ibid., 18:544.

[38]Bonzano to USLHB, October 2, 1866, Lighthouse Letters, RG 26, NA.

[39]Lighthouse Site Files, RG 26, NA; Site Files, Coast Guard Headquarters, Washington, DC.

[40]Edward W. Sloan, "The Roots of a Maritime Fortune: E.K. Collins and the New York-Gulf Coast Trade, 1821-1848," *Gulf Coast Historical Review* 5, no. 2 (Spring 1990):119-120; USLHB, *Annual Reports*, 1869 and 1870; V. Sheliha to J. F. Gilmer, *ORN*, Ser. I, 21:563; Light List, 1875.

[41]*Submerged Anomolies*, p. 65; New Orleans *Times Picayne*, October 21, 1893; Lighthouse Site Files, RG 26, NA.

[42]USLHB, *Annual Reports*, 1871, 1872, and 1873.

[43]USLHB, *Annual Report*, 1906.

[44]USLHB, *Annual Reports*, 1879 and 1889; Title Records, Site Files, Coast Guard Headquarters, Washington, DC; *Submerged Anomolies*, p. 28; Light List, 1951.

[45]Mistovich and Knight, *Cultural Resources*, p. 21; U.S. Department of Commerce and Labor, Light-House Board, *Laws Relative to the Light-House Establishment passed at the Third Session of the Fifty-Eighth Congress, 1904-1905* (Washington: Government Printing Office, 1905), p. 22; USLHB, *Annual Reports*, 1883 and 1885.

[46]USLHB, *Annual Report*, 1885.

[47]USLHB, *Annual Report*, 1905; Light List, 1907.

[48]*Mobile Bay Monthly*, December 1988, p. 62; Light List, 1916.

[49]Site Files, Coast Guard Headquarters, Washington, DC; News Release dated September 14, 1981, Alabama Historical Commission; Lighthouse Database, National Park Service.

[50]Sullivan, *The Mississippi Gulf Coast*, p. 64; *Message from the President of the United States*, H. Doc. 7, 21st Cong., 1st sess., pp. 14-15; *Submerged Anomolies*, p. 27; Mistovich and Knight, *Cultural Resources*, p. 19.

[51]Sullivan, *The Mississippi Gulf Coast*, p. 64; USLHB to Bonzano, June 28, 1865, Lighthouse Letters, RG 26, NA.

[52]Jenkins to Bell, January 15, 1864, *ORN*, Ser. I, 21:36; Farragut to Alex. Gibson, February 8, 1864, ibid., p. 91; U.S. Navy Department, *Report of the Secretary of the Navy, 1864* (Washington: Government Printing

Office, 1864), p. 389; Albert J. Myer to Farragut, July 13, 1864, *ORN*, Ser. I, 21:371-72.

[53]Bonzano to USLHB, August 19, 1864, Lighthouse Letters, RG 26, NA; USLHB to Bonzano, December 15, 1864, June 28, 1865, and May 22, 1866, ibid.; USLHB, *Annual Reports*, 1866 and 1873.

[54]USLHB, *Annual Report*, 1873; Maps and Plans, Cartographic Division, RG 26, NA.

Notes to Chapter 6, Mississippi Sound (Mississippi)

Significant material was derived from Charles L. Sullivan, *The Mississippi Gulf Coast* and B.F. French, *Historical Collections of Louisiana and Florida*. The 53,000-page James M. Stevens Collection in the Biloxi Public Library also provided extensive information, as did the archives of the museums of the City of Biloxi.

[1]T. Kane Harnett, *The Golden Coast* (Garden City, NY: Doubleday & Co., 1959), p. 51.

[2]U.S. Treasury Department, *Statement of Appropriations and Expenditures*, p. 421; Pleasonton to Robert Mitchell, July 27, 1829, Lighthouse Letters, RG 26, NA; President Andrew Jackson to Speaker of the House, December 16, 1829, in *Message from the President of the United States*, H. Doc. 7, 21st Cong., 1st sess., 1829, pp. 7-11.

[3]Lighthouse Site Files, RG 26, NA; U.S. State Department, *Register of Officers, 1847*, p. 127; L. M. Powell to Charles Morris, February 5, 1841, in *Report from the Secretary of the Navy*, S. Rept. 38, 27th Cong., 1st sess., 1841, p. 14; Deeds and Contracts, RG 26, NA.

[4]Deeds and Contracts, RG 26, NA; Lighthouse Site Files, ibid.; John W. Bingey to U.S. Treasury Secretary, November 18, 1831, Letters Sent to the Secretary of the Treasury, ibid.

[5]Inspection Report, December 5, 1846, Lighthouse Letters, RG 26, NA; Pleasonton to New Orleans Collector, April 28, 1851, ibid.

[6]USLHB, *Annual Report*, 1855.

[7]Ibid., 1856 and 1860; USLHB to 8th District Engineer, November 15, 1859, Lighthouse Letters, RG 26, NA; Light List, 1858; Sullivan, *The Mississippi Gulf Coast*, p. 73; Frank Heideroff, New Orleans *Times*, June 4, 1871, in M. James Stevens Collection, City of Biloxi, MS, Library.

[8]USLHB, *Annual Reports*, 1860 and 1868; *Harper's Weekly*, May 10, 1862.

[9]Shieldsboro [Bay St. Louis] Customs District Pay Slips, June 30, 1861, CSLHB, RG 56, NA; Bonzano to USLHB, January 30, 1863, Lighthouse Letters, RG 26, NA.

[10]Bonzano to USLHB, June 1, 1863, Lighthouse Letters, RG 26, NA; USLHB, *Annual Reports*, 1868,

1870, and 1872; U.S. Treasury Department, *Statement of Appropriations and Expenditures*, p. 421.

¹¹USLHB, *Annual Report*, 1872; Lighthouse Site Files, RG 26, NA.

¹²USLHB, *Annual Reports*, 1880, 1882, 1900, and 1901; Lighthouse Site Files, RG 26, NA.

¹³U.S. Coast Guard Public Information Division, *The Coast Guard at War* (Washington, DC: Government Printing Office, 1949), vol. 15, *Aids to Navigation*, p.40; Site Files, Coast Guard Headquarters, Washington, DC.

¹⁴Edmund and George W. Blunt, *Blunt's American Coast Pilot*.

¹⁵Light-House Board, *Laws*, p. 132; George Bowditch to Dennis Prieur, May 13, 1847, Maps and Plans, Cartographic Division, RG 26, NA; Pleasonton to Prieur, August 9, 1847, Lighthouse Letters, ibid.; Deeds and Contracts, ibid.

¹⁶Department of the Interior, *Register of Officers*, 1849; Pleasonton to U.S. Treasury Secretary, April 3, 1848, Lighthouse Letters, RG 26, NA; Pleasonton to Prieur, April 21, December 18, 1848, June 6, 1849, ibid.; Prieur to U.S. Treasury Secretary, May 3, 1848, ibid.; New Orleans *Daily Picayune*, August 31, 1852, in Stevens Collection; Light-House Board, *Laws*, p. 181; USLHB, *Annual Reports*, 1853 and 1855; Thornton Jenkins to John Slidell, April 8, 1854, Lighthouse Letters, RG 26, NA; Light List, 1858.

¹⁷Melancton Smith to Wm. Mervine, July 9, 1861, *ORN*, Ser. I, 16:581; Henry French to Mervine, September 13, 1861, in Stevens Collection.

¹⁸W. K. Mayo to H. H. Bell, September 12, 1863, *ORN*, Ser. I, 20:587; Site Files, Coast Guard Headquarters, Washington, DC; Bonzano to USLHB, October 17, 1862, Lighthouse Letters, RG 26, NA; USLHB to Bonzano, November 13, 1862, ibid.; Henry Edler, oath of office, October 3, 1864, in Site Files, Coast Guard Headquarters, Washington, DC.

¹⁹USLHB, *Annual Report*, 1891; New Orleans *Daily Picayune*, October 5, 1893, in Stevens Collection; S. Wike to Speaker of the House, May 15, 1894, in U.S. Congress, House, *Letter from the Acting Secretary of the Treasury recommending an amendment for the sundry civil bill providing for the reestablishment, upon a safer site near-by, of the Chandeleur, La., light station, which was wrecked October 1, 1893*, H. Ex. Doc. 225, 53d Cong., 2d sess., 1894, pp. 1-2.

²⁰*Statutes at Large*, 28:375; USLHB, *Annual Reports*, 1895, 1895, and 1897; Department of the Interior, *Official Register, July 1, 1899*, p. 343.

²¹Malcom F. Willoughby, *Rum War at Sea* (Washington, DC: U.S. Coast Guard, 1964), p. 121.

²²Title Records, Site Files, Coast Guard Headquarters, Washington, DC.

²³U.S. Congress, Senate, *Memorial of The Legislature of Mississippi, Praying a survey of the coast of that State, and the erection of fortifications on the same*, S. Doc. 281, 26th Cong., 1st sess., 1840; James K. Polk to U.S. Senate, December 10, 1845, in U.S.

Congress, Senate, *Message from the President of the United States, in answer to a resolution of the Senate, respecting a fort or forts on Ship Island, on the coast of Mississippi*, S. Doc. 9, 29th Cong., 1st sess., 1845, pp. 1-3.

²⁴Jefferson Davis, quoted in Vicksburg *Sentinel*, July 21, 1846, in Stevens Collection; Light-House Board, *Laws*, pp. 135, 149; Pleasonton to Jefferson Davis, February 13, 1849, Lighthouse Letters, RG 26, NA.

²⁵Pleasonton to W.M. Meredith, December 29, 1849, in USLHB, *Light-House Papers*, p. 535; Pleasonton to John J. McCaughern, June 10, 1850, Lighthouse Letters, RG 26, NA; USLHB to New Orleans Superintendent, Jan 7, 1854, ibid.; Lighthouse Site Files, ibid.; USLHB, *Annual Report*, 1853; Light List, 1858.

²⁶Charles L. Dufour, *The Night the War Was Lost* (Garden City, NY: Doubleday & Company, Inc., 1960), pp. 48-54.

²⁷Smith to William W. McKean, September 20, 1861, *ORN*, Ser. I, 16:677, 678; Greensburg [LA] *Imperial*, October 5, 1861, in Stevens Collection; J. G. Devereaux, report, September 17, 1861, *ORA*, Ser. I, 53:740; Bonzano to USLHB, November 24, 1862, Lighthouse Letters, RG 26, NA.

²⁸J. W. Phelps to Benjamin F. Butler, December 5, 1861, *ORA*, Ser. I, 6:465-468; Bonzano to USLHB, August 30, October 17, December 3, 1862, March 31, 1863, Lighthouse Letters, RG 26, NA.

²⁹USLHB, *Annual Reports*, 1886, 1887, 1901, and 1906; Light List, 1888.

³⁰Department of Commerce, *Lighthouse Service Bulletin*, 5:172; Site Files, Coast Guard Headquarters, Washington, DC.

³¹Rowland, *Official Letter Books of W. C. C. Claiborne*, 5:103; Richard W. Updike, "Winslow Lewis and the Lighthouses," *American Neptune*, 28:253; Light-House Board, *Laws*.

³²Richard Delafield to Charles Gratiot, July 6, 1829, in *Message from the President of the United States*, H. Doc. 7, 21st Cong., 1st sess., 1829; Pleasonton to Mitchell, July 7, 1829, May 6, 1830, Lighthouse Letters, RG 26, NA.

³³Deeds and Contracts, RG 26, NA; Department of the Interior, *Register of Officers*, 1831.

³⁴Bingey to U.S. Treasury Secretary, November 18, 1831, Letters Sent to the Secretary of the Treasury, RG 26, NA.

³⁵Pleasonton to New Orleans Collector, August 22, 1839, Lighthouse Letters, RG 26, NA; Department of the Interior, *Register of Officers*, 1845; U.S. State Department, *Register of Officers*, 1847, p. 127; Department of the Interior, *Register of Officers*, 1873, p. 206; idem, *1875*, p. 218; idem. *1877*, p. 185; Caroline M. Hunt to Z[achary] Taylor, February 25, 1850, Lighthouse Letters, RG 26, NA.

³⁶Site Files, Coast Guard Headquarters, Washington, DC; USLHB to 8th District Engineer [undated, c. 1859], Lighthouse Letters, RG 26, NA;

Holland, *America's Lighthouses*, p. 144; U.S. Treasury Department, *Statement of Appropriations and Expenditures*, p. 422.

[37]Mobile Deputy C.S. Collector to Martin, storage contract, [undated, c. 1861], CSLHB, RG 56, NA; Bonzano to USLHB, January 30, 1863, June 28, September 30, 1865, August 16, October 2, 1866, Lighthouse Letters, RG 26, NA; USLHB to Bonazano, July 5, 1865, August 6, 1866, ibid.; USLHB, *Annual Report*, 1866; Foreman P. Engmann to Bonzano, September 12, 1866, Lighthouse Letters, RG 26, NA.

[38]USLHB, *Annual Reports*, 1878, 1882, and 1883; Maps and Plans, Cartographic Division, RG 56, NA; Lighthouse Site Files, RG 26, NA.

[39]Ibid.

[40]USLHB, *Laws*, p. 93; Pleasonton to U.S. Senate, March 21, 1832, Lighthouse Letters, RG 26, NA.

[41]Pleasonton to Noah Porter, May 5, 1832, Lighthouse Letters, RG 26, NA; Pleasonton to U.S. Treasury Secretary, April 2, 1834, ibid.; Deeds and Contracts, ibid.

[42]"Round Island Blockade and Embargo," New Orleans *Daily Delta*, September 1, 1849, in Stevens Collection; "Second Grand Exploit of the Round Island Blockaders," September 9, 1849, ibid.; V. M. Randolph to "The Persons Encamp'd on Round Island," August 28, 1849, ibid.; Pleasonton to John J. Walker, November 21, 1849, Lighthouse Letters, RG 26, NA.

[43]USLHB, *Annual Reports*, 1854, 1855, 1866, and 1859; *Light List*, 1858; U.S. Treasury Department, *Statement of Appropriations and Expenditures*, p. 423.

[44]J. C. Colsson to Martin, January 5, 1862, CSLHB, RG 56, NA; Bonzano to USLHB, February 17, June 28, September 30, 1865, ibid.

[45]New Orleans *Daily Picayune*, September 19, 1860, in Stevens Collection; Thorwald Hansen, station log, quoted in Ray M. Thompson, "Round Island," *Down South*, March-April 1964, p. 20.

[46]Site Files, Coast Guard Headquarters, Washington, DC; *Light List*, 1947.

[47]Pleasonton to Prieur, August 9, 1847, Lighthouse Letters, RG 26, NA; James M. Stevens, "Traffic Lights of the Sea," unpublished manuscript, October 1974, in Stevens Collection; Pleasonton to Murray and Hazlehurst, January 17, August 9, 1847, Lighthouse Letters, RG 26, NA.

[48]*Minutes of Evidence Taken Before the Select Committee on Lighthouses*, June 16, 1845, xxx, xxxi, Parliament, United Kingdom; Pleasonton to William D. Mosely, April 28, 1847, Lighthouse Letters, RG 26, NA.

[49]Pleasonton to Congress, February 19, 1846, Lighthouse Letters, RG 26, NA; Pleasonton to Prieur, April 16, 1846, ibid.; Pleasonton to John Walker, October 13, 1847, ibid.

[50]Pleasonton to New Orleans Collector, April 4, 1848, ibid.; New Orleans Collector to Pleasonton, May 11, 1848, ibid.; Biloxi *Daily Herald*, February 6, 1933; M. James Stevens, "Biloxi's First Lady Light House

Keeper," *The Journal of Mississippi History*, 36 (February 1974):39-41; Jenkins to W. P. Harris, January 31, 1854, Lighthouse Service Letters to Congress, RG 26, NA; Department of Commerce, *Lighthouse Service Bulletin*, 3:96; New Orleans *Daily Picayune*, October 21, 1893, in Stevens Collection; Mobile Deputy C.S. Collector, Mobile District Pay Slips, June 30, 1861, CSLHB, RG 56, NA; Sullivan, *The Mississippi Gulf Coast*, p. 79.

[51]USLHB, *Annual Report*, 1854.

[52]Sullivan, *The Mississippi Gulf Coast*, p. 79; James Fewell to Frank Hatch, February 5, 1862, CSLHB, RG 56, NA; Bonzano to USLHB, August 30, 1862, Lighthouse Letters, RG 26, NA.

[53]Bonzano to USLHB, October 2, 1866, October 21, 1867, Lighthouse Letters, RG 26, NA; USLHB to Bonzano, November 14, 15, 22, 1866, ibid.; Bonzano, Notice to Mariners, New Orleans *Times*, November 13, 1866.

[54]USLHB, *Annual Report*, 1854.

[55]USLHB, *Annual Report*, 1902, 1907; U.S. Commerce Department, *Annual Report, 1927*; Site Files, Coast Guard Headquarters, Washington, DC.

[56]Sullivan, *The Mississippi Gulf Coast*, p. 35; Rowland, *Official Letter Books of W. C. C. Claiborne*, 5:103.

[57]Engineer Department, report, to Lewis Cass, November 15, 1835, in U.S. Congress, Senate, *Report from the Engineer Department* in *Annual Report of the Secretary of War*, S. Doc. 1, 24th Cong., 1st sess., 1835, p. 109; U.S. Treasury Department, *Statement of Appropriations and Expenditures*, p. 422; Richard Evans to U.S. Treasury Secretary, January 27, 1851, in U.S. Congress, House, *Letter from the Secretary of the Treasury, Transmitting a report respecting light-houses*, H. Ex. Doc. 52, 31st Cong., 2d sess., 1851, p. 5.

[58]U.S. Coast Survey Annual Report, 1853, in U.S. Congress, Senate, *Report of the Superintendent of the United States Coast Survey for 1853*, S. Ex. Doc. 14, 33d Cong., 1st sess., 1853, p. 175; USLHB, *Annual Reports*, 1853 and 1855; Title Records, Site Files, Coast Guard Headquarters, Washington, DC; USLHB Journal, September 5, 1854, Lighthouse Letters, RG 26, NA; U.S. Treasury Department, *Statement of Appropriations and Expenditures*, p. 422.

[59]Bonzano to USLHB, October 2, 1866, August 15, 1868, Lighthouse Letters, RG 26, NA; USLHB, *Annual Report*, 1868.

[60]USLHB, *Annual Report*, 1888; Site Files, Coast Guard Headquarters, Washington, DC; *Statutes at Large*, 25:792; Department of the Interior, *Official Register, 1887*, p. 219; idem, *1891*, p. 239.

[61]Wike to Speaker of the House, January 29, 1894, in U.S. Congress, House, *Letter from the Acting Secretary of the Treasury, transmitting prsonal statements of losses sustained by keepers of light stations and other employés of the Light-House Establishment in the Sixth Light-House District during the cyclones on August 27 and 28, 1893*, H. Ex. Doc. 91, 53d Cong., 2d sess., 1894, pp. 1-3; New Orleans *Times Picayune*, October 21, 1893, in

Stevens Collection; USLHB, *Annual Reports*, 1894 and 1907; Light List, 1907; Site Files, Coast Guard Headquarters, Washington, DC; Title Records, Site Files, Coast Guard Headquarters, Washington, DC.

[62]B. F. French, *Historical Collections of Louisiana and Florida* (New York: J. Sabin and Sons, 1869), p. 43; John J. Walker to Provisional USLHB, October 24, 1851, Lighthouse Letters, RG 26, NA.

[63]USLHB, *Laws*, p. 191; USLHB, *Annual Report*, 1853; U.S. Treasury, *Report on the Finances*, 1856, Lighthouse Letters, RG 26, NA; Bonzano to USLHB, July 28, 1868, ibid.

[64]USLHB, *Annual Report*, 1868; USLHB, *Specifications for metalwork of screw-pile light-houses to replace light-vessels* (Washington, DC: Geo. W. Bowman, Public Printer, 1860, amended 1872).

[65]USLHB, *Annual Report*, 1874; Department of the Interior, *Register of Officers*, 1875; David Farragut to Gideon Welles, August 12, 29, 1864, *ORN*, Ser. I, 16:420; James Alden, log entry, August 25, 1864, ibid., p. 785; James S. Palmer, log entry, August 25, 1864, ibid., p. 803.

[66]USLHB, *Annual Reports*, 1880, 1882, 1883, and 1884; Light List, 1880.

[67]USLHB, *Annual Reports*, 1885 and 1887; Light List, 1888; New Orleans *Times Picayune*, October 21, 1893, in Stevens Collection.

[68]USLHB, *Annual Reports*, 1887, 1889, 1900, and 1901.

[69]Department of the Interior, *Official Register*, 1905,; Putnam, *Lighthouses and Lightships*, p. 113; Site Files, Coast Guard Headquarters, Washington, DC.

[70]*Statutes at Large*, 34:995; USLHB to Congress, January 30, 1907, in Site Files, Coast Guard Headquarters, Washington, DC; USLHB, *Annual Reports*, 1907 and 1908; U.S. Commerce Department, Coast and Geodetic Survey, *United States Coast Pilot, Atlantic Coast, Section E*, (Washington, DC: Government Printing Office, 1916), p. 90.

[71]*United States Coast Pilot*, 1916; Adamson, *Keepers of the Lights*, p. 400; Light List, 1981.

[72]USLHB, *Laws*, p. 131; George Bowditch to Prieur, May 13, 1847, Maps and Plans, Cartographic Division, RG 26, NA; USLHB, *Annual Report*, 1857; USLHB to Walter H. Stevens, September 7, 1859, July 9, 31, 1860, Lighthouse Letters, RG 26, NA; Sullivan, *The Mississippi Gulf Coast*, p. 76; Shieldsboro District Pay Slips, July 30, 1861, CSLHB, RG 56, NA.

[73]Bonzano to USLHB, November 1, 24, December 1, 2, 1862, March 31, May 22, July 30, 1863, July 24, 1866, Lighthouse Letters, RG 26, NA; USLHB to Bonzano, December 15, 1862, ibid.; USLHB, *Annual Reports*, 1863 and 1866.

[74]USLHB, *Annual Reports*, 1880 and 1884.

[75]New Orleans *Daily Picayune*, October 9, 1893, in Stevens Collection; USLHB, *Annual Report*, 1906; Light Lists, 1932, 1933, 1936, 1947, 1981; Site Files, Coast Guard Headquarters, Washington, DC.

[76]Jackson to Speaker of the House, December 16, 1829, in *Message from the President of the United States*, H. Doc. 7, 21st Cong., 1st sess., 1829, p. 15.

[77]USLHB, *Laws*, pp. 108, 131, 191; Lawrence Rousseau to Pleasonton, October 29, 1838, in *Letter from the Secretary of the Treasury*, H. Doc. 24, 25th Cong., 3d sess., p. 114.

[78]Walker to Provisional USLHB, October 24, 1851, Lighthouse Letters, RG 26, NA; USLHB, *Laws*, p. 191; USLHB, *Annual Reports*, 1855 and 1859; U.S. Treasury Department, *Statement of Appropriations and Expenditures*, p. 423; Title Records, Site Files, Coast Guard Headquarters, Washington, DC; Raphael Semmes to R. Eager, December 21, 1860, CSLHB, RG 56, NA; R. Eager to USLHB, January 3, 1861, Lighthouse Letters, RG 26, NA; Shieldsboro District Pay Slips, June 30, 1861, CSLHB, RG 56, NA; Bonzano to USLHB, January 30, 1863, Lighthouse Letters, RG 26, NA.

[79]Bonzano to USLHB, April 12, 1865, Lighthouse Letters, RG 26, NA; USLHB, *Annual Report*, 1867.

[80]Ibid.

[81]USLHB to Bonzano, December 23, 1867, Lighthouse Letters, RG 26, NA; USLHB, *Annual Reports*, 1868 and 1869.

[82]USLHB, *Annual Reports*, 1873, 1878, 1879, 1884, and 1886.

[83]Ibid., 1887-1890.

[84]Light List, 1888; New Orleans *Times Picayune*, October 21, 1893, in Stevens Collection.

[85]USLHB, *Annual Reports*, 1878, 1886, 1887, 1889, and 1890; Lighthouse Site Files, RG 26, NA; Department of the Interior, *Register of Officers*, 1891.

[86]New Orleans *Times Picayune*, October 2, 1893, in Stevens Collection; Bay St. Louis *Sea Coast Echo*, September 25, 1909, ibid.; USLHB, *Annual Reports*, 1908 and 1911; *Statutes at Large*, 35:20.

[87]Site Files, Coast Guard Headquarters, Washington, DC; Lighthouse Site Files, RG 26, NA.

[88]J. D. B. DeBow, *The Commercial Review*, 1 (January 1846):86, 3 (June 1847):360; Work Projects Administration, *Louisiana*, p. 83.

[89]Pleasonton to John Davis, March 31, 1848, Lighthouse Letters, RG 26, NA; USLHB, *Laws*, p. 135; Pleasonton to Prieur, August 22, 1848, July 6, 29, 1850, Lighthouse Letters, RG 26, NA; Danville Leadbetter to USLHB [copy, undated] Lighthouse Site Files, ibid.

[90]Department of State, *Civil Service Register, September 30, 1853*, p. 45; USLHB, *Annual Reports*, 1854 and 1855.

[91]USLHB, *Laws*, p. 135; USLHB, *Annual Reports*, 1856, 1858, and 1860; Light List, 1858; Hatch to Martin, November 22, 1861, CSLHB, RG 56, NA; USLHB Journal, October 1, 1860, Lighthouse Letters, RG 26, NA.

[92]USLHB, *Annual Reports*, 1868, 1870, and 1871; U.S. Treasury Department, *Statement of Appropriations and Expenditures*, 1873, p. 171.

Notes to Chapter 7, Louisiana's Lake Country

Hundreds of general references are available which discuss the early maritime development of this region. Significant material was derived from: B.F. French, *Historical Collections of Louisiana and Florida*; Dunbar Rowland, *Official Letter Books of W.C.C. Claiborne*, vols. 1-6; and W. Adolphe Roberts, *Lake Pontchartrain*. Personal journals include Maj. Amos Stoddard, *Sketches, Historical and Descriptive, of Louisiana*, (1812), and Capt. Philip Pittman, *European Settlements on the Mississippi*, (1770). Snapshots of economic factors affecting early navigation and lighthouses are available in the various issues of J. D. B. Debow's *Commercial Review*, and other Debow publications. One of the best and most accessible repositories of historical data lies in the Historic New Orleans collection in that city.

[1]Pleasonton to William Haile, October 7, 1830, Lighthouse Letters, RG 26, NA; USLHB, *Laws*, p. 93.

[2]Martin Gordon to Treasury Secretary, April 7, 1831, Letters Sent to the Secretary of the Treasury, RG 26, NA; Pleasonton to Gordon, February 23, 1832, Lighthouse Letters, ibid.

[3]Deeds and Contracts, RG 26, NA; R.B. Taney to Speaker of the House, February 21, 1834, in U.S. Congress, House, *Letter from the Secretary of the Treasury*, H. Doc. 124, 23d Cong., 1st sess., 1834, p. 3; Pleasonton to M. Gordon, April 30, December 30, 1833, March 3, 1840, Lighthouse Letters, RG 26, NA; Pleasonton to Denis Prieur, September 21, 1839, ibid.

[4][unsigned] to Pleasonton, December 5, 1846, Lighthouse Letters, RG 26, NA; Pleasonton to Alexander Gordon, August 4, 1842, September 30, 1843, ibid.; Pleasonton to Thomas G. Morgan, May 22, 1843, March 27, April 11, 1844, ibid.; U.S. Congress, House, *Message from the President of the United States, transmitting a report from the Secretary of the Treasury, in compliance with the resolution of the House of Representatives of the 21st ultimo, respecting appointments to office, &c., since 4th April, 1841*, H. Doc. 192, 27th Cong., 2d sess., 1842, p. 15; Department of the Interior, *Register of Officers*, 1843.

[5]Pleasonton to Prieur, September 21, 1839, Lighthouse Letters, RG 26, NA; Light Lists, 1839 and 1858.

[6]Bonzano to USLHB, August 30, September 30, December 1, 1862, Lighthouse Letters, RG 26, NA; USLHB, *Annual Report*, 1866.

[7]USLHB, *Annual Reports*, 1866, 1878, and 1879; USLHB to 8th District Engineer, April 25, 1874, Lighthouse Site Files, RG 26, NA; Department of the Interior, *Register of Officers, 1871*, p. 81; idem, *1875*, pp. 218-19.

[8]Lighthouse Site Files, RG 26, NA.

[9]U.S. Treasury Department, *Statement of Appropriations and Expenditures*, p. 373; John W. Bingey to U.S. Treasury Secretary, August 28, 1832, Letters Sent to the Secretary of the Treasury, RG 26, NA; USLHB, *Laws*, p. 375; USLHB, *Annual Report*, 1856; Light List, 1858.

[10]Frank Hatch to Martin, November 2, 1861, CSLHB, RG 56, NA; William A. Goodwin to USLHB, August 5, 1862, Lighthouse Letters, RG 26, NA; Bonzano to USLHB, November 1, 1862, ibid.; USLHB to Bonzano, February 13, 1863, ibid.; Department of the Interior, *Official Register, 1899*, p. 343.

[11]USLHB, *Annual Reports*, 1869 and 1870; U.S. Commerce Department, *Annual Report*, 1917.

[12]Department of Commerce, *Lighthouse Service Bulletin*, 2:244; Light List, 1945.

[13]French, *Historical Collections of Louisiana and Florida*, p. 45; Holland, *America's Lighthouses*, p. 146; Charles Gayarre, *History of Louisiana, The French Domination* (New York: William J. Widdelton, 1866), pp. 351-53; Ellicott, *The Journal of Andrew Ellicott*, p. 188.

[14]Frank N. Schubert, ed., *The Nation Builders, 1838-1863* (Ft. Belvoir, VA: U.S. Army Corps of Engineers, 1988), p. 9; Deeds and Contracts, RG 26, NA; William C. C. Claiborne to Albert C. Gallatin, November 12, 1808, in Rowland, *Official Letter Books of W. C. C. Claiborne*, 4:248; Gallatin to Thomas Newton, December 20, 1808, RG 26, NA; Gallatin to Thomas H. Williams, May 3, 1810, Letters Sent to the Secretary of the Treasury, ibid.

[15]Williams to Gallatin, August 5, December 11, 1811, Letters Sent to the Secretary of the Treasury, RG 26, NA; Pleasonton to New Orleans Collector, May 16, 1821, Lighthouse Letters, ibid.; Secretary of the Interior, *Register of Officers*, 1821.

[16]Contract, March 18, 1811, Letters Sent to the Secretary of the Treasury, RG 26, NA; Williams to Gallatin, December 11, 1811, ibid.; Bingey to Treasury Secretary, August 28, 1832, ibid.; Lighthouse Site Files, ibid.

[17]Henry C. Castellanos, *New Orleans As It Was* (New Orleans, LA: The L. Graham Co. Ltd., 1895), p. 332.

[18]USLHB, *Laws*, p. 109; Pleasonton to James M. Breedlove, October 7, 1837, January 25, 1838, Lighthouse Letters, RG 26, NA; U.S. House of Representatives, report, in U.S. Congress, House, *Executing Law of Last Session for Building Lighthouses, etc., with List of Sites Approved and Rejected also Number of Light-houses in Each State on 1st January 1833*, H. Doc. 27, 25th Cong., 2d sess., 1838, p. 12.

[19]Levi Woodbury to Speaker of the House, January 10, 1839, in *Letter from the Secretary of the Treasury*, H. Doc. 131, 25th Cong., 3d sess., p. 4; Breedlove to Pleasonton, March 31, 1839, Lighthouse Letters, RG 26, NA; Pleasonton to Woodbury, April 1, 1839, ibid.; Light List, 1839.

[20]Pleasonton to Prieur, January 8, 1840, Lighthouse Letters, RG 26, NA; USLHB, *Annual Reports*, 1853-1856.

[21]USLHB, *Annual Report*, 1860; J. P. Kofts Key, inventory, December 24, 1861, CSLHB, RG 56, NA; Bonzano to USLHB, September 25, 1862, Lighthouse Letters, RG 26, NA.

[22]Lighthouse Site Files, RG 26, NA; Bonzano to USLHB, December 1, 1866, October 5, 1868, Lighthouse Letters, ibid.; USLHB, *Annual Report*, 1869.

[23]"The Joys of Milneburg," *New Orleans Magazine* 1 (May 1981):17; W. Adolphe Roberts, *Lake Pontchartrain* (New York: The Bobbs-Merrill Company, 1946), p. 234; Pontchartrain Rail Road Corporation to Treasury Secretary, August 8, 1835, Letters Sent to the Secretary of the Treasury, RG 26, NA; USLHB, *Laws*, p. 97.

[24]Bingey to Treasury Secretary, October 5, 1836, Letters Sent to the Secretary of the Treasury, RG 26, NA; Breedlove to Treasury Secretary, November 9, 1836, ibid.

[25]U.S. Treasury Department, *Statement of Appropriations and Expenditures*, p. 375; Woodbury to Speaker of the House, January 30, 1839, in *Letter from the Secretary of the Treasury*, H. Doc. 131, 25th Cong., 3d sess., 1839, p. 4; Deeds and Contracts, RG 26, NA; New Orleans Collector to Pleasonton, February 13, 1839, Lighthouse Letters, ibid.

[26]Deeds and Contracts, RG 26, NA; Lighthouse Site Files, ibid.

[27]U.S. Coast Survey Annual Report, 1852, in *United States Coast Survey*, S. Ex. Doc. 58, 32d Cong., 2d sess., pp. 99-100; USLHB Journal, RG 26, NA; USLHB, *Laws*, p. 190.

[28]Maps and Plans, Cartographic Division, RG 26, NA; Lighthouse Site Files, ibid.

[29]Lighthouse Site Files, ibid.; Hatch to Martin, November 22, 1861, CSLHB, RG 56, NA; Goodwin to USLHB, August 5, 1862, Lighthouse Letters, RG 26, NA; Bonzano to USLHB, October 23, 1863, October 31, 1864, ibid.

[30]USLHB, *Annual Report*, 1880; Light List, 1880, 1888; Lighthouse Site Files, RG 26, NA; Department of the Interior, *Official Register*, 1883, p. 231; idem, *1895*, p. 293; idem, 1905, p. 1123; U.S. Commerce Department, *Annual Report*, 1915; Commerce Secretary to Mrs. W. E. Coteron, May 26, 1929, in Lighthouse Site Files, RG 26, NA.

[31]USLHB, *Laws*, p. 109; Breedlove to Pleasonton, September 20, 1837, Maps and Plans, Cartographic Division, RG 26, NA; Woodbury to Speaker of the House, January 30, 1839, in *Letter from the Secretary of the Treasury*, H. Doc. 131, 25th Cong., 3d sess., 1839, p. 4; Deeds and Contracts, RG 26, NA.

[32]U.S. Department of State, *Register of Officers*, 1847, p. 127; Department of the Interior, *Register of Officers*, 1871, p. 81; idem, 1895, p. 293; Pleasonton to New Orleans Collector, June 12, 1850, Lighthouse Letters, RG 26, NA; New Orleans *Item Tribune*, June 26, 1932.

[33]Pleasonton to Morgan, May 22, 1843, Lighthouse Letters, RG 26, NA; USLHB, *Annual Reports*, 1853-1856.

[34]Hatch to Martin, November 22, 1861, CSLHB, RG 56, NA; Bonzano to USLHB, September 29, 1862, Lighthouse Letters, RG 26, NA; USLHB to William A. Waldo, December 15, 1862, ibid.

[35]USLHB, *Annual Report*, 1881; Light List, 1888.

[36]New Orleans *Item Tribune*, June 26, 1932; Department of Commerce, *Lighthouse Service Bulletin*, 1:186.

[37]Department of Commerce, *Lighthouse Service Bulletin*, 3:155; Light List, 1932.

[38]USLHB, *Laws*, p. 97; James M. Breedlove, "Advertisement for Bids, June 10, 1837," July 1, 1837, *The Bee* (New Orleans); Woodbury to President of the Senate, February 21, 1838, in U.S. Congress, Senate, *Report from the Secretary of the Treasury*, S. Doc. 235, 25th Cong., 2d sess., 1838, p. 4; Deeds and Contracts, RG 26, NA; Pleasonton to New Orleans Collector, December 13, 1837, Lighthouse Letters, ibid; Pleasonton to oil contractor, September 21, 1838, ibid.

[39]Light List, 1858; Bonzano to USLHB, October 2, 1866, March 7, June 20, 1867, Lighthouse Letters, RG 26, NA; Lighthouse Site Files, ibid.; Thornton A. Jenkins to David Farragut, August 8, 1864, *ORN*, Ser. I, 21:457.

[40]Work Projects Administration, *Louisiana*, p. 445; *St. Tammany News-Banner*, December 4, 1985; George Bowditch to New Orleans Collector, May 13, 1847, Lighthouse Letters, RG 26, NA.

[41]U.S. Congress, Senate, *Resolution of the General Assembly of Louisiana to obtain an appropriation for the erection of a light-house on the Bayou Bonfouca*, S. Doc. 348, 26th Cong., 1st sess., 1840; U.S. Congress, House, *Resolution of the Legislature of Louisiana, praying for a light-house at Bayou Bonfouca*, H. Doc. 6, 27th Cong., 1st sess., 1841; Pleasonton to Thomas Barrett, September 9, 1844, Lighthouse Letters, RG 26, NA; Pleasonton to Congress, December 13, 1844, ibid.; USLHB, *Laws*, p. 131; *St. Tammany News-Banner*, December 4, 1985.

[42]*St. Tammany News-Banner*, December 4, 1985; Deeds and Contracts, RG 26, NA.

[43]Pleasonton to New Orleans Superintendent of Lights, March 16, April 17, 1848, June 6, 1849, Lighthouse Letters, RG 26, NA; *St. Tammany News-Banner*, December 4, 1985.

[44]Bonzano to USLHB, October 5, 1862, Lighthouse Letters, RG 26, NA.

[45]André Penicaut, quoted in Roberts, *Lake Pontchartrain*, p. 25; Bonzano to USLHB, October 5, 1868, Lighthouse Letters, RG 26, NA.

[46]U.S. Treasury Department, *Statement of Appropriations and Expenditures*, p. 375; USLHB, *Annual Reports*, 1872-1875; Title Records, Site Files, Coast Guard Headquarters, Washington, DC.

[47]USLHB, *Annual Report,* 1872; Light List, 1875.

[48]USLHB, *Annual Reports,* 1888, 1889, 1890, and 1902; U.S. Commerce Department, *Annual Report,* 1917.

[49]Title Records, Site Files, Coast Guard Headquarters, Washington, DC; Site Files, U.S. Coast Guard Eighth District, New Orleans; Lighthouse Site Files, RG 26, NA.

[50]Bureau of Topographical Engineers, *Professional Papers of the Corps of Topographical Engineers, United States Army* (Washington, DC: War Department, 1861), p. 5; Philip Pittman, *The Present State of the European Settlements on the Mississippi* (London: 1770; ed. Frank Heywood Hodder, Cleveland, Ohio: The Arthur H. Clark Company, 1906), pp. 64-65.

[51]U.S. Treasury Department, *Statement of Appropriations and Expenditures,* p. 375; Woodbury to Speaker of the House, January 30, 1839, in *Letter from the Secretary of the Treasury,* H. Doc. 131, 25th Cong., 3d sess., 1839, p. 5; Pleasonton to New Orleans Collector, January 16, 1839, Lighthouse Letters, RG 26, NA.

[52]Pleasonton to Prieur, January 8, 1840, March 31, 1841, July 30, November 7, 1845, Lighthouse Letters, RG 26, NA; Morgan to Pleasonton, August 13, 1843, ibid.; Pleasonton to Morgan, May 22, 1843, ibid.; Deeds and Contracts, ibid.

[53]Lighthouse Site Files, RG 26, NA; Maps and Plans, Cartographic Division, ibid.; Light List, 1848; Pleasonton to Lawrence Garvey, [undated, c. March 1847], Lighthouse Letters, RG 26, NA.

[54]USLHB, *Annual Report,* 1855; Keeper B. Williams to New Orleans Collector, September 28, 1849, Lighthouse Letters, RG 26, NA; U.S. Congress, House, *Letter from the Secretary of the Treasury, communicating statements of the receipts and expenditures of the United States for the year ending June 30, 1858,* H. Ex. Doc. 20, 35th Cong., 2d sess., 1859, p. 36; Light Lists, 1858 and 1865; USLHB, *Annual Report,* 1859; Hatch to Martin, November 22, 1861, CSLHB, RG 56, NA.

[55]Bonzano to USLHB, October 2, December 1, 1866, January 16, October 21, 1867, Lighthouse Letters, RG 26, NA; Lighthouse Site Files, ibid.

[56]Site Files, U.S. Coast Guard Eighth District, New Orleans.

[57]Pittman, *European Settlements on the Mississippi,* pp. 64-67; Rowland, *Official Letter Books of W. C. C. Claiborne,* 2:7; Roberts, *Lake Pontchartrain,* p. 270.

[58]USLHB, *Annual Report,* 1856; U.S. Treasury Department, *Statement of Appropriations and Expenditures,* p. 372.

[59]U.S. Treasury Department, *Statement of Appropriations and Expenditures,* p. 372; USLHB, *Annual Report,* 1880; *Statutes at Large,* 21:263; Site Files, U.S. Coast Guard Eighth District, New Orleans.

Notes to Chapter 8, America's Marine Highway: Delta to Natchez (Louisiana)

[1]Adamson, *Keepers of the Lights,* p. 186; Lighthouse Site Files, RG 26, NA; Leonard V. Huber, *A Pictorial History of Louisiana* (New York: Charles Scribner's Sons, 1975), pp. 48-49; J.D.B. De Bow, *The Industrial Resources, Etc., of the Southern and Western States* (New Orleans: De Bow's Review, 1853), p. 5.

[2]Gayarre, *History of Louisiana,* pp. 30, 121, 358, 518; David Joel Morgan, "The Mississippi River Delta," *Geoscience and Man* 26 (Baton Rouge: Louisiana State University, 1977), p. 66; Lighthouse Site Files, RG 26, NA.

[3]James Alexander Robertson, *Louisiana Under the Rule of Spain, France and the United States 1785-1807,* 2 vols. (Cleveland, Ohio: The Arthur H. Clark Company, 1911), 2:332; John Pintard to Albert Gallatin, September 14, 1803, in Clarence Edwin Carter, ed. and comp., *The Territorial Papers of the United States,* vol. 9, *Territory of New Orleans, 1803-1812* (Washington, DC: Government Printing Office, 1940), 53; Rowland, *Official Letter Books of W. C. C. Claiborne,* 2:42.

[4]USLHB, *Laws,* p. 48; U.S. Army, *Professional Papers,* p. v; Benjamin Henry Boneval Latrobe, *Impressions Respecting New Orleans, Diary and Sketches, 1818-1820,* ed. Samuel Wilson, Jr. (New York: Columbia University Press, 1951), pp. 74, 123, 126.

[5]Weiss, *The Lighthouse Service,* p. 4; Hore Brousa Trist to Gallatin, June 29, 1804, Letters Sent to the Secretary of the Treasury, RG 26, NA.

[6]William Brown to Gallatin, December 24, 1804, January 14, 1805, Letters Sent to the Secretary of the Treasury, RG 26, NA; M. Laffon, plan for *Phare du Mississippi,* 11 Janvier 1805, Maps and Plans, Cartographic Division, ibid.

[7]Gallatin to B. H. B. Latrobe, May 6, 1807, Letters Sent to the Secretary of the Treasury, ibid.; Gallatin to Thomas Newton, House Commerce Committee, January 4, 1810, ibid.; Gallatin, advertisement for bids, May 16, 1807, Deeds and Contracts, ibid.; Latrobe, *Impressions Respecting New Orleans,* pp. xii, xiii, xviii.

[8]Henry S. B. Latrobe, plan for lighthouse, November 7, 1816, Maps and Plans, Cartographic Division, RG 26, NA; Hamlin, *Benjamin Henry Latrobe,* p. 293; Updike, "Winslow Lewis and the Lighthouses," 28:43.

[9]Updike, "Winslow Lewis and the Lighthouses," 28:43; Winslow Lewis to Robert W. Winthrop, May 16, 1842, in *Light-House Establishment,* H. Rept. 811, 27th Cong., 2d sess., 1842, p. 106.

[10]Winslow Lewis to Robert W. Winthrop, May 16, 1842, in *Light-House Establishment,* H. Rept. 811, 27th Cong., 2d sess., 1842, p. 106; USLHB, *Lighthouse Papers,* p. 311; Latrobe, *Impressions Respecting New Orleans,* pp. xxii, 139, 170; Samuel Smith to Beverly Chew, November 10, 1819, Lighthouse Letters, RG 26, NA; Inventory of property at Frank's Island, May 1, 1820,

in Lighthouse Site Files, ibid.; Pleasonton to Lewis, May 20, 1820, Lighthouse Letters, ibid.

[11]Pleasonton to Newton, March 12, 1822, in *Light-House Establishment*, H. Rept. 811, 27th Cong., 2d sess., 1842, p. 94.

[12]Richard Delafield to Charles Gratiot, July 6, 1829, in *Message from the President of the United States*, H. Doc. 7, 21st Cong., 1st sess., 1829, p. 10.

[13]Latrobe, *Impressions Respecting New Orleans*, p. 15; USLHB to Danville Leadbetter, August 3, 1853, Lighthouse Letters, RG 26, NA; Leadbetter to USLHB, May 30, 1854, Lighthouse Site Files, ibid.

[14]USLHB, *Laws*, p. 181; USLHB to Leadbetter, August 3, 1853, Lighthouse Letters, RG 26, NA; USLHB to Congress, March 16, 1854, ibid.; USLHB, *Annual Reports*, 1853-1854; Lighthouse Site Files, RG 26, NA; Bonzano to USLHB, January 19, 1863, Lighthouse Letters, ibid.

[15]Welles, "Extinguishing the Lights," 19:303-304, 307; James Russell Soley, *The Navy in the Civil War*, in *The Blockade and the Cruisers* (New York: Charles Scribner's Sons, 1883), 7:27, 121; Semmes, *Memoirs*, pp. 110-11; Frank Hatch to Martin, November 22, 1861, CSLHB, RG 56, NA.

[16]Semmes, *Memoirs*, p. 111; Thos. F. Wade, receipt for property removed, July 10, 1861, CSLHB, RG 56, NA.

[17]William A. Goodwin to USLHB, August 5, 1862, Lighthouse Letters, RG 26, NA; Bonzano to USLHB, January 3, 16, 19, March 4, 1863, ibid.

[18]Bonzano to USLHB, January 19, April 3, 1863, ibid.; USLHB to Bonzano, July 25, 1863, ibid.

[19]USLHB, *Annual Reports*, 1868 and 1877; Light Lists, 1858, 1865, 1868, 1880; Site Files, Coast Guard Headquarters, Washington, DC.

[20]Light List, 1888; George R. Putnam, *Sentinels of the Coasts: The Log of a Lighthouse Engineer* (New York, W. W. Norton & Company, Inc., 1937), p. 276; USLHB, *Annual Report*, 1902; Light List, 1907.

[21]U.S. Coast Pilot, 1916; Title Records, Site Files, Coast Guard Headquarters, Washington, DC; Lighthouse Site Files, RG 26, NA; Light List, 1951.

[22]Delafield to Gratiot, July 6, 1829, in *Message from the President of the United States*, H. Doc. 7, 21st Cong., 1st sess., 1829, p. 7; USLHB, *Laws*, p. 93.

[23]Maps and Plans, Cartographic Division, RG 26, NA; Pleasonton to Martin Gordon, October 11, 1831, Lighthouse Letters, ibid.; Louis McLane to Speaker of the House, February 9, 1832, in *Letter From the Secretary of the Treasury*, H. Doc. 114, 22d Cong., 1st sess., 1832, p. 4.

[24]Deeds and Contracts, RG 26, NA.

[25]Pleasonton to Treasury Secretary, March 29, 1832, Lighthouse Letters, RG 26, NA; Pleasonton to Gordon, April 16, November 17, 1832, ibid.; Pleasonton to Boston Collector, July 23, 1832, ibid.; B. Willis to William Breedlove, October 21, 1837, ibid.

[26]Denis Prieur to Pleasonton, December 18, 1839, ibid.; Pleasonton to Prieur, January 8, August 17, 1840, ibid.; Thomas Gibbs Morgan to Pleasonton, January 26, 1842, ibid.; Winslow Lewis to Winthrop, May 16, 1842, in *Light-House Establishment*, H. Rept. 811, 27th Cong., 2d sess., 1842, p. 107.

[27]Pleasonton to Winthrop, May 13, 1842, in *Light-House Establishment*, H. Rept. 811, 27th Cong., 2d sess., 1842, p. 107; Deeds and Contracts, RG 26, NA; Pleasonton to Prieur, March 31, 1846, Lighthouse Letters, ibid.; Jos. E. Bell to New Orleans Collector, September 10, December 26, 1846, November 15, 1847, ibid.

[28]USLHB, *Annual Report*, 1857; Welles, "Extinguishing the Lights," p. 301.

[29]Welles, "Extinguishing the Lights," p. 304.

[30]Hatch to Martin, November 22, 1861, CSLHB, RG 56, NA; Goodwin to USLHB, August 5, 1862, Lighthouse Letters, RG 26, NA; Bonzano to USLHB, August 30, September 4, 22, 1862, ibid.; USLHB, *Annual Reports*, 1867 and 1869.

[31]USLHB, *Annual Report*, 1878; *Statutes at Large*, 20:56, 214, 381; Light List, 1880.

[32]USLHB, *Annual Reports*, 1882 and 1890; Light List, 1888; *Statutes at Large*, 25:444.

[33]Light List, 1951; Site Files, Coast Guard Headquarters, Washington, DC.

[34]Department of Commerce, *Lighthouse Service Bulletin*, 1:278-79, 3:23; Light List, 1932.

[35]Deeds and Contracts, RG 26, NA; Delafield to Gratiot, July 6, 1829, in *Message from the President of the United States*, H. Doc. 7, 21st Cong., 1st sess., 1829, p. 7; Pleasonton to Treasury Secretary, March 29, 1832, Lighthouse Letters, RG 26, NA; Pleasonton to Gordon, April 16, 1832, ibid.; Henry D. Hunter, report, April 1834, ibid.

[36]Henry D. Hunter, report, April 1834, Lighthouse Letters, RG 26, NA; Pleasonton to Gordon, November 17, 1832, ibid.; W. Knight to Pleasonton, November 12, 1834, ibid.

[37]Pleasonton to Breedlove, April 19, 1837, ibid.; Breedlove to Pleasonton, May 31, 1837, ibid.; Willis to Breedlove, October 21, 1837, ibid.

[38]Pleasonton, advertisement for bids, August 7, 1838, Lighthouse Site Files, RG 26, NA.

[39]Deeds and Contracts, RG 26, NA; Pleasonton to Boston Collector, September 1, 1838, Lighthouse Letters, ibid.; Pleasonton to I. W. P. Lewis, January 30, March 9, May 13, 1839, ibid.; Pleasonton to Hammond & Dexter, February 11, 1839, ibid.

[40]Report of the commander, *USRC Woodbury*, May 30, 1843, Lighthouse Letters, RG 26, NA; Lighthouse Site Files, ibid.; George M. Bowditch, report, February 8, 1850, ibid.

[41]USLHB, *Report of Officers Constituting the Light House Board* in *Light House Establishment*, H. Ex. Doc. 55, 32d Cong., 1st sess., 1852; U.S. Treasury

Department, *Statement of Appropriations and Expenditures,* p. 377.

[42]Manuel Mareno to Hatch, February 6, March 31, June 22, 1861, quoted in Welles, "Extinguishing the Lights," pp. 299-305; David D. Porter to William Mervine, July 4, 1861, *ORN,* Ser. I, 16:573.

[43]USLHB to Bonzano, September 15, 1862, Lighthouse Letters, RG 26, NA; Bonzano to USLHB, September 29, 1862, July 30, 1863, ibid.; Moreno to Hatch, February 6, 1861, quoted in Welles, "Extinguishing the Lights," p. 299.

[44]Bonzano to USLHB, July 16, 30, 1863, Lighthouse Letters, RG 26, NA; Light List, 1865; USLHB, *Annual Report,* 1866; U.S. Treasury Department, *Statement of Appropriations and Expenditures,* p. 377; U.S. Congress, House, *Letter from the Secretary of the Treasury, Transmitting Estimates of Appropriations required for the Service of the Fiscal Year Ending June 30, 1871,* H. Ex. Doc. 5, 41st Cong., 2d sess., 1869, p. 195.

[45]USLHB, *Annual Reports,* 1870, 1871, 1873 and 1874; David Porter Heap, *Ancient and Modern Lighthouses* (Boston: Ticknor & Company, 1889), pp. 161-63.

[46]USLHB, *Annual Reports,* 1894 and 1895.

[47]U.S. Commerce Department, *Annual Report,* 1928; Light Lists, 1953 and 1954; Site Files, Coast Guard Headquarters, Washington, DC.

[48]Secretary of the Interior, *Register of Officers,* 1837; Pleasonton to Senate Commerce Committee, September 20, 1850, Lighthouse Letters, RG 26, NA; USLHB, *Laws,* p. 50; Richard Evans to Pleasonton, January 27, 1851, Lighthouse Letters, RG 26, NA.

[49]*New Orleans Daily Crescent,* advertisement for bids, April 5, 1851.

[50]Pleasonton to William Freret, April 26, May 22, 1851, Lighthouse Letters, RG 26, NA; Pleasonton to John J. McCaughan, May 24, 1851, ibid.

[51]USLHB, *Laws,* p. 181; Light List, 1854; Bonzano to USLHB, October 30, 1862, Lighthouse Letters, RG 26, NA.

[52]James Fisher to Hatch, June 20, 1861, quoted in Welles, "Extinguishing the Lights," p. 304; Chart of Head of Passes, c. 1857, *ORN,* Ser. I, 16:637.

[53]Bonzano to USLHB, Jan 15, March 31, 1863, February 5, 1864, Lighthouse Letters, RG 26, NA; H. H. Bell to Bonzano, September 14, 1863, *ORN,* Ser. I, 20:587; USLHB, *Annual Reports,* 1866-1868, 1872, and 1874; New Orleans Collector to Bonzano, September 24, 1866, Letters Received by 8th and 9th District Engineers, RG 26, NA.

[54]Lighthouse Site Files, RG 26, NA; USLHB, *Annual Reports,* 1888 and 1890.

[55]Pleasonton to Andrew Marshcaulk, June 12, 1826, Lighthouse Letters, RG 26, NA; Pleasonton to Gideon Tomlinson, House Commerce Committee, December 20, 1826, ibid.; Pleasonton to Senate Commerce Committee, February 2, 1827, ibid.

[56]Pleasonton to Marschaulk, March 23, 1827, ibid; Marschaulk, contract, signed May 22, 1827, ibid.; Pleasonton to Treasury Secretary, November 22, 1827, ibid.; Pleasonton to Boston Collector, April 26, May 26, 1828, ibid.; Pleasonton to John Quincy Adams, May 22, 1828, ibid.; Deeds and Contracts, RG 26, NA.

[57]Quote of Joseph Holt Ingraham, as cited in Eaton, *A History of the Old South.*

[58]Pleasonton to Natchez Superintendent of Lights, May 10, 11, June 13, 1836, Lighthouse Letters, RG 26, NA; Pleasonton to Treasury Secretary, January 8, 1838, ibid.

[59]Pleasonton to William Gannt, June 21, 1841, ibid.; *Principal Marine Disasters Since 1831,* (U.S. Coast Guard, Washington, DC, n.d.)

Notes to Chapter 9, Bayou Country (Louisiana and Texas)

[1]Robert C. Vogel, "John Lafitte, the Baratarians, and the Historical Biography of Piracy in the Gulf of Mexico," *Gulf Coast Historical Review* 5, no. 2 (Spring 1990):64.

[2]*Report of the Superintendent of the United States Coast Survey,* S. Ex. Doc. 14, 33d Cong., 1st sess., 1853, pp. 51-52; Roberts, *Lake Pontchartrain,* pp. 116-19.

[3]Work Projects Administration, *Louisiana,* pp. 419-20; J.D.B. De Bow, *The Commercial Review* 3 (June 1847):310.

[4]USLHB Letters to 9th District Inspector, August 12, 1856, RG 26, NA; *Report of the Superintendent of the United States Coast Survey for 1853,* S. Ex. Doc. 14, 33d Cong., 1st sess., 1853, p. 52.

[5]U.S. Treasury Department, *Statement of Appropriations and Expenditures,* p. 373; USLHB Letters to 9th District Inspector, December 31, 1856, March 19, September 29, 1857, RG 26, NA; Department of the Interior, *Register of Officers,* 1857.

[6]Light List, 1858; USLHB Journal, September 15, 1859, RG 26, NA.

[7]Lighthouse Clerk to Secretary of Treasury, RG 26, NA; USLHB, *Annual Report,* 1864; Lighthouse Letters, RG 26, NA; Letters to Superintendents, January 3, 1865, ibid.; Light List, 1865.

[8]USLHB, *Annual Report,* 1894; Updike, *Winslow Lewis and the Lighthouses,* pp. 368-69; Adamson, *Keepers of the Lights,* p. 401; USLHB, *Annual Report,* 1897.

[9]Light List, 1947.

[10]*Report of the Superintendent of the United States Coast Survey,* S. Ex. Doc. 14, 33d Cong., 1st sess., 1853, pp. 52-53.

[11]USLHB, *Laws,* p. 191; U.S. Treasury Department, *Statement of Appropriations and Expenditures,* p. 378; Secretary of the Interior, *Register of Officers,* 1857.

[12]USLHB, *Annual Report,* 1935; Snow, *Famous Lighthouses,* p. 220; Light List, 1951.

[13]USLHB, *Annual Report,* 1864; Letters Sent to USLHB 8th and 9th District Engineers, New Orleans, June 27, July 18, 1865, RG 26, NA; Letters Sent to Superintendents, September 20, 1865, ibid.

[14]Miscellaneous Letters Received by 8th and 9th District Engineers, July 12, 1866, RG 26, NA; Holland, *America's Lighthouses,* p. 147; Snow, *Famous Lighthouses,* p. 220.

[15]USLHB, *Annual Report,* 1867; Letters sent to USLHB by 8th and 9th District Engineers, New Orleans, October 21, 1867, RG 26, NA; Holland, *America's Lighthouses,* p. 148.

[16]Letter from the Secretary of War, *Estimate of Appropriations, 1869,* H. Doc. 224, 40th Cong., 2d sess., 1868, p. 59; U.S. Treasury Department, *Statement of Appropriations and Expenditures,* p. 378; USLHB, *Annual Report,* 1869; Act of March 3, 1871, contained in a compilation of laws relative to the Light-house Establishment, Coast Guard Historian's Office; USLHB, *Annual Reports,* 1871 and 1875.

[17]USLHB, *Annual Report,* 1881.

[18]USLHB, *Annual Report,* 1894; Coast Guard Data Sheet on Timbalier, Site Files, Coast Guard Headquarters, Washington, DC; List Lists, 1901, 1903; U.S. Commerce Department, *Annual Report,* 1917; National Archives Site Files.

[19]National Archives Site Files; U.S. Commerce Department, *Annual Report,* 1917; Department of Commerce, *Lighthouse Service Bulletin,* 3:155; USLHB, *Annual Reports,* 1927 and 1928; Department of Commerce, *Lighthouse Service Bulletin,* 4:81.

[20]Work Projects Administration, *Louisiana,* p. 699.

[21]USLHB, *Annual Report,* 1856.

[22]U.S. Congress, Senate, *Resolution of the Legislature of Louisiana, in favor of the erection of light-houses at the mouth of the Sabine, and on the west end of Last Island,* S. Misc. Doc. 134, 30th Cong., 1st sess., 1848; USLHB, *Report of Officers,* p. 128; USLHB, *Annual Report,* 1852.

[23]USLHB, *Annual Report,* 1852

[24]USLHB, *Laws; Report of the Superintendent of the United States Coast Survey for 1853,* S. Ex. Doc. 14, 33d Cong., 1st sess., 1853, p. 176; U.S. Treasury Department, *Statement of Appropriations and Expenditures,* p. 377.

[25]USLHB Letters to 9th District, January 13, 1858, September 27, 1858, RG 26, NA; Light List, 1858.

[26]C.S. Treasury Letters, RG 365, NA; USLHB Letters Sent by 8th and 9th District Engineers, January 30, 1863, RG 26, NA.

[27]Lighthouse Letters, RG 26, NA; USLHB, *Annual Report,* 1864; Department of the Interior, *Register of Officers, 1865,* p. 79.

[28]Letters Sent to USLHB by 8th and 9th District Engineers, October 1, 1866, RG 26, NA; USLHB, *Annual Report,* 1867; Light List, 1868.

[29]USLHB, *Annual Report,* 1866; Coast Guard Data Sheet on Ship Shoal, Site Files, Coast Guard Headquarters, Washington, DC; USLHB, *Annual Report,* 1870.

[30]USLHB, *Annual Report,* 1874; Coast Guard Data Sheet on Ship Shoal, Coast Guard Historian's Office, Washington, DC.

[31]Lighthouse Contracts, RG 26, NA; Site Files, Coast Guard Headquarters, Washington, DC; National Archives Site Files.

[32]U.S. Congress, House, *Letter from the Secretary of Treasury, transmitting a report of the expenditures of the light-house establishments, &c.,* H. Doc. 140, 27th Cong., 2d sess., 1842, p. 92; Blunt, *The American Coast Pilot,* p. 408.

[33]U.S. Congress, *American State Papers: Commerce and Navigation* 7:839.

[34]Ibid.; USLHB, *Laws,* p. 70.

[35]Ibid.

[36]Ibid.; Lighthouse Letters, May 1, August 9, 1826, RG 26, NA; U.S. Treasury Department, *Statement of Appropriations and Expenditures,* p. 377; U.S. Congress, House, *Letter from the Secretary of the Treasury,* H. Doc 101, 19th Cong., 2d sess., 1927; Lighthouse Contracts, RG 26, NA.

[37]Lighthouse Letters, September 19, September 20, 1826, RG 26, NA; *Letter from the Secretary of the Treasury,* H. Doc 101, 19th Cong., 2d sess., 1927; Site Files, Coast Guard Headquarters, Washington, DC.

[38]Light List 1842 in *Letter from the Secretary of Treasury,* H. Doc. 140, 27th Cong., 2d sess., 1842, p. 49; Mills, *The American Pharos,* p. 95; U.S. Congress, Senate, *Report from the Secretary of the Treasury, in relation to the erection of light-houses, &c., in compliance with the 2d section of the act of March 3, 1837, "making appropriations for building light houses, light-boats, beacon-lights, bouys, and dolphins",* S. Doc. 15, 25th Cong., 2d sess., 1837, p. 24; U.S. Congress, Senate, *Message from the President of the United States to the Two Houses of Congress, at the Commencement of the Third Session of the Twenty-Seventh Congress,* S. Doc. 1, 27th Cong., 3d sess., 1842, p. 300.

[39]Lighthouse Letters, RG 26, NA.

[40]Willard Flint, *Lightships and Lightship Stations of the U.S. Government* (Washington, DC: U.S. Coast Guard, 1989), index 89.

[41]USLHB, *Annual Reports,* 1855 and 1857; Letters to 9th District Inspector, January 4, 1856, RG 26, NA; Light List, 1855.

[42]USLHB, *Annual Report,* 1864.

[43]Site Files, Coast Guard Headquarters, Washington, DC; USLHB, *Annual Report,* 1864; Site Files, U.S. Coast Guard Eighth District, New Orleans.

[44]U.S. Treasury Department, *Statement of Appropriations and Expenditures,* p. 377; USLHB Letters to 9th District Inspectors, August 8, 1859, RG 26, NA.

[45]USLHB Letters to 9th District Inspectors, February 6, 1858, RG 26, NA.

[46]Ibid., July 24, 1858; USLHB, *Annual Report,* 1859.

[47]Ezra Leonard to H. K. Thatcher, June 21, 1865, *ORN,* Ser. I, 22:232; Letters Sent to USLHB by 8th and 9th District Engineers, New Orleans, RG 26, NA.

[48]USLHB, *Annual Report,* 1867.

[49]Ibid., 1867 and 1868.

[50]Ibid., 1872 and 1875; U.S. Treasury Department, *Statement of Appropriations and Expenditures,* p. 377.

[51]U.S. Commerce Department, *Annual Report,* 1916.

[52]*Statutes at Large,* 30:1,017; Department of Commerce, *Lighthouse Service Bulletin,* 1:4; U.S. Coast Pilot, 1916.

[53]Site Files, Coast Guard Headquarters, Washington, DC; National Maritime Initiative files, National Park Service, Washington, DC.

[54]Pleasonton to Breedlove, September 16, 1837, Lighthouse Letters, RG 26, NA; USLHB, *Laws,* 1835, p. 108.

[55]Pleasonton to Boston Collector, June 27, 1839, Lighthouse Letters, RG 26, NA; Pleasonton to Thomas G. Morgan, August 6, 1841, ibid.; *Letter from the Secretary of Treasury,* H. Doc. 140, 27th Cong., 2d sess., 1842, p. 92; U.S. Department of State, *Register of Officers,* 1841; *Message from the President of the United States,* H. Doc. 192, 27th Cong., 2d sess., 1842, p. 15; *Report of the Secretary of the Treasury,* S. Ex. Doc. 31, 31st Cong., 1st sess., 1850, p. 4; National Archives Site Files.

[56]Benjamin F. Sands, January 15, 1855, in U.S. Congress, Senate, *Report of the Superintendent of the Coast Survey, Showing the Progress of the Survey during the Year 1855,* S. Ex. Doc. 22, 34th Cong., 1st sess. 1856, p. 413; USLHB Letters to 9th District Inspector, April 7, 1855, RG 26, NA; USLHB, *Annual Report,* 1855.

[57]USLHB, *Annual Report,* 1855; USLHB, *Laws,* p. 191; Letters from USLHB to 9th District Inspector, September 15, 1856, RG 26, NA.

[58]USLHB Journal, RG 26, NA; Lighthouse Contracts, ibid.; USLHB, *Annual Report,* 1859; Light List, 1865.

[59]Letters Sent to USLHB by 8th and 9th District Engineers, New Orleans, July 18, 1865, RG 26, NA; Ezra Leonard to H. K. Thatcher, June 21, 1865, *ORN,* Ser. I, 22:232; USLHB, *Annual Report,* 1865.

[60]Letters Sent to USLHB by 8th and 9th District Engineers, New Orleans, October 12, 30, 1867, RG 26, NA.

[61]U.S. Treasury Department, *Statement of Appropriations and Expenditures,* p. 376.

[62]Holland, *America's Lighthouses,* p. 148; USLHB, *Annual Reports,* 1870 and 1972.

[63]Act of March 3, 1871, contained in a compilation of laws relative to the Light-house Establishment, Coast Guard Historian's Office; U.S., Congress, House, *Letter from the Secretary of the Treasury, Transmitting Estimates of Appropriations required for the Service of the Fiscal Year Ending June 30, 1873,* H. Ex. Doc. 5, 42d Cong., 2d sess., 1871, p. 177; U.S. Treasury Department, *Statement of Appropriations and Expenditures,* p. 378; USLHB, *Annual Report,* 1873.

[64]USLHB, *Annual Reports,* 1874 and 1875.

[65]USLHB, *Annual Reports,* 1875 and 1876; *Statutes at Large,* 20:380; U.S. Treasury Department, *Statement of Appropriations and Expenditures,* p. 378.

[66]USLHB, *Annual Reports,* 1894 and 1904.

[67]Ibid., 1903.

[68]Ibid., 1904; Department of the Interior, *Register of Officers,* 1905, p. 1124.

[69]Light List, 1947.

[70]USLHB, *Annual Report,* 1853.

[71]*Resolution of the Legislature of Louisiana,* S. Misc. Doc. 134, 30th Cong., 1st sess., 1848; USLHB, *Laws,* p. 144; U.S. Lighthouse Establishment, *Lighthouse Papers,* p. 539.

[72]USLHB, *Report of Officers,* pp. 130-31; *Report of the Secretary of the Treasury on the state of the finances,* S. Doc. 22, 32d Cong. 2d sess., 1853, p. 97; *Report of the Superintendent of the United States Coast Survey for 1853,* S. Ex. Doc. 14, 33d Cong., 1st sess., 1853, p. 177.

[73]*Report of the Superintendent of the United States Coast Survey for 1853,* S. Ex. Doc. 14, 33d Cong., 1st sess., 1853, p. 177.

[74]U.S. Coast Guard, *Sabine Pass Light Station History Sheet* (Washington, DC), n.d.; USLHB Letter to 9th District Inspector, February 20, 1855, RG 26, NA.

[75]C.S. Treasury Letters, RG 365, NA.

[76]A. Read to Gideon Welles, April 10, 1863, *ORN,* Ser. I, 20:128, 147-52; Letters Sent to the USLHB by 8th and 9th District Engineers, New Orleans, September 30, 1865, RG 26, NA; USLHB, *Annual Report,* 1866.

[77]USLHB, *Annual Report,* 1886; Department of Commerce, *Lighthouse Service Bulletin,* 1:181-82; T. Lindsay Baker, *Lighthouses of Texas* (College Station, Texas: Texas A&M University Press, 1991), p. 75.

[78]Maury Darst, "Texas Lighthouses: The Early Years, 1850-1900," *Southwestern Historical Quarterly* 79, no. 3 (1976):316; Baker, *Lighthouses of Texas,* p. 82; Title Records, Site Files, Coast Guard Headquarters, Washington, DC; Baker, *Lighthouses of Texas,* p. 78; National Maritime Initiative lighthouse files, National Park Service, Washington, DC.

[79]USLHB, *Annual Reports,* 1898 and 1899.

[80]Baker, *Lighthouses of Texas,* p. 82.

[81]USLHB, *Annual Reports,* 1904 and 1905; Baker, *Lighthouses of Texas,* p. 82.

[82]Light Lists, 1907, 1916, and 1919.

[83]Department of Commerce, *Lighthouse Service Bulletin* 1:181-82.

[84]U.S. Commerce Department, *Annual Report,* 1923.

[85]Kelsie B. Harder, *Illustrated Dictionary of Place Names* (New York: Van Nostrand Reinhold, 1976), p. 74; USLHB, *Annual Report,* 1855; USLHB, *Laws,* p. 192; *Report of the Superintendent of the Coast Survey,* S. Ex. Doc. 22, 34th Cong., 1st sess., 1856, p. 414; U.S. Treasury Department, *Statement of Appropriations and Expenditures,* p. 373.

[86]U.S. Treasury Department, *Statement of Appropriations and Expenditures,* p. 373.

[87]Act of March 3, 1871, contained in a compilation of laws relative to the Light-house Establishment, Coast Guard Historian's Office; USLHB, *Annual Reports,* 1870 and 1872.

[88]USLHB, *Annual Report,* 1873.

[89]Ibid, 1874; U.S. Treasury Department, *Statement of Appropriations and Expenditures,* p. 374; Department of the Interior, *Register of Officers,* 1877, p. 186.

[90]USLHB, *Annual Report,* 1887; Department of Commerce, *Lighthouse Service Bulletin* 1:181, 2:97.

[91]Department of Commerce, *Lighthouse Service Bulletin* 2:237.

Notes to Chapter 10, Galveston Bay (Texas)

[1]Elinor DeWire, "The Guardian Eyes of Texas," *Texas Weekly Magazine* (October 13, 1984):4; Baker, *Lighthouses of Texas,* p. 57; USLHB, *Laws,* p. 132.

[2]*Light-house Establishment,* House Ex. Doc. 27, 30th Cong., 1st sess., 1848, p. 132.

[3]Bolivar Point Lighthouse File, Coast Guard Historian's Office; Title Records, Site Files, Coast Guard Headquarters, Washington, DC.

[4]Pleasonton to Bell, October 23, 1851, Lighthouse Letters, RG 26, NA; U.S. Treasury Department, *Statement of Appropriations and Expenditures,* p. 469; U.S. Lighthouse Establishment, *Lighthouse Papers,* p. 540.

[5]USLHB, *Report of Officers,* pp. 128, 130-31; Flint, *Lightships and Lightship Stations,* Index 92.

[6]U.S. Congress, House, *List of Light House Contracts,* H. Ex. Doc. 43, 32d Cong., 1st sess., 1852.

[7]National Archives clips, RG 26, NA; *Report of the Secretary of the Treasury on the state of the finances,* S. Doc. 22, 32d Cong., 2d sess., 1853; USLHB, *Annual Reports,* 1852 and 1858.

[8]*Report of the Superintendent of the United States Coast Survey for 1853,* S. Ex. Doc. 14, 33d Cong., 1st sess., 1853, p. 177.

[9]USLHB, *Annual Reports,* 1857 and 1858; Baker, *Lighthouses of Texas,* p. 59.

[10]Holland, *America's Lighthouses,* pp. 149-50; Letters to USLHB by 8th and 9th District Engineers, New Orleans, RG 26, NA.

[11]Hamilton Cochran, *Blockade Runners of the Confederacy* (New York: Bobbs-Merrill Co., Inc., 1905), p. 21; Holland, *America's Lighthouses.*

[12]USLHB Letters, July 7, 1865, RG 26, NA; Baker, *Lighthouses of Texas,* p. 59; Light List, 1968; USLHB, *Annual Reports,* 1869 and 1870; U.S. Treasury Department, *Statement of Appropriations and Expenditures,* p. 469.

[13]USLHB, *Annual Reports,* 1871, 1872, and 1873; Baker, *Lighthouses of Texas,* p. 61; USLHB, *Annual Report, 1881.*

[14]USLHB, *Annual Report,* 1902; Herbert Molloy Mason, Jr., *Death From the Sea: Our Greatest Natural Disaster the Galveston Hurricane of 1900* (New York: The Dial Press, 1972), pp. 162-63.

[15]USLHB, *Annual Report,* 1902; Putnam, *Lighthouses and Lightships.*

[16]Putnam, *Lighthouses and Lightships;* Adamson, *Keepers of the Lights,* pp. 187-88; Department of Commerce, *Lighthouse Service Bulletin,* 1:181-83.

[17]Darst, "Texas Lighthouses," p. 316; Bolivar Point Lighthouse File, Coast Guard Historian's Office.

[18]U.S. Commerce Department, *Annual Reports,* 1919 and 1920.

[19]USLHB, *Annual Reports,* 1894, 1895, 1901, and 1905; U.S. Congress, House, *Constructing Lights at Galveston Harbor, Texas,* H. Rept. 1219, 53d Cong., 2d sess., 1894, pp. 1-2.

[20]USLHB, *Annual Reports,* 1905 and 1907.

[21]Ibid., 1911; Department of Commerce, *Lighthouse Service Bulletin,* 1:91, 135, 166-67, 178, 181.

[22]U.S. Commerce Department, *Annual Reports,* 1918 and 1919.

[23]U.S. Department of Commerce Press Releases, Galveston Lighthouse File, Coast Guard Historian's Office.

[24]U.S. Congress, Senate, *Annual Report of the Superintendent of the Coast Survey, showing the progress of that work during the year ending November, 1851,* S. Ex. Doc. 3, 32d Cong., 1st sess., 1852, pp. 504-505.

[25]Ibid.; USLHB, *Laws,* p. 158.

[26]Deeds and Contracts, RG 26, NA.

[27]Letters from USLHB to 9th District Inspectors, USLHB to Superintendents, December 8, 1853, passim, RG 26, NA; USLHB, *Annual Report,* 1855; Light List, 1858.

[28]Annual Report of District Engineers, October 5, 1868, USLHB Letters to 8th and 9th District Engineers, RG 26, NA; USLHB, *Annual Report,* 1868; Light List, 1868.

[29]USLHB, *Annual Report,* 1895.

[30]Clarence Ousley, *Galveston in Nineteen Hundred* (Atlanta: William C. Chase, 1900), p. 189; USLHB, *Annual Report,* 1900.

[31]Ousley, *Galveston*, p. 189; Department of Commerce, *Lighthouse Service Bulletin*, 1:182; Light List, 1936.

[32]*Annual Report of the Superintendent of the Coast Survey*, S. Ex. Doc. 3, 32d Cong., 1st sess., 1852, pp. 504-06.

[33]Light List, 1858; USLHB, *Annual Report*, 1855.

[34]USLHB, *Annual Report*, 1869.

[35]Mason, *Death From the Sea*, pp. 159-60; Ousley, *Galveston*, pp. 189, 292.

[36]USLHB, *Annual Report*, 1902.

[37]USLHB Letters to 9th District Inspector, RG 26, NA; Darst, "Texas Lighthouses," p. 312; National Archives Clips, RG 26, NA.

[38]*Annual Report of the Superintendent of the Coast Survey*, S. Ex. Doc. 3, 32d Cong., 1st sess., 1852, pp. 504-506; Light List, 1858; USLHB, *Annual Report*, 1855.

[39]USLHB, *Annual Reports*, 1880 and 1888.

[40]National Archives Clips, RG 26, NA; Title Records, Site Files, Coast Guard Headquarters, Washington, DC; Department of the Interior, *Register of Officers*, 1883, p. 231; Darst, "Texas Lighthouses," pp. 312-13.

[41]National Archives Clips, RG 26, NA; Light List, 1888; USLHB, *Annual Report*, 1898.

[42]USLHB Letters, March 28, 1859, RG 26, NA; USLHB, *Report of Officers*, pp. 130-31; U.S. Treasury Department, *Statement of Appropriations and Expenditures*, p. 470.

[43]USLHB, *Annual Report*, 1893.

[44]Ibid.; Title Records, Site Files, Coast Guard Headquarters, Washington, DC; Baker, *Lighthouses of Texas*, p. 41; USLHB, *Annual Report*, 1896; Department of the Interior, *Official Register, 1897*, p. 320.

[45]USLHB, *Annual Report*, 1902; Baker, *Lighthouses of Texas*, p. 42; Putnam, *Lighthouses and Lightships*, p. 257; Department of Commerce, *Lighthouse Service Bulletin*, 1:182.

[46]Baker, *Lighthouses of Texas*, p. 45.

Notes to Chapter 11, Lower Texas Coast

[1]Baker, *Lighthouses of Texas*, p. 28.

[2]*Light-house Establishment*, H. Ex. Doc. 27, 30th Cong., 1st sess., 1848, p. 13; Title Records, Site Files, Coast Guard Headquarters, Washington, DC; Earl F. Woodward, "Internal Improvements in Texas in the Early 1850's," *Southwestern Historical Quarterly* 76 (October, 1972):168; Source 170 - sec. citing; Pleasonton to Governor Bell, October 23, 1851, Lighthouse Letters, RG 26, NA.

[3]*List of Light House Contracts*, H. Ex. Doc. 43, 32d Cong., 1st sess., 1852; Elizabeth Lewis, "Guiding Lights," *Texas Highways* 36, no. 2 (February, 1989):28; Pleasonton to Cooper, October 29, 1851, Lighthouse Letters, RG 26, NA; Thornton Jenkins to 9th District Inspector, April 1, 1854, USLHB Letters to 9th District Inspector, ibid.; Light List, 1858; Descriptive list of Lighthouses, circa 1858, RG 26, NA; *Report of the Secretary of the Treasury*, S. Doc. 22, 32d Cong., 2d sess., 1853.

[4]U.S. Congress, Senate, *Report on the United States and Mexican Boundary Survey*, by William H. Emory, S. Ex. Doc. 108, 34th Cong., 1st sess., 1856; USLHB, *Annual Report*, 1855.

[5]USLHB, *Annual Report*, 1857; DeWire, "The Guardian Eyes of Texas," p. 4; USLHB Letters to 9th District Inspector, October 26, 1857, June 11 and July 16, 1958, RG 26, NA; Light List, 1858.

[6]CSA Files, RG 365, NA; Holland, *America's Lighthouses*, p. 150; USLHB, *Annual Reports*, 1864, 1867, and 1869; Light List, 1868; Baker, *Lighthouses of Texas*, p. 30; James Trathen to William W. McKean, December 18, 1861, *ORN*, Ser. I, 17:6; Allen Morris, *Florida Place Names*, (Coral Gables, FL: University of Miami Press, 1974), p. 30; Lewis, "Guiding Lights," p. 30.

[7]Title Records, Site Files, Coast Guard Headquarters, Washington, DC; Baker, *Lighthouses of Texas*, p. 30; USLHB, *Annual Reports*, 1870, 1873, and 1874; National Archives Clips, RG 26, NA.

[8]USLHB, *Annual Report*, 1887.

[9]Department of Commerce, *Lighthouse Service Bulletin*, 2:46.

[10]Baker, *Lighthouses of Texas*, p. 33; Collection of notes on Point Isabel Lighthouse, Texas Parks and Wildlife Department, 1984; Lewis, "Guiding Lights," p. 34.

[11]USLHB, *Annual Report*, 1855; *Report of the Superintendent of the Coast Survey*, S. Ex. Doc. 22, 34th Cong., 1st sess., 1856, p. 400; USLHB Letters to 9th District Inspector, February 6, November 10, 1858, RG 26, NA.

[12]USLHB, *Annual Report*, 1864; Letters Sent to USLHB by 8th and 9th District Engineers, New Orleans, September 16, 1865, RG 26, NA; Letters Sent to 9th District Inspectors, October 27, 1866, ibid.; Blunt, *The American Coast Pilot*, p. 412; USLHB, *Annual Report*, 1870.

[13]USLHB, *Annual Report*, 1872.

[14]USLHB Letters, June 26, 1858, RG 26, NA.

[15]*Letter from the Secretary of the Treasury, communicating statements of the receipts and expenditures of the United States for the year ending June 30, 1858*, H. Ex. Doc. 20, 35th Cong., 2d sess., 1859, p. 37; U.S. Treasury Department, *Statement of Appropriations and Expenditures*, p. 469; Descriptive List of Lighthouses, RG 26, NA; Light List, 1858.

[16]C.C. Sibley to Adjutant-General, U.S. Army, *ORA*, Ser. I, 1:561; Report Collector at LaSalle, November 21, 1861, CSA Files, RG 365, NA; USLHB, *Annual Report*, 1868.

[17]USLHB, *Annual Reports*, 1864 and 1869.

[18]USLHB, *Annual Reports*, 1870 and 1872.

[19]Ibid., 1872.

[20]Ibid., 1876; Department of the Interior, *Register of Officers*, 1873, p. 219.

[21]National Archives clips, RG 26, NA.

[22]USLHB, *Annual Reports*, 1853 and 1855; USLHB, *Laws*, p. 192; *Report of the Superintendent of the Coast Survey*, S. Ex. Doc. 22, 34th Cong., 1st sess., 1856, p. 406; Descriptive List of Lighthouses, RG 26, NA; USLHB Letters to 9th District Inspectors, October 10, 24, 1859, ibid.

[23]USLHB, *Annual Report*, 1868; Annual Report of District Engineer to 8th and 9th District, USLHB, October 5, 1868, RG 26, NA.

[24]National Archives clips, RG 26, NA; USLHB, *Annual Reports*, 1888 and 1902; Light List, 1907.

[25]Baker, *Lighthouses of Texas*, p. 39; DeWire, "The Guardian Eyes of Texas," p. 4; Lewis, "Guiding Lights," p. 34.

[26]Updike, *Winslow Lewis and the Lighthouses*, p. 95; Blunt, *Blunt's American Coast Pilot*.

[27]USLHB, *Laws*, p. 158; Baker, *Lighthouses of Texas*, p. 22.

[28]*Annual Report of the Superintendent of the Coast Survey*, S. Ex. Doc. 3, 32d Cong., 1st sess., 1852, pp. 507-08.

[29]*United States Coast Survey*, S. Ex. Doc. 58, 32d Cong., 2d sess., 1852, pp. 133-34; *Report of the Superintendent of the United States Coast Survey for 1853*, S. Ex. Doc. 14, 33d Cong., 1st sess., 1853, p. 178; Maps and Plans, Cartographic Division, RG 26, NA.

[30]Maps and Plans, Cartographic Division, RG 26, NA.

[31]U.S. Treasury Department, *Statement of Appropriations and Expenditures*, p. 469.

[32]CSA Files, RG 365, NA; Engineering Secretary to Bonzano, October 27, 1866, Letters Sent to 9th District Inspector, RG 26, NA.

[33]Holland, *The Aransas Pass Light Station*, pp. 41, 47; E. P. Turner to DeBray, December 25, 1862, X. B. DeBray to Hobby, December 25, 1862, X. B. DeBray to Buchel, December 26, 1862, *ORA*, Ser. I, 15:909, 910, 912; Lewis, "Guiding Lights," p. 36.

[34]USLHB, *Annual Reports*, 1866 and 1867.

[35]Department of Commerce, *Lighthouse Service Bulletin*, 1:230, 236, 2:32, 97; U.S. Commerce Department, *Annual Report*, 1918; *Statutes at Large*, 40:375.

[36]Darst, "Texas Lighthouses," p. 316; Baker, *Lighthouses of Texas*, p. 27; "History of Egmont Key Light Station," p. 36, Site Files, Coast Guard Headquarters, Washington, DC; Adamson, *Keepers of the Lights*, p. 402.

[37]Deeds and Contracts, RG 26, NA.

[38]U.S. Treasury Department, *Statement of Appropriations and Expenditures*, p. 469.

[39]Descriptive List of Lighthouses, RG 26, NA.

[40]National Archives Site Files; National Archives clips, RG 26, NA.

[41]Corpus Christi Lighthouse file, Corpus Christi Library Manuscript Collection.

[42]Thornton A. Jenkins to 8th District Inspector, November 19, 1870, Letters Sent to 8th District Inspector, RG 26, NA.

[43]Harder, *Illustrated Dictionary of Place Names*, p. 436.

[44]Snow, *Famous Lighthouses*, p. 221; Darst, "Texas Lighthouses," p. 305; USLHB, *Laws*, p. 150.

[45]Report of Captain Richard Evans, January 27, 1851, Lighthouse Letters, RG 26, NA; Pleasonton to John S. Rhea, May 22, 1851, National Archives Site Files, ibid.

[46]National Archives Site Files, RG 26, NA; Contract to John E. Carey, December 6, 1851, Deeds and Contracts, ibid.; Baker, *Lighthouses of Texas*, pp. 18-19.

[47]Snow, *Famous Lighthouses*, p. 221; USLHB Letters to 9th District Inspector, June 27, 1857, RG 26, NA; Collection of notes on Point Isabel Lighthouse, Texas Parks and Wildlife Department, 1984.

[48]USLHB, *Annual Report*, 1855; National Archives Clips, RG 26, NA; CSA Files, RG 365, NA.

[49]Texas Parks and Wildlife Department, *Port Isabel Lighthouse, State Historic Structure, Preservation Plan and Program* (July 1884), p. 44; Snow, *Famous Lighthouses*, p. 221.

[50]Texas Parks and Wildlife Department, *Port Isabel Lighthouse*, p. 44.

[51]Collection of notes on Point Isabel Lighthouse, Texas Parks and Wildlife Department, 1984; USLHB, *Annual Reports*, 1866, 1878, and 1881; Texas Parks and Wildlife Department, *Port Isabel Lighthouse*, p. 49.

[52]Baker, *Lighthouses of Texas*, p. 20; Texas Parks and Wildlife Department, *Port Isabel Lighthouse*, p. 36.

[53]USLHB, *Annual Report*, 1888.

[54]Darst, "Texas Lighthouses," p. 313; Texas Parks and Wildlife Department, *Port Isabel Lighthouse*, p. 37.

[55]Arnold Burges Johnson, *The Modern Lighthouse Service* (Washington, DC: Government Printing Office, 1890), p. 11; Title Records, Site Files, Coast Guard Headquarters, Washington, DC.

[56]Department of the Interior, *Register of Officers, 1895*, p. 293; Port Isabel File, Coast Guard Historian's Office; Collection of notes on Point Isabel Lighthouse, Texas Parks and Wildlife Department, 1984.

[57]Title Records, Site Files, Coast Guard Headquarters, Washington, DC; Verna Jackson McKenna, *Old Point Isabel Lighthouse, Beacon of Brazos Santiago* (Port Isabel State Park, n.d.), p. 3.

[58]Letters Received by 5th Auditor from Superintendent of Lights, November 7, 26, December 23, 1851, May 15, 1852, RG 26, NA.

[59]Pleasonton to Rhea, April 5, 1852, Letters Sent by 5th Auditor, RG 26, NA; Department of the Interior, *Register of Officers*, 1853.

[60]USLHB Letters to 9th District Inspector, January 7, July 11, 1854, National Archives Site Files; Letters Sent to USLHB by 8th and 9th District Engineers, New Orleans, December 31, 1863, RG 26, NA.

[61]USLHB Letters to 9th District Inspector, November 15, 1859, RG 26, NA; Letters to Superintendents, November 9, 1865, ibid.

[62]USLHB, *Annual Report*, 1872.

[63]Ibid., 1875.

[64]U.S. Treasury Department, *Statement of Appropriations and Expenditures*, p. 469; USLHB, *Annual Report*, 1878; Title Records, Site Files, Coast Guard Headquarters, Washington, DC.

[65]USLHB, *Annual Report*, 1879; Holland, *America's Lighthouses*, p. 150; Light List, 1888.

[66]Light List, 1939; Adamson, *Keepers of the Lights*, p. 42; Baker, *Lighthouses of Texas*, p. 17.

Notes to Chapter 12, Lightships

[1]Robert F. Cairo, "Notes on Early Lightship Development," *Engineer's Digest* 188 (July-August-September, 1975):4.

[2]Trist to Secretary of Treasury, June 29, 1804, *Correspondence of the Secretary of the Treasury with Collectors of Customs 1789-1833*, General Records of the Department of the Treasury, RG 56, NA.

[3]Gallatin to Trist, April 16, 1804, ibid.

[4]U.S. Congress, House, *Letter from the Secretary of the Treasury Transmitting a Report of the Fifth Auditor of the Treasury, of the Progress Made in the Erection of the Light House at the Mouth of the Mississippi*, H. Doc. 97, 16th Cong., 1st sess., 1820, p. 4.

[5]*Letter from the Secretary of the Treasury*, H. Doc. 48, 17th Cong., 1st sess., 1822; Deeds and Contracts, RG 26, NA.

[6]September 2, 1820, Lighthouse Letters, RG 26, NA.

[7]Pleasonton to Chew, January 16, 1821, ibid.

[8]Ibid.; National Archives Site Files.

[9]Holland, *America's Lighthouses*, p. 146; *Light-House Establishment*, H. Rept. 811, 27th Cong., 2d sess., 1842, p. 94.

[10]Lighthouse Letters, RG 26, NA; U.S. Treasury Department, *Receipts and Expenditures For the Year 1823*, p. 61.

[11]Lighthouse Letters, RG 26, NA.

[12]*Message from the President of the United States*, H. Doc. 7, 21st Cong., 1st sess., 1829, p. 14.

[13]Pleasonton to Collector at Norfolk, October 13, 1847, Lighthouse Letters, RG 26, NA; Pleasonton to Prieur, June 3, 1848, ibid.; *Light-house Establishment*.

H. Ex. Doc. 27, 30th Cong., 1st sess., 1848, p. 11; National Archives Letters, RG 26, NA.

[14]USLHB, *Annual Report*, 1855; USLHB Journal, RG 26, NA; U.S. Coast Guard, *Record of Movements, Vessels of the U.S. Coast Guard, 1790-1933* (Washington, DC: Government Printing Office, 1934), p. 109; Putnam, *Lighthouses and Lightships*, p. 203; Light List, 1848.

[15]Photo, Coast Guard Historian's Office.

[16]USLHB, *Annual Report*, 1860; E. H. Riddell to Bonzano, September 15, 1866, Miscellaneous Letters Received by 8th and 9th District Engineer, RG 26, NA.

[17]National Archives Site Files.

[18]Ibid.

[19]Pleasonton to Davis, March 1, 1848, Lighthouse Letters, RG 26, NA; USLHB, *Laws*, p. 135.

[20]U.S. Congress, House, *A Letter from the Secretary of the Treasury Transmitting Exhibits of contracts made by the Treasury Department, during the years 1847 and 1848*, H. Ex. Doc. 53, 30th Cong., 2d sess., 1849, p. 8; Secretary of the Interior, *Register of Officers*, 1849.

[21]Light List, 1851.

[22]USLHB Letters to 9th District Inspector, June 7, 1854, RG 26, NA; USLHB, *Annual Report*, 1855.

[23]USLHB Letters to 9th District Inspector, August 8, 1859, July 16, 1860, RG 26, NA; USLHB, *Annual Reports*, 1855 and 1856.

[24]*Resolution of the Legislature of Louisiana*, S. Misc. Doc. 134, 30th Cong., 1st sess., 1848, p. 139; USLHB, *Laws*, p. 135; Pleasonton to Davis, June 12, 1848, Lighthouse Letters, RG 26, NA; Pleasonton to Winslow Foster, June 10, 1848, Lighthouse Letters, ibid.; Pleasonton to John Davis, June 12, 1848, ibid.

[25]Pleasonton to Superintendent, New Bern, May 7, 1849, RG 26, NA; Pleasonton to Ocracoke Collector, October 3, 1849; Pleasonton to Congress, December 29, 1849, ibid.; Lighthouse Letters, ibid.

[26]Light List, 1851; Pleasonton to Secretary of the Treasury, December 29, 1849, in U.S. Lighthouse Establishment, *Lighthouse Papers*, p. 537.

[27]USLHB, *Annual Report*, 1852; National Archives Site Files; *Report of the Superintendent of the United States Coast Survey for 1853*, S. Ex. Doc. 14, 33d Cong., 1st sess., 1853, p. 176.

[28]USLHB, *Annual Reports*, 1855 and 1856; USLHB to 9th District Inspector, February 3, 1857, RG 26, NA.

[29]USLHB Letters to 9th District Inspector, April 18, 1860, RG 26, NA.

[30]Coast Guard Historian's Office files; USLHB, *Annual Report*, 1882; Light List, 1883.

[31]USLHB, *Annual Reports*, 1883 and 1890.

[32]U.S. Congress, House, *Letter from the Acting Secretary of the Treasury, relative to the discontinuance of the light-vessel on Trinity Shoal, Gulf of Mexico, and recommending the establishment of a light-ship in the Gulf of Mexico off the South Pass of the Mississippi River,*

on the coast of Louisiana, H. Ex. Doc. 218, 53d Cong., 2d sess., 1894, pp. 1-2; USLHB, *Annual Report,* 1894.

[33]U.S. Congress, House, *Light-ship at South Pass, off the jetties of the Mississippi River,* H. Rept. 859, 47th Cong., 1st sess., 1882, pp. 1-2; USLHB, *Annual Report,* 1894.

[34]*Statutes at Large,* 28:375; USLHB, *Annual Reports,* 1894 and 1895.

[35]USLHB, *Annual Report,* 1895; Flint, *Lightships and Lightship Stations,* Index 85.

[36]USLHB, *Annual Report,* 1896; Flint, *Lightships and Lightship Stations,* Index 85.

[37]USLHB, *Annual Reports,* 1901 and 1912.

[38]U.S. Commerce Department, *Annual Report,* 1914.

[39]Flint, *Lightships and Lightship Stations,* Index 85.

[40]Ibid.; U.S. Commerce Department, *Annual Reports,* 1934 and 1935.

[41]U.S. Commerce Department, *Annual Report,* 1913; Department of Commerce, *Lighthouse Service Bulletin,* 1:50.

[42]Department of Commerce, *Lighthouse Service Bulletin,* 1:50; Flint, *Lightships and Lightship Stations,* Index 86.

[43]U.S. Commerce Department, *Annual Report,* 1917; Flint, *Lightships and Lightship Stations,* Index 86.

[44]Letter, U.S. Coast Guard Headquarters to Robert Fraser, undated, Coast Guard Historian's Office.

[45]U.S. Congress, Senate, *Petition of Citizens of Texas, praying the erection of a light-house on or near the north breakers at the entrance of the harbor of Galveston, and the restoration of the light-vessel lately removed from the entrance of that harbor,* S. Misc. Doc. 56, 36th Cong., 1st sess., 1860, p. 1.

[46]U.S. Congress, Senate, *Report of the Secretary of the Treasury, with statements of contracts authorized by that department, of payments for the discharge of miscellaneous claims, and of expenditures from the marine hospital fund for the relief of sick and disabled seamen,* S. Ex. Doc. 31, 31st Cong., 1st sess., 1850, p.5.

[47]Letters from USLHB to 9th District Inspector, June 8, 1853, RG 26, NA.

[48]*Annual Report of the Superintendent of the Coast Survey,* S. Ex. Doc. 3, 32d Cong., 1st sess., 1852, p. 508; U.S. Congress, House, *Letter from the Secretary of the Treasury, Transmitting a Report from the Light-house Board, &c.,* H. Ex. Doc. 114, 32d Cong., 1st sess., 1852, p. 28.

[49]Baker, *Lighthouses of Texas,* p. 53; Letters from USLHB to 9th District Inspector, May 17, June 8, August 22, 1853, RG 26, NA.

[50]USLHB, *Annual Report,* 1857; USLHB Miscellaneous Documents, RG 26, NA; USLHB, *Annual Report,* 1860; Coast Guard Historian's Office.

[51]*Petition of Citizens of Texas,* S. Misc. Doc. 56, 36th Cong., 1st sess., 1860, pp. 1-15.

[52]National Archives Site Files.

[53]USLHB, *Annual Report,* 1872.

[54]USLHB, *Annual Reports,* 1876 and 1880.

[55]Coast Guard Historian's Office files; Light List, 1880.

[56]Galveston County Historical Museum exhibit text, Coast Guard Historian's Office files, p. 12; USLHB, *Annual Report,* 1901.

[57]Coast Guard Historian's Office files; Baker, *Lighthouses of Texas,* p. 56; USLHB, *Annual Report,* 1911; *Statutes at Large,* 36:536.

[58]Baker, *Lighthouses of Texas,* p. 66; USLHB, *Annual Report,* 1901.

[59]USLHB, *Annual Reports,* 1901 and 1903; *Statutes at Large,* 32:1092.

[60]Coast Guard Historian's Office files; USLHB, *Annual Report,* 1905; Light List, 1907.

[61]Department of Commerce, *Lighthouse Service Bulletin,* 3:155.

[62]Flint, *Lightships and Lightship Stations,* Index 91.

Bibliography

Manuscript and Document Collections

Alabama Historical Commission

City of Biloxi, Mississippi, Library

    M. James Stevens Collection

Corpus Christi Library Manuscript Collection

    Corpus Christi Lighthouse file

Historic Mobile Preservation Society

Museum of the City of Mobile, Alabama

    Matthew Fontaine Maury Papers

National Archives, Washington, DC

    National Archives Site Files

    Record Group 26, Records of the United States Coast Guard

    Record Group 56, Records of the Department of the Treasury

    Record Group 77, Records of the Office of the Chief of Engineers

    Record Group 365, Treasury Department Collection of Confederate Records

National Park Service. Lighthouse Database, National Maritime Initiative, Washington, DC

Pensacola Historical Society

Texas Parks and Wildlife Department. Collection of notes on Point Isabel Lighthouse, 1984

U.S. Coast Guard Eighth District Site Files, New Orleans, Louisiana.

U.S. Coast Guard Historian's Office

U.S. Coast Guard Seventh District Site Files, Miami, Florida

U.S. Coast Guard Site Files, Washington, DC (recently discarded by the Coast Guard)

Government Documents

Bureau of Topographical Engineers. *Professional Papers of the Corps of Topographical Engineers, United States Army.* Washington, DC: War Department, 1861.

Statutes at Large of the United States of America, 1789-1873. 17 vols. Washington, DC: 1850-73.

U.S. Army Corps of Engineers. *Identification and Evaluation of Submerged Anomalies, Mobile Harbor, Alabama.* Mobile, Alabama: Army Corps of Engineers, 1984.

U.S. Coast Guard Public Information Division. *The Coast Guard at War,* Vol. 15, *Aids to Navigation.* Washington, DC: Government Printing Office, 1949.

U.S. Coast Guard. *Lighthouses Then and Now.* Washington, DC: n.d.

_____. *Principal Marine Disasters Since 1831.* Washington, DC, n.d.

_____. *Record of Movements, Vessels of the United States Coast Guard, 1790-December 31, 1933.* Washington, DC: U.S. Coast Guard, n.d.

U.S. Congress. *American State Papers.*

U.S. Congress. House. *A Letter from the Secretary of the Treasury transmitting exhibits of contracts made by the Treasury Department, during the years 1847 and 1848.* H. Ex. Doc. 53, 30th Cong., 2d sess., 1849.

_____. *Annual Report of the Superintendent of the Coast Survey, showing the progress of that work during the year ending November, 1851.* H. Ex. Doc. 26, 32d Cong., 1st sess. Washington, DC: Robert Armstrong, Printer, 1852.

_____. *Constructing Lights at Galveston Harbor, Texas.* H. Rept. 1219, 53d Cong., 2d sess., 1894.

_____. *Executing Law of last session for building light-houses, etc., with list of sites approved and rejected; also number of light-houses in each state on 1st January 1833.* H. Doc. 27, 25th Cong., 2d sess., 1838.

_____. *Letter from the Acting Secretary of the Treasury, transmitting personal statements of losses sustained by keepers of light stations and other employés of the Light-House Establishment in the Sixth Light-house District during the cyclones on August 27 and 28, 1893.* H. Ex. Doc. 91, 53d Cong., 2d sess., 1894.

_____. *Letter from the Acting Secretary of the Treasury transmitting statements under acts of 21st April, 1808, and 2d March 1909.* H. Ex. Doc. 52, 30th Cong., 1st sess., 1848.

_____. *Letter from the Acting Secretary of the Treasury recommending an amendment for the sundry civil bill providing for the reestablishment, upon a safer site near-by, the Chandeleur, La., light station, which was wrecked October 1, 1893.* H. Ex. Doc. 225, 53d Cong., 2d sess., 1894.

_____. *Letter from the Acting Secretary of the Treasury, relative to the discontinuance of the light-vessel on Trinity Shoal, Gulf of Mexico, and recommending the establishment of a light-ship in the Gulf of Mexico off the South Pass of the Mississippi River, on the coast of Louisiana.* H. Ex. Doc. 218, 53d Cong., 2d sess., 1894.

_____. *Letter from the Secretary of the Treasury transmitting a Report of the Fifth Auditor of the Treasury, of the progress made in the erection of the light house at the mouth of the Mississippi,* H. Doc. 97, 16th Cong., 1st sess., 1820.

_____. *Letter from the Secretary of the Treasury transmitting statements of contracts authorized by the Treasury Department during the year 1838.* H. Doc. 131, 25th Cong., 3d sess., 1839.

_____. *Letter From the Secretary of the Treasury transmitting statements relative to public contracts with that department, &c.* H. Doc. 159, 28th Cong., 1st sess., 1844.

_____. *Letter from the Secretary of the Treasury, transmitting estimates of appropriations required for the service of the Fiscal Year Ending June 30, 1871.* H. Ex. Doc. 5, 41st Cong., 2d sess., 1869, Washington, DC: Government Printing Office. 1869.

_____. *Letter from the Secretary of the Treasury, transmitting estimates of appropriations required for the service of the Fiscal Year Ending June 30, 1873.* H. Ex. Doc. 5, 42d Cong., 2d sess., 1871, Washington, DC: Government Printing Office. 1871.

_____. *Letter from the Secretary of the Treasury, communicating statements of the receipts and expenditures of the United States for the year ending June 30, 1858,* H. Ex. Doc. 20, 35th Cong., 2d sess., 1859.

_____. *Letter from the Secretary of the Treasury, transmitting a Report of the Fifth Auditor, in relation to the execution of the act of 7th July last, for building light-houses, light-boats, etc.* H. Doc. 24, 25th Cong., 3d sess., 1838.

_____. *Letter from the Secretary of the Treasury, accompanied by a Report of the Fifth Auditor, upon the subject of light-houses.* H. Doc. 19, 19th Cong., 1st sess., 1825.

_____. *Letter from the Secretary of the Treasury, transmitting statements of payments made at the Treasury, during the year 1821.* H. Doc. 48, 17th Cong., 1st sess., 1822.

_____. *Letter from the Secretary of the Treasury, transmitting a Report of the Fifth Auditor in relation to the light-houses, &c.* H. Doc. 62, 28th Cong., 1st sess., 1844.

_____. *Letter from the Secretary of the Treasury, transmitting a Report from the Light-House Board, &c.* H. Ex. Doc. 114, 32d Cong., 1st sess., 1852.

_____. *Letter from the Secretary of the Treasury, transmitting a Report respecting Light-Houses.* H. Ex. Doc. 52, 31st Cong., 2d sess., 1851.

_____. *Letter from the Secretary of the Treasury, transmitting a statement of contracts, &c., made in that department.* H. Doc. 152, 28th Cong., 2d sess., 1845.

_____. *Letter from the Secretary of the Treasury.* H. Doc 101, 19th Cong., 2d sess., 1927.

_____. *Letter from the Secretary of the Treasury.* H. Doc. 124, 23d Cong., 1st sess., 1834.

_____. *Letter From the Secretary of the Treasury.* H. Doc. 114, 22d Cong., 1st sess., 1832.

_____. *Letter from the Secretary of Treasury, transmitting a report of the expenditures of the light-house establishments, &c.* H. Doc. 140, 27th Cong., 2d sess., 1842.

_____. *Letter from the Secretary of War, in answer to a resolution of the House of the 18th instant, making revised and reduced estimates of appropriations required for harbor and river improvements for the year ending June 30, 1869.* H. Doc. 224, 40th Cong., 2d sess., 1868.

_____. *Letters from the Secretary of the Treasury, transmitting estimates of additional appropriations required for the service of the Fiscal Year ending June 30, 1867, and also estimates of appropriations required for the service of the Fiscal Year ending June 30, 1868.* H. Ex. Doc. 2, 39th Cong., 2d sess. Washington, DC: Government Printing Office, 1866.

_____. *Letters from the Secretary of the Treasury, tranmitting estimates of additional appropriations required for the Service of the Fiscal Year ending June 30, 1869, and previous years; and also estimates of appropriations required for the Service of the Fiscal Year ending June 30, 1870.* Washington, DC: Government Printing Office, 1868.

_____. *Light-House at Cape San Blas, in Florida,* H. Rept. 1973, 47th Cong., 2d sess., 1883.

_____. *Light-House at St. Joseph's Point, Florida, Report from the Committee on Commerce.* H. Rept. 423, 51st Cong., 1st sess., 1890.

_____. *Light-House Establishment.* H. Ex. Doc. 27, 30th Cong., 1st sess., 1848.

_____. *Light-House Establishment.* H. Rept. 811, 27th Cong., 2d sess., 1842.

_____. *Light-ship at South Pass, off the jetties of the Mississippi River.* H. Rept. 859, 47th Cong., 1st sess., 1882.

_____. *List of Light House Contracts.* H. Ex. Doc. 43, 32d Cong., 1st sess., 1852.

_____. *Message from the President of the United States, transmitting copies of surveys made in pursuance of Acts of Congress, of 30th April, 1824, and 2d March, 1829.* H. Doc. 7, 21st Cong., 1st sess., 1829.

_____. *Message from the President of the United States, transmitting a report from the Secretary of the Treasury, in compliance with the resolution of the House of Representatives of the 21st ultimo, respecting appointments to office, &c., since 4th April, 1841.* H. Doc. 192, 27th Cong., 2d sess., 1842.

_____. *Report of Officers Constituting the Light-House Board.* H. Ex. Doc. 55, 32d Cong., 1st sess., 1852.

_____. *Report of the Fifth Auditor in relation to lighthouses.* H. Doc. 38, 28th Cong., 1st sess., 1844.

_____. *Report of the Superintendent of The United States Coast Survey.* H. Ex. Doc. 41, 36th Cong., 1st sess., 1859.

_____. *Resolution of the Legislature of Louisiana, praying for a light-house at Bayou Bonfouca.* H. Doc. 6, 27th Cong., 1st sess., 1841.

_____. *Treasury Statements, 1829.* H. Doc. 57, 21st Cong., 1st sess., 1830.

U.S. Congress. Senate. *Annual Report of the Superintendent of the Coast Survey, showing the progress of that work during the year ending November, 1851.* S. Ex. Doc. 3, 32d Cong., 1st sess. Washington, DC: Robert Armstrong, Printer, 1852.

_____. *Documents on Light-House Establishment of the United States.* S. Doc. 258, 25th Cong., 2d sess., 1838.

_____. *Expediency of deepening channel, erecting light-house, and establishing port of entry at St. Marks, and removing ostructions in Apalachicola and Ocilla Rivers in Florida.* S. Doc. 50, 20th Cong., 1st sess., 1828.

_____. *Memorial of The Legislature of Mississippi, praying a survey of the coast of that sate, and the erection of fortifications on the same.* S. Doc. 281, 26th Cong., 1st sess., 1840.

_____. *Memorial of W.H. Gleason, asking that a light-house be constructed at the harbor of Punta Rassa, on Sanibel Island, Florida.* S. Misc. Doc. 106, 42d Cong., 2d sess., 1872.

_____. *Message from the President of the United States to the Two Houses of Congress, at the commencement of the Third Session of the Twenty-Seventh Congress.* S. Doc. 1, 27th Cong., 3d sess., 1842.

_____. *Message from the President of the United States, in answer to a resolution of the Senate, respecting a fort or forts on Ship Island, on the coast of Mississippi.* S. Doc. 9, 29th Cong., 1st sess., 1845.

_____. *Message From The President of the United States to Two Houses of Congress, at the commencement of the Second Session of the Twenty-first Congress.* S. Doc. 1, 21st Cong., 2d sess., 1830.

_____. *Petition of Citizens of Texas, praying the erection of a light-house on or near the north breakers at the entrance of the harbor of Galveston, and the restoration of the light-vessel lately removed from the entrance of that harbor.* S. Misc. Doc. 56, 36th Cong., 1st sess., 1860.

_____. *Report from the Committee of Commerce.* S. Rept. 577, 50th Cong., 1st sess., 1888.

_____. *Report from the Committee of Commerce.* S. Rept. 578, 50th Cong., 1st sess., 1888.

_____. *Report from the Committee on Commerce.* S. Rept. 1034, 50th Cong., 1st sess., 1888.

_____. *Report from the Engineer Department* in *Annual Report of the Secretary of War.* S. Doc. 1, 24th Cong., 1st sess., 1835.

_____. *Report from the Secretary of the Navy, transmitting, in compliance with a resolution of the Senate, a report of the survey of the coast from Appalachicola Bay to the mouth of the Mississippi River.* S. Rept. 38, 27th Cong., 1st sess., 1841.

_____. *Report from the Secretary of the Treasury, relative to light houses and buoys, on the coast of Florida and Gulf of Mexico.* S. Doc. 17, 18th Cong., 2d sess., 1825.

_____. *Report from the Secretary of the Treasury, in relation to the erection of light-houses, &c., in compliance with the 2d section of the act of March 3, 1837, "making appropriations for building light houses, light-boats, beacon-lights, buoys, and dolphins."* S. Doc. 15, 25th Cong., 2d sess., 1837.

_____. *Report from the Secretary of the Treasury, in compliance with a resolution of the Senate of the 25th instant, transmitting copies of the representations made to him relative to the light-houses of the United States, by the Messrs. Blunt of New York, &c.* S. Doc. 138, 25th Cong., 2d sess., 1838.

_____. *Report from the Secretary of the Treasury.* S. Doc. 235, 25th Cong., 2d sess., 1838.

_____. *Report of the Secretary of the Treasury, communicating a report from the Superintendent of the Coast Survey, in relation to the survey of the coast of Florida.* S. Ex. Doc. 30, 30th Cong., 2d sess., 1849.

_____. *Report of the Secretary of the Treasury, communicating a report of the Superintendent of the Coast Survey, showing the progress of that work during the year ending November, 1848.* S. Ex. Doc. 1, 30th Cong., 2d sess., 1848.

_____. *Report of the Secretary of the Treasury, on the state of the finances.* S. Doc. 22, 32d Cong., 2d sess., 1853.

_____. *Report of the Secretary of the Treasury, with statements of contracts authorized by that department, of payments for the discharge of miscellaneous claims, and of expenditures from the marine hospital fund for the relief of sick and disabled seamen.* S. Ex. Doc. 31, 31st Cong., 1st sess., 1850.

_____. *Report of the Superintendent of the Coast Survey showing progress during the year ending November 1849.* S. Ex. Doc. 5, 31st Cong., 1st. sess., 1850.

_____. *Report of the Superintendent of the Coast Survey, showing the progress of the survey during the Year 1855.* S. Ex. Doc. 22, 34th Cong., 1st sess. Washington, DC: A.O.P. Nicholson, Printer, 1856.

_____. *Report of the Superintendent of the United States Coast Survey for 1853.* S. Ex. Doc. 14, 33d Cong., 1st sess., 1853.

_____. *Report of the Superintendent of the United States Coast Survey for 1852.* S. Ex. Doc. 58, 32d Cong., 2d sess., 1852.

_____. *Report on the United States and Mexican Boundary Survey,* by William H. Emory. S. Ex. Doc. 108, 34th Cong., 1st sess., 1856. Washington, DC: A.O.P. Nicholson, 1857.

_____. *Resolution of the General Assembly of Louisiana to obtain an appropriation for the erection of a light-house on the Bayou Bonfouca.* S. Doc. 348, 26th Cong., 1st sess., 1840.

_____. *Resolution of the Legislature of Florida, relative to the erection of a light-house on Egmont Key.* S. Doc. 130, 29th Cong., 2d sess., 1847.

_____. *Resolution of the Legislature of Louisiana, in favor of the erection of light-houses at the mouth of the Sabine, and on the west end of Last Island.* S. Misc. Doc. 134, 30th Cong., 1st sess., 1848.

U.S. Department of Commerce and Labor. Light-House Board. *Laws Relative to the Light-House Establishment passed at the Third Session of the Fifty-Eighth Congress, 1904-1905.* Washington: Government Printing Office, 1905.

U.S. Department of Commerce. Lighthouse Service. 1912-1939. *Lighthouse Service Bulletin.* 5 vols. Washington, DC: Government Printing Office.

_____. U.S. Coast and Geodetic Survey. *United States Coast Pilot, Atlantic Coast, Section E, Gulf of Mexico from Key West to the Rio Grande.* Washington, DC: Government Printing Office, 1916.

U.S. Light-House Board. *Specifications for metalwork of screw-pile light-house to replace light-vessels.* Washington, DC: Geo. W. Bowman, Public Printer, 1860, amended 1872.

_____. *Annual Report to the Secretary of the Treasury, 1855.* Washington, DC: Government Printing Office, 1855.

_____. *Laws of the United States relating to the establishment, support, and management of the light-houses, light-vessels, monuments, beacons, spindles, buoys, and public piers of the United States from August 7, 1789, to March 3, 1855.* Washington, DC: A.O.P. Nicholson, Public Printer, June 30, 1855.

_____. *Report of Officers Constituting the Light-house Board.* Washington DC: A. Boyd Hamilton, printer, 1852.

U.S. Light-house Establishment. *Light-house Papers, Compilation of public documents and extracts, 1789-1871.* Washington, DC: Government Printing Office, 1871.

U.S. Navy Department. *Report of the Secretary of the Navy, 1863.* Washington, DC: Government Printing Office, 1863.

_____. *Report of the Secretary of the Navy, 1864.* Washington, DC: Government Printing Office, 1864.

U.S. Treasury Department. *An account of the receipts and expenditures of the United States for the year 1823.* Washington, DC: E. de Krafft, Printer, 1824.

_____. *Statement of Appropriations and Expenditures for public buildings, rivers and harbors, forts, arsenals, armories, and other public works, from March 4, 1789, to June 30, 1882.* Washington, DC: Government Printing Office, 1882.

United Kingdom. Parliament. *Minutes of Evidence Taken Before the Select Committee on Light-houses.* London: 1845.

Work Projects Administration. *Louisiana: A Guide to the State.* New York: Hastings House, 1941.

Bibliography

_____. *Texas: A Guide to the Lone Star State.* New York: Books, Inc., 1940.

Published Annual Reports of the Lighthouse Service

These are listed in chronological order. From 1852 to 1872 the reports are found in the "Report on the Finances" in the Treasury Department annual report. Beginning in 1873, they were published by the Lighthouse Service as separate documents until 1939.

U.S. Treasury Department. Light-House Service. Light-House Board. "Report of the Light-House Board....January 15, 1852." Pp. 70-175 in *Report of the Secretary of the Treasury...* S. Ex. Doc. 22, 52d Cong., 2d sess., Washington, DC: A.O.P. Nicholson, Printer, 1853.

_____. Light-House Service. Light-House Board. "Report of the Light-House Board...Nov. 19, 1853." Pp. 180-271 in *Report of the Secretary of the Treasury...1853.* Washington, DC: A.O.P. Nicholson, Printer, 1854.

_____. Light-House Service. Light-House Board. "Report of the Light-House Board.... October 31, 1854." Pp. 286-348 in *Report of the Secretary of the Treasury...1854.* Washington, DC: A.O.P. Nicholson, Printer, 1854.

_____. Light-House Service. Light-House Board. "Report of the Light-House Board.... October 31, 1855." Pp. 250-422 in *Report of the Secretary of the Treasury...1855.* Washington, DC: Beverly Tucker, 1856.

_____. Light-House Service. Light-House Board. "[Report of the Light-House Board.]... November 1, 1856." Pp. 250-422 in *Report of the Secretary of the Treasury...1855.* Washington, DC: Cornelius Wendel, Printer, 1856.

_____. "[Report of the Light-House Board.]... November 1, 1857." Pp. 229-59 in *Report of the Secretary of the Treasury...1857.* Washington, DC: Cornelius Wendel, Printer, 1857.

_____. Light-House Service. Light-House Board. "[Report of the Light-House Board.]... October 1, 1858." Pp. 281-90 in *Report of the Secretary of the Treasury...1858.* Washington, DC: William A. Harris, Printer, 1858.

_____. Light-House Service. Light-House Board. "[Report of the Light-House Board.]... October 25, 1859." Pp. 286-97 in *Report of the Secretary of the Treasury...1859.* Washington, DC: George W. Bowman, Printer, 1860.

_____. Light-House Service. Light-House Board. "[Report of the Light-House Board.]... October 22, 1860." Pp. 363-371 in *Report of the Secretary of the Treasury...1860.* Washington, DC: Thomas H. Ford, Printer, 1860.

_____. Light-House Service. Light-House Board. "[Report of the Light-House Board.]... November 26, 1861." Pp. 203-206 in *Report of the Secretary of the Treasury...1861.* Washington, DC: Government Printing Office, 1861, 1862, 1863, 1864, 1865, 1866, 1867, 1868, 1869, 1870, 1871, 1872, 1873, 1874, 1875, 1876, 1877, 1878, 1879, 1880, 1881, 1882, 1883, 1884, 1885, 1886, 1887, 1888, 1889, 1890, 1891, 1892, 1893, 1894, 1895, 1896, 1897, 1898, 1899, 1900, 1901, 1902.

U.S. Department of Commerce and Labor. Light-House Service. Light-House Board. *Annual Report of the Light-house Board to the Secretary of Commerce and Labor, October 15, 1903.* Washington, DC: Government Printing Office, 1903.

_____. *Annual Report of the Light-house Board to the Secretary of Commerce and Labor, June 30, 1904.* Washington, DC: Government Printing Office, 1904, 1905, 1907, 1908, 1911, 1912.

U.S. Department of Commerce. Lighthouse Service. Bureau of Lighthouses. Commissioner. *Annual Report of the Commissioner of Lighthouses to the Secretary of Commerce for the Fiscal Year Ended June 30, 1913.* Washington, DC: Government Printing Office, 1913, 1914, 1915, 1916, 1917, 1918, 1919, 1920, 1923, 1927, 1928, 1934, 1935, 1938.

Register of Officers

Official Register of Employees of the United States. Washington, DC: Government Printing Office, 1831, 1837, 1843, 1845.

U.S. Department of State. *Register of all Officers and Agents, Civil, Military, and Naval, in the Service of the United States, on the Thirtieth September, 1847.* Washington, DC: J. & G.S. Gideon, 1847.

Official Register of Employees of the United States. Washington, DC: Government Printing Office, 1849.

U.S. Department of State. *Civil Service Register, September 30, 1853.*

Official Register of Employees of the United States. Washington, DC: Government Printing Office, 1857.

U.S. Department of the Interior. *Register of Officers and Agents, Civil, Military, and Naval, in the Service of the United States, on the Thirtieth September 1865.* Washington, DC: Government

Printing Office, 1866, 1871, 1873, 1875, 1877, 1883, 1885, 1887, 1891, 1895, 1897, 1899, 1903, 1905.

Light Lists–chronologically ordered

U.S. Treasury Department. Lighthouse Service. *The Light-houses, Beacons and Floating Lights of the United States in Operation on the 1st December, 1839.* Washington, DC: Blair and Rives, 1939.

_____. *List of Lighthouses, Beacons, and Floating Lights of the United States 1848*, Gideon and Company, 1849.

U.S. Treasury Department. Lighthouse Service. *List of Light-houses, Lighted Beacons, and Floating Lights of the United States*, Washington: William A. Harris, Public Printer, 1854.

U.S. Treasury Department. U.S. Light-House Board. *List of Light-houses, Lighted Beacons and Floating Lights of the Atlantic, Gulf and Pacific Coasts of the United States*, 1858, 1865, 1868, Corrected to January 1, 1875, Corrected to January 1, 1880, Corrected to January 1, 1884, Corrected to January 1, 1885, Corrected to January 1, 1888, Corrected to January 1, 1889, Corrected to January 1, 1907.

U.S. Department of Commerce. Lighthouse Service. *Light List Atlantic and Gulf Coast of the United States.* Washington, DC: Government Printing Office, 1919.

_____. Lighthouse Service. *Local Light List, including lights, fog signals, buoys, and daymarks, Gulf Coast: Key West to the Rio Grande Porto Rico and adjacent U.S. Islands.* Washington, DC: Government Printing Office, 1932, 1933, 1936, 1939.

U.S. Treasury Department. Coast Guard. *Light List Atlantic and Gulf Coast of the United States,* Washington, DC: Government Printing Office, 1945, 1947,,1951,,1953, 1954.

U.S. Department of Transportation. U.S. Coast Guard. *Light List Volume II, Atlantic and Gulf Coast of the United States.* Washington, DC: Government Printing Office, 1969.

_____. *Light List Atlantic and Gulf Coast of the United States, From Little River, South Carolina to Rio Grande, Texas and the Antilles.* Washington, DC: Government Printing Office, 1981.

_____. *Light List, Vol. IV, Gulf of Mexico.* Washington, DC: Government Printing Office, 1993.

Newspapers and Periodicals

Commercial Bulletin (New Orleans)

Commercial Register (Mobile)

Daily Herald (Biloxi)

Daily Picayune (New Orleans)

Floridian (Pensacola)

Gazette (Pensacola)

Harper's Weekly

Journal (Pensacola)

New Orleans Daily Crescent

News-Banner (St. Tammany, Louisiana)

Press Register (Mobile)

Times Picayne (New Orleans)

Primary Books and Articles

Adamson, Hans Christian. *Keepers of the Lights.* New York: Greenburg, 1955.

Bauer, K. Jack. *A Maritime History of the United States.* Columbia: University of South Carolina Press, 1988.

Blunt, Edmund and George W. *Blunt's American Coast Pilot.* New York: E. & G.W. Blunt, 1861.

Blunt, Edmund and George W. *Blunt's American Coast Pilot.* New York: E. & G.W. Blunt, 1847.

Blunt, Edmund M. and Blunt, George W. *The American Coast Pilot.* New York, George W. Blunt, 1867.

Boyd, Mark F. "The Fortifications at San Marcos de Apalache." *Florida Historical Society Quarterly* 15, no. 1 (July 1936):3-34.

Breedlove, James M. "Advertisement for Bids, June 10, 1837." *The Bee* (New Orleans) July 1, 1837.

Bushnell, Amy Turner. "How to Fight a Pirate: Provincials, Royalists, and the Defense of Minor Ports During the Age of Buccaneers." *Gulf Coast Historical Review* 5, no. 2 (Spring 1990):18-35.

Cairo, Robert F. "Notes on Early Lightship Development." *Engineer's Digest*, 188 (July-August-September, 1975):4.

Carter, Clarence Edwin. ed. and comp. *The Territorial Papers of the United States.* 14 vols. Washington, DC: Government Printing Office, 1940.

Castellanos, Henry C. *New Orleans As It Was.* New Orleans, LA: The L. Graham Co. Ltd., 1895.

Chadwick, F.E. "Aids to Navigation." *Proceedings of the United States Naval Institute* 17, no. 3 (1881):1-8.

Civil War Naval Chronology. Washington, DC: Navy Department, Naval History Division, 1971.

Cochran, Hamilton. *Blockade Runners of the Confederacy.* New York: Bobbs-Merrill Co., Inc., 1905.

Darst, Maury. "Texas Lighthouses: The Early Years, 1850-1900," *Southwestern Historical Quarterly* 79 no. 3 (1976):301-316.

Davis, T. Frederick. "Juan Ponce de Leon's Voyages to Florida." *Florida Historical Society Quarterly* 14, no. 1 (July 1935):3-49.

Davis, William Watson. *The Civil War and Reconstruction in Florida,* New York: Columbia University, 1913.

De Bow, J.D.B. *The Commercial Review.* 1, no. 1 (January 1846):86, 3, no. 6 (June 1847).

_____. *The Industrial Resources, Etc., of the Southern and Western States.* 3 vols. New Orleans: De Bow's Review, 1853.

de Charlevoix, Francois Xavier. *Journal of a Voyage to North America.* trans. Louise Phelps Kellogg. Chicago: The Caxton Club, 1923.

DeBrahm, Gerald. *Report of the General Survey in the Southern District of North America.* Columbia: U.S. Car Press, 1971.

DeWire, Elinor. "The Guardian Eyes of Texas." *Texas Weekly Magazine* (December 4, 1984):4-5.

Dufour, Charles L. *The Night the War Was Lost.* Garden City, NY: Doubleday & Company, Inc., 1960.

Eaton, Clement. *A History of the Old South.* New York: Macmillan Publishing Co., Inc., 1975.

Ellicott, Andrew. *The Journal of Andrew Ellicott, Late Commissioner on Behalf of the United States, etc.* Philadelphia: Budd & Hartram, for Thomas Dobson, 1803.

Findlay, Alexander George. *Memoir, Descriptive and Explanatory, to Accompany the Charts of the Northern Atlantic Ocean; and Comprising Instructions, General and Particular, for the Navigation of that Sea.* London: R.L. Laurie, 1845.

Flint, Willard. *Lightships and Lightship Stations of the U.S. Government.* Washington, DC: U.S. Coast Guard, 1989, Index 89.

Florida Department of Natural Resources. "San Marcos de Apalache State Historic Site." Division of Recreation and Parks, n.d.

French, B.F. *Historical Collections of Louisiana and Florida.* New York: J. Sabin and Sons, 1869.

Gayarré, Charles. *History of Louisiana, The French Domination.* New York: William J. Widdleton, 1866.

Hamilton, Peter J. *Colonial Mobile.* Tuscaloosa: University of Alabama, 1976.

Hamlin, Talbon. *Benjamin Henry Latrobe.* New York: Oxford University Press, 1955.

Harder, Kelsie B. *Illustrated Dictionary of Place Names.* New York: Van Nostrand Reinhold, 1976.

Harnett, T. Kane. *The Golden Coast.* Garden City, NY: Doubleday & Co., 1959.

Heap, David Porter. *Ancient and Modern Light-houses.* Boston: Ticknor & Company, 1889.

Holland, Francis Ross, Jr. *America's Lighthouses: Their Illustrated History since 1716.* Brattleboro, VT: The Stephen Greene Press, 1972.

Holland, Francis Ross, Jr. *Aransas Pass Light Station, A History.* Corpus Christi, Texas: By the Author, 1976.

Huber, Leonard V. *A Pictorial History of Louisiana.* New York: Charles Scribner's Sons, 1975.

Hurley, Neil E. *Keepers of Florida Lighthouses, 1820-1939.* Alexandria, VA: Historic Lighthouse Publishers, 1990.

Johnson, Arnold Burges. *The Modern Light-house Service.* Washington, DC: Government Printing Office, 1890.

Kmen, Henry A. "The Joys of Milneburg." *New Orleans Magazine,* 1 no. 1 (May 1981).

Latrobe, Benjamin Henry Boneval. *Impressions Respecting New Orleans, Diary and Sketches, 1818-1820.* Edited by Samuel Wilson, Jr. New York: Columbia University Press, 1951.

Lewis, Elizabeth. "Guiding Lights," *Texas Highways* 36, no. 2 (February, 1989).

Martin, Sidney Walter. *Florida during the Territorial Days.* Athens, GA; University of Georgia Press, 1944.

Mason, Herbert Molloy, Jr. *Death From the Sea: Our Greatest Natural Disaster, the Galveston Hurricane of 1900.* New York: The Dial Press, 1972.

McKenna, Verna Jackson. *Old Point Isabel Lighthouse, Beacon of Brazos Santiago.* Port Isabel State Park, n.d.

Mills, Robert. *The American Pharos, or Light-house Guide.* Washington: Thompson & Homans, 1832.

Mistovich, Tim S. and Knight, Vernon James, Jr. *Cultural Resources Survey of Mobile Harbor, Alabama.* Mobile: U.S. Army Corps of Engineers, 1983.

Moore, Frank, ed. *Rebellion Record: A Diary of American Events.* New York: G.P. Putnam, 1861-1868.

Morgan, David Joel. "The Mississippi River Delta." *Geoscience and Man,* 26. Baton Rouge: Louisiana State University, 1977.

Morris, Allen. *Florida Place Names*. Coral Gables, Florida: University of Miami Press, 1974.

Ousley, Clarence. *Galveston in Nineteen Hundred*. Atlanta: William C. Chase, 1900.

Pittman, Philip. *The Present State of the European Settlements on the Mississippi*. London: 1770. Reprint, with introduction, notes, and index by Frank Heywood Hodder. Cleveland, Ohio: The Arthur H. Clark Company, 1906.

Putnam, George R. *Lighthouses and Lightships of the United States*. Boston: Houghton Mifflin Co., 1917.

_____. *Sentinels of the Coasts: The Log of a Lighthouse Engineer*. New York, W.W. Norton & Company, Inc., 1937.

Roberts, W. Adolphe. *Lake Pontchartrain*. New York: The Bobbs-Merrill Company, 1946.

Robertson, James Alexander. *Louisiana Under the Rule of Spain, France and the United States 1785-1807*. 2 vols. Cleveland, Ohio: The Arthur H. Clark Company, 1911.

Rowland, Dunbar. ed. *Official Letter Books of W.C.C. Claiborne*. 6 vols. Jackson: Mississippi Department of Archives and History, 1917.

Rush, Richard et al., eds. *Official Records of the Union and Confederate Navies in the War of the Rebellion*. 31 vols. Washington, DC: Government Printing Office, 1894-1927.

Schubert, Frank N. ed. *The Nation Builders, 1838-1863*. Ft. Belvoir, VA: U.S. Army Corps of Engineers, 1988.

Scott, R.N., et al. *The War of the Rebellion: A Compilation of the Official Records of the Union and Confederate Armies*. 128 vols. Washington, DC: Government Printing Office, 1880-1901.

Semmes, Raphael. *Memoirs of Service Afloat during the War between the States*. Baltimore: Kelly, Piet & Co., 1869.

Sloan, Edward W. "The Roots of a Maritime Fortune: E.K. Collins and the New York-Gulf Coast Trade, 1821-1848." *Gulf Coast Historical Review* 5, no. 2 (Spring 1990):104-113.

Snodgrass, Paul. "Beacons of the Sea." *Gulfshore Life* (October 1990):78-81.

Snow, Edward Rowe. *Famous Light Houses of America*. New York: Dodd, Mead & Co., 1955.

Soley, James Russell. *The Navy in the Civil War*. Vol. 7, *The Blockade and the Cruisers*. New York: Charles Scribner's Sons, 1883.

Stevens, M. James. "Biloxi's First Lady Light House Keeper." *The Journal of Mississippi History* 36 (February 1974):39-41.

Sullivan, Charles L. *The Mississippi Gulf Coast*. Northridge, CA: Windsor Publications, 1985.

Texas Parks and Wildlife Department. *Port Isabel Lighthouse, State Historic Structure, Preservation Plan and Program*. Austin: July 1984.

Thompson, Ray M. "Round Island." *Down South* (March-April 1964):20.

Tindall, George Brown. *America, a Narrative History*. New York: W.W. Norton & Co., 1984.

Turner, Maxine. *Navy Gray: A Story of the Confederate Navy on the Chattahoochee and Apalachicola Rivers*. Tuscaloosa: University of Alabama Press, 1988.

Updike, Richard W. "Winslow Lewis and the Lighthouses." *American Neptune*, 28:31-48.

Vogel, Robert C. "John Lafitte, the Baratarians, and the Historical Biography of Piracy in the Gulf of Mexico." *Gulf Coast Historical Review* 5, no. 2 (Spring 1990):62-77.

Ware, John D., and Rea, Robert R. *George Cault, Surveyor and Cartographer of the Gulf Coast*. Gainesville: University of Florida Press, 1982.

Weiss, George. *The Lighthouse Service: Its History, Activities and Organization*. Baltimore: The John Hopkins Press, 1926.

Welles, Carol. "Extinguishing the Lights: 1861." *Louisiana History* 19 (Spring 1978):297-307.

Wells, Tom Henderson. *The Confederate Navy, A study in organization*. Tuscaloosa, AL: The University of Alabama Press, 1971.

Whitnah, Donald ed. *Government Agencies*. Wesport, Connecticut: Greenwood Press, 1983.

Willoughby, Malcom F. *Rum War at Sea*. Washington, DC: U.S. Coast Guard, 1964.

Wise, Stephen R. *Lifeline of the Confederacy: Blockade Running during the Civil War*. Columbia: University of South Carolina Press, 1988.

Woodward, Earl F. "Internal Improvements in Texas in the Early 1850's." *Southwestern Historical Quarterly* 76 (October, 1972):161-182.

Index
